The Frontier Club

The Frontier Club

Popular Westerns and Cultural Power, 1880–1924

CHRISTINE BOLD

OXFORD
UNIVERSITY PRESS

OXFORD

UNIVERSITY PRESS

Oxford University Press is a department of the University of Oxford.
It furthers the University's objective of excellence in research, scholarship,
and education by publishing worldwide.

Oxford   New York
Auckland   Cape Town   Dar es Salaam   Hong Kong   Karachi
Kuala Lumpur   Madrid   Melbourne   Mexico City   Nairobi
New Delhi   Shanghai   Taipei   Toronto

With offices in
Argentina   Austria   Brazil   Chile   Czech Republic   France   Greece
Guatemala   Hungary   Italy   Japan   Poland   Portugal   Singapore
South Korea   Switzerland   Thailand   Turkey   Ukraine   Vietnam

Oxford is a registered trademark of Oxford University Press in the UK and
certain other countries.

Published in the United States of America by
Oxford University Press
198 Madison Avenue, New York, NY 10016

Library of Congress Cataloging-in-Publication Data
Bold, Christine, 1955–
The frontier club : popular westerns and cultural power, 1880–1924 / Christine Bold.
p. cm.
ISBN 978–0–19–973179–4—ISBN 978–0–19–991302–2   1. American literature—West (U.S.)—
History and criticism.   2. Western stories—History and criticism.   3. Frontier and pioneer
life in literature.   4. West (U.S.)—In literature.   I. Title.
PS271.B65 2013
810.9'3278—dc23
2012024725

ISBN 978–0–19–973179–4
978–0–19–991302–2

1 3 5 7 9 8 6 4 2
Printed in the United States of America
on acid-free paper

To Ric
again

CONTENTS

LIST OF ILLUSTRATIONS

ACKNOWLEDGMENTS

It's a long way round for a shortcut. Thirty years ago, I completed a doctoral dissertation on popular westerns, which became my first book, *Selling the Wild West*. I still owe thanks to Professor Stephen Fender (and, subsequently, Mick Gidley and Eric Mottram) for supporting what was regarded by some, at that time, as a rather dubious endeavor. Many years later, as I was emerging from an onerous stint of university administration, Robert Paul Lamb and G. R. Thompson invited me to contribute an essay on print westerns to their Blackwell *Companion to American Fiction, 1865–1914*. I will be forever grateful to them; not only did this work reconnect me with the field, but I began to recognize some of the blind spots—at times amounting to tunnel vision—of my earlier work and set about enlarging my frame of reference. The eventual result was this book.

Along the way, I have enjoyed an astonishing level of support. As an archivally rich project, this work has depended on generous funding from the Social Sciences and Humanities Research Council of Canada, the American Heritage Center at the University of Wyoming, and the College of Arts Research Enhancement Fund and the Undergraduate Research Assistantships Program at the University of Guelph. I have depended greatly on the support of Lori Barnsley in the Dean of Arts office, University of Guelph. Graduate and undergraduate research assistants who have provided invaluable aid include (at the University of Guelph) Shannon Boucher, Liz Groeneveld, and Morvern McNie and (at the University of Wyoming) Kirsty Callaghan.

Innumerable archivists have contributed their expertise and time; again, this work would have been impossible without their generosity. I thank the staff of the K. Ross Toole Archives, Mansfield Library, University of Montana-Missoula (including Donna McCrea and Amy Casamassa); the Glacier National Park Archives, Montana (particularly Deirdre Shaw and Fred Manicke); the Glacier National Park Library, Montana (especially Sheree West); the American Heritage Center, University of Wyoming (including Carol Bowers, Leslie Carol Waggener,

John R. Waggener, Shannon Bowen, Ginny Kilander, D. C. Thompson, and Rick Walters); the McCracken Research Library, Buffalo Bill Historical Center, Cody, Wyoming (especially Linda Clark and Mary Robinson); the Western History and Genealogy Division, Denver Public Library (including Judy Brown, Roger Dudley, and Ellen Zazzarino); Archives and Special Collections, University of Nebraska-Lincoln; the Historical Society of Pennsylvania, Philadelphia; the College of Physicians, Philadelphia; The New York Public Library Manuscripts and Archives Division; the Frederic Remington Art Museum, Ogdensburg, New York (especially Laura A. Foster); Princeton University Library, Manuscripts Division (especially Don C. Skemer); Manuscripts and Archives, Yale University Library; the Moorland-Springarn Research Center, Howard University, Washington, DC (especially Marva Belt); and the Manuscripts Division, Library of Congress, Washington, DC (especially Bruce Kirby and Jeffrey Flannery). Earnest Heavy Runner, Cultural Advisor, the Blackfeet Heritage Center and Art Gallery, Browning, Montana, gave generously of his time and knowledge. Although this work is thick with references to publications on which I depended, I have drawn so fundamentally on the work of three scholars that I want also to acknowledge my debt here: to Darwin Payne for his finely detailed biography of Owen Wister, to Richard Slotkin for his magisterial trilogy on "the frontier," and to G. Edward White for his first, provocative excavation of connections between the eastern establishment and the West.

At Oxford University Press, I am indebted to Shannon McLachlan, Stephen Bradley, and Elyse Turr, the anonymous manuscript readers, and most especially to Brendan O'Neill for his unstintingly professional guidance. I also greatly appreciate the punctilious attention of Sravanthi Sridharan at Newgen Knowledge Works and my copy-editor Michele Bowman.

While all errors and omissions are of course mine, I could not have completed the project without the Western Literature Association, a community of scholars unparalleled in its combination of collegiality, acuteness, and engagement. Among the members of the association whom I thank for their memorable conversations and thought-provoking suggestions are Chad Allen, José Arando, Susan Bernardin, Neil Campbell, J. J. Clark, Krista Comer, Sara Humphreys, Katy Halverson, Michael K. Johnson, Susan Kollin, Carmen Pearson, Karen Ramirez, Lisa Tatonetti, Steve Tatum, Nicole Tonkovich, and Nicolas Witschi. Heartfelt thanks also to Nancy Cook for her critical help with my Montana research, Melody Graulich for her unfailing support on many fronts, Bill Handley for his detailed and very generous reading of my work, and Victoria Lamont and Susan Nance for sustaining me with their constant and knowledgeable enthusiasm. Members of the Canadian Association for American Studies and the American Historical Association also provided very valuable feedback. Over the years, several invitations to talk about the project helped it along: much thanks to Don Chambers and the Extended Learning Opportunities group in Erin, Ontario; Gary Kelly, Kirsten MacLeod, and the Pop Print conference committee at the University of Alberta; Mark Simpson and the Department of English and Film Studies at the University of Alberta; Cheryl Suzack and the Lansdowne Lectureship at the University of Victoria, British Columbia; and Percy Walton and "The Production of Literature" PhD program at Carleton University, Ottawa. My friend Cressida McKean gave me an extraordinary gift with her invitation to talk about the project in the Pocono Lake Preserve lecture series, where I was honored to meet some members of the current generation of redoubtable Wistar women.

I have also bent the ear of many a generous friend and colleague in far-flung places. I have learned a great deal from conversations and correspondence with Richard Abel, John Benson, John Dorst, Mike Epp, Tara Kathleen Kelly, Eric Sandeen, Shelley Streeby, Cheryl Suzack, Mark Simpson, Mary Swan, George B. Ward, and Chris Wilson. For pointing me beyond the frontier club, I especially thank Philip Adams, Gloria Miguel, Monique Mojica, Yvette Nolan, and Michelle St. John. I dedicate the book to Ric Knowles, who has stuck with it, and me, for many a year. He has been my chauffeur from Philadelphia to Wyoming, my unpaid research assistant from Washington, DC to Glacier National Park, my constant sounding board, my first and best reader, and my indispensable companion.

Earlier formulations of some of this book's arguments appeared in the following publications: "Exclusion Acts: How Popular Westerns Brokered the Atlantic Diaspora," *American Exceptionalisms*, ed. Sylvia Söderlind and James Taylor Carson (Albany, NY: SUNY Press, 2011), 93–123; "Westerns," *U.S. Popular Print Culture, 1860–1920*, ed. Christine Bold (Oxford: Oxford University Press, 2011), 317–36; "Where Did The Black Rough Riders Go?," in *War*, ed. Michael H. Epp, Spec. Issue of *Canadian Review of American Studies* 39.3 (2009): 273–97 (material reprinted with permission from University of Toronto Press www.utpjournals.com); "'Rough Riders of the World': The Frontier Club and the Atlantic Diaspora," in *Americas' Worlds and the World's Americas*, ed. Amaryll Chanady et al. (Ottawa, ON: University of Ottawa/ Legas, 2006), 369–78; "'The Frontier Story': The Violence of Literary History," in *A Companion to American Fiction, 1865–1914*, ed. Robert Paul Lamb and G. R. Thompson (Oxford: Blackwell, 2006), 201–21. I gratefully acknowledge these publishers and thank all the editors and readers involved for their very helpful feedback.

PREFACE

For better and for worse, we owe a lot to the group I call "the frontier club" (Fig. P.1). At the turn of the twentieth century, this network of patrician easterners created the western as we now most commonly know it, yoking the genre to their interests in hunting and conservation, open-range ranching, mass publishing, Jim Crow segregation, immigration restriction, and American Indian assimilation. They clinched the formula which has long served as the most popular face of America, nationally and internationally, and they created recreational spaces that continue to benefit some of us while others count the cost.

Frontier club members include more and less well remembered names: Theodore Roosevelt, who became president of the United States in 1901; George Bird Grinnell, leading conservationist, anthropologist, and editor of *Forest and Stream*; Owen Wister, author of the 1902 bestseller *The Virginian*; Winthrop Chanler of the Astor clan, sportsman and soldier; Madison Grant, eugenicist and founder of the New York Zoölogical Society; Henry Cabot Lodge, long-time Republican congressman, then senator; and Caspar Whitney, editor of the sporting journal *Outing*. On the fringes, in one sense, stood Dr. Silas Weir Mitchell, the famous nerve doctor, and, in another, Frederic Remington, western artist and illustrator *par excellence*. Forty-five years ago, G. Edward White cracked open the influence of the eastern establishment on western myth-making by exploring the triad of Remington, Roosevelt, and Wister. Subsequently, Richard Slotkin put particular emphasis on Roosevelt's formative role in generating a frontier myth that privileged aristocratic violence. Building on this groundbreaking scholarship, my study draws heavily on archival records to trace a more intricate mesh of alliances and exclusions among nine key easterners. Through their extended club network, these men popularized a version of the West which furthered their own cultural, political, and financial interests while violently excluding less powerful groups. This power play happened in print, just at the dawn of moving pictures, decades before paperback books and

Figure P.1. The Frontier Clubmen around the Turn of the Twentieth Century

television shows, and much about the western has changed with these developments. Yet the clubmen's fingerprints are still legible on the formula.

The laconic white cowboy, the shootout on main street, the "neck tie party,"
the pacifist schoolma'am come west, the cowering townspeople in need of
defense, the ever-present threat of "savages," and, above all, the gentrification
of violence are frontier club legacies. As members of the eastern establishment
threatened by rapid and volatile change, frontier clubmen sought to shore up
their cultural power by influencing public opinion and federal policy in the key
areas of land control, race politics, and emerging mass culture. They worked their
political connections, mounted magazine campaigns, spearheaded advocacy
organizations, and produced popular writings which, in complementary ways,
promoted a club mentality of privilege and exclusion. From this constellation

of mutually reinforcing narratives emerged what would become the trademark motifs of the western. By delving into the clubmen's archives of personal papers and organizational records, we can recover the cultural baggage carried by the genre and appreciate how deeply its making depended on those whom the frontier club sought to exclude: women, African Americans, "new" immigrants, and Indigenous peoples. This book makes newly visible how, in whose interests, and at what cost a central trope of U.S. culture was made.

In order to demonstrate what was at stake in this story, I begin by revisiting the collusion of clubmen east and west in the most graphic act of violence to fuel the frontier club western. Then I excavate, chapter by chapter in a somewhat recursive structure, the buried cultural, political, and financial connections that undergirded its success. Chapter One addresses the centerpiece of the frontier club network, the Boone and Crockett Club, exploring how its creation of the proto-western connected to its vision of conservation. Chapter Two brings publishing history into the story, tracing how open-range ranching and mass publishing—both heavily contested terrains—overlapped and paralleled each other, economically and culturally, and how the frontier club western functioned as the linchpin in this relationship. Chapter Three focuses on the women who have been erased from the cultural history of the western: the wives, mothers, daughters, and mentors of frontier clubmen without whom the modern western as we know it would not exist. Chapter Four zeroes in on another group conventionally excluded from the history of the popular western—African Americans—who were both fundamental to and suppressed by the writings of frontier clubmen. Chapter Five traces the contribution of frontier club writings to federal policy on immigration and American Indian assimilation—in other words, to the regulation of American citizenship. Chapter Six goes beyond the frontier club by recovering other writers and performers—Indigenous figures, African Americans, and white women—who attempted to popularize the West in very different terms during the same period and were pushed to the margins. By way of conclusion, I map the continuing imprint of frontier club patterns and values on mainstream western movies.

These intimations of orchestrated effort, collective creation, and mutually reinforcing interests sound very different from the still orthodox claim that Owen Wister single-handedly created the modern western with his bestselling novel of 1902, *The Virginian*. Wister himself got the ball rolling in 1928, when he declared, "*The Virginian*...suddenly created the popular taste which has demanded Western stories ever since" ("Preface" xxxix). His fans reinforced this message: his daughter, for example, said in 1958, "This one novel set the tradition of the West permanently" (F. Wister, *Owen* 2). And, in the 1960s and 70s, when popular literature entered academic study in a big way, critical consensus followed. In 1968, Leslie Fiedler announced of the formula western,

"The pattern is set once and for all in Owen Wister's *The Virginian*," a judgment that was repeated by such influential scholars as John Cawelti, Richard Etulain, and Ray Allen Billington.[1] As Lee Clark Mitchell puts it: "Choose any history of the Western" and it will cite *The Virginian* as "responsible all by itself for making the restrained, soft-spoken, sure-shooting cowboy into a figure worthy of sustained popular interest" (95). This one-man-genre narrative mirrors the western formula itself: it upholds triumphant individualism, expunging both collective effort and competing models, then and thereafter.

Resituating the novel within the frontier club network challenges this perspective. The novel was successful (it enjoyed fifteen reprintings in its first year alone and has never been out of print) precisely because its way was prepared by influential figures and discourses and because its telling of western adventure underwrote their values. In addition to bringing alive a social group and its cultural power, then, this account also tells the history of a book and the making of popularity at the moment when the international literary marketplace was hardening into the coordinates we live with today.

The Frontier Club Western

An Introduction

Lynch law. On the evening of April 5, 1892, a group of clubmen—English aristocrats, Ivy League alumni, and big ranch managers—boarded a private train in Cheyenne, Wyoming, joining a carful of Texas mercenaries behind drawn blinds. The combined force, about fifty men in all, disembarked in Casper before dawn the next day, saddled up, checked their arms, then rode north on the sagebrush flats to the small KC ranch where they surrounded a cabin containing two cowboys. They shot down Nick Ray then set the cabin alight to smoke out Nate Champion, whom they gunned down as he blundered out of the flames in his stocking feet. Ten years later almost to the month, another clubman in Philadelphia, a friend of the vigilantes, published a highly fictional version of this lynching. In the most famous western of all time, *The Virginian*, Owen Wister transformed this event in two astonishingly successful ways. He turned a brutal murder by a power elite into a democratic uprising, a case of "your ordinary citizen" taking back the power of the U.S. constitution on the wild frontier, and he converted an incident of mob violence into an image of heroic individualism (436). In this sleight of hand we see the force that created the modern western: a cultural elite violently protecting its privilege in the name of democracy—in other words, the frontier club mentality.

I begin with this explosion of violence and its conversion into popular print because they go to the heart of the frontier club western. This moment in history is not just a dramatic (and often told) incident in a Wyoming range war; it is a crystallization of the stakes in the making of a genre. This chapter introduces the key players, organizations, and literary activity that together seized the West as a source of cultural power in the late nineteenth century. This network was subtended by more deeply buried alliances and exclusions—social, political, and financial—to which I return in subsequent chapters. First, I set the stage by rehearsing the coming together of three crucial forces: clubmen, cattle interests, and popular print culture.

Frontier Clubmen

America's most popular form was shaped by a group of influential easterners who were prominent in politics and professional life—as well as being published authors—and who inhabited the most privileged class in Victorian America. They clustered around the most exclusive college and gentlemen's clubs of the period—including the Porcellian and Dickey at Harvard, the Philadelphia and Rittenhouse Clubs in Philadelphia, the Somerset in Boston, the Metropolitan in Washington, DC, and the Manhattan in New York City.[1]

As Ivy-League-educated, Anglo-American "old stock," these men were habituated to wielding considerable public influence in politics, publishing, the law, medicine, and the arts. In Gilded Age America, however, this class—G. Edward White calls them America's "preindustrial eastern upper class"—felt threatened by rapid industrial, urban, and demographic change (6). They feared the rise of new financial power brokers and non-Anglo groups (while their private and public writings are peppered with racial epithets, they reserved their most vicious characterizations for Jewish Americans, who combined these two threats). Exclusive clubs functioned as cultural enclaves, keeping unwanted groups at bay while enabling members to shore up social, political, and financial alliances among themselves and with their transatlantic counterparts. Behind the walls of these venerable establishments, homosocial rituals bolstered members' manhood, class position, and Anglo-Saxon superiority: college clubmen indulged in boyish hi-jinks, gentlemen clubmen gathered for more dignified repasts, political connections were made, publishing deals were struck, lobby groups met, while committees spun out the arcane rules of club inclusion and exclusion. In these and other ways, the club network simultaneously protected members from a modernizing world and gave them power within it.

In 1887, this club culture emphatically connected with the American West when Theodore Roosevelt (Harvard 1880) met with a hand-picked group of friends to found the Boone and Crockett Club. The membership consisted of self-styled "gentlemen hunters"—the vast majority of them easterners who had already won election to the exclusive gentlemen's clubs—who wanted to reserve western lands for their sporting pleasure. The club became a powerful lobby group, promoting several congressional bills concerning hunting, conservation, and forestry, and it remains today a force to be reckoned with on gun legislation, hunting rights, and wildlife policy.[2]

As part of the effort to extend the reach of Anglo-American cultural capital over the West, the Boone and Crockett Club also developed a distinctive literary culture. In 1893, Roosevelt and George Bird Grinnell (Yale 1870) edited the first of what became a seven-volume series of members' hunting tales and conservation essays—about ninety essays in all—faithfully shepherded by Grinnell over the next forty years. Contributors—who included Wister (Harvard 1882), Winthrop Chanler (Harvard 1885), and Caspar Whitney (who claimed to have graduated from Harvard in 1882)—strategized about how to popularize without "vulgarizing" their vision of the West.[3] Members' tales mapped first the American West then an expanding global network of hunting locations with the attitudes and hierarchies of gentlemen hunters, reaching across Mexico, Alaska, Canada, Africa, India, Russia, Chinese Turkestan, Korea, Mongolia, and Tibet. As these writings were traded back and forth among Boone and Crockett members for comment and editorial emendation, they developed a remarkably consistent voice, and they crystallized the western's fundamental features: the tenderfoot narrator, the laconic hero, the stylized violence, the exclusive right of white men to carry the gun, and the vast, beautiful landscapes that become enclaves of whiteness, emptied out of women and threatened by savage forces. Together, these features resolve what Lee Clark Mitchell calls the problem that most deeply haunts the western, "the problem of becoming a man" (4). Some members extended the values and tropes of these hunting tales into other spheres. Henry Cabot Lodge (Harvard 1872) helped to convert Boone and Crockett values into congressional action on conservation and immigration; Madison Grant (Yale 1889) echoed his Boone and Crockett publications in his writings on race suicide. None of these men lived long-term in the West, yet they succeeded in stamping its most popular representation with their values and interests.

The frontier club network went beyond Boone and Crockett membership, although that organization was the central consolidating force. Dr. Silas Weir Mitchell, Philadelphia clubman, preferred fishing to hunting and never joined the Boone and Crockett Club (though his son, John K. Mitchell, also a doctor and his father's coauthor, was a long-time member). Nevertheless, Mitchell helped to give the frontier club western its start. As a renowned nerve doctor, he mythologized the West as manly space; as a bestselling author, he brought drawing-room manners to the western formula; and as cousin and mentor to Owen Wister, he gave his young relative his entrée to the publishing world. These so-called "quality" publishers—centrally, J. Henry Harper of Harper & Brothers and George Brett, editor at Macmillan—were also prominent figures on the club scene and used Manhattan club quarters to wine, dine, and on occasion celebrate their western authors.

The joker in this pack was Frederic Remington. As a visual artist, he was central to the dominant popularization of the West, he illustrated many frontier club works, and he enjoyed friendship of sorts with several of the clubmen. But he hovered on the edge of the elite social institutions without winning full acceptance. He was not of the aristocratic class, he did not have the same Ivy League pedigree—although he attended Yale Art School, he did not graduate, and he never won membership in the most exclusive clubs—and, contrary to conventional wisdom, he was not a member of the Boone and Crockett Club.[4] His literary work serves as a kind of limit case, for what it reveals about the cost of frontier club values.

Vigilante Clubmen

Meanwhile, on the western plains, an outpost of the frontier club had formed which was destined to expose the brute force at the heart of the eastern take-over of the West. It was a particular example of the violence which, as Louis Owens points out, was inherent in "the American establishment" treating the West as "a capitalist resource"—whether for ranching, big-game hunting, or popular entertainment (85). In 1880, the Cheyenne Club was organized by big cattle ranchers, led by Boston blue-bloods, European remittance men, and Ivy League alumni (some—such as Hubert Teschemacher, Frederic deBillier, and Dick Trimble—were Porcellian clubmates and some became staunch Boone and Crockett Clubmen).[5] All had come to Wyoming to make a quick killing on the "bonanza frontier" of open-range ranching (Slotkin, *Gunfighter* 18). They determined to erect their own gentlemanly enclave, replicating the opulent trappings, gentlemanly rituals and exclusive membership of the metropolitan clubs: "the Somerset moved West," as one of the founders put it.[6]

The Cheyenne Club was, however, the velvet glove over the iron fist of the Wyoming Stock Growers Association, the organization through which the cattle kings controlled open-range ranching and policed the activities of small ranchers, whom they suspected of cattle stealing and dubbed "rustlers." After the disastrous winter of 1886–1887—when temperatures dropped to -43 degrees centigrade and 900,000 cattle died on the overstocked plains—the big cattle ranchers felt increasingly threatened by homesteaders encroaching on what they had come to assume was their territory and became increasingly violent in their methods.[7] The club provided a genteel mantle for their activities, privacy in which they could hatch their plans, a place to wine and dine opinion makers—local politicians, newspaper editors, municipal leaders—and, briefly in 1892, the most open and luxurious of jails for lynchers under federal arrest.[8]

Although there were frequent rumors of WSGA intimidation, ambushing, and assassination, two recorded acts of terrorism stand out. In July 1889 six big cattle ranchers led by Albert Bothwell, a Cheyenne Club stalwart with Ivy League pretensions and anglophile airs, lynched settlers Ellen Watson and Jim Averell. The couple had staked homestead claims on the beautiful, fertile Sweetwater Valley, infringing on the parcel of land illegally seized by Bothwell—who was operating according to standard cattle king practice—and cutting across his access to water. The only hanging of a woman in Wyoming, the act was so shocking that the WSGA had to move quickly to manipulate public opinion, coercing the local press into representing Watson and Averell as cattle thieves guilty of "extraordinary provocation" in preying on the big ranchers' property (Hufsmith 15). The Cheyenne newspapers reached for recognizably dime novel conventions to vilify Watson—"Cattle Kate," they called her—in particular (Fig. I.1). The *Cheyenne Daily Leader* and the *Daily Sun* claimed that she was a prostitute, bank-robber, and husband-poisoner:

> The female was the equal of any man on the range. Of robust physique she was a daredevil in the saddle, handy with a six-shooter and adept with the lariat and branding iron. Where she came from no one seems to know, but that she was a holy terror all agreed. She rode straddle, always had a vicious broncho for a mount and seemed never to tire of dashing across the range. (Quoted in Hufsmith 11)

The tactics worked. A grand jury absolved the lynchers.

Three years later, the WSGA did it again. The attack on the KC ranch in April 1892 was the climax of the so-called Johnson County War. The big cattle ranchers had launched an offensive against "small operators"—homesteaders, maverickers, cowboys on the WSGA blacklist—whom they suspected of stock

Figure I.1. Ella "Cattle Kate" Watson

rustling, conveniently ignoring how many of their own number had employed the same techniques to build their spreads in earlier days.[9] They drew up a "death list" which has been reported as consisting of anywhere from 19 to 70 alleged rustlers clustered in Johnson County, hired a score of Texas gunmen with the promise of a $50 bounty a head, and moved north from Cheyenne, first on their specially commissioned train then by horseback (Fig. I.2). The cabin at the KC ranch on the Powder River held four men: two trappers, whom the vigilantes let go, and the independent cowboys Ray and Champion, who had openly defied the WSGA monopoly. The siege was a blundering comedy of errors from the first—it took two days for fifty men to overpower the two cowboys—and news of the murders spread to incensed homesteaders in the area. Over 400 took up arms—small ranchers, along with workingmen, mechanics, and assorted citizens of Douglas, the local county seat—and they, in turn, laid siege to the self-styled "invaders" at the TA ranch, a posse member's spread just north of the KC, to which the vigilantes had retreated in disarray. Eventually the vigilantes' powerful friends in Washington, DC, broke the stalemate. After receiving "a nocturnal visit" from two Wyoming senators and some insistent telegrams from the acting state governor (all statesmen with links to the WSGA), President Benjamin Harrison ordered the 6th Cavalry to take the vigilantes into custody (O'Neal 147). The cattle barons were ostensibly brought to justice, but all escaped conviction.

The Cheyenne Club celebrated the murderers' acquittal in best club style, what one of the vigilantes (William C. Irvine, who later became state treasurer, then senator) called "The grand finale to the whole affair.... a Banquet without regard to expense."[10] It included unlimited champagne, a wild send-off to the Texans, and the presentation of a silver cup which rewrote the lynching as a heroic act: the engraving reads, "In grateful remembrance of untiring devotion on our behalf during the trying time of the Wyoming invasion of 1892."[11]

The Virginian

The conflict between big and small ranchers was accompanied by a running battle over who got to tell the story and in what terms.[12] Part of Jim Averell's threat to the cattle barons lay in his eloquent letters about the land-grabbers printed in the Wyoming press, which the WSGA tried to counter with their newspaper "propaganda barrage" in the wake of lynching Watson and Averell (H. H. Smith 127). When the vigilantes set out for Johnson County, they took along two newspapermen—one local, one from Chicago—to ensure that their version of events received national coverage. Nate Champion wrote the story of his own murder, from inside the burning cabin, on a notebook whose

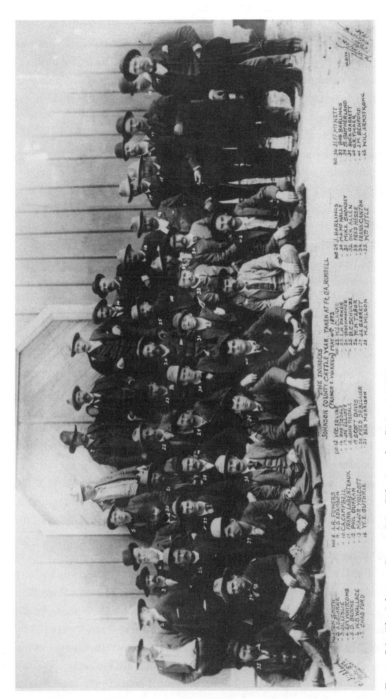

Figure I.2.   The Johnson County War, "The Invaders," May 4, 1892

contents were published a week later in the Chicago *Herald* before mysteriously disappearing. Jack Flagg, leader of the independent cowboys, began to serialize "A Review of the Cattle Business in Johnson County, Wyoming, Since 1882, and the Causes That Led to the Recent Invasion" in the Buffalo (Wyoming) *Bulletin* just weeks after the killing of Champion and Ray.[13] The first denunciation of the cattle barons to make it into book form, *The Banditti of the Plains; or, The Cattlemen's Invasion of Wyoming in 1892 (The Crowning Infamy of the Ages)* by Cheyenne newspaper proprietor A. S. Mercer, was published in 1894 only to be burned in the West and suppressed in the East—"Even the copyright copies disappeared from the Library of Congress" (Mercer xvi). Almost a century later, Michael Cimino's 1980 film *Heaven's Gate*, which ran wildly over budget and is reputed to have helped to bring down United Artists, fingered the class and race hatred behind the cattle barons' brutality. The film had a catastrophic reception. Kris Kristofferson, one of its stars, argued that it was a case of "political assassination" by the newly installed administration of Ronald Reagan, determined to stamp out negative portrayals of U.S. history.

Owen Wister worked within a different political and literary framework. He brought the cultural resources of clubmen in the East in support of the violence of clubmen in the West and created a bestselling novel. *The Virginian* weaves participants and events from the Wyoming range violence into a story of romance and adventure, switching up the power dynamics so that intimidation becomes heroism, manliness equals class fealty, and independence translates into insurrection. Read against its historical moment, the novel also reveals the logic connecting an exclusive club mentality with its ultimate expression in the act of lynching.

Wister was introduced to the Cheyenne Club by his Porcellian clubmate Dick Trimble in 1885, on his first trip to the Territory of Wyoming. He fell in love with the club's ambience—he called it "the pearl of the prairies"—and became an unblushing apologist for the cattle barons.[14] On a return trip to Wyoming in 1889, he met one of the ranchers who had murdered Watson and Averell, recording in his diary: "Sat yesterday in smoking car with one of the gentlemen indicted for lynching the man and the woman—He seemed a good solid citizen—and I hope he'll get off—Sheriff Donell said, 'All the good folks say it was a good job: it's only the *wayward* classes that complain.'"[15] His sympathies in the Johnson County War were entirely with his clubmates. Cheyenne Club founders and Porcellian members Teschemacher, deBillier, and Trimble all joined the 1892 posse, as did Dr. Charles Penrose, Wister's Philadelphia clubmate. The vigilantes were led by Major Frank Wolcott, who hosted Wister on his first trip west, as manager of the VR ranch in which Wister's Philadelphia friends had financial interests.

In *The Virginian* Wister updated the West of James Fenimore Cooper and the dime novelists for the twentieth century. He moved the setting from the forested wilderness to the Wyoming plains and the hero from hunter to cowboy—here, the laconic Southerner known only as "the Virginian." Three plot strands hold the episodic structure together: the evolving relationship between the eastern tenderfoot narrator (who sounds very much like Wister) and the Virginian; the Virginian's courting of Molly Wood, an eastern schoolma'am come west (who shares a name and some attitudes with Wister's wife); and the Virginian's rise through the ranching hierarchy, which includes his shooting down one rustler and lynching two more on the orders of his boss, Judge Henry.

The cowboy's heroism is proven through one violent act of exclusion after another, presented sometimes as comical, at other times as tragic, but always as necessary. Wister first disposes of Ella Watson in a joke, tossed off in the novel's opening pages. As the eastern narrator arrives at Medicine Bow station, he encounters the Virginian in the midst of joshing an aged local about his attempts to find a young bride: "you'd most got united with Cattle Kate, only—" the victim, Uncle Hughey, expostulates, "—only she got hung" (5). This comic strain runs throughout the novel, as the Virginian makes a fool of "Jew drummers," jokes about "I-talians" and Chinese, and sings racist ditties about African Americans, making it clear that none of these groups belong in the pure boyish community of the West.

Also running throughout the novel is the mano-a-mano combat between the Virginian and Trampas, in which the hero's moral righteousness is conflated with the big rancher interests which he represents. Trampas is the ultimate demonization of the rustler. Modeled partly on Jack Flagg, he proves his villainy in his disrespectful attitude to Molly, his bucking of the Virginian's authority as ranch foreman, his recruitment of weak-willed cowboys into his gang of thieves, and his murder of one of that gang. (The character provides practically one-man vindication of Governor Barber's wild telegram to President Harrison, in which he claimed that Wyoming was facing "insurrection" and successfully begged for federal troops to protect the vigilantes [quoted in H. H. Smith 224]). The Virginian repeatedly humiliates Trampas, from the first time he draws a gun on him, with the famous line, "When you call me that, *smile!*," to his ridiculing of him with a tall tale, to the ultimate confrontation in their shootout. When the Virginian kills Trampas, there is no question that honor has vanquished villainy. The Virginian's reward is marriage to the eastern schoolma'am, entrance into the rancher class, land ownership, and status as "an important man, with a strong grip on many various enterprises" (503).

Before that ending comes the sequence of chapters in which Wister most directly whitewashed the vigilantism of the WSGA. He conflated the murders of 1889 and 1892 in a scene in which the Virginian leads a posse in hanging two cattle thieves, the Virginian's erstwhile friend Steve, who has been turned bad by Trampas, and his partner-in-crime Ed. The lynching is represented as a fraternal ritual undertaken with reluctance. It is the endpoint of a contract—a game, as Steve repeatedly calls it—on whose rules rustlers and ranchers agree, and the chief perpetrator—the Virginian—suffers pangs of remorse much worse than anything the hanging victims endure. Since the narrator is of the eastern establishment, his sympathies for the lynchers suggest both that there is something deeply gentlemanly about the act and that it enjoyed a country-wide climate of support.

The most explicit apologia is delivered by Judge Henry, when he defends the act to Molly, the Virginian's bride-to-be, who is horror-struck by the news of her fiancé's violence. Judge Henry is recognizably based on Frank Wolcott, a justice of the peace who had been promoted to major in the Civil War and had served as a United States marshal in Wyoming. Where Judge Henry is wise, affable, and courteous, however, Major Wolcott was bullying, murderous, a vigilante leader, and quite possibly a briber of juries.[16] Wolcott-cum-Henry's first and most insistent point is the distinction between "burning Southern negroes in public" and "hanging Wyoming cattle-thieves in private" (433). When Molly drily returns that she can see no difference in principle between the two acts, he repeats his words:

> in all sincerity I see no likeness in principle whatever between burning Southern negroes in public and hanging Wyoming horse-thieves in private. I consider the burning a proof that the South is semi-barbarous, and the hanging a proof that Wyoming is determined to become civilized. We do not torture our criminals when we lynch them. We do not invite spectators to enjoy their death agony. We put no such hideous disgrace upon the United States. (434)

He proceeds to lead Molly through a series of specious arguments, including the familiar claim that Wyoming juries refused to convict rustlers, a canard which Helena Huntington Smith exposed when she researched the court records in preparation for her excoriating history of the Johnson County War. Step-by-step Judge Henry's defense turns a violent power elite into "we, the people," the bedrock of U.S. justice: "when they lynch they only take back what they once gave." Molly's counter-arguments dwindle in the face of his logic. Finally, she has no rebuttal.

The making of the modern western coincided with what has been called "a frenzy of lynching": "Between 1869 and 1922, there were 3,436 lynchings committed in the United States with less than a dozen of the perpetrators ever punished" (Tolnay and Beck 3; King 147). The largest number of lynching victims were African American, but between 1910 and 1925, Jewish Americans, Italian Americans, Asian Americans, political dissidents, and union organizers also "were identified as legitimate targets for vigilantism" (Slotkin, *Gunfighter* 192). Anti-lynching activists raised their voices against the assertion that extra-legal violence was necessary to sustain social order. In the 1880s, Ida B. Wells, African American spokeswoman, led the way in bringing public attention to the ways in which a southern racist agenda underlay the myths and justifications promoted by the lynching establishment. White women followed her lead; by 1930, the Association of Southern Women for the Prevention of Violence was visibly active in fifteen southern States, its central goal "to break the circuit between the tradition of chivalry and the practice of mob murder" (J. Hall, "Mind" 337).

The justification mounted by Judge Henry-cum-Major Wolcott in *The Virginian* wades into this debate, without acknowledging its existence, and brings several rhetorical maneuvers to bear on it. First, in distinguishing legitimate western violence from southern brutality, the novel attempts to profit from the southern associations of its title and chivalric hero while distancing itself from the looming underbelly of that image. This tactic is part of the larger post-bellum reconciliation of white men at the expense of southern blacks, what Nina Silber calls "the whitewashed road to reunion" which "paved the way for northern acceptance of some of the most virulent forms of racism which American society had ever produced" (124). The maneuver involves considerable historical inaccuracy. *Pace* Judge Henry's distinction between southern and western vigilantism, the first "spectacle lynching" took place in Texas, and such acts were a known quantity in the West and Southwest, as well as the South.[17] His protestations that Wyoming does not burn its victims ring particularly hollow in light of accusations that the big cattlemen burned Nick Ray's body, whose charred remains went on public display.[18] The novel also undermines the women's lobby: when the judge's apologia silences the educated, eastern Molly, a representative woman becomes complicit in the logic of lynching—and, of course, her objection involves no presumption of innocence. Taking the culpability of the rustlers as proven, she is concerned not for the victims but the perpetrators. In defending the Cheyenne Club vigilantes in these terms, Wister joined the efforts of other frontier clubmen to shape the debate on extra-legal violence to their own purposes. Theodore Roosevelt tried to join a group of Montana vigilantes in 1884, arguing that this was a necessary resort against suspected horse rustlers. Henry Cabot Lodge blamed the lynching of Italians in 1891 on the government's policy of unrestricted immigration. And the group as a whole worked steadily at distinguishing between legitimate and illegitimate uses of violence in terms that shored up their class and race privileges.

In Wister's hands lynching and its defense became increasingly central to the western and its place in a progressive narrative of American history. When he adapted the novel for the stage in 1903, he reoriented the action around lynching and made the connection to the Johnson County War explicit. His script synopsis opens:

> The scene is laid in Wyoming Territory during the era of the great ranches and before the coming of the wire fences. Cattle and horse thieves threaten the prosperity of the ranchmen and the law is unable to protect them; consequently the ranchmen have taken the matter in their own hands and any thief they catch they hang.[19]

Act One sees the big ranchers justifying their violence in an extended debate. They agree on a blacklist of cowboys gone bad, adding fictional names—Trampas, Steve, Shorty—to the historical figures targeted and murdered by the WSGA: Jack Flagg, Nate Champion, Pete [sic] Ray. Wister also ratcheted up the racial dynamic, renaming Steve's sidekick "Spanish Ed" and making the Hispanic connotations of Trampas's name more emphatic with the addition of a first name "Sorgy" (an emphasis which was redoubled when Frank Campeau performed the role in vaquero-type costume).[20] In Act Two the Virginian consents to lead the "lynching bee" in the face of Molly's repeated protests. The climax comes in Act Three, where Wister has his lynching victims endorse the Cheyenne Club version of history. The rustlers are chuckling over the security offered by stacked juries—Steve crows, "The whole of Johnston [sic] county's on our side," and Trampas sneeringly responds, "Johnston county is about tired of these big ranch owners and swell-heads, like Judge Henry"—when they are surprised by the Virginian's posse.[21] The act ends with the Virginian's agony at hanging his friend while "the moon rises, throwing upon a flat face of rock the black shadow of Steve as he hangs in mid-air."[22]

Wister insisted on this emphasis in the face of objections by his co-playwright, Kirke LaShelle (a theatrical entrepreneur with very different sensibilities from the frontier club) and his mother (who was perennially critical of his western subject matter). In terms of popular acclaim, he was proved right. Reviewers consistently praised the lynching scene, and audiences emphatically preferred this version to another, pre-Broadway version that played down the vigilantism. This dramatization was the bridge to the remakes—numerous stage revivals, five film versions between 1914 and 2000, and a weekly television show in the 1960s.[23]

So the ideology of cattle barons became embodied in the quintessential cowboy hero. Men whom even John Clay, erstwhile president of the WSGA, subsequently judged to be guilty of "ill-luck, mismanagement and greed" are celebrated in *The Virginian* as wise mentors and stabilizing forces, the bedrock of the national triumphalism being played out in the West (quoted in H. H. Smith 35). In the longer view, we can see how the attempt first collectively mounted by the Boone and Crockett Clubmen in their publications—the attempt to reserve the privilege of honorable killing for their class and race—bodily entered mass entertainment, firmly hooked to the rise of American history.

Coda

The Johnson County War as reconfigured by Wister illuminates the key elements of the frontier club power play, in terms of white masculinity, club culture, and the mutually reinforcing structures of the cattle and publishing industries.

The moment is equally significant for what it suppresses, especially in terms of race. African Americans, who are invisible in frontier club westerns, in fact featured as a pawn in the WSGA end-game. In June 1892, while awaiting arraignment in Cheyenne, Frank Wolcott and others wired Wyoming Senator Joseph M. Carey to arrange for members of the African American 9th Cavalry to be sent out to watch over the citizens of Johnson County. The WSGA vigilantes aimed to exploit racism to their own benefit. They calculated that ratcheting up tensions could lead to more violence and deaths among their adversaries, or at least to the undermining of their credibility and the further distraction of local law enforcement. With a coded reference to the independent cowboy leader Jack Flagg, who had come up from Texas, and his associates they insisted: "The colored troops will have no sympathy for Texan thieves, and these are the troops we want" (quoted in Schubert, "Suggs" 60). Within two weeks, the secretary of war had complied and the black troops were stationed on the Powder River near the town of Suggs. Predictably, racial hostility, exacerbated by locals' suspicion that the black soldiers were doing the dirty work of big cattlemen, erupted in what is known as "the Suggs Affray."[24] For several days, the cavalrymen were subjected to discrimination and racist epithets, then Private Abraham Champ of G Troop was attacked. As told by Frank N. Schubert, based on official records, the confrontation reads like a counterpoint to Wister's famous "son-of-a—" scene:

> Private Champ went into town on June 16 to see a prostitute he had known previously. The woman refused Champ's requests to enter her house, so he headed toward a local saloon for a drink. At the saloon he was accosted by a white man with a drawn gun. "Ain't your mother a black bitch?" he threatened. (63)

The cavalryman escaped only to return with a large group of his fellow soldiers the next night. They opened fire on the town and the ensuing fight left one black soldier dead and two injured.

As we will see, this was only one of many occasions on which Wister specifically and frontier clubmen more generally rendered the black presence invisible. The climactic showdown between white men in the western repeatedly aims to deny the claims of others (including, crucially, the Indigenous peoples on whose land the Johnson County War was fought) to their part in the story. This example of how alliance and exclusion go violently hand in hand reverberates throughout this book.

1

Boone and Crockett Writers

On the evening of January 11, 1893, during the lame-duck days between President Harrison's defeat at the ballot box in November and President-Elect Cleveland's inauguration in March, the gentlemen of the Boone and Crockett Club held their most sumptuous banquet to date. They gathered in the exclusive confines of the Metropolitan Club—within walking distance of the White House, it had served as the most discrete refuge of Washington's power elite since 1863—dining on saddles of elk and mountain sheep shipped in from Montana and making merry until after one o'clock in the morning.[1] These gentlemen hunters included some of the most influential figures of the new generation: Theodore Roosevelt, Boone and Crockett Club president and currently the headline-grabbing civil service commissioner, and George Bird Grinnell, the club's cofounder, who was becoming a powerhouse lobbyist as editor of *Forest and Stream*, headed a list of names who were rising to the top of the political, military, literary, financial, academic, professional, and social elite. On that evening, their guests ranged from the secretary of the interior to the popular sports editor of *Harper's Weekly*. The purpose of the meeting was to announce their new cultural program, consisting of their first exhibit, at the World's Columbian Exposition, and the launching of a book series.

Within the decade, these hunter-writers would successfully lay claim to the American West by establishing the dominant blueprint for conservation and the manual for the modern western. This chapter tells the organizational and literary back-story to that success. It traces the emergence of the Boone and Crockett Club program, from its Washington dinner to its Chicago exhibition to its book series. A core group of clubmen shaped this development; I sketch the biographies of eight men who played key roles in bringing together hunting, lobbying, and writing and in forging a collective club voice from these individual lives. The genre that they crafted did triple duty. In the larger frame, it participated in the centuries-old ritualization of "regeneration through violence" that Richard Slotkin has established as central to the formation of American national identity. In the more immediate context, the

14

Boone and Crockett hunting narrative mutated into a model for the formula western and it served as a lobbying tool for a range of frontier club causes. The chapter ends by exploring how those latter two developments dovetailed and reinforced each other.

The Boone and Crockett Club, 1893

The Boone and Crockett Club remains an influential sporting organization, with considerable clout in the hunting and gun lobbies—and it continues to hold lavish annual dinners. It is famous for having codified the rules of fair chase—adherence to hunting seasons, bag limits, protected species, and hunting methods—and having shaped America's first national conservation policies. At the Metropolitan Club dinner, they toasted the success of their influence "first, in making a great timber reserve in Wyoming in the country adjoining the Yellowstone Park; next, in setting aside and protecting from depredators the sequoia groves in California; and finally, in creating on an island on the Alaskan coast a reservation for the protection of seals, salmon, and sea birds, which breed thereon in myriads."[2] What is less remembered is the writing culture that they developed in the late nineteenth century and its role in shaping some fundamental terms that long dominated public debate, government policy-making, and the popularization of the frontier West.

For all their power and privilege, the gentlemen in evening dress lounging around the long dining table also felt themselves to be beleaguered. The changes of the era threatened their entitlements: rapid industrialization and urbanization, labor organization and its violent suppression, economic boom-and-bust cycles, and demographic shifts were transforming the face of postbellum America. New migration patterns—African Americans escaping the South, "new" immigrants from southern and eastern Europe—were visibly changing the cities—Philadelphia, New York, Boston, Washington, DC—in which these gentlemen lived and worked. Many had invested in the open-range cattle industry which, after severe over-grazing, went bust in the winter of 1886–1887; in familiar perpetrator-victim reversal, these would-be cattle kings tended to blame small homesteaders for crowding them out. At the same time, a *nouveau riche* class of tycoons was assembling a new corporate power base, further eroding the traditional economic and social underpinnings of the old-stock aristocracy. And the gentlemen hunters were losing their sport: the last of the great buffalo herds was decimated by 1883, elk and grizzly had disappeared from the western badlands, and even the antelope were thinning.[3] When the Boone and Crockett Club rallied around the cause of big-game preservation, it responded to a larger landscape of loss.

As united a front as the Metropolitan Club display suggested, fissures and frustration were also creeping into the group. For several years, Boone and Crockett Clubmen had supported the bill put forward by one of their members, Senator George Vest of Missouri, ensuring the protection and maintenance of Yellowstone National Park, which had been created in 1872, but they were continuously thwarted by the development, railroad, and mining lobbies—what Grinnell called "some of the sharpest intellects, some of the best business ability in the country" backed by "unlimited money with which to influence legislation" (quoted in Punke 154). For a while, Roosevelt had become persuaded that a railroad should be allowed into the park, until Grinnell, threatening to "throw him overboard," managed to change his mind (quoted in Reiger, *American* 157). Then both Vest and another club member, Arnold Hague, head of the Geological Survey, caved in to pressure to back the "segregation bill" promoted by commercial interests to return over six hundred square miles of the park to private development. In December 1892, Grinnell declared himself "sick of this whole Park business" (quoted in Reiger, *American* 161). Now this club of predominantly Republican stalwarts had lost Harrison as their champion in the White House, and were rallying to keep the pressure on Cleveland.

One of their challenges was to find an effective way of entering the court of public opinion. The clubmen were well connected in the congressional corridors of power, but they also had to persuade "the people"—the amorphous public who were becoming an increasing consideration in the modern age. This was not a simple task for this closed, patrician group, "apparently concerned only with their own recreation," as Grinnell himself put it ("Brief" 490). The emerging mass culture was at once the threat and the solution. Clubmen hated and feared the mechanisms of mass society that delivered the hoi polloi to the regions they aimed to reserve for their private recreation: the railroad networks, the fledgling tourist industry, the Yellowstone Park syndicate, and, above all, the market hunter—"that camp follower of industrialism's advance into the Western wilderness" (Reiger, *American* 133). But these forces had also delivered new communications media—mass magazines, popular fiction— which could mould the opinions of the public whose support they needed. In Grinnell's words:

> It would have been natural and easy for the Club to have confined its
> activities to meeting at intervals to dine, and discuss abuses and dan-
> gers, and to pass stirring resolutions, about them. Instead of this, it
> has had a small body of intelligent men, scattered all over the country,
> working individually and constantly in behalf of things once laughed
> at or unknown, but now as familiar to the public mind as household

words. The results accomplished by the Boone and Crockett Club bear testimony to the alertness and energy of its members, and to the success of the methods which they have pursued. ("Brief" 491)

Those "methods" were central to the program announced in the Metropolitan Club in January 1893.

Six months later, the clubmen reassembled at the Columbian Exposition in Chicago in their "Hunter's Cabin." According to James Trefethen, this exhibit represented "perhaps the only time in its history that the Club in its own name conducted anything resembling a publicity campaign," and it had targeted a mass audience: collectively, at 28 million visitors, the fair represented the largest mass of American public ever gathered in one place.[4] In several ways, the exhibit embodied the club's strategies for popularizing their vision. The cabin was positioned close to the power center of the fair, the immense, neoclassical buildings of White City, on a peaceful wooded island in the middle lagoon, well away from the raucous commercialism of the Midway Plaisance. Securing that favored spot had necessitated considerable leverage. Originally, the island had been reserved for the Japanese temple and gardens, a refuge from the noisy throngs "to be sacred to public comfort" (quoted in Bolotin and Laing 14). Then space was found for Sioux performers who, it was felt, would provide a good fit with this terrain. But this was precisely the kind of space the clubmen were setting out to dominate: they flexed their political muscle, the Sioux were ousted, and the Hunter's Cabin took its place on a tiny islet en route to the Japanese display.

The cabin's design disguised that power behind a façade of authentic western simplicity. Among the fair's towering displays of international achievement—the world's first Ferris Wheel, the brilliant lights powered by a giant electrical dynamo, replicas of Columbus's caravels sailed from Spain, a plethora of mechanical wonders in the Machinery Hall and electrical inventions in the Electricity Hall, the breathtaking scale and international diversity of the Manufactures and Liberal Arts Building—the "long, low cabin of unhewn logs" looked decidedly modest (Grinnell, "Boone" 49). In contrast to the displays of both European classicism and the latest technological wizardry, the cabin's interior was hung with big-game skins, trophy heads, and early hunting weapons. The curator was Elwood "Billy" Hofer, a Montana guide brought in to talk to visitors (he had also supplied the saddles of game for the Washington banquet). All this simplicity cost the club a tidy $2,500.[5] When Grinnell announced the exhibit in *Forest and Stream*—"a log cabin of the ordinary type"—he repeated the word "ordinary" four times in as many sentences.

On June 15, 1893, the cabin showed a different face again when its doors were temporarily closed to the public, it became an enclave for the clubmen to consort with each other and the fair dignitaries (the organization's first and only clubhouse for its first two decades), and the champagne corks began to pop.[6] This time, they dined "well and simply, camp fashion," as Owen Wister put it: planked whitefish, beefsteak, and salt pork complete with fine wine, silverware, and black waiters.[7] Another clubman, Winthrop Chanler, declared, "The dinner went off like a cork out of a bottle" (M. Chanler, *Winthrop* 51). Roosevelt had wanted to stick to "simple drinks"—whisky and beer—appropriate to the western atmosphere, but Wister and Chanler—Dan and Winty, in this company— insisted on champagne.[8] They had much to toast. Later, the champagne would become a matter of grief for the clubman who organized the supper. Charles Deering complained that the surplus had not been returned to the supplier, and he was stuck with the bill. "I am inclined to think that the n[...] waiters stole it," he told Roosevelt (the elision is mine), the violence of privilege under siege welling again behind the discreet façade.[9]

Boone and Crockett Clubmen

There are many declarations about the significance of the World's Columbian Exposition to American culture. It has been called the real beginning of the twentieth century, the true launching of the United States on the international stage, and Chicago's coming of age. It has been credited with showcasing the West as commercial spectacle—Buffalo Bill's Wild West took up fourteen acres just outside the fair's main entrance—and as scholarly concept—Frederick Jackson Turner delivered his influential Frontier Thesis to the American Historical Association, which met in conjunction with the exposition a month after the Boone and Crockett Club shindig. When we consider the company gathered in the Hunter's Cabin, it is no more hyperbolic to claim that this was one of the fair's most concentrated sites of cultural power.

The company of men that toasted itself that June evening had hand-picked each other from their exclusive club, college, and kinship networks. They restricted access to their hunting club with entrance requirements (to qualify for consideration, candidates had to have shot one—later, it was upped to three—of a designated list of big-game animals with the rifle), quotas (membership was initially limited to thirty, later expanded to one hundred), and rules of nomination (a candidate had to be nominated and seconded by two members, followed by a write-in ballot; a single nay would disqualify him). The club's innermost circle was forged by a combination of social status, passion for hunting, and prolific writing. Although quite a number of club authors wend in and out of this story, I here detail a core group of eight who shaped the hunting tale-cum-western and its wider sphere of influence. The common thread in their biographies is the way in which the intertwining of hunting and writing fashioned their identities as much as their vision of the western spaces they aspired to control.

Theodore Roosevelt

The life and soul of the party, the architect of the Hunter's Cabin, and of the Boone and Crockett Club as a whole, was Theodore Roosevelt. In December 1887, he had gathered twelve men at his Manhattan residence to propose the idea of the club, which was officially constituted early the following year. The name was his idea: Daniel Boone and Davy Crockett were for him "the tutelary deities of American hunting lore."[10] Roosevelt's social and political connections were central to the success of the club's lobbying. Once he reached the Oval Office in 1901, he brought in by executive order a slew of policies on natural resource management, protection, and restoration (including "scenic vistas, wildlife ranges, fossil sites, cliff dwelling, Indian artifacts" [Trefethen, *American* 125]).

Hunting was one of the leitmotifs of desire running through Roosevelt's life, from his first years as a member of New York's Knickerbocker aristocracy. He first shot a bird at age 14, for the purposes of anatomical study.[11] Throughout his sickly boyhood and his student years at Harvard (1876–1880), he disciplined himself in "the strenuous life" partly with hunting trips through the Adirondacks in northern New York State and the north woods of Maine. In the fall of 1883, with his political career, as an assemblyman in the New York legislature, taking off, he headed west to the Dakota territory to shoot buffalo. Roosevelt spent sixteen days in the badlands, during which time he hired a guide, shot his first buffalo after prolonged and exhausting hunting, bought the Maltese Cross cattle herd for $14,000, and hired two locals to manage his new ranch. On the strength of this experience and investment, that fall he campaigned for speaker of the legislature as "a man of Harvard, Albany, and the Dakota Territory" (quoted in Brinkley 165).

In February 1884, personal tragedy and political disaster hit the rising star. On February 12, his wife, Alice Lee Roosevelt, gave birth to their first child. Two days later, she and his mother died within hours of each other. Then in June, at the Republican National Convention in Chicago, Roosevelt and his political ally Henry Cabot Lodge suffered humiliating defeat. First failing to block the nomination of James G. Blaine then refusing to bolt the party, they found themselves political outcasts, spurned by the Independents with whom they had conspired and with many of whom they shared close social ties, and denounced by the Reform press. Roosevelt fled to Dakota, into what has typically been characterized as deep withdrawal. Owen Wister said that he "disappeared into the West"; more recently, Richard Slotkin and Edmund Morris represent this period as two years of immersion in "the therapeutic emptiness of the Bad Lands."[12]

The record suggests, rather, that Roosevelt frenetically shuttled back and forth on the Pacific Northern Railroad, with intense bursts of hunting and ranching activity in the West, a month or two at a time, interspersed with periods of equally intense political activity in the East—conferring with Lodge, responding to "shoals of letters, pathetic and abusive" from his critics, and stumping in support of Lodge's run for Congress and Blaine's for president, both of which failed (Morison 76). Even in the midst of the most rugged hunting trips and exhausting labor of the roundup, Roosevelt remained deeply engaged with the minutiae of political, social, and literary life in the East. He corresponded frequently and voluminously with Lodge, his sisters Anna and Corinne ("Darling Bysie" and "Darling Pussie"), and several East Coast editors, keeping up with political developments, justifying and strategizing his and Lodge's maneuvers, and trading literary critiques, all the while detailing his hunting and ranching adventures at length. Even those were oriented eastwards, as he imagined bringing his trophy heads home to his Sagamore Hill mansion, whose hallway would ultimately be decked with his first buffalo head, which he christened Pow-Pow, an elk head named Boom, and a blacktail buck head named Pop-pop-pop.

Roosevelt's correspondence consistently dwelt on the rigors of his western life: "Having been off on a four days hunt after antelope …," "I have just come in from spending *thirteen* hours in the saddle," "I am now writing under difficulties, being in the cattlemen's hut …," "You must pardon the paper and general appearance of this letter, as I am writing out in camp, a hundred miles or so from any house" (Morison 72, 73, 74, 79). For all that, his life sounds quite sociable—and, of course, his very need to write about hunting made it a social activity. On hunts, he was accompanied with one or more guides and sometimes encountered other eastern and European gentry. On the ranch he shared accommodation with his managers who provided rudimentary domestic service. At first, he lived on the Maltese Cross with the Canadians William Merrifield and Sylvane Ferris, then he bought a second ranch, 30 miles further north, and brought out Will Sewall and Wilmot Dow—his former Maine guides—as managers and, subsequently, their wives and children. He shuttled between his ranches, socialized with selected neighbors and townspeople in nearby Medora, organized and chaired meetings of the Little Missouri Stockmen's Association, gave public speeches, and entertained a number of eastern visitors.

This back and forth pattern lasted until October 1886, when he left more permanently, first to campaign (unsuccessfully) as "the Cowboy of Dakota" for mayor of New York, and then to marry his second wife, Edith Carow (Morris 350). While they were on a three-and-a-half-month honeymoon in Europe, the blizzards hit the badlands. Desperate, skeletal cattle huddled in Medora gnawing frozen garbage and tarpaper siding, Roosevelt's herds were decimated, and he lost heart in his western adventure. He wrote to Anna: "I am bluer than indigo about the cattle; it is even worse than I feared; I wish I was sure I would lose no more than half the money ($80,000) I invested out here" (Morison 126–27). After that time, he returned only for hunts and visits, about a month each year, sometimes with friends and family.

From the first, in order for Roosevelt fully to realize his hunting experience, he needed to write about it. When he could not find solitude enough in the West to write the book that he planned—another indication of the sociability of his circumstances—he retreated to Manhattan at the end of December 1884 for an intense three months of composition. *Hunting Trips of a Ranchman*, published in mid-1885, was his second book and the first of his ten volumes addressing hunting or the West. In it, Roosevelt crafts the authoritative persona that he would bring to the Boone and Crockett Club. The first-person voice that he adopts pretends to considerably more western expertise than his time in Dakota—at that point, an accumulated five months at most—would support. Species by species, from water-fowl and grouse to buffalo, elk, and grizzly bear, he describes his pursuit of game, carefully specifying seasons without dates so that it is unclear how many hunts of what duration he has undertaken. He paints his "home ranch-house" as a scene of work-hardened men, relaxing "round the hearthstone, while the pine logs roar and crackle," the room bedecked with antlers, horns, animal skins, and bookshelves—all this at a time when the Elkhorn ranch house did not even yet have a roof.[13]

In a period when voices were already being raised against the slaughter of the northern buffalo herd and other species local to his hunting grounds around the Little Missouri, Roosevelt skillfully merges his roles as independent hunter and property-owning rancher so that each justifies and heroizes the other. His hunting exploits mask the commercial and managerial orientation of his ranching enterprise, while the needs of his ranch crew enable him to gloss over how much of his activity was trophy and how much subsistence hunting: "On many of the ranches—on my own, for instance—the supply of fresh meat depends mainly on the skill of the riflemen, and so, both for pleasure and profit, most ranchmen do a certain amount of hunting each season," though not "such extended trips as are made by some devotees of sport who are so fortunate as to have no every-day work to which to attend" (*Hunting* 3). That insistence that his activity is work, not leisure, recurs throughout (to literary critic Brander Matthews, Roosevelt typically insisted, "I didn't play; I *worked*, while on my ranch") as does the adjective "average"—much like Grinnell's "ordinary"—as his favorite way of characterizing his life in the West (Morison 411). Finally, by framing hunting and open-range ranching as "ephemeral" and "evanescent" phases that inevitably pass, he adroitly avoids grappling with his own complicity in processes of extermination: he had whoopingly rejoiced in killing one of the few remaining buffalo on his first trip to Dakota, he continued to search out scarce game as trophy heads to display in his eastern mansions, and he imported more and more cattle, which contributed to the over-grazing of the badlands. When he wrote to Anna about the scarcity of game—"the cattle men have crowded it out"—he finessed the contradiction between his two roles, complaining as a hunter without acknowledging his own culpability as a rancher (Morison 73–74).

George Bird Grinnell

The reviews of *Hunting Trips of a Ranchman* on both sides of the Atlantic were enthusiastic. One man, however, caught Roosevelt out in his inflated self-representation, and said so in print. George Bird Grinnell, nine years older than Roosevelt, had gone west earlier, farther, and for more extended periods, and he called the author out on his point of pride: his authority. Grinnell praised many of the book's narrative and visual qualities but noted: "We are sorry to see that a number of hunting myths are given as fact, but it was after all scarcely to be expected that with the author's limited experience he could sift the wheat from the chaff and distinguish the true from the false" ("New" 451). Back in Manhattan when the review appeared, Roosevelt rushed indignantly around to the *Forest and Stream* office on Park Row, where, in Grinnell's cryptic words, they "talked freely about the book, and took up at length some of its statements" ("Introduction" xv). Roosevelt was apparently convinced of the older man's credentials (Grinnell claimed, "He at once saw my point of view"), and they became close allies in lobbying for wildlife protection legislation, founding the Boone and Crockett Club, and editing its book series.

Like Roosevelt, Grinnell belonged to a distinguished upper-class family—of long New England lineage, in his case—and he was brought up mainly on Manhattan island; in his wistful recollection, "in those days, which now seem so long ago, a very considerable proportion of the men of any class in New York knew most of the other men in their class."[14] His youth was spent in Audubon Park, the former estate of the great ornithologist whose widow, Lucy Audubon, was Grinnell's boyhood teacher. Among other things, Audubon Park introduced him to hunting implements: on the walls of the Audubon sons' houses "were the antlers of deer and elk, supporting rifles and shotguns, with powder horns and shot, and ball pouches. There were many trophies from the Missouri River."[15] Like Roosevelt, Grinnell began hunting birds as a boy with budding naturalist interests and he also had an Ivy League education, attending Yale from 1866 to 1870 (where he was elected to the Scroll and Key Society), then returning for doctoral studies in osteology and vertebrate paleontology, which he completed in 1880. His life was touched more closely by the financial upheavals of the period. His father was investment broker for the Vanderbilt dynasty, the partner of Horace B. Clark, Cornelius Vanderbilt's son-in-law, with whom he became involved in vast railroad stock speculations.[16] George inherited the brokerage firm with much reluctance (he "had always had a settled dislike for the business") when his father retired (Reiger, *Passing* 80). Weeks later, the Panic of 1873 burst the bubble, at which point the firm went bankrupt. Although Grinnell Sr. came out of retirement to settle the firm's debts, once the business was back in good standing (and his father back in retirement), George sold it off.

Never keen to enter the financial world, Grinnell had, by this time, discovered his lasting passion. In 1870, he had been one of the young Yale graduates accompanying Professor Othniel C. Marsh on a fossil-hunting expedition that ranged across Nebraska, Wyoming, Utah, and California. In five months of rugged travel, he rode with cavalrymen and Pawnee scouts, encountered trappers and members of many Plains nations, survived prairie fire, and fell in love with big-game hunting. Thirty-four years later, he remembered it as "the untrodden west, the fenceless land which stretched away as one travelled mile after mile, day after day and week after week and month after month."[17] In the summers of 1872 and 1873, he returned to participate in what turned out to be the last Pawnee buffalo hunt and an elk hunt, both times with Luther North, who captained his brother Major Frank North's Pawnee scouts. Once Grinnell sold the family business and returned to study with Marsh at Yale's Peabody Museum, he served as geologist on two more expeditions of several months' duration—into the Black Hills with Lieutenant Colonel George Armstrong Custer in 1874, then into Yellowstone National Park with Colonel William Ludlow in 1875—sustaining almost annual trips, to hunt, collect fossils, ranch, explore, and conduct ethnologies of Native people for the next forty years. (In a frisson of history, he was too busy at the Peabody to accept Custer's invitation to return to the Black Hills with him in 1876, thereby missing the Battle of the Little Bighorn.)

Grinnell crafted an authorial voice that is the most complex of the clubmen's and remains least recognized in terms of its contribution to the popularization of the West. In 1873, partly as distraction from his financial problems, he began to publish hunting tales in Charles Hallock's new sporting magazine, *Forest and Stream*. His persona as a hunter-writer was much more restrained and self-effacing than Roosevelt's; Grinnell staged himself not as the lone hunter-rancher but as part of a hunter-scientist fraternity. His stories show him always hunting with companions—sometimes the Pawnee, at other times his fellow paleontologists—and he writes himself back into the scientific community at day's end. In one tale, the party gather round the campfire in recognizable club formation: "college songs, so well known 'neath the grand old elms of New Haven, but new to these regions, broke the stillness of the clear night air and were echoed back from the mountains in a grand refrain" ("Day" 196). The following week's story welds the hunting and scientific more closely still in a scene of a dozen young men round a glowing fire: "Bearded, bronzed by exposure to all weathers, and clothed in buckskin, you might take them all at first glance for a party of trappers; but their speech betrays their occupation, and shows you that they are members of some scientific expedition ... The two last are John N—and myself" ("Green" 212).

Among other influences on which Grinnell rings the changes in these scenes are the western adventure stories of Mayne Reid (for whom Grinnell and Roosevelt shared a youthful passion).[18] Remembering his frame of mind on his first trip west, Grinnell commented: "I had been brought up, so to speak, on the writings of Captain Mayne Reid ... I had always been eager to visit the scenes he described, but had supposed they were far beyond my reach."[19] While James Fenimore Cooper was formative to the creation of rugged individualism in the wilderness, Reid provided a vision of fraternity as in, for example, his coterie of Santa Fe traders in The Scalp-Hunters (1851). Grinnell's campfire scenes are close echoes except that his boyish adventurers are scientists, part of a larger scheme of federally sponsored exploration, which William Goetzmann has argued was a major, often underestimated, force in the colonization of the West. That scientific streak, sometimes amounting to clinical detachment, remains threaded through Grinnell's hunting tales. It surfaces, for example, when he chillingly details the course of his bullet through a fawn's body and when he tries to cross the racial divide in defense of his Mexican guide. Señor Josè Alleyo Felemanches "belonged to that despised class denominated in frontier parlance, 'greasers'" but is "a very favourable specimen of his class"—phrasing that makes the man sound more geological find than human being ("Trip" 670; "Day" 196). That note of detachment, or disinterested objectification, would come to loom large in the frontier club western.

In 1876 Grinnell was invited to become Natural History editor for Forest and Stream, then in 1880 he maneuvered his own financial take-over, with his father, when they secured enough stock to oust Hallock and install the younger Grinnell as president of the company and editor of the magazine—a position he would hold from 1881 to 1911. With a weekly editorial in addition to his natural history pieces and book reviews, he developed a strong lobbying voice, campaigning ceaselessly for the enforcement of game laws, from the Adirondacks in the East to the giant redwoods in the West. In his drive to preserve wilderness and wildlife, he became increasingly adept at constituting and galvanizing his readership as a democratic force. In an editorial lambasting the Yellowstone Park Improvement Company, for example, he invoked "the people" and "the public" fifteen times in one column, cajoling ("Well, now, what are the people going to do about it?"), characterizing ("The people are a little tired of having the public domain given away with a lavish hand"), and relentlessly repeating ("all that [the monopolists] have said about their patriotism and their love for the people and people's interest is a mere tissue of misrepresentations, by means of which they have hoped to hoodwink the people, and above all, the representatives of the people") ("Park" 461). He enrolled his readers' services as lobbyists, providing leaflets to distribute to their congressmen and other influential figures, which they did in great numbers. When the *New York Times* reprinted his *Forest and Stream* pieces and petitions, he reached an even larger reading public.[20]

Grinnell also folded justice for Native people into his lobbying efforts. From about 1884, his editorial campaigns to enforce game laws and create wildlife refuges were accompanied by smaller pieces protesting government treatment of starving tribes, corruption on reservations, and the breaking of treaties. This concern represented a considerable change of attitude from the 21-year-old hunter with his Mayne Reid vision of Natives as trophy kills. In his first letter home, he tells his parents about an extended fossil-hunting trip he has made out from Fort Bridger into "a region where but few white men, and they only old hunters and trappers, had ever been before." There is a sudden, chilling shift of tone, from the reassuring son to the man with the gun: "We all enjoyed excellent health and are feeling much better for the trip. Only one indian [sic] was seen and no one was able to get a shot at him."[21] Soon, however, Grinnell was hunting with the Pawnee, and by 1873 he was crediting them with teaching him an incipient conservationism. Their thrifty use of buffalo—"Every ounce of this will be saved"—contrasted starkly with the profligacy of white hunters who downed big game only for their hides and trophy heads, leaving huge carcasses "to rot upon the prairie" ("Buffalo" 306). By 1904, Grinnell was squarely blaming "the white man" for the buffalo's extinction ("Bison" 112). He increasingly became advocate for and ethnographer of Indigenous peoples in the West, and a large body of his writing—probably now the best known of the two dozen books and hundreds of essays and articles that he produced during his long lifetime—documents the stories and lifeways of the Pawnee, Blackfeet, and Cheyenne. By 1923, in *The Cheyenne Indians*, he insisted that "the Indian" was not "a museum specimen"; "fundamentally they are like ourselves" (xvi).

These attitudinal shifts put Grinnell at odds with his Boone and Crockett club-mates. He disputed the blame that many of them placed on Native hunters for the destruction of big game and the virulent racial stereotypes they propagated. In time, his preservationist attitude even turned him against killing—the club's original *sine qua non*. By 1897 he was arguing with Roosevelt about the merits of conducting a fair chase that eschewed the final kill (Roosevelt gently chided him, "I think we want to beware of getting into the merely sentimental stage").[22] Later still, Grinnell confessed himself thoroughly weary of destructive big-game hunting: "it is not likely that I shall ever again fire a shot at any big game animal. Of that sort of hunting I have done all I need, in fact all I want to."[23]

In becoming the most progressive face of the Boone and Crockett Club, Grinnell also most clearly exposed its deeply conservative core values. For all their differences, Grinnell never broke with his clubmates' fundamental assumptions. He remained the Boone and Crockett Club's most tireless champion, serving in one executive capacity after another, as book series editor, and on innumerable club committees throughout his life. He negotiated compromises that allowed the club to develop its particular vision of conservation, which was centrally concerned with preserving gentlemen hunters' sporting privileges. When Roosevelt and Grinnell joined forces in 1887 to create the Boone and Crockett Club, the former's vision was enshrined in the club's first constitutional object—"To promote manly sport with the rifle"—and the latter's in the third: "To work for the preservation of the large game of this country, and, so far as possible, to further legislation for that purpose, and to assist in enforcing the existing laws" (Roosevelt and Grinnell, *American* 337). Compromise was possible because none of the clubmates' disagreements touched the core value they shared: preserving the authority of their own class.

Grinnell's key role in massaging the clubmen's image is evident in *Forest and Stream*, which he made into what he called the club's "natural mouthpiece" ("Brief" 452). In one editorial, he trades on the club's upper-class affiliations while claiming that it transcends them. He opens with the club's constitutional objects, then acknowledges that the members come from the wealthy class, which has, in the past, been most guilty—"excepting, of course, the 'skinners' and the meat hunters"—of wantonly butchering game for fun. Boone and Crockett Clubmen are, however, leading the way in carving out a new class, based on character:

> This club discountenances the bloody methods of all game butchers without regard to occupation, wealth or social status, and no man who is guilty of slaughtering game can expect consideration from, or fellowship with, its members. These members are not slow to express their views about the folly and the wrong of wanton butchery, and their opinions on sport are therefore spread among that very class which in the past has given most offense in this respect... those who used to boast of their slaughter are now ashamed of it, and it is becoming a recognized fact that a man who wastefully destroys big game, whether for the market, or only for heads, has nothing of the true sportsman about him. ("Boone" 513)

Later, speaking for the Boone and Crockett Game Preservation Committee, he would put it more pithily: "the sportsman must conduct his sport like a gentleman" ("Game" 427). This conflation of sportsmanship and class standing would indelibly stamp the club's mark on American popular culture.

Owen Wister

Seeking out hunter-writers for the club, Roosevelt had brought on board Owen Wister, the writer destined to become the biggest best-seller of the group. Wister had been elected to the club in 1892, just as he began to publish in the Harper magazines, and he was immediately appointed to the small executive committee charged with the World's Fair exhibit and book publication plans.

Wister came from a distinguished Philadelphia family with roots both in the South and England—his grandmother was the actress Fanny Kemble. He grew up in a country estate just outside Philadelphia, and was active athletically, but hunting did not loom large in his activities; the closest he came was collecting birds' eggs. At age seventeen, he wrote wistfully to his mother from the elite St. Paul's school: "I have never camped out and gone shooting and lots of boys have and I feel a big desire to do so too...I don't want to be a 'house boy'" (quoted in Vorpahl, *My* 6). Many years later, when he portrayed himself in Caspar Whitney's journal *Outing* as a schoolboy playing wilderness hunter, there is a strong sense of his making himself over to fit the present company. Stealing away from "the populous playground" in moccasins, bought with his pocket money from Quebec, he prowled through "the secret pine woods," imagining himself as Meriwether Lewis with buckskin shirt and trusty rifle "until the distant bell recalled him from the upper waters of the Missouri to Todhunter's Algebra for Beginners" ("Wilderness" 251). Only when he entered Harvard, in 1878, did he acquire a shotgun and begin to hunt occasionally.[24] His more obvious passions revolved around music and cultural life, which he fed by extended education and travel in Europe, and he studied music at Harvard, as well as composing and performing in several comic operas that won acclaim within and beyond the university. What presaged his involvement in the Boone and Crockett Club at this stage was his intense attraction to elite clubs. Wister's great need to belong was still palpable half-a-century later when he described himself waiting, trembling and anxious in his bed, to learn if he had been elected to Harvard's secret society, the Dickey:

> Was that roving midnight chorus, whose progress he could mark in the distance, going to approach and stop beneath his window with its jaunty serenade announcing he was "in," and so send thrills of triumph and joy through his young body ...? To be left out of the Dickey meant that your social future at Harvard was likely to be in the back seats.... Some wrong ones we took in, some right ones we left out—but not many of either sort...Bless the old merry brutal ribald orgiastic natural wholesome Dickey! (*Roosevelt* 9, 12)

He also won election to the Porcellian, the most exclusive of all the university's social clubs. One of the leading lights of these clubs was Roosevelt, two years his senior, whom Wister admired tremendously.

Wister's real hunting experiences began in 1885, when he was sent west as a cure for neurasthenia. Like Roosevelt, he had undergone a crisis and, like Grinnell, it involved a brush with the financial sector. After graduating from Harvard, Wister had travelled to Europe in the hope of following a musical career. His work was admired by Franz Liszt, but his father objected vehemently to him pursuing such a vocation and, after an intense struggle, Wister caved in to the expectation that he would enter the professional world. Through social connections with the first families of Boston, Wister was offered a position with the brokerage firm Lee, Higginson, and Company, although a downturn in their business meant that, in fact, he ended up in their Union Safety Deposit Vaults as a clerk, in 1883. Bored and restless, Wister next agreed to apprentice with Francis Rawle, a Philadelphia lawyer, and to enter Harvard Law School. At this point, the strain of disappointment, family tensions, and perhaps sheer tedium broke his health, and he was sent to the VR ranch in Wyoming, for vigorous outdoor activity and a change of environment. (Unbeknownst to Wister at the time, he was closely following the footsteps of Grinnell who, seven years earlier, had traveled to Wyoming, sleeping on the station floor in Medicine Bow as, later, both Wister and his narrator in *The Virginian* slept on the town's dry-goods store counter.)

Wister fell in love with the West, and this trip was followed by frequent expeditions over the next fifteen years. He undertook regular hunting trips as part of these western sojourns, usually in the company of several Philadelphia and Harvard friends (many of whom became fellow Boone and Crockett Club members), as well as white, mixed-race, and Native guides. In a few years, he had shot a grizzly, some mountain sheep, and wild goats; he qualified for Boone and Crockett membership, which Roosevelt extended to him in 1892. This sealed Wister's acceptance by the hunting fraternity, a kind of social embrace that seems to have been the main point for him.

If Roosevelt's writings blend the hunter and rancher, and Grinnell's the hunter and scientist, Wister's conjoin the hunter and the cowboy. Although he documented his hunting experiences copiously in his journals and letters, Wister did not write a hunting tale proper until his contribution to the first Boone and Crockett Club book in 1893. But a hunting motif wends its way through his earliest western fiction. His first western story, begun early in 1891 and never completed, was titled "The Story of Chalkeye." Wister's first fictional character in the West sounds exactly the type targeted by Grinnell's lambasting editorials. Mr. Ludlow Weeks, a New Yorker related to the Vanderbilts, is returning from a two months' hunting trip in the mountains of northwestern Wyoming:

It was his first experience of hunting; and his party had been successful enough to kill so many more elk than they could dismantle of their
horns and hides, or eat up in camp, that twenty carcasses, weighing
each some six hundred pounds, had been left behind untouched, rot-
ting where they fell among the hills, as witnesses of the sportsman-like
spirit and skill of their slayers.[25]

Mr. Weeks, having experienced "the most poignant thrill of pleasure he had yet
known...pump[ing] lead into the grave, staring animals" proceeds to shoot a
tame elk calf, the pet of Chalkeye (Mr. James Hilary, long since of New Jersey),
a small cattle rancher. As the story unfolds, various western types spar with the
eastern tenderfoot over the term "cowboy," whether it applies to Chalkeye and
whether it is a term of opprobrium, inappropriate for one who has his own modest land claim and heads of stock. As Wister's writings developed, he moved the
emphasis from hunter to cowboy. But the fundamental patterns of action and
character remained, wending through the tales of adventure and welding the values and tropes of the hunting tale to what became the popular western.

Winthrop Chanler

On that June night in the Hunter's Cabin, Wister clinked glasses with another
Roosevelt nominee, his Harvard clubmate and close friend, Winthrop Chanler.
Chanler made no such momentous contribution to popular culture, but he lived
a life that in several respects embodied the Boone and Crockett Club spirit at its
most unabashed, as well as the voice that went with it. Even in his older age, when
his wife, Margaret Terry Chanler, chided him that hunting "is after all not the only
thing in the world" (he was about to sacrifice the family home in its pursuit), he
answered, "Well, but, you see, for me it is" (quoted in M. Chanler, *Autumn* 207).
    Chanler enjoyed the typical clubman's privileged pedigree uneasily touched,
again, by the commercialism that they disdained. On his mother's side, he
belonged to the Astor family, whose acceptance into New York high society
occurred only in the 1850s, after the death of the patriarch John Jacob Astor,
America's first millionaire who made his fortune in western fur-trading and
whom the elite widely scorned as a crude parvenu; his father served for a time
as congressman from New York.[26] "Shielded from the outside world by that wall,
money," he was tutored at home in the family estate on the Hudson River until
being sent to Eton (Kavaler 99). He belonged to a glittering, if eccentric, family:
after his parents' deaths, he and his nine surviving siblings were known as the
"Astor orphans," their young lives ruled by a committee of Astor relatives. His
Harvard years (1881–1885) were devoted to the same clubs and Boston social
circles as Wister and Roosevelt, though he applied himself rather less than they

to his studies. His academic performance was so poor that his degree was initially withheld, much to his unjustified annoyance: "It makes me foam at the mouth to think of those—blunderers & boobies with all their endless arrays of books, ledgers & records being unable to keep their hands from picking & stealing & their tongues from lying in such a way that a poor cuss is swindled out of his degree."[27] One commentator calls him "restless" and "attractive"; another says he had "the typical Chanler insouciance" (Morison 352; Kavaler 99). Ten years after graduation, he retained his taste for carousing: after one reunion, Roosevelt wrote to his sister that "Winty…showed in somewhat startling manner the effects of an enjoyable Commencement day at the Porcellian."[28] His inheritance allowed him to enjoy a life of "energetic idleness" (O'Connor 311). His wife and, eventually, seven children flitted back and forth across the Atlantic, living sometimes in Rome, sometimes in Washington, DC, sometimes in other European and American East Coast locations. His wife summed up his life: "hunting mouflon in Sardinia, elk in Colorado, a quite unsuccessful search for oil-wells in Morocco, the Cuban War, relief-work after the Messina earthquake, fox-hunting in Ireland, lastly the Great War were among the most important adventures that took him away from us; the minor ones were innumerable" (M. Chanler, *Winthrop* 6).

From his election in 1892, Chanler gave stalwart service to the Boone and Crockett Club. He was the longest-serving member of the executive committee, with five terms from 1893 until his death in 1926, including a long stint as vice president. His only published writings are the essays he wrote for the Boone and Crockett Club book series, although he wrote at least three chapters of what sounds like a hunting book, which he passed by Wister periodically for commentary ("Pray use your claws in critiquing me. I am *really* humble, & shan't take, even the severest sort of strictures on my work, in any but the most thankful spirit").[29] Roosevelt judged that Chanler had "the real literary gift"—a judgment that is supported by his voluminous, narratively rich correspondence, which he half-jokingly called "the story of my life."[30]

Chanler's correspondence provides the clearest articulation of the clubmen's shared voice and its efficacy in demarcating outsiders from insiders. One sequence of letters from 1890 charts his journey from England to Colorado on a hunting trip. Crossing the Atlantic, he finds himself hemmed in on board by companions not of his choosing. The clubmen generally had a fear of crowds, which they routinely disdained as "mobs" and in animalistic terms. Chanler similarly complains of his fellow passengers: "Such ruffians, such a mob! I am at a table with a darkey and some wild beasts from Chicago." As he reaches the Midwest, he launches a diatribe that closely echoes Wister's description of "the commercial hog ridden Middle of the U.S.A."[31] Chanler complains to his wife, "The air round me is full of the babble of money-grabbing apes. Real estate, stocks and bonds. And all so solemn and provincial and dirty" (M. Chanler, *Winthrop* 6). As his train journey comes to its final stretch, his nostalgia for the frontier of the past and his welcoming of empty Colorado spaces could be any of the gentlemen hunters making their way west and regretting its modernization: "all day we have been crossing the plains. They have changed woefully in the last eight years...Little beastly houses and Artesian wells like palm trees all over the country. Now at last we seem to be in the real old-fashioned prairie with only an occasional herd of cattle and a solitary hut in sight" (M. Chanler, *Winthrop* 16).

Chanler embodied his wife's definition of the aristocrat, demonstrating "a certain half-conscious aloofness, a shrinking from the crowd in the market-place, and all vulgar contact, a natural exclusiveness" (M. Chanler, *Memory* 46). Because he wrote so little for publication, he did not need to develop "the common touch" that Roosevelt, Grinnell, and Wister, in their different ways, did. (It may have been precisely because he was not willing to negotiate the print marketplace that Chanler did not act on his literary gift.) He did not shy away from displays of anglophone privilege: as avid a fox hunter as big-game hunter, he regularly rode to hounds—these were the years in which opposition to the practice as evidence of entrenched aristocratic interests grew more vehement—ultimately serving as Master of the Genesee Valley Hunt for several years.[32] He did not struggle to appeal to or find a way of being part of "the people." Significantly, there is no record of him joining the conservationist lobby, or ever speaking in those terms.

Within the protective confines of club culture, Chanler sustained a very different persona and voice which, again, were typical of white male privilege in those years. He played the eternal boy, whose youthful high spirits enliven his club correspondence. In his hands the stately Rittenhouse Club becomes the "Chicken house club," Owen Wister becomes "Omar" (short for "Omar dear Daniel").[33] His letters are peppered with limericks and comic rondelles, while his vocabulary—everything in life is either "bully" or "beastly"—exactly echoes the vigorous expression traded behind club walls and in clubmen's writings. That dual voice—exclusionary distaste combined with fraternal ebullience— was the quintessentially frontier club voice, and it audibly fueled their writings. Again perhaps more clearly than anyone else, Chanler saw that the club was the ultimate author. When Wister published his 1895 essay, Chanler wrote: "The 'Evolution of the Cowpuncher' is the best thing (with the exception of my new man-child) the Porcellian has produced in years," referring to the essay as "our joint production."[34]

Madison Grant

Other members who passed through the Hunter's Cabin that year suggest the range of the club's associations and alliances. Madison Grant was another upper-class New Yorker, whose path—his childhood interest in animals on his family's summer estate, his travels and education abroad, his years at Yale (1884–1887) and Columbia Law School, his hunting trips across North America—followed closely those of many of his clubmates. Grant was nominated to the Boone and Crockett Club by George Bird Grinnell in 1893, with considerable approval from Roosevelt, who quickly judged him "a genuine acquisition" and "a good fellow."[35] He was immediately pressed into service, spearheading the Adirondack Deer Law, the Alaska Game Law, the creation of the New York Zoölogical Society (which he headed from 1895), and working closely with Grinnell on the creation of Glacier National Park. Grant was voted on to the executive committee in 1897, rose to secretary in 1903, vice president in 1913, and president in 1928.

Grant seems a closeted figure, in several senses. Because his private papers have been systematically destroyed, he survives almost exclusively as a public figure, defined by his intense organizational attachments.[36] What is known of his private life is that it was deeply homosocial: his friends and his organizations were all-male; when he finally moved out of the family home at age 61, he took up a bachelor brownstone next door to his younger brother.[37] Given his intense commitment to upper-class male enclaves, it makes sense that his prolific writings made most explicit the racial implications of the club's exclusivity and conservationism (the hybrid figure that he contributed to the club's pantheon was the hunter-white supremacist). "The old order" to which he was dedicated was equally pure-blood big-game animals (preserved in the Bronx Zoo and in national parks) and old-stock, "Nordic" Americans (quoted in Spiro 22). Grant's best-known work, *The Passing of the Great Race* (1916), secured his position as America's leading eugenicist and "prophet of scientific racism" (Spiro xii).

Henry Cabot Lodge

The link to the crafting and passing of legislation was provided by several high-powered congressmen, many of whom occupied the Boone and Crockett Club's "Associate Member" category, created for those who did not qualify as big-game hunters but whom the club wished to gather within its fold. Of those, the most prolific writer and most influential statesman was Henry Cabot Lodge.[38] After editing the highly prestigious *North American Review* from 1873 to1876 and practicing law, Lodge entered politics, first as a member of the Massachusetts House of Representatives, then as the state's congressman in the U.S. House of Representatives, until finally, in 1893, entering the Senate, where he served until his death in 1924.

Lodge was a Boston Brahmin, Harvard graduate, and Porcellian Clubman, often described as cold-blooded and elitist, a man who used his privilege and learning to exact public humiliation on his rivals. A Massachusetts editor described "his metallic voice, rasping 'like the tearing of a bed sheet'" and "his 'repellently cold' manner" (Garraty 61). He was experienced somewhat differently by members of his inner circle, however. Again the motif of boyishness comes forward: Roosevelt, his great friend and political ally, for example, wrote to his sister Anna in 1888, that "dear old Cabot…was the same delightful, big-boyish personage as ever" (Morison 141). Lodge was a scholar and historian who wrote extensively—once in collaboration with Roosevelt—but never directly for the Boone and Crockett Club series. (Roosevelt did report, however, that in the Dakota winter evenings he discovered "my cowboys reading and in large part comprehending" Lodge's *Studies in Literature* [quoted in Hagedorn 228]). In Congress, Lodge gave what Chanler called "golden aid," acting as backstop on forest and game preservation measures introduced by other associate club members—Secretary of the Interior John W. Noble, Congressman John F. Lacey of Iowa, and Senator George G. Vest of Missouri—and leading the way in turning the club's more extended interests, especially around immigration restriction, into law.[39]

Caspar Whitney

On the fringes of the club in another sense, and underlining the deeply social uses of big-game hunting, especially in written form, was Caspar Whitney. In 1893 he attended the Boone and Crockett Club Metropolitan dinner as a guest and by 1894 was a member.[40] Despite his name, which connected him at some distance to one of New York's most prominent families, Whitney seems to have been decidedly middle-class in upbringing and occupation yet determined to break into the ranks of the elite. A member of "what appears to have been a staunchly middle-class family in Boston" and educated at "the obscure St. Matthews College" in California, Whitney successfully muddied the waters by claiming a Harvard education, which he did not have (T. Kelly, "Hunter" 134, 142). In 1889, in his magazine *This Week's Sport*, he selected and published the first college "All-American football team" (135). By 1893, he was sports columnist and editor at *Harper's Weekly*, preaching "the cult of amateurism" as the keystone of American manliness (138). The values he espoused—transcendence of financial consideration, manly vigor and discipline, and Anglo-American superiority—aligned him with the upper classes, a connection he industriously cemented. He established himself as arbiter of Ivy League sporting practices, he inveterately dropped names of the socially prominent, and he "sought out every chance to hobnob with the wealthy" (136). Whitney's presence at the Metropolitan Club dinner took him a step closer to making himself over as a gentleman hunter, an identity he consolidated with a musk-ox hunting expedition to the Barren Grounds of Canada, the repeated publication of his adventures, and entrance to the Boone and Crockett Club (as well as the undying envy of Roosevelt who, in his lifelong hunting career, never managed to kill a musk-ox).

If Whitney needed the club to fulfill his social aspirations, the club had equal need of him. On *Harper's Weekly*, he had a popular following that far outstripped Grinnell's on *Forest and Stream*, and he was training them to accept the values and leadership of the club class. The increased access to a broad reading public he provided was further enhanced in 1900, when he became co-owner and editor of the outdoor monthly magazine *Outing*, which also put the resources of the Outing Publishing Company at his disposal. Within five years, Whitney increased the magazine's readership fivefold. He filled a good chunk of the magazine with his own editorial commentary, which embraced big-game hunting and amateur athletics, game laws and sporting rules, thereby connecting wilderness hunting with social hierarchies. This maneuver served equally to popularize the clubmen's values and to reinforce Whitney's social credentials (when, for example, he used his disquisition on the U.S. Golf Association as a thin excuse to digress at length about "a personal experience on a tiger hunt in the Malay Peninsula").[41] It was consistent with this urge to popularize that, when the club debated increasing its membership in 1901, Whitney spearheaded the "ayes." He argued vigorously for "developing the club's might along the lines on which it was organized thirteen years ago" and preventing it from dwindling into "a dining club" (he was supported by Grinnell, among others, who was also keen to enlarge the club's influence, especially by introducing more westerners into its membership).[42] But the majority of members, worried about the "levelling down" effect, were not convinced; his case was voted down by a 2-to-1 margin.[43]

Whitney strove to inject the Boone and Crockett Club voice into *Outing*, partly in his own editorial rhetoric. When he advocated, for example, "the strenuous life which makes for the upbuilding of a virile, progressive, respected nation," it could have been Roosevelt speaking.[44] His repeated celebration of the "wholesome out-of-door spirit," "sport for its own sake," and invocation of the need for Protection, Preservation, and Enforcement all toe the club line. He also made mighty efforts to publish Boone and Crockett members, soliciting them repeatedly (and sometimes successfully) for material for his magazine and book projects, for which he promised top payment rates. However, he never felt that the hunter-writers entirely came through for him. Just a few months into his new venture, he was wrangling with Grinnell over payment rates and by 1903 he was writing plaintively to Wister: "I can't say that I have been over-powered by support from Boone & Crockett Club members in my endeavor to publish a magazine that would be the highest exponent of the particular field in which they are supposedly so much interested; especially you and Roosevelt could have helped out greatly when we needed it...Now, we have passed beyond the need of help, I am glad to say, from anybody."[45] In 1904, he managed to chivvy both Wister and Grinnell into joining him as co-authors of *Musk-Ox, Bison, Sheep and Goat,* a volume in his American Sportsman's Library, thereby binding himself, as Tara Kelly puts it, "between covers with two of the cream of the elite" ("Hunter" 151).

Three times over—as writer, editor, and publisher—Whitney showed the power of print for the consolidation of gentleman-hunter influence. Yet his position in the inner circle was never secure. It is a sad postscript to his efforts that in 1910 he declared bankruptcy, and, when he died in 1929, Grinnell and Grant agreed not to mark the event in the Club's book. Grant wrote: "I do not think it important to put an obituary notice of the death of Casper [sic] Whitney. We have gone far enough in the matter of obituaries and I think it is a mistake to do this except for important officials."[46]

Frederic Remington

One final name needs to be mentioned in this company, although he was not of the company. If Whitney was positioned on the febrile edge of club culture, Frederic Remington occupied the outlier position.[47] Remington's visual art and sculptures of the West were—and remain—the most instantly recognizable face of the frontier club western, and his name is closely linked with Roosevelt and Wister in particular. However, he was never invited to join the Boone and Crockett Club, and his work does not appear in any club publication.

Remington belonged to small-town Upper New York State, son of a country journalist and Civil War colonel. Without the blue-blood origins or inherited income, he traced a path parallel to, but always separate from, the clubmen's. He attended Yale School of Fine Arts—which, as a recently created professional school, was outside the circle of elite gentlemen students—but left after just over a year. He went west to Montana in 1881, hoping to make his fortune, but he did not have sufficient capital for cattle investment. Instead, two years later, he invested in sheep-ranching in Kansas; once that venture failed, he moved on to a hardware store, then a saloon in Kansas City, Missouri. Like the clubmen, he believed in Anglo-Saxon racial superiority, and he was a skilled hunter (though he developed different rituals and companions in the woods around his home and the nearby Adirondacks, and he did not loom large in the conservation effort).[48] He also understood the power of claiming western authenticity: one letter from Peabody, Kansas home to Canton, New York interrupts itself melodramatically, "Man just shot down street—must go"; later, he learned to represent himself as "an ex cow-puncher," which he never was (quoted in Samuels, *Frederic* 42, 92).

He did, however, find his sketching subjects in the West—again, like so many of the clubmen, his western art narrowly saved him from clerical work—and he began to sell illustrations to *Harper's Weekly.* When he and his wife moved to New York, he began a steady relationship with the Harpers, who sent him off on western sketching expeditions, as well as publishing illustrations in *Outing* (at that point edited by Poultney Bigelow, whom Remington knew at Yale) and other magazines. In 1887, in the face of his rising popularity, Roosevelt requested him as illustrator of *Ranch Life and the Hunting Trail*; subsequently, Harper & Brothers initiated a long collaboration with Wister; and Remington illustrated Whitney's series of articles on the Barren Grounds.[49] In Remington's studio, frontier clubmen's books lined his shelf—Grinnell's *Pawnee Hero Stories and Folk-Tales* next to Wister's *Red Men and White*, Whitney's *On Snow Shoes to the Barren Grounds* up against Roosevelt's *Winning of the West*—and clearly he felt himself making common cause with them.[50]

But Remington never entered the inner circle. Roosevelt looked down on sheep farmers—"No man can associate with sheep and maintain his self-respect"—and Remington, a large, raucous man, lacked the gentlemanly manners valued by the aristocratic set (*Hunting* 128). Roosevelt's approach to Remington to illustrate his volume, at the very moment he was conceiving of his hunting club, did not include an invitation to that select group. At the Columbia Exposition, Remington's focus was the Midway Plaisance and Buffalo Bill's Wild West, not the Hunter's Cabin. Wister welcomed the collaboration with Remington: when he first bumped into him in Yellowstone Park, just after his World's Fair visit in 1893, he noted, "Remington is an excellent American—that means, he thinks as I do about the disgrace of our politics, and the present asphyxiation of all real love of country."[51] Yet he kept the illustrator at arm's length; after several years of working together, Remington considered himself a friend of Wister's and was hurt to discover that he had never been privy to his intimate nickname "Dan" (Vorpahl, *My* 117). Knowingly or otherwise, Chanler also discounted Remington's contribution to "The Evolution of the Cowpuncher" when he celebrated the essay as a Porcellian Club production. Surviving correspondence shows that Remington in fact first urged Wister to write "an article on the evolution of the puncher" and provided him with information and critique, as well as illustrations.[52] Given this treatment, it is not surprising that Remington remained inordinately sensitive to comments about himself (he confided to his diary close to the end of his life, "There is one thing a man who does anything in America can figure on—a d— good pounding").[53]

Essentially, the clubmen treated Remington as an adjunct—illustrator rather than co-creator of their vision. In Remington's visual art, Alexander Nemerov has read a self-conscious meta-commentary on the fabrications at work, while Stephen Tatum has traced, especially in the late nocturnes, a movement between "a dialectic of estrangement and attachment" (141). Remington's writings brought to the surface his difference in outlook from the frontier club (further discussed in Chapters Four and Five, this volume). As outsider, he illuminated the ugly exclusions at the heart of this powerful network.

The Books of the Boone and Crockett Club

Although Boone and Crockett Clubmen often hunted together in twos and threes, their group meetings were as committee men, lobbyists, and bon vivants, gathering at club dinners, as one member put it, to "swap lies and get acquainted" and, if a congressman was present, "to get him in a corner and talk to him."[54] The place where they came together as a larger fraternity of hunters was in the pages of their book series. Initiated and shaped by Roosevelt and Grinnell, the series grew to seven volumes, about ninety essays by over fifty members—mostly big-game hunting tales, with some pieces arguing the case for big-game reserves and conservation areas—between 1893 and 1933.[55] The publication of the series was clustered in the years when the literary market-place was shaking down into "quality" versus cheap houses and a mass audience was up for grabs (see Chapter Two). Grinnell and Roosevelt had both entered the book business around 1880. Grinnell's stock takeover of *Forest and Stream* included the book publishing arm of the same name, while Roosevelt entered into a partnership with G. P. Putnam's Sons, maintaining an office with them even after he withdrew his financial investment. They were followed by Whitney in the 1900s, when he added book publishing to the *Outing* operation and produced an "American Sportsman's Library," which closely imitates the Boone and Crockett Club series. Several clubmen had close ties with established publishers who positioned themselves as "quality" producers—Wister and Whitney with Harper & Brothers, Grant and Lodge with Scribner's, and the ever-prolific Roosevelt with both.

Shaping the Voice

When the Boone and Crockett Club launched its book series in 1893, its members put those publishing connections, know-how, and rhetoric to work. Grinnell and Roosevelt edited, financed, and published the first volume, using Roosevelt's private resources and Grinnell's Forest and Stream book publishing wing.[56] For a later volume, they turned to Harper & Brothers, which circulated a full series set.[57] Hunting tales went back to classical times, generating tropes that equated hunting and war, and the deer hunt and sexual love, a tradition with which these Ivy League-educated men would have been familiar.[58] With the first volume of the Boone and Crockett Club series, Roosevelt and Grinnell began to chart a distinctively American hunting literature, featuring big-game hunting books by Boone and Crockett Clubmen, among others. In this lineage, the foundational text was *The Still-Hunter* (1882), by associate member Theodore Strong Van Dyke, which defined stalking as the manly, character-making version of big-game hunting and headed the list that Roosevelt had earlier imagined on the "rough board shelves" of his not-yet-existent ranch-house (*Hunting* 12). They also position their club's contribution above their marketplace competitors, which they dismiss as commercial trash—"there does not exist a more dismal species of literature than the ordinary cheap sporting volume"—while the quality of their own product is signaled by its manliness: "The best books are those written by the rare men who, having actually done the things, are also capable of writing well about them when done" (Roosevelt and Grinnell, *American* 321). Boone and Crockett volumes "contain material of permanent value" that is "more than merely pleasant reading" and "of a lasting character" (Grinnell and Roosevelt, *Trail* 7, 10).

What Boone and Crockett Clubmen knew better than anyone else in the publishing business was how to wield books as lobbying tools. The club strategized at length over the distribution of complimentary copies to senators, congressmen, and officials in states (and Canadian provinces) concerned with big game (at one point, the list grew to nearly six hundred names). They debated back and forth whether to undertake a mass distribution of books during the 1904 election, especially in light of Roosevelt's run for a second term in the White House. Ultimately, they agreed, as Grant put it, that "immediately after the election excitement is past we could arrange to have them handed to members of Congress when they first get together in Washington."[59] One member called their fourth volume "the very best campaign document that we can possibly send out in preparation for next season's legislative campaign."[60] Grinnell agreed that they should "hit that body hard" with book distribution, adding, "I do not think the club could do a more useful thing."[61] Congressman John Lacey, their point man on conservation legislation, advised them on tailoring their material to follow up on congressional appropriations made in their interests. At the same time, Grinnell knew they had to keep an eye on the readership at large: "we desire as wide a public for our books as possible."[62] As a closed patrician group learning to win over public opinion, they knew well the value of print culture.

As editors, Roosevelt and Grinnell worked to fine-tune the clubmen's common voice, vigorously pursuing members for contributions and blue-penciling the results, sometimes over lunch at Delmonico's. Tone was a major issue. While it was appropriate to be jocular—Grinnell complimented Roosevelt on his account of one hunt, "I laughed 'plenty' over your description of the suffering of travelling with a pack train"—slapstick humor crossed the line.[63] Of one member's contribution, Roosevelt wrote to his co-editor, "all of the would-be funny parts must be cut out ruthlessly. If there exists any particularly vulgar horror on the face of the globe it is the 'funny' hunting story"; three weeks later he was still at work on it, telling Grinnell, "I will slash it up into about a third of the space it now occupies" (Morison 636, 658). One comic paragraph by Wister in his tale of a white goat hunt—a digression about the Marquis of Lorne falling off his horse at the Queen's Jubilee parade—passed muster with the editors, but they had reckoned without transatlantic sensibilities. While Wister was out of touch in Yellowstone Park, Grinnell was approached by the Edinburgh publisher David Douglas who agreed to take five hundred copies of the book on the condition this account was excised, "as it would hurt the feelings of many of his readers—especially as he published for the Marquis's wife and sister." After consultation with the editorial committee (that is, Roosevelt and Chanler), Grinnell agreed, sending profuse apologies to Wister, who seemed more amused than otherwise.[64] Wister appears to have been one of the most amenable revisers, trading his writings back and forth with other members, offering and receiving feedback.

The strength of the editors' shaping hand was vividly illustrated when they approached clubmate and distinguished painter Albert Bierstadt for a contribution.[65] Bierstadt's qualifications for club membership rested mainly on the famously large moose that he had shot on a hunting expedition in Maine thirteen years earlier (its antlers were, at that time, the eighth-largest known in the world), and Roosevelt eagerly sought the story for the club's first volume. He wrote Bierstadt several letters of solicitation, ultimately cornering him in his studio ("I want that moose article!" he wrote on his calling card, promising to return). Bierstadt's literary facility was not equal to his visual artistry, but he did eventually deliver a manuscript. Presumably Roosevelt's consternation was considerable when he arrived at the climactic moment of the story only to discover that Bierstadt had not shot the moose; his Native guide John had. Not only did the sequence of events potentially invalidate Bierstadt's membership, it undermined the gentlemen hunters' racial hierarchy. Of the moose, Bierstadt wrote:

> Did I feel like taking his life? No. This was a case of the survival of the fittest and my love for seeing him enjoying his breakfast, unconscious of the presence of the enemy, made me respect him. John looked at me in amazement, a hunter who did not want to kill! He said "what you come here for?" I handed him the rifle and a moment later regretted it for I saw the greatest Moose, desperately wounded he ran a few rods and turned to look at us. I took the rifle then and ended his misery. (Quoted in Nye and Hoem 462)

Roosevelt went at the essay with his blue pencil, emending it phrase by phrase and line by line, cleaning up the expression and moving the action along at a swifter pace, and adroitly changing this passage so that the exact source of the first shot is unclear. Bierstadt agreed to the publication of the revised essay with some discomfort, stipulating that it must appear anonymously, a condition Roosevelt and Grinnell could not accept. The rejected essay suggests the degree to which Boone and Crockett tales were massaged to fit a common template, reinforcing the "insider pool" whose solidarity outweighed their individual differences (Punke 166).

Clearing the Enclave

What story of the West did the clubmen craft into a lobbying tool? Cumulatively, their hunting tales and conservation essays recreate the American West as a network of white enclaves reserved for superior species, animal and human, fringed and threatened by degenerate species. This vision is an extension of the clubmen's social outlook. They saw their organization, and their class more generally, as a beleaguered enclave of upper-class whiteness. Its only protection from the forces of modernization was what Arthur Erwin Brown, in arguing against increasing the club membership, termed "rigid selection." (Brown, who was a Philadelphia friend of Wister's, acknowledged, "This may be non democracy, but it is good biology and I will take my stand in it.")[66]

One tale after another opens with a beautiful, panoramic landscape cleared of certain forms of animal and human life. One of the Boone and Crockett Club's foundational documents specified the hierarchy of animals to be protected. Article IV of the club's constitution strictly classifies "big game": "Bear, buffalo (bison), mountain sheep, caribou, cougar, musk-ox, white goat, elk (wapiti), wolf (not coyote), pronghorn antelope, moose, and deer" (Roosevelt and Grinnell, *American* 338). Vermin to be exterminated include muskrat, skunk, fox, and sheep. These distinctions—"wolf (not coyote)"—are what the book series enacts and preserves. The casting out of non-Anglo human elements is equally obsessive. "Jew drummers" ritualistically encountered on the way west are despicably commercial; Chinese cooks are a joke; Mexicans are "cut-throat, horse-stealing" thieves; "half-witted 'Portugee'" in California are "a drug in the market"; African Americans are simply absent (Whitney, "Cougar" 238; Sampson 207, 208).

The essays' language lines up categories of human and animal degeneracy so that the distinction between them disappears. Grant worries that the moose he kills has a "Jewish cast of nose" ("Canadian" 104). "Tramp sheep" that intrude on ranching lands deserve to be shot (Sampson 188). Whitney writes of "herding up Mexicans" ("Cougar" 238). Speaking for the club's collective logic, Alden Sampson explains: "It is well known that men who habitually care for any animal come in time to resemble him," therefore Mexican sheep-herders inevitably suffer "fatty degeneration of the intellect" (203, 204). Clubmen freely used the term "vermin" within and beyond their book series: Whitney famously called working-class athletes "vermin" in *A Sporting Pilgrimage*, his 1894 volume from Harper & Brothers; the next year, Wister wrote of new immigrants as "hordes of encroaching alien vermin" in "The Evolution of the Cowpuncher."[67] (The interdependence of the club's animal and human taxonomies showed up in 1920, when the club struggled with new complications concerning "the question of Vermin and Non-Vermin" in the face of changing pelt values in the West, just at the time when they were fretting over their racial hierarchies in the face of "new" immigrants.)[68]

Even the Indigenous people on whom the gentlemen hunters routinely depended as guides threaten the pure space of big-game hunting. One essayist after another—always excepting Grinnell—insist that Natives (along with wolves) are most guilty of "indiscriminate slaughter."[69] Repeatedly, Native guides are at once necessary, lazy, and untrustworthy, the best trackers but the worst shots. According to Roosevelt, the Sioux "are not good shots, but they hunt in great numbers, killing everything, does, fawns and bucks alike...they cause great destruction to game" ("Hunting" 290). Grant, among others, asserts that they are without doubt the most rampant breakers of the sportsman's code: "An Indian with a gun will shoot at anything he sees until his ammunition is gone" ("Condition" 373). In clubmen's tales, race suicide narratives that are convenient to their purposes predominate. They tell, for example, how deer in Newfoundland were decimated by the wasteful Native peoples who subsequently died of starvation and exposure—allowing the deer to increase again and be available for trophy killing.[70]

Having organized vast, beautiful landscapes, emptied out of non-Anglo men (and women, a topic I take up in Chapter Three), the essays repopulate the space with its rightful inhabitants. The central figure turns out to be a sort of Leatherstocking-turned-clubman. Roosevelt and Grinnell introduce him in the first essay of the first volume:

> The rifle-bearing hunter, whether he goes on foot or on horseback, whether he voyages in a canoe or travels with a dog-sled, must be sound of body and firm of mind, and must possess energy, resolution, manliness, self-reliance, and capacity for hardy self-help. In short, the big-game hunter must possess qualities without which no race can do its life-work well; and these are the very qualities which it is the purpose of this Club, so far as may be, to develop and foster. (*American* 14–15)

Tales typically take this man through a rite of passage, from jittery tenderfoot to stoical killer (thus delivering on its members' youthful fantasies—Grinnell and Roosevelt stalking through Audubon Park and Long Island Sound, Wister pretending to be Meriwether Lewis—among other effects). This maturation is most often narrated from a jocular, self-deprecating, first-person point of view, which seems to offer intimacy. The gentleman hunter not only addresses the reader directly—"Reader, what would you have given to have seen, as I have, a band of two hundred and fifty bull-elk ...?"—but he also confides his failures, initially poking fun at his own immaturity and mishaps (Rogers 102). The sense that the reader was being drawn into the inner circle was of course illusory for all except the club class, but the use of the narrative "I" can be understood as an effective method of persuasion. It also confirms that Anglo, eastern gentlemen have the racial right to bear the gun. As one hunting tale emphasizes, the "degradation of the 'gun' is to rest upon the hip of a degenerate sheep-herder, half Spaniard, half Indian and half coyote" (Sampson 205).

The hunting tales pit one superior species against another, as "a vigorous, masterful people" go up against "the master of the herd" (Roosevelt and Grinnell, *American* 14, 18). This is an honorable confrontation between equals. Grant, for example, describes a moose hunt: "the moose is pitting his acute senses against the encroaching rifleman in the struggle for survival"—a phrasing that also makes it crystal clear why Grant was so perturbed by that "Jewish cast of nose" ("Distribution" 383). The "intellect and intelligence" of the grizzly bear are "not many grades in the process of evolution" below the hunter; "Strip him of his hide, stand him erect on his hind feet, stick a plug hat on his upper end, and he resembles in anatomy and general appearance that 'noblest work of god'—man" (Pickett 214, 215). This trope becomes literal in another (presumably apocryphal) tale, when a hunter in the Sierra Madre Mountains divests himself of his clothes "with the rapidity of a lightning-change artist" and drops to all fours to confront an advancing grizzly (Thompson 65). The drive to protect these spaces is as much about the preservation of a particular class and race of man—embodied in the gentleman hunter—as the big-game animals and their wilderness spaces.

The contest is highly ritualized around the Boone and Crockett Club rules of fair chase, by which the big-game hunter demonstrates, repeatedly, the fine etiquette of killing honorably. This is "the sportsman's code" which, John Reiger argues, was adopted by the American upper classes from aristocratic Europe as a means "at least partly to separate themselves from the 'common' hunter and fisherman," systematically hardening the line between market hunter and sportsman which was hazy until the middle of the nineteenth century (*American* x). The code is virulently anti-commercial; true sportsmen kill only for recreation, never for money. The code is highly self-disciplined; true sportsmen never kill female animals, never waste meat or skin, kill only what they need for food or an unusually fine trophy head. The ritual includes the expression of regret. On killing his first white goat—a deed for which he traveled almost three thousand miles, much of it in great discomfort—Wister typically reports, "I had my invariable attack of remorse on looking closely at the poor harmless old gentleman"; but "We had all the justification that any code exacts" ("White" 42, 56). The code also insists on the matching of human and animal wits under circumstances of equality: true sportsmen do not blind animals with fire ("jack-lighting"), trap them in water, or mire them in deep snow ("crusting").

True sportsmen stalk and bait and still hunt: "The enjoyment of sport increases in proportion to the amount of danger to man and beast engaged in it" (Roger Williams, "Wolf-Coursing" 327). The central action is the stalk, in the Van Dyke formulation to which the clubmen adhered. Extended passages tell of the hunter, rifle in hand, suspensefully pursuing his game on foot, following fresh "sign," climbing and crawling as silently as possible, peering at the animal through the cover of foliage and over rock ledges, "taking forty minutes for some four hundred yards" (O. Wister, "White" 49). Sometimes the tables are turned and the animal stalks the hunter. Pursuing Rocky Mountain sheep, Archibald Rogers congratulates himself on making "a most successful stalk" when he realizes that he has become part of a larger chain, "I sneaking down after the rams, and the panther sneaking down upon me" (97, 98). The climax of the tale is most often face-to-face confrontation; it is almost routine in Boone and Crockett stories for hunters to be charged by the bear or moose or elk they have just wounded. Daniel Moreau Barringer faces a female grizzly: "I instinctively knew that we would have it out then and there, and that there was no use in running" ("In" 309). Rogers fires at one bear—"up came her head, her jaws flew open like clockwork, and a snort came forth. But right between the eyes went the deadly messenger, smashing her skull." Then the hunter turns swiftly to her "partner": "He had been taking it all in, and was ready for a fight...he had true grit, and faced us; but it was an unequal battle" (118). Winty Chanler kills an elk: "Instinctively my rifle went to my shoulder, my finger pressed the trigger, the elk plunged forward and fell on his knees. As he struggled to rise, I shot him again" ("Day" 58).

Writing the Frontier Club Western

Fast forward through the decades, and it becomes startlingly clear that this was the moment when the ur-western was made. Change the rifle to a six-shooter, the hunting trail to the dusty main street, and you have what has become the classic western scene in print and on film. The hunter becomes the honorable cowboy or sheriff—"the gentleman with a gun" whom Robert Warshow analyzed as the moral center of western movies in his famous 1954 essay of that title. This gentlemanly figure stalks his enemy through the dangerous streets culminating in a man-to-man shoot-out on main street, the villain keeled over by the hero's lightning-fast draw. *High Noon* (1952) is the quintessential filmic example; *Shane* (1953) typifies the variant in which the climactic confrontation occurs in a saloon. Critical to this encounter is the racial compatibility of the combatants—as Boone and Crockett tales reserve confrontation for "superior species," so does the western formula face white men off against each other (hence the shock when revisionist westerns re-choreograph the showdown to include a black, Native, Asian, or Hispanic gunslinger).[71] The sportsman's code mutates into the Code of the West, which similarly teaches the art of honorable killing to the tenderfoot who rightfully bears the gun. Even the Boone and Crockett Club voice stamps the modern western. Cumulatively, the book series promotes a quasi-democratic gee-shucks tone that finesses the contradictions in the gentlemen hunters' image, democratizing their aristocratic status. The legacy of this voice is apparent in every Jimmy Stewart or John Wayne hero, who repeatedly undergoes the same journey from self-deprecation to stoicism, his violence and elitism cloaked by the same rhetorical cover. And, of course, all this takes place in the kind of enclaves created by Boone and Crockett hunter-writers: the vast, ostensibly empty spaces—panoramas of grasslands and desert—fringed by threatening forces and structured around clear hierarchies of race and power that become the ruling trope of western fiction and film.

To trace the line from the Boone and Crockett Club hunting tale to the formula western as we still most commonly know it, we can usefully return to the Columbian Exposition. A fortnight after the clubmen's celebratory dinner in June 1893, Wister went back to the Hunter's Cabin alone. He had brought his mother to the fair to show her the sights, but had temporarily abandoned her to female friends from Philadelphia, including his future wife, because he was facing an imminent deadline from Henry Mills Alden, his editor at Harper & Brothers. In the refuge of the clubhouse, he found inspiration and dashed off a draft of his sixth western story, "The Winning of the Biscuit Shooter," which he subsequently circulated among his family and friends for feedback before forwarding it to Alden. The moment was typical of the frontier club's writing culture. These upper-class men removed themselves from the social masses into an intensely masculine enclave of whiteness—their clubs, their hunting parties, this cabin, but also their western writings—which shielded them from the modern world of change while giving them power within it. Wister's story also constitutes one of several steps by which the frontier club western was made.

In the draft of "The Winning of the Biscuit Shooter" that Wister carried away from the Hunter's Cabin, he transferred many Boone and Crockett narrative characteristics from the western hunting scene to the cattle land of Wyoming. The action concerns the efforts of a young cowboy, Lin McLean, to win the hand of Katie Peck, the "biscuit shooter" (or railroad station waitress) of the title, and best his rival suitor 'Rapaho Dick.[72] The tale is recounted by a first-person narrator (an eastern tenderfoot) who combines the mixture of naivety and jocular self-deprecation familiar from the hunting tales (he accepts, for example, the reproach in the cowboy's "glance of slight pity" at his blundering inability to understand their unspoken code), while the cowboy heroes exhibit more of the laconic stoicism into which seasoned hunters grow.

The scene is yet another enclave of whiteness. A fraternity of white cowpunch-ers, whose paths will cross intermittently throughout Wister's fiction, come together "after an interval of gathering and branding all over the country" in an isolated frontier settlement of a schoolhouse and one cabin, occupied by a white family and visitor. The sportsman's code looms large in the story, functioning as a central sign of Lin's superior manhood. On a hunt, he refuses to shoot a she-bear (whose gambols with her cubs echo innumerable Boone and Crockett bear-hunt tales) whereas his rival goes ahead, in order to cater to Katie's demand for a bear skin.

The story culminates in boyish high jinks, with Lin and his Virginian cow-boy companion masquerading as screeching Crow warriors circling the cabin to expose the cowardice of Dick, who is discovered trembling under the kitchen table. Lines of distinction—by gender, race, and class—are clearly laid down on this landscape. The virtuous, upper-class eastern schoolma'am, Miss Wood, is separated off spatially from the character whom Wister would develop as the bigamous, working-class "biscuit shooter": they occupy opposite ends of the cabin and when, at the height of the "Indian" attack, Katie rushes out in her nightdress, Miss Wood remains discreetly out of sight "but I thought I heard her mocking treble laughter coming from somewhere." As in Boone and Crockett hunting tales, the scene is free of non-Anglo presences, Natives figuring only as savage figments of the cowboy imagination. Lin and the Virginian, playing Indian, literally ring the white enclave. 'Rapaho Dick folds a tribal name into his own as a sign of his vaunted fighting prowess which, the Virginian tells the narra-tor, is based on seeing "a heap of Injuns in Buffalo Bill's show"—the same show as was drawing record crowds just a few blocks from the hunter's cabin in which Wister was writing this tale.

Another step in the transformation of the Boone and Crockett "sportsman's code" into the familiar "Code of the West" occurred in the second volume of their book series, when the rituals of fair chase were transferred onto a man-hunt. In 1894, as the club ramped up the pressure on the Cleveland administra-tion to enact legislation enforcing game laws in Yellowstone National Park, a hunter named Ed Howell was caught by Scout Burgess in the act of killing buf-falo from the park's last herd. Grinnell immediately broadcast the story, sending his ace reporter, Emerson Hough, to write it up for *Forest and Stream*. Hough was not of the social class necessary to club membership, but his vision was heav-ily influenced by Grinnell's magazine—he called it "a gentleman's paper, owned by a gentleman, and offered to gentlemen"—and he wrote up the pursuit and capture in terms familiar from the Boone and Crockett Club formula (*Getting* 140). He made scouting for a poacher sound very much like tracking big game: "A poacher's trail has to be followed hard and sharp, with no let-up and no return-ing" ("Account" 377). He also worked to make the final stalk and showdown a contest between equals, however morally despicable Howell was, and he did so by employing the familiar trope of vast, empty space:

> I learned how utterly small, lonely and insignificant a man looks and feels in the midst of solitude so vast, so boundless, so tremendous and so appalling. Then I knew that the man Howell was in his brutal and misguided way a hero in self-reliance, and that Scout Burgess was also in courage and self-reliance a hero, nothing less.

A narrative formula that was only partly about animals in the first place transferred easily and effectively back onto human relations.

The story attracted a wave of interest. It galvanized *Forest and Stream* readers to join forces as lobbyists in a government mail-in campaign, and it became the springboard for Hough's career as a popularizer of the West. In 1896, Grinnell recommended him to Ripley Hitchcock at D. Appleton & Co. (another "quality" publisher) as a replacement for Roosevelt, who was too busy to write the book about cattle ranching that Hitchock wanted from him—Grinnell vouched, "I am altogether disposed to believe that Mr. Hough can lay aside his news paper style and treat the book in a dignified and serious spirit, and at the same time can retain the snap of his style."[73] The result was *The Story of the Cowboy* (1897). This was Hough's in with the publishing network he had been attempting to access for years, and it established his credentials as a frontier club author. Roosevelt wrote him a letter of congratulations—"it has been done better than I could have done it myself" (quoted in Hough, *Getting* 155). Whitney courted him to contribute regularly to *Outing* (a move Grinnell blocked as inappropriate for a *Forest and Stream* employee).[74] For Hough, this was the turning point in his career: "I now saw not only fame but also fortune immediately within my grasp."[75]

Meanwhile Wister—with a lot of feedback and advice from his clubmates—was producing western stories apace. Among other initiatives, he had upgraded the cowboy who appeared as Lin's sidekick in "The Winning of the Biscuit Shooter" and built around him the best-selling *Virginian* of 1902. The novel is again set in Wyoming's cattle land cleared of its Native and African American inhabitants—an "unfeatured wilderness"; "this voiceless land, this desert, this vacuum"; "a space across which Noah and Adam might come straight from Genesis" (7, 58, 13). The tenderfoot voice belongs to the same eastern establishment narrator as appeared in earlier stories, his self-deprecating accounts of his western education sustaining the Boone and Crockett tone. The role of honorable, stoical killer is fulfilled by the Virginian, the natural gentleman from the South, come west as cowboy. The climactic action of the novel—in which the Virginian and the villain Trampas close in on each other through the town's back alleys at sundown, culminating in a shootout on main street—codifies the stalk-and-showdown sequence so familiar in the Boone and Crockett Club hunting tale as the culminating action of the cowboy western. Wister, in fact, said that he planned the novel's climactic episode in "1896, while hunting mountain sheep in the Tetons."[76]

Other Boone and Crockett Clubmen helped to consolidate the frontier club western. Whitney, always with an eye on the main chance, swiftly saw the gain to be made in the cowboy connection. When he wrote up the 1896 version of his musk-ox hunt on the Barren Grounds of northern Alberta, he painted Edmonton as the new frontier with little sense of Canadian difference—"the atmosphere was continuously shattered by cowboy whoops and leaden pellets"—and crafted the pacing and final showdown to maximize the suspense (quoted in T. Kelly, "Hunter" 146). During the same period in which Wister was refining the laconic Virginian as natural gentleman, Whitney imported a remarkably similar figure into his *Outing* editorials: "the sportsman is simply a fair-minded, manly-acting, outspoken, courteous gentleman—and I mean gentleman in the sense that implies natural instinct, not clothes and general outward appearance. Many a good sportsman I have known in cowhide boots and with a somewhat limited vocabulary."[77] (The borrowing, of course, worked in two directions: Wister's rendition of the lynching scene—"A Stable on the Flat"—in *The Virginian* is full of the vocabulary of game and sportsmanship that could be from Whitney's pen.) Finally, when *The Virginian* went to the top of the bestseller list in 1902, Whitney wrote to Wister asking for "a story anything of the nature of the Virginians [sic]" for serialization in *Outing*.[78] Perhaps more than any other clubman, Whitney understood that sportsman, hunter, and cowboy were all clubmen of the same stripe.

George Bird Grinnell also contributed to the new formula, when he applied the Boone and Crockett template to a seven-volume series of westerns for young readers, published between 1899 and 1913. The "Jack" books (beginning with *Jack, The Young Ranchman*) propagate familiar settings, action, voices, and values, bringing together hunting and ranching adventures and literalizing the motif of boyishness. Madison Grant turned late in life to writing western fiction, with *Hank, His Secrets and His Lies* in 1931, reviving once more the hunting template as the site of core values in an attempt to combat what he saw as the degeneration of the western. (For more on Grinnell's and Grant's fiction, see Chapter Five, this volume).

The transition from frontier club hands to the wider cultural arena was facilitated by at least two writers connected, but not belonging, to the group. Hough parlayed the early opportunities offered by Grinnell into a highly successful career as a writer of western fiction. In 1905, he worked closely with an editor at Macmillan (publisher of *The Virginian*) to produce *Heart's Desire*, a comic version of Wister's novel.[79] Remington began to illustrate his work. In 1922, Hough published *The Covered Wagon* in response to a request from the editor of the

Saturday Evening Post that he follow the Wister prototype more closely.[80] The novel became a best-seller and was made into a major motion picture. With the publication of his trail-drive novel, *North of 36*, in 1923, the critic Douglas E. Branch judged him a better writer of westerns than Wister (203).

Even as the formula western developed beyond this group and its class coding gradually changed, the frontier club connections and imprint remained visible. The next best-selling author of westerns, Zane Grey, was also a hunter with a particular interest in buffalo. He was friend and biographer of Charles Jesse "Buffalo" Jones, the reformed buffalo hunter who became the protector of buffalo and the breeder of the doomed "cattalo," an attempt to combine "the best attributes of cattle and buffalo" (quoted in Punke 220). Remington sketched Jones for Harper's in 1890, and Roosevelt and Grinnell supported his appointment as the Yellowstone National Park Game Warden in 1902, where one of his main tasks was to construct a gigantic corral for pure-blooded buffalo, segregated from interbred animals. In 1908, Grey published his hagiography of Jones, *Last of the Plainsmen*, with Whitney's Outing Publishing Company. In 1910, Harper & Brothers, trying to reconnect with the genre after losing its star author Wister, published Grey's first best-selling western, *The Heritage of the Desert*, then proceeded to publish another sixty-one westerns by him over the next fifty-three years, along with many of his hunting, outdoors, sporting, and boys' books (with more after the company became Harper & Row). Although Grey would famously introduce to the genre an explicit sexuality foreign to the frontier club western, he also reinforced the natural right of the white hero to bear the gun, adhered to the suspenseful stalk-and-showdown sequences, and ramped up the symbolism of the enclave, with his shut-off valleys in *Riders of the Purple Sage* (1912) and *The Rainbow Trail* (1915). Whatever variations developed, the frontier club coordinates became stock features of innumerable pulps, paperbacks, and classic and B westerns. The rest, as they say, is history.

Lobbying the Federal Government

What makes this lineage more than the story of a single genre is the reach, influence, and transferability of the frontier club template. The formula that issued in the western also provided "the simplified categories of conservation" that informed federal consideration of western land use, specifically, and issues of citizenship more generally (Jacoby 38). The cumulative rhetoric of Boone and Crockett Club books recreated, first, the American West, second, the nation and, third, an international group of nations as a network of enclaves designed to protect animal and human hierarchies.

The story of the poacher Ed Howell that played such a significant role in the development of the western, and in the career of Emerson Hough, also serves to illustrate the efficacy of the Boone and Crockett hunting tale as lobbying tool. A year after Hough's piece in *Forest and Stream*, Roosevelt and Grinnell rehearsed the story two more times, in the second book of the Boone and Crockett Club, *Hunting in Many Lands* (1895). In addition to penning their own account of the man-hunt, they commissioned an essay by Captain George S. Anderson, head of the park's military detail (and associate member of the club). Even more closely than Hough's, these pieces adhere to the suspenseful stalk-and-shoot-out formula. Howell is cast as the fearsome animal, tracked by the usual manly pairing— scout plus sidekick—and the suspense builds as they stalk the "desperate criminal armed with a rifle" through the snow (Anderson 308). Burgess the scout stumbles on the poacher, "so occupied in removing the scalp from one of his bison," that the scout, armed only with a .38 caliber revolver, was able to close in "within four or five yards of him undiscovered." The rules of fair chase apply: "It would have been easy enough to kill him then, but it was too much like cold-blooded murder to do so at that range; at 200 or 300 yards it would have seemed entirely different" (Anderson 398). The kill never quite happens, but its threat is kept alive: when Howell makes a step towards his rifle, "Burgess told him to stop or he would shoot"; "It must have been difficult for the scout at that moment not to forget that ours is a Government of law, and to refrain from making as summary an end of Howell as Howell had made of the buffalo" (Anderson 399; "Yellowstone" 414). The ending of the story is new. After years of effort by the Boone and Crockett Club, this story finally convinced President Cleveland to sign an Act on May 7, 1894 "to protect the birds and animals in Yellowstone National Park, and to punish crimes in said park, and for other purposes" ("Yellowstone" 403).

Another source confirms the strong belief that the Boone and Crockett hunting tale changed the face of game legislation. Billy Hofer, hunting guide to Grinnell and other clubmen in Montana, the man who supplied the elk for the 1893 Metropolitan Club dinner and served as guide to the Hunter's Cabin at the World's Fair, made his own fierce claim on the story of Ed Howell. Hofer had led Hough into the park that winter of 1894, and until the end of his days he insisted that it was he who had seen the potential lobbying power of the man-hunt narrative. Three decades after the event, he was still complaining to Grinnell about Hough turning the story to his own benefit:

> Hough was more interested in getting a picture of Howell than in getting an account of his capture.... I told Hough to rush through the message, night letter, to Forest and Stream.... I saw a chance for the story to stir up the country about the park.[81]

A year later again, irked by Hough's celebrity status in the wake of the success of the film of *The Covered Wagon*, Hofer reiterated:

> Yes he was a hard man to get along with on that snowshoe trip. I had to urge and had to *make* him send that dispatch about Ed Howell killing the Buffalo. That gave us Law in the Park.[82]

Hofer was right. The simplified story of good-vs-evil, and the threat to noble sport represented by the greedy local, redoubled the authority of the gentlemen hunters in the legislative arena.

From the second volume onwards, the goal of federal legislation became increasingly explicit in Boone and Crockett Club books. As the hunting tales tallied up the gentlemen hunters' trophies, the books' prefaces charted their legislative successes. As the series proceeded and hunting adventures receded further into the past for these aging clubmen, the policy imperative became even more pronounced. Where earlier volumes teach the mechanics of hunting, volume six in 1925 teaches the mechanics of lobbying—meetings, coordination, leadership, campaigning, banquet, publicity. The Boone and Crockett executive instructs all outdoor magazines to substitute the term "game administration" for "game protection"—"every possible means should be taken to get it into the thoughts of the people"—as the first step towards crafting legislation that will ensure the survival of fair hunting rights, according to the club's definition, wildlife refuges, and national parks (500, 510). Once Roosevelt entered the Oval Office in 1901, more attention than ever was trained on winning over the electorate. Roosevelt himself wrote in the 1904 volume: "The work of preservation must be carried on in such a way as to make it evident that we are working in the interest of the people as a whole, not in the interest of any particular class," and he flattered westerners who support conservation by saying that they "show patriotic good sense" (24, 44). Grinnell also sounded the democratic note, supporting Roosevelt in his argument that "such refuges should be established for the benefit of the man of moderate means and the poor man, whose opportunities to hunt and to see game are few and far between" (20). The club's language becomes politically sensitive to the times, stressing the economic benefits of conservation above all others. In 1925—by which time the club was incorporated so that it could fund-raise—the language of business and modernity appears: "game is an asset"; its use must be "coordinated with all industrial uses in such a way that our national life will enjoy the maximum benefits of all our resources"; the club advocates "plain common sense management" (501).

These rhetorical maneuvers impacted entire economies and cultural communities in the West. Their real-life consequences were starkest among those people whom the clubmen represented as the threatening fringe to their pure hunting and conservation spaces. The game and conservation laws promoted by the gentlemen hunters criminalized many long-standing practices of local people: hunting and fishing were redefined as poaching, foraging as trespassing, the seasonal setting of fires as arson, tree-cutting as timber theft, and settlers as squatters.[83] Native hunters practicing their traditional rights were arrested and incarcerated as law-breakers. The Boone and Crockett Club reinforced these legal reclassifications not only by harping on the dangerous wastefulness of Indigenous peoples in their hunting and conservation essays but also by submitting formal motions to the federal government. In 1889, for example, the club passed a resolution, at the urging of Roosevelt and Grinnell, enjoining government regulation of the Bannock, Shoshone, and Crow around Yellowstone National Park: the "destruction of forests and of game caused by these Indian hunting parties... [is] a serious evil" (quoted in Jacoby 91). Lewis S. Thompson's Boone and Crockett tale adeptly lines up multiple threats when it parallels the army's protection of settlers from rampaging Natives with their protection of superior animal species from poachers.

The potential scope of the Boone and Crockett Club's influence increased exponentially when its racial scheme went global. From the first, the club situated itself within an imperial network: Roosevelt said that he had modeled it on London's Alpine Club, and Grinnell claimed that it had international influence, an effect which Edmund Morris says was hastened by the book series when it "won acclaim on both sides of the Atlantic, and prompted the establishment of Boone & Crockett-type clubs in England and various parts of the British Empire."[84] The formulaic narrative of gentlemanly killing also served to fold many nations into the clubmen's network of power, reinforcing a "transnational racial community."[85] As the tales range abroad, Boone and Crockett members write of bumping into compatriots, fellow clubmen, and high-placed Englishmen—colonial officials, military officers, planters, merchants—who smooth their way, extending an Anglo-American alliance across the continents. The rituals of the hunting tale and their attendant hierarchies remain identical across Mexico, Alaska, Canada, Africa, India, Russia, Chinese Turkestan, Korea, Mongolia, and Tibet. Widely distant parts of the world tell the same story about the white hunter's centrality, the contest between superior races, and the inferiority and threat of others. The big-game species may differ (ibex, wildebeest, eland, letchwi, mpallah, tigers, rhinoceros, elephants, giraffes, wild yak), but they are anthropomorphized, measured, and ranked according to the same conventions, and they provoke the same hunting rituals, gentlemanly codes, and racial positions. International links also come to be strengthened through legislative examples, such as the measures taken by Germany and the UK to protect reserves in Africa.

One difference is that, outside the United States, black- and brown-skinned figures can come into view—sometimes in massive numbers, as with the 130 Zanzibaris accompanying William Chanler, Winthrop's brother; and the 200 Indian beaters who served as retinue to Elliot Roosevelt, Theodore's brother— so that their subordination be made explicit. "The Anglo-Saxon idea of sport" is a superior concept that has to be introduced to the subservient Natives, from the black "boys" and "Kaffirs" of Rhodesia to the "coolies" of India, who serve as guides, servants, and cooks.[86] In telling of his hunting trip in East Africa, William Chanler instructs the reader in how to distrust and handle black workers, such as his boatman, "the negro," and his Swahili gun-bearer (19). William Lord Smith and his English hunting companion demonstrate both their dependence on and the threat of contamination by Africans when they are carried through high seas to the coast on the shoulders of Natives who are immediately demeaned as money seekers: "the water about the dhows swarmed with black heads, all eager to earn a little silver by carrying things ashore" (81). As in Theodore Roosevelt's first hunting book, these foreign adventurers are strongly oriented homewards, incorporating the fruits of these foreign expeditions, along with their racial attitudes, into the domestic realm. Their trophy heads and skins stocked the great museums that reinforced America's national identity and the private mansions that reinforced their own (William Chanler, for example, caps his African expedition by triumphantly bringing his rhino kill home: "I have a table at home made of a piece of this animal's hide, and supported in part by one of its horns").[87]

The template that the Boone and Crockett Club laid on the American West and other countries' wild spaces—the spatial enclave with its embedded racial hierarchies—served them as a lobbying tool not only on game and conservation laws but on federal legislation more broadly. Madison Grant most systematically enabled the transfer of terms from animal to human spheres. Many of his Boone and Crockett essays argue for big-game preserves—"proper sanctuaries...thoroughly controlled"—for certain species that are "the very culmination of their respective genera," such as giant moose in Alaska and wild buffalo in Yellowstone Park ("Condition" 371, 368). He adapted that vision to urban space when he argued successfully for the creation of a zoological park in New York City. Designed according to "those principles of game preservation advocated by the Boone and Crockett Club," it would save from extinction "herds—not merely individuals—of each of the large North American quadrupeds" ("Origin" 313, 317). Twenty years later, when he delivered his eugenics diatribe in *The Passing of the Great Race*, he reproduced the same logic once more, arguing that superior species of Nordic Americans should be preserved by being isolated from inferior, mixed-race presences. Owen Wister made the same connection more wittily. The sight of a mountain sheep tethered to a post outside Livingston, Montana leads him to a disquisition on the distinction between the bourgeois domestic sheep and the aristocratic mountain sheep which "has, even beyond the bull elk, that same secure, unconscious air of being not only well bred, but *high* bred, not only game but *fine* game, which we still in the twentieth century meet sometimes among men and women...nature scorns universal suffrage; and when our houses have ceased to contain gentlefolk, we shall still be able to find them in the zoölogical gardens" ("Mountain" 183).

The Boone and Crockett Club was assiduous in re-stocking western game preserves—transplanting pure-bred bison from the New York Zoo to an Oklahoma refuge, for example—but their ambitions did not rest there. The hunter-writers made clear that they aimed to re-populate the nation. Another member, D. M. Barringer, in his account of dog sledging in the north, notes the "magnificent specimens" of animals and men and is particularly impressed by "primitive" Icelanders: "They are much more neat and cleanly than many of the immigrants who come to the United States... [they] would make good citizens" ("Dog" 124, 138). As Daniel Herman puts it: "Hunting is not just about hunting; it is about the meaning of citizenship in a republic" ("Hunting" 31). The culminating acts in this vision came with two pieces of legislation in 1924—the National Origins Act and the Indian Citizenship Act—whose story is told in Chapter Five of this volume.

Conclusion

The dominant western formula was forged within a network of power from which it benefited and which it reinforced. In shoring up their hunting and other privileges, Boone and Crockett Club writers more generally shored up an aristocratic class that felt itself beleaguered on several fronts and sought means of extending its influence over federal policy and public opinion. This power play was explicitly focused on the American West, but it connected with a larger constellation of national and international efforts around masculinity, race, and citizenship.

The Boone and Crockett Club was perennially frustrated at not being able to exert control directly over western lands. Its members tried to enforce game laws by offering rewards for the capture of poachers, a scheme that rebounded to their disadvantage when their lack of local knowledge led to them being swindled by various means. Reluctantly, the executive committee conceded in 1902 "that we have not the means at our disposal for an effective prosecution of offenders against the Game Laws."[88] What they did have, however, as they had been convincingly reminded a couple of months earlier that year with the success of Wister's novel, was the power of print. Henry Fairfield Osborn, honorary clubman and eugenicist, was confident that "What the Club can do is to spread information and thoroughly enlighten the people, who always act rightly when they understand" (373). Who belonged to "the people" or "the public" whom they sought to influence, however, was not a straightforward question. Certainly, the category did not include the Indigenous peoples displaced by the Dawes Act (which took their land away to give to "the public") in the same year that the Boone and Crockett Club was formed, nor any of the "degenerate" types who appear on the fringes of their hunting tales. It was also the case that compliance was not assured; sometimes "that public required to be governed" (Grinnell, "Brief" 452). Club writings aimed to define, persuade, and govern the public—including the reading public—in one fell swoop.

Read from this perspective, the hunting tale-turned-western began as one big lobbying mechanism, designed to win over a popular audience from whom clubmen shrank and on whom they depended. From the books of the Boone and Crockett Club, tentacles of influence extended, from Roosevelt, Grinnell, Wister, Chanler, Whitney, and Grant, through Remington, Hough, Grey, and beyond. What remains the most familiar version of the western in print and on screen carries the imprint of the clubmen's voice, action, landscape, and cultural agendas, both the manifest and the more hidden. There was, however, one narrative element that the Boone and Crockett Clubmen were not best positioned to provide: heterosexual romance. This, as the next chapter explores, came from a different quarter, bringing with it additional cultural baggage and new opportunities for cultural prestidigitation.

2

Cowboys and Publishers

Owen Wister had his own myth of the modern western's origin. In September 1891, he had just returned from his fifth trip west and repaired to the Philadelphia Club for a hearty meal with Walter Furness, son of the eminent Shakespearean scholar Horace Howard Furness. As Wister told it:

> And so one Autumn evening of 1891, fresh from Wyoming and its wild glories, I sat in the club dining with a man as enamoured of the West as I was.... From oysters to coffee we compared experiences. Why wasn't some Kipling saving the sage-brush for American literature, before the sage-brush and all that it signified went the way of the California forty-niner, went the way of the Mississippi steam-boat, went the way of everything? Roosevelt had seen the sage-brush true, had felt its poetry; and also Remington, who illustrated his articles so well. But what was fiction doing, fiction, the only thing that has always outlived fact?...Was Alkali Ike in the comic papers the one figure which the jejune American imagination, always at full-cock to banter or to brag, could discern in that epic which was being lived at a gallop out in the sage-brush? To hell with tea-cups and the great American laugh! We two said, as we sat dining at the club. The claret had been excellent.
>
> "Walter, I'm going to try it myself!" I exclaimed to Walter Furness. "I'm going to start this minute." (*Roosevelt* 29)

Whereupon, Wister dashed up to the club library and wrote his first western story—"Hank's Woman"—in one sitting. By this telling, popular western fiction was created in the oldest and most exclusive gentlemen's club in America by the man who, forty-two years later, would become its honorary president.

While this account is apocryphal—Wister's first attempt at a western did not take place in the Philadelphia Club and was not "Hank's Woman"—it points to a larger truth. Wister's entrée to the West and the western did come partly through his Philadelphia Club connections, specifically the "very Proper Philadelphian"

Dr. Silas Weir Mitchell (Baltzell 154). Mitchell introduced Wister to both cow-boys and publishers, sending his young protégé to the cattle-country West, help-ing him to shape his fiction about it, and smoothing his path to publication. The appearance of his western stories in *Harper's Weekly* and *Harper's Monthly Magazine* in1892 brought Wister back to "the full sunshine" of Roosevelt's attention—the two men having lost touch since Harvard days—and election to the Boone and Crockett Club that year (*Roosevelt* 30). By combining those two influences, Wister brought the frontier club western one step closer to fruition.

The Philadelphia Club is a quite different starting point from the Boone and Crockett Club, though there are convergences, both in membership and in the view of the West as a place for the temporary immersion and renewal of eastern privilege. This chapter traces the journey of Owen Wister from Philadelphia to Wyoming to Manhattan, a journey linked by a series of elite clubs: of metropoli-tan gentlemen, cattle kings, and quality publishers. Along the way, the frontier club western accrued several formative elements. From Philadelphia, his place of birth and adult residence, Wister learned to incorporate the drawing room manners and heterosexual romance that the Boone and Crockett Club template lacked. In Wyoming he met the cattle kings with whom he developed common cause within and beyond his fiction. And in Manhattan he forged a mutually sup-portive relationship with quality publishers, who needed this emerging genre as much as it needed them.

In each case, and in parallel ways, these personal and professional relation-ships helped to resolve one of the frontier clubmen's perennial problems: their relationship to the marketplace. Many of them, like their class more generally, were embroiled in financial speculation—ranching and publishing were among their favorite fields of investment—while experiencing deep discomfort with the mass market to which these industries belonged. The Philadelphian Silas Weir Mitchell, as a physician-writer, popularized a diagnostic narrative in which the West cured upper-class men contaminated by contact with the marketplace. He also demonstrated how this medical prognosis could be converted into popular fiction invested with drawing-room manners and morality. The Wyoming cattle kings, who became the heroes of frontier club westerns, showed how the iron fist of investment capital could nestle in the velvet glove of club culture. And the publishers of frontier club writings worked to bifurcate the new literary market-place into "quality" houses that ostensibly transcended market considerations and "cheap" houses that were consumed by them, a narrative that frontier club authors, Wister first among them, were keen to promote.

As we follow Wister's movements among those genteel markets, the parallels and overlaps between them accumulate. The degree to which the cattle and pub-lishing industries were fighting the same battle is evident in their echoing termi-nology. Both cattle kings and quality publishers practiced "book counts," both inveighed against "pirates" ("range pirates" in the one case, copyright "pirates" in the other), and both agreed not to "jump another's claim." The two spheres shared commercial structures and rhetorics of power. In both, cultural stratification was wielded by established interests that felt themselves to be losing control of the marketplace—in a shrinking market on the cattle range and an expanding market in the book industry. The frontier club western capitalized on and facilitated this strategy in a series of maneuvers that began far from the West, in Proper Philadelphia.

A Very Proper Philadelphian

The Philadelphia upper class of the late nineteenth century was at once wealthy, intensely cultured, and in the throes of change. Since the city's founding, its network of elite families—what E. Digby Baltzell famously dubbed "Proper Philadelphia"—had repeatedly negotiated changing circumstances (9, *passim*). The colonial generation owed its power to mercantile wealth—they were merchants, lawyers, doctors, bankers. In the antebellum period, the balance of power began to shift to industrial wealth—mining, railroads, manufacturing. After the Civil War, investment finance and real estate speculation produced the fantastically wealthy robber barons of the Gilded Age. The struggle of the hereditary upper class to retain its standing in the face of this plutocracy was at its most intense in Philadelphia, where the family network was most conservative and the social upheavals over the decades—population explosion, sectarian conflict, anti-black riots, attacks on immigrants, strikes—among the most violent.[1] Historians have identified various social institutions and cultural projects by which the old elites selectively absorbed the new—among them, the *Social Register* and the Philadelphia Exposition of 1876.[2] Baltzell is unequivocal: "The circulation of elites in America and the assimilation of new men of power and influence into the upper class takes place primarily through the medium of urban clubdom"—the *sanctum sanctorum* of which was the Philadelphia Club (340).

The clubman who most closely translated these social, family, and club dynamics into popular writings was Dr. Silas Weir Mitchell, "Philadelphia's leading author and physician in the Victorian Age" (Baltzell 126). Mitchell belonged to the same family lineage as Wister—he was a distant cousin on the mother's side—and he was a leading figure in the city's most glittering literary circle: his "'Saturday evenings after nine' were famous for excellent food, wine, and conversation."[3] They regularly included members of the Furness and Wister families—who were also connected by marriage—as well as out-of-town literati such as Oliver Wendell Holmes and James Russell Lowell (a distant cousin of Mary Cadwalader Mitchell).

Mitchell also intimately lived the threats to upper-class status and the accommodations necessary for its survival. Although he came from a distinguished medical family, he experienced brushes with poverty and had to interrupt his own education to support his family when his father fell ill, and he struggled to secure a preferred medical position in the city. In his funeral eulogy, Wister praised Mitchell: "he had carried upon his shoulders a family heavy with misfortune; he had triumphantly lived down patronizing distrust and indifference" ("Owen"). Perhaps for this reason, Mitchell "eagerly lapt up adulation."[4] Sarah Butler Wister teasingly accused him of having a "vanity which finds perpetual incense," however many honors he piled up (quoted in Earnest 241). Only with his second marriage, into the Cadwalader family (a most distinguished founding family of Philadelphia, a member of whom served as the first president of the Philadelphia Club), was his social position unassailable. He moved to one of the city's most fashionable addresses—1524 Walnut Street, near Rittenhouse Square. He was invited to Manhattan's most exclusive social event, the Patriarchs' Ball at Delmonico's, a rare privilege for a Philadelphia aristocrat.[5] And he summered at Newport, Rhode Island, which he celebrated as "a large, highly cultivated, intellectual life," which included his membership in the Town and Country Club, restricted to fifty families for the purposes of scientific, cultural, and educational entertainments.[6] There, his Philadelphia circle was joined by luminaries from Manhattan (including Mrs. John Jacob Astor, to whose clan Winthrop Chanler belonged) and Boston (including Colonel Higginson, a good friend of Lodge and part of the family with which Owen Wister first found employment and into which Roosevelt first married). Even within this enclave, however, Mitchell was alive to the pressure of the Gilded Age *nouveaux riches*: "The charm of this interesting society was broken as people of large means, merely socially ambitious, began to build extravagant houses and to substitute for what we lost the unequalled folly of rapidly acquired wealth.... The change of tone in the society finally drove us out and sent us to Bar Harbor."[7]

Frontier Club Neurasthenia

Mitchell epitomizes the fabric of the larger frontier club network. He moved in the same circles as the Boone and Crockett Clubmen, but he did not belong to their hunting club. A generation older than most of them, he shared interests (and a profession) with Owen Wister's father, and his sport was salmon fishing in Quebec rather than big-game hunting in the West. His generation of the eastern establishment sought their manhood status in their professional work, rather than in their recreational pursuits, and therefore frankly approached field sport as leisure (although they shared the younger generation's attitude to the land: the Cascapedia Club and Ristigouche Salmon Club in which Mitchell held membership attempted to appropriate Quebec's rivers in ways closely parallel to the aristocrats' attempts to appropriate the western wilderness).[8] He shared membership in the Philadelphia Club with several Boone and Crockett Clubmen. They included his son, Jack Mitchell, who also became a doctor and was Owen Wister's close friend and first hunting companion in Wyoming, and the Penrose brothers, one of whom (Boies) became U.S. senator from Pennsylvania in 1897 and another of whom (Charles), again a close friend of Wister, played a prominent role as physician to the Johnson County War Invaders. Mitchell's medical practice also served these upper echelons of society. One of Chanler's sisters-in-law (Amélie Rives) was a patient in Mitchell's Philadelphia clinic in the 1890s, particularly under the care of his assistant, Dr. John Madison Taylor.[9] Taylor also visited Roosevelt at his Dakota ranch and passed the test of ruggedness, Roosevelt pronouncing him "a good deal of a man" (Morison 106–07). Mitchell himself chose not to approach Roosevelt too closely, observing: "I have always had for him great respect and no very great liking."[10] Mitchell's most lasting contribution to the frontier club came through his writings, medical and fictional.

Given Mitchell's intense investment in his own prestige, it is ironic that his role in medical and literary history is most often remembered nowadays in a negative light. He is the villain behind Charlotte Perkins Gilman's "The Yellow Wall-paper" of 1892, a short story still read by millions of students across and beyond North America. Mitchell, having diagnosed Gilman as neurasthenic, relegated her to the extended bed rest whose hellish effects she vividly fictionalized in her story and sent to him in castigation of his methods. Throughout the 1870s and 1880s, Mitchell had published treatises on the neurological diagnoses and treatment that made him internationally famous, especially for his "rest cure," known in Europe (much to his gratification) as "the Mitchell system." This was Mitchell's highly gendered response to the new condition named "neurasthenia" by his compatriot George Beard in 1869: a nervous disorder or exhaustion that Beard identified as specifically modern and originating in America. When Mitchell diagnosed neurasthenia in women, he recommended absolute bed rest, absence of intellectual or creative activity, massage, over-feeding and, in a later refinement, electro-therapy. This regime enraged Gilman and killed the daughter of Mitchell's literary friend William D. Howells. (In time, Mitchell would revise his prescription for women; he applied the results less disastrously to Edith Wharton, among others.) When Mitchell diagnosed neurasthenia in men, he prescribed a trip west, with as much vigorous outdoor activity and the recording of closely observed detail as possible. Mitchell's medical writings were massively popular: the first edition of *Wear and Tear, Or Hints for the Overworked* (1871) sold out within ten days, issued in eight more editions and continues to be reprinted.[11]

Mitchell's diagnosis targeted not just individuals but modern society as a whole. As he announced in *Fat and Blood* (1877), he was intent on "renewing the vitality of feeble people" both as individuals and as a class (9). Responding to the recurrent economic upheavals of the period, he diagnosed society's disease as "the modern American marketplace, with its demands and depletions" (Will 298). In *Wear and Tear* he cited some of the most prominent features of the Gilded Age: "the cruel competition for the dollar...the racing speed which the telegraph and railway have introduced into commercial life, the new value which great fortunes have come to possess as means towards social advancement" are all overtaxing "the nervous system of certain classes of Americans" (9). He was concerned about "young men suddenly cast into business positions," particularly if they involve "the responsibilities of great manufactories...especially with borrowed capital" (63). The antidote is to go west, engage in "the sturdy contest with Nature," and thus "store up a capital of vitality" which enables the manly man to return to successful labor (8). As the tropes accumulate, the parallels in Mitchell's analysis become clear. As men and women need different versions of the rest cure, so modern society needs the balance of conventional Victorian gender roles. Both the body and the economy need periodic replenishment to their "capital" in order to thrive. Mitchell's "neurasthenic logic" echoes and supports the social logic of the gentlemen's clubs: both offer a method by which the genteel upper class retains its vitality by selectively accepting the injection of new commercial sources and types (Will 299).

Several members of the frontier club suffered breakdowns. Theodore Roosevelt was diagnosed with neurasthenia as a boy and struggled with various ailments, nervous and otherwise, throughout his life.[12] George Bird Grinnell was also diagnosed with neurasthenia as a young man, and well into the 1890s he regarded the West as an antidote to what he called "a good deal of trouble with my head"; in 1894, he told Luther North, "I want to go somewhere where I can be in camp and do some hard physical work for a little while so as to straighten out my physical and mental condition, for I am not very well."[13] Henry Cabot Lodge was frail in his youth and repeatedly collapsed from nervous exhaustion as he aged. Jack Mitchell recurrently descended into depression, and at least one of the cattle kings involved in the Johnson County lynching, Frederic deBillier, broke down in the wake of that violence. Neurasthenia was one condition Frederic Remington did share with the clubmen. Owen Wister most closely fitted Mitchell's template of the neurasthenic gentleman. Wister broke down in 1885, after surrendering his musical career in accordance with his father's wishes and engaging with the worlds of business and law. Mitchell diagnosed him as suffering from neurasthenia and prescribed a trip to Wyoming.

Wister's approach to the West was heavily conditioned by Mitchell's analysis: he went west understanding that he and his class were sick and that the West held the cure for both. He also worked to inculcate the "strong clinical-like power of observation" which Mitchell prescribed for men embarking on the "West cure"

(Lovering 75; Tuttle, "Rewriting"). (From a different direction, Mitchell's advice echoes both the clinical precision with which Grinnell documented his killing of a fawn in one hunting tale and the injunction by Grinnell and Roosevelt in the Boone and Crockett book series: "the closer a man's habits of observation the more speedily will he become a good hunter" [*Trail* 11]). The diary Wister faithfully kept on his first and subsequent trips closely alternated between monitoring the state of his own health and recording the landscape around him, echoing Mitchell's journal of his trip to Yellowstone Park six years earlier. The younger man, like the older, compares the Rockies to the Alps (the Matterhorn in Mitchell's case, the Dolomites in Wister's) and reaches for European imagery (Mitchell describes "the Dante like horror of the pines slain & now half burned grim grey spectres of trees," while Wister notes "the most ominous and forbidding chasm of rocks I ever saw in any country—Deep down below a camp fire is burning—It all looked like Die Walkure").[14] One of Wister's first observations on arrival in Wyoming—"I'm beginning to be able to feel I'm something of an animal and not a stinking brain alone" sounds like textbook Mitchell.[15]

A Man's Gotta Do …

As Wister began to convert his journal notes into fiction, from 1891, his character types also owed much to Mitchell. From his first published short story—"Hank's Woman" in *Harper's Weekly* in 1892—to his culminating western novel—*The Virginian* in 1902—and beyond, the first-person eastern narrator carries both the tenderfoot voice refined in the Boone and Crockett Club and the neurasthenic symptoms identified by Mitchell: the narrator suffers from nervous exhaustion, irritability, and physical weakness which can be cured only by a recurrent "return to the earth" in the West which, in turn, enables him to return to his life in the East (Mitchell, *Wear* 8). His western hero also personifies and proves the efficacy of Mitchell's prescription. The Virginian's superb physicality is directly linked to his active, outdoors life ("it has made me want to become the ground," he says of the camping life); his energy also delivers healthy financial success (493). In the course of the novel, the Virginian is, as Mitchell prescribed, "gradually trained to naturally and slowly increasing burdens"; his employer promotes him from cowboy to foreman to ranch partner (*Wear* 63). By the end of the novel, he has become a mature, successful man of business, profiting from both cattle rearing and mineral extraction, who retains his vitality and masks his entrepreneurial relationship to the land with recurrent returns to outdoor living.

If Mitchell's "neurasthenic view of the world" clearly stamped Wister's westerns, so did his fictional techniques (Will 296). As "a neurologist-novelist whose dual identities informed and fertilized one another," Mitchell moved easily from medical case histories to fictional character studies (Micale,

"Medical" 184). He had a prolific literary output—poetry, thirty to forty short stories and novelettes, and thirteen novels—in which, more intimately than any other writer, he explored the history, manners, and morals of Proper Philadelphia. He fictionalized clubland most directly in his "conversation novels"—*Characteristics* (1891) and *Dr. North and his Friends* (1900)—which are modeled on the conversations and personalities of his own literary circle (including Horace Howard Furness, Talcott Williams, John Cadwalader, and Sarah Butler Wister).[16] He also contributed to the selective assimilation of the Gilded Age tycoon by writing the "robber financier" into his fiction (*Characteristics* 27). He developed a character named Xerxes Z— in *Characteristics* and fleshed him out as Xerxes Crofter in *Dr. North*, a western railroad magnate understood to be an amalgamation of Collis P. Huntington, Cornelius Vanderbilt, and Andrew Carnegie, with the last of whom Mitchell had life-long dealings.[17] Mitchell returned to such a figure several times, in, for example, Rufus Hood, the northern millionaire in *Constance Trescot*, and Roger Grace, the tortured self-made millionaire in *Circumstance*. In their violent speculation, these figures initially breach the clubmen's code of honor but gradually learn how to use their commercial talents more honorably. They remain threatening figures (Hood, for example, is indirectly responsible for the murder of one of Mitchell's gentleman heroes), never secure within the inner circle but tolerated by those who are.

Several of Mitchell's novels (including his bestselling *Hugh Wynne* of 1896) are historical romances that plot the history of Colonial and Reconstruction Philadelphia, weaving in families and places (Cadwaladers, Wisters, Newport, Harvard) that made up Mitchell's social world in the present. The romances also revolve around Mitchell's class, teasing out the minutiae of character, family, and drawing-room manners through a central love story. A recurrent issue is a gentleman's honor, often debated between man and woman. *In War Time* (serialized in 1884), for example, dramatizes a confrontation between Colonel Fox, an ex-Confederate soldier, and the widow Alice Westerley, Proper Philadelphian to a "T." Fox's code of honor compels him to reveal an act of cowardice by Alice's lover, Dr. Wendell, another Philadelphian—knowing that she cannot marry a coward—and to inform Wendell that he has done so. Alice's pragmatic response to the information staggers Fox: she sees no need to call off the wedding, given that the act is past and secret, nor to let Wendell know. Fox passionately refutes the logic of her morality and, ultimately, he is proved right. Wendell's moral weakness leads him into a second cowardly act that Alice cannot ignore, and he retreats west, a broken man. The novel's ending hints that Alice and Fox may ultimately wed.

Mitchell's writing served, quite literally, as one of Wister's templates. The younger man often sought his elder's advice about his writing, and their correspondence shows them debating their fellow writers—particularly W. D. Howells and Henry James—in terms of style, plotting (on which neither was strong), and characterization. In 1896, Wister adapted one of Mitchell's long dramatic poems, with Thomas Wharton, into a play: "Francois Villon: A Romantic Drama in Four Acts with Songs." Wister also collaborated with Mitchell's younger son, Langdon. By 1909, an anonymous story by Wister was mistaken as Mitchell's work, so close was their style.

Wister's westerns are in many ways, like Mitchell's fiction, studies of historical manners. In the preface to the first edition of *The Virginian*, Wister drew attention to the similarity, commenting that several newspapers had mistaken the title for a historical novel "meaning (I take it) a colonial romance" and pointing out that his book is indeed historical "quite as much so as any colonial romance. Indeed, when you look at the root of the matter, it is a colonial romance. For Wyoming between 1874 and 1900 was a colony as wild as was Virginia one hundred years earlier" (vii). Citing Mitchell's *Hugh Wynne* as the paradigmatic historical novel, he positions *The Virginian* within the genre. By the same token, although the Rocky Mountain territories seem far removed from Mitchell's urban, east coast locations, the West hovers suggestively in the margins of the elder man's early work. It is the location, for example, in *In War Time* from which several male figures emerge and in which they undergo complicating experiences, as well as the place of banishment for the male protagonist at the end of the novel. When Wister fleshed out that West, he borrowed from Mitchell the central business between man and woman that is missing from the Boone and Crockett Club writings. In *The Virginian* much of the courtship between the eastern schoolma'am Molly and the southern cowboy the Virginian consists of literary debate that sounds like snippets from the conversations of Mitchell's Dr. North and his intimates— and, indeed, Mitchell's real-life literary circle. As Molly introduces her lover to the literary canon, they debate the merits of Shakespeare and Walter Scott versus Jane Austen and George Eliot, and analyze the meanings and effects of Robert Browning's poetry.

Wister extends Mitchell's attention to the rules of conduct from the parlor to the outdoors, bringing the rules of Philadelphia genteel society and Boone and Crockett hunting codes to bear, together, on questions of honor and violence. The confrontation played out between Fox and Alice in her Germantown drawing-room is closely echoed between the Virginian and Molly in his Wyoming hotel room before the climactic shootout. The Virginian insists that his only honorable course is to face the slanderous Trampas; any other way would give the appearance of cowardice, and Molly would not wish to marry a coward. Molly, like Alice, holds to a pragmatic line, arguing that everyone knows that the Virginian is not a coward, so why does he not simply sidestep the confrontation with Trampas and they can marry straightaway. The outcome is different, swifter and more violent than in Mitchell's model (the Virginian insists on facing the shootout with Trampas, kills his man, and returns to Molly, who then capitulates to his logic and they marry), but the morality is identical.[18] Buried in this dynamic is an additional echo, in the Virginian's origins. Mitchell, whose family had emigrated to Pennsylvania from Scotland via Virginia, said he learned from his father "the Virginia code of honor," which is a recurrent characteristic of his fictional heroes (Earnest 7). In the same year that Wister published *The Virginian*, Mitchell printed his "autobiography" of his own "Virginia gentleman," George Washington (Earnest 182).

The sense that the two men were telling essentially the same story was reinforced as their works developed. Mitchell's unpublished short story, "An Adventure on Fifth Avenue," is annotated by Wister and very similar in tone and action to the second story he published, "How Lin McLean Went East."[19] In both stories, the action revolves around a western cowboy who goes east (to Manhattan in one case, Boston in the other), only to find himself ridiculed by eastern club society, which he ultimately betters and rejects. Because Mitchell's story is undated, it is impossible to identify the direction in which the influence traveled in this case, but it is more evidence of an ongoing conversation between them about the West.

In 1905, Mitchell seemed to take on the challenge of violence set by *The Virginian*, while teasing out the moral complications it avoided, in his novel *Constance Trescot*. This work takes a young married couple from New England to Missouri, here named "the wilder west" (168). The husband, lawyer Hugh Trescot, is challenged to a duel by the creole villain Greyhurst. Trescot resists the challenge, debating issues of cowardice, violence, and honor at some length (Greyhurst's very racial lineaments, of course, would have disqualified him as a duelist according to the Boone and Crockett Club code). Ultimately, however, Greyhurst, after first fortifying himself with drink (like Trampas before his final shootout), shoots the unarmed Trescot as he reaches innocently into a pocket. His self-justification—"according to his Western code, he was justified"—is accepted by the community, and he goes unpunished (222). Constance's response, however, echoes Molly's in the face of the Virginian's resolve to meet Trampas in a shoot-out. Molly cries out, "It's murder!" to which her lover responds "sternly," "Don't call it that name" (473-74). Constance confronts Greyhurst: "You have murdered an unarmed man," and she spends the rest of the novel hounding Greyhurst, eventually to the point of suicide (221). Point-by-point, it reads like a darker, more complex resolution of the crisis facing Molly and the Virginian.

Almost immediately after Mitchell went west with this novel, Wister went south, turning to Reconstruction Charleston in *Lady Baltimore* (1906). This novel, which Wister dedicated to his mentor, tells of some *nouveaux riches* Northerners invading the genteel networks of aristocratic Southerners and testing the honor of one young southern gentleman in particular, whom Langdon Mitchell spotted as a close copy of Winthrop Chanler.[20] The vocabulary, tone, pacing, and detail are almost identical to Mitchell's. The similarity is more pronounced still in *Romney*, Wister's novel of Philadelphia in the 1880s—the same time period as *The Virginian*—which he began in 1912 but was never able to finish. Here Wister, like Mitchell before him, took on the figure of the robber baron in the ruthless colossus Jupiter. This character was modeled on the financier who most haunted Wister: J. Pierpont Morgan (sometimes nicknamed Jupiter or Zeus), the world's banker who was said to hold the national and transatlantic economies in the palm of his hand.

Morgan was a particular threat to the club enclave "since he qualified for membership in both the old and new elites," at least in the shifting social scene of New York (Strouse 217). The older Philadelphia elite was more resistant to the man denounced by Senator La Follette as "a beefy, red-faced, thick-necked, financial bully, drunk with wealth and power," yet he unquestionably arrived at their gates when, in 1871, he joined forces with the prominent Philadelphia banker, Anthony J. Drexel ("La Follette"). In 1885, Morgan saved the Pennsylvania Railroad—the other preeminent Proper Philadelphia institution identified by Baltzell, besides the Philadelphia Club—when he brokered an agreement between it and the New York Central with which it was in suicidal competition.[21] Several years after Wister, Morgan's son Jack attended the same school—St. Paul's—and university—Harvard—and in time won election to the Boone and Crockett Club.[22] Morgan resurfaces fleetingly but influentially throughout the frontier club story.

Thus did Proper Philadelphia put its mark on the frontier club western. Silas Weir Mitchell, diagnostician and defender of his class, framed the West as an antidote to individual disease and market culture and carved out the concept of honor, like the "West cure," as exclusively available to gentlemen. Wister ran with this vision, writing into his westerns the hallmarks, conversations, and preoccupations of the eastern establishment, but resolving their problems with much greater ease (and Boone and Crockett-style violence) in the new world of "simple categories" and simple resolutions. Part of what he had to learn for himself was how to make this vision square with the violent hierarchies of capital and labor that he and his frontier club fellows encountered out west.

Aristocrats out West

When Mitchell pointed Wister west, he was sending him towards company of his own class. Throughout the nineteenth century, the old families of the urban northeast became preoccupied with strengthening their class boundaries in the face of shifting power structures. As Eric Homberger has pointed out, in a republic that had abolished entail and primogeniture, the foundations of European aristocratic lineage, American aristocracy had to remake itself through rituals and social institutions. One challenge took the form of new money—the power base of the industrial Robber Barons, millionaires' club, or *nouveaux riches* as they were variously styled—which the aristocratic class wanted to both profit from and transcend. Part of the answer to this conundrum lay in cattle country.

Frontier Club Investments

A new form of finance took off in the nineteenth century—T. J. Stiles lays its invention primarily at the feet of the steamboat-cum-railroad magnate who had touched Grinnell's life most closely, Cornelius Vanderbilt—in the form of stocks-and-bonds investment. Investment culture was attractive to the aristocrats, "with their upper-class condescension toward men of commerce": its abstractness kept investors at arm's length from the marketplace, the requirement for intensive capitalization kept the investor group selective, and the profits to be reaped from speculative booms were enormous (G. E. White 135). The resources of the American West were integral to the transatlantic expansion of capitalism, especially with large-scale international investment in the "bonanza frontier" of open-range cattle ranching.[23] After the Civil War, a vision of endless free grass, stretching from Texas to Montana, Nebraska to Idaho, attracted a wave of ranchers who brought hundreds of thousands of cattle to the range in the belief that they would be self-sustaining, winter and summer. John Clay, the canny Scottish banker, manager, and rancher who roamed the plains in these years, was only slightly exaggerating when he declared: "we had only to brand our calves when dropped and ship our beeves when fat" (245). The numbers tell a story of unbridled enthusiasm: during the 1880s, sixty British companies were formed, "most decked out with titled and ornamental directors," to raise cattle and settle land in the West; nearly 850 cattle brands were registered in Cheyenne, Wyoming by 1884; and, by 1899, $2,625 million had poured in from British investors.[24] Clay called it "a minor South Sea bubble" (35).

Among the investors in big ranching were the frontier club and their associates, as family members, friends, and clubmates encouraged each other to join "the investment clique" (Gressley 64). In 1882, Roosevelt purchased a $10,000 stock certificate in the Wyoming ranching venture of his Porcellian clubmates Hubert Teschemacher and Frederic deBillier, then the next year began to sink what finally amounted to $80,000 in his own Dakota ranches.[25] In 1883, Grinnell bought a sheep outfit, which he soon turned into a horse and cattle ranch, in Wyoming's Shirley Basin.[26] Although he never adopted the ranching persona to such a degree as Roosevelt, he did masquerade at times—when, for example, he wrote to Luther North complaining about the need for lobbying: "I would rather break bronchos for a living than talk to congressmen about a bill" (quoted in Punke 160). Clarence King, Boone and Crockett Clubman and first director of the U.S. Geological Survey, sank a large proportion of his capital in several cattle ranching schemes.[27] Henry Lee Higginson, Boston broker and Wister's benefactor, became deeply embroiled in the Union Cattle Company in Wyoming, serving on its board of directors and working his blue-blood Boston connections when further injections of money were needed.[28] The investment web even spread to President Benjamin Harrison, who used his office to support both the Boone and Crockett Club and the Johnson County Invaders; his son was an influential cattleman and secretary of the Montana Stock Growers Association.[29]

When Wister left the confines of the Philadelphia Club to travel westward on Dr. Mitchell's orders at the end of June 1885, among the cultural baggage that accompanied him was a conundrum. As framed under Mitchell's close tutelage, the West was the opposite and antidote to the marketplace that threatened the health of the old established classes. Yet Wister must have been intimately familiar with the West *as* marketplace. Although there is no evidence of him personally sinking funds in the West until 1911, he must have been familiar with the investment buzz over port and cigars in the club.[30] He also frequented the circle of Henry Lee Higginson during the years of his most active ranch investment: 1883, the year that Higginson joined the board of directors of the Union Cattle Company, was also the year that Wister went into his employ, and they remained in close contact long after 1892, when Higginson took a leading role in managing the company's liquidation.

A tipping point for Wister came in Omaha, Nebraska. As he embarked on the Pennsylvania Railroad on his first transcontinental railway journey, his diary shows him palpably yearning to be ever westward. Half an hour out of Philadelphia, he celebrates, "am further West than ever before in the 25 years."[31] He continues to chart their mile-by-mile progress—to Chicago, beyond Chicago, across the Mississippi River, across the Missouri River—finally hitting Omaha after two days' travel and joyfully declaring: "This place is pure west.... Omaha could not be an Eastern town by any possibility"; "future America is just bubbling and seething in bare legs and pinafores here." He sounds understandably taken aback, then, when he discovers that the face of Wall Street has followed him westwards. Lunching in Omaha at the home of some friends of friends, Wister is startled to recognize the image of Proper Philadelphia's bête noir (and recent savior): "Curious to come here and ... see a photograph of hon. Pierpont Morgan in a rack on the wall." The curiousness would grow into dread: "The nouveau riche element in New York will damn this western expanse of virgin soil if it doesn't look out.... If not, good day to my theory of an American civilization here—It will slowly New Yorkify, and rot."

A few hours later and a few blocks south, on the station platform, Wister met up with the man who would point him towards a resolution to this conundrum. This was Dick Trimble, his Porcellian clubmate from Harvard days (who would also become a staunch Boone and Crockett Clubman). As part of the wave of eastern gentlemen, Trimble had come west in 1882 to help run the Teschemacher & deBillier Cattle Company, started north of Cheyenne by his Harvard classmates one year after their 1878 graduation.[32] Trimble was smitten and became a booster for cattle country, working energetically to attract more eastern investors.[33] He boarded the train with Wister, accompanying him to Cheyenne, where he took him to the Cheyenne Club for an eve-of-4th-of-July drink. This was home away from home for Wister and more fitted to Mitchell's vision than he could have imagined: an entirely familiar enclave of gentlemen, consolidating their standing as patricians of the plains, discreetly converting the ugly commercialism of speculation into gentlemanly rituals, and selectively training a new class to assimilate with their upper-class ways. Wister, too, was smitten, declaring, "It's the pearl of the prairies" and returning regularly to the club over the next ten years.[34]

The Cheyenne Club

The Cheyenne Club was founded in 1880 by a group of Wyoming cattle barons who decided that an exclusive social club would serve their social and economic interests (Fig. 2.1). They compiled a list of fifty names, approaching them in explicitly anglophile, exclusive terms. William Sturgis, a Boston blueblood and club secretary, wrote to the Harvard alumnus-turned-ranchman, Frederic deBillier, "We purpose having a *good* club on an eastern basis—have limited the numbers to 50 in order to be able to control the social status most satisfactorily."[35] To others, Sturgis evoked the stately white granite frontage of one of Boston's oldest (and most pro-slavery) clubs, by describing the Cheyenne Club as "the Somerset moved West," which "will fill a want long felt by those of us hailing from the East" and provide a mechanism for excluding "undesirables."[36] Sturgis was even blunter in his invitation to Clarence King: the exclusive membership list was designed "so that we may keep it full at all times and avoid blackballing too many 'natives.'"[37] Another invitation put it most succinctly: "Trusting you will be 'one of us.'"[38] By 1884, more than one member of the eastern establishment judged it "one of the best clubs in the United States."[39]

Like the eastern club enclaves, the "we" that was in the making in the Cheyenne Club involved several class negotiations. Open-range ranching was primarily financed by east coast and European investors, many with social and familial

Figure 2.1. The Cheyenne Club, 1888

connections in the upper echelons of society, and some ranchers belonged to that social bracket. Often a degree of insecurity undermined their aristocratic position. The Europeans who came west tended to be remittance men, younger sons of wealthy families who crossed the Atlantic temporarily to make the fortune that had been denied them by the rules of primogeniture; sometimes called "supernumerary gentlemen," more often "gentlemanly failures," they had a reputation as freespenders and dissolutes (Cannadine 429). Prominent examples in Wyoming include Moreton Frewen, a younger son of a Sussex squire and a good friend of Henry Cabot Lodge, who developed and lost the famous 76 brand in Powder River Basin, and Horace Plunkett, the younger son of the Irish peer Lord Dunsany. Wister met both Frewen and Plunkett at the Cheyenne Club.[40] William Moncreiff, the fourth son of the seventh baronet of the Scottish Moncreiffs of that Ilk, became a friend of Roosevelt (and Bill Cody).[41]

Some of the American ranchers were equally precariously positioned, and there was the more general sense that American aristocrats still had to prove their status. Take Harry Oelrichs, the youngest son of the wealthy Oelrichs family of New York and in-law to the Vanderbilts, for example. His older brother Hermann inherited the family's shipping firm, married the heiress of the Comstock Lode, and came to have his name splashed across the society pages of the eastern press as owner of Rosecliff, one of the grandest mansions at Newport, modeled after the Grand Trianon at Versailles (and doubtless one of the "extravagant houses" that drove Mitchell and his circle out to Bar Harbor). Meanwhile, Harry took the younger brother's route, treating the West as a resource to be exploited for eastern profit, pleasure, and cultural compensation. He went west as superintendent of the Anglo-American Cattle Company of Dakota Territory and had his name splashed across the western press (which mistook him as British, presumably because of his English education) as one of the Cheyenne Club's most vivid members, colorful maker and breakers of rules.[42]

The financing model added another layer of tension to the relationship between investor and manager. Teschemacher and deBillier, for example, fell in the uncomfortable position of investor-managers. Both sank their own money into their cattle company, using their social connections to raise additional funds. "Teschie," as his friends knew him, was particularly well connected through his European upbringing. "An intimate of presidents and princes," his success in attracting eastern capital was said to have been due as much "to his recreational pursuits in his club" as to "his knocking on office doors in Boston's Federal Square" (Clay 283; Gressley 62–63). At the same time, the two young ranchers were salary men, paid for managing their three ranches' affairs, and answerable to their board of directors. When times got tough, the awkwardness of the arrangement rose to the surface. In 1886, when Teschie and Fred voted themselves salary raises, one of their investors exploded: "The lone item that has improved in your financial statement since last year is your salary! Don't you think you could suffer along with the rest of us?" (quoted in Gressley 150). Other managers were of a different class again, middlemen working on behalf of European speculators. In this period, Scotland in particular became the headquarters for an international "client capitalism" (Szasz 88). While Cheyenne was "overrun with Britishers," more of the aristocrats "stayed home" (Woods 87, 193). The resulting mix on the plains was "almost a domestic microcosm of the British Empire itself" (Woods 192). One of the troubling strains of these imperial relations was that managers were strongly dissuaded from building independent bases; employers thousands of miles away perennially suspected them of rustling their stock (a suspicion that was, in turn, passed on from managers to cowboys).

The exclusive society the Cheyenne Club helped to carve out on the plains, then, served a double function. It confirmed the superiority of upper-class anglophiles while training aspirants to identify with that class interest. The club imitated its British and East Coast models in enforcing exclusive membership requirements and the strictest protocols of behavior. Elaborate rules governed committee elections, meetings, and minutes. On July 7, 1881, the Board of Governors passed a rule that "The making of wagers of any description for money in the public rooms of the Club House is positively prohibited." The by-law must have been ineffective, because on October 20, 1881 Harry Oelrichs stiffened it with a long resolution against "boisterous and disorderly conduct," re-fortifying this social enclave. The nub of the motion was that club house rules were being violated by "guests of improper character and by gambling" and that the Board of Governors should "strongly condemn" and publicly "reprimand" offending members. The motion was carried unanimously.[43]

The comforts the club so zealously protected closely replicated the forms of privileged British life. Its accoutrements and activities included cards and billiards, polo and horse racing, its own tennis courts, and the most elegant dining available, with European cuisine and an international array of foods and wines shipped out to the barren plains. A fortune was spent on supplies from the legendary Park & Tilford of Broadway: standing orders ran to Champagne Geisler, Champagne Goulet, Burgundy Chambertin, 1848 Brandy, Jamaica Rum, St. Cruz Rum, Liebfraumilch, Mumms Extra Dry, Delatour Soda, Old Tom Gin, and Reina Victoria cigars, "the best brand of Manila Cheroots" (although even the resources of the Cheyenne Club could not conjure many of the luxury items during the winter because of the risk of their freezing on the long journey out).[44] This island of privilege on the plains was "famous the world over" (Spring 53). A story circulated through clubs on several continents of Horace Plunkett simultaneously conducting a game of tennis, calling chess plays to two opponents on the club piazza, and refreshing himself with swigs of bourbon.[45]

Living high on the hog was expensive. One club dinner for twenty guests, celebrating "an exceptionally good cattle sale," cost $5,000. At another, when British club members entertained American members, the forty-two diners drank sixty-six bottles of champagne and twenty bottles of red wine.[46] Club records show that, in one night in the bar, Trimble, Teschemacher, deBillier, and Oelrichs each easily spent the equivalent of a week's worth of cowboy wages (and more than two weeks' worth of the wages paid to the club's Chinese laundryman). Such over-indulgence inevitably led to considerable boisterousness: Oelrichs and Teschemacher more than once fell foul of the rules that Oelrichs was so quick to propose. On one uproarious September night in 1882, Harry Oelrichs attacked another member verbally, his brother Charles attacked the barkeeper physically, and Teschemacher somehow got mixed up in the fray. The board of governors posted their censure of the miscreants then, when Oelrichs tore down the notice, deemed his action "a scandalous breach of Club discipline and an insult to the entire Club," resolving "That Mr. Harry Oelrichs is hereby suspended from the privileges of the Club House for a period of one year from this date, and beyond that time until he shall make an acceptable apology to the Governors of the Club for his action."[47]

What these rituals and hi-jinks masked was the fact that the Cheyenne Club was also a "business center" for international capital (Clay 74). The club was the headquarters of the Wyoming Stock Growers Association (WSGA), the organization of wealthy Anglo-American ranchers who held sway over the mainly unfenced northern plains. By 1885, early assumptions about endless natural resources free for the taking—the myth of inexhaustibility—were changing as too many animals were crowded onto the plains, and the WSGA was organizing to protect their capital-intensive investment by fencing in water, lobbying to privatize public lands, and policing the small, independent outfits that threatened their dominance. The uncomfortable truth was that the WSGA was a financial cartel that enforced its monopoly on grazing lands in particularly violent ways. The carefully controlled "we" of the club drew a social line around those who claimed their privilege as the first occupiers of public domain lands (as always, of course, ignoring the rights of Indigenous peoples), buttressing their solidarity with rituals, rules, and regulations, and excluding and intimidating small ranchers and farmers. In the flow of investment capital and returns, the WSGA also embodied the new transatlantic economies, bringing together "reticent Britisher, cautious Scot, exuberant Irishman, careful Yankee, confident Bostonian, worldly New Yorker, chivalrous Southerner and delightful Canadian" (Clay 73). In 1885, the year in which Wister first landed in Cheyenne, Thomas Sturgis, William's brother and WSGA secretary, reported that the association "is now the largest in the world" (quoted in Clay 251).

The clubbiness promoted by the WSGA and the Cheyenne Club was closely complementary to Boone and Crockett Club dynamics, despite the fact that in some respects the organizations were at odds. There was much western resistance to the kinds of hunting restrictions for which the Boone and Crockett men vigorously lobbied. But there were also common class and race interests, and their rhetoric, structures, and procedures were parallel. Both groups implemented their ideological outlook through committees, resolutions, and federal lobbying campaigns. Both emphasized the need for protection, law enforcement, and national policy on public lands. In the case of the WSGA, the point was more immediately to do with property rights, but in both cases the larger issue was economic and cultural dominance.

George Bird Grinnell had been working to develop this common ground as early as 1880. In *Forest and Stream* he celebrated the WSGA for joining the newly formed Game Protective Association in Wyoming as a body and as individuals: "the stock growers have pledged themselves as individuals to prosecute violators of the laws, and from such action on the part of such a body of men the best results are to be expected" ("Game" 423). The niceness of Grinnell's diplomacy becomes evident when he reveals that his own class—the clubmen's class—is most at fault: "The worst slaughter of game in Wyoming does not come from the killing by skin hunters" but from "Parties of hunters from the East, men who slaughter simply for count and to boast of their bags when they get back to civilization." When Roosevelt went west in 1884, he also became involved with stock growers' associations, though in a more aggressive vein. He tried to join the Montana group that was engaging in vigilante action; having failed in that attempt (they considered him too high profile to be an effective vigilante), he turned to organizing the Little Missouri Stockmen's Association.

Grinnell was also the first of the frontier club to bring his narrative skills to the task of resolving conservation and ranching interests. Before Roosevelt's *Hunting Trips of a Ranchman* (1885) and long before Wister began to write western fiction, Grinnell argued for the common ground of different western interests in a hunting tale based on his own ranch experiences, published in 1883. In the midst of a stalk in the Shirley Basin, Wyoming, Grinnell pauses the action for a disquisition on stockmen's growing support for game laws and antipathy to the "wanton slaughter" of big game. They are coming to "realize that while they can supply their ranches and camps with wild meat they are putting a certain amount of absolute cash in their pockets; that every time they bring in an elk, it saves them a steer, and whenever an antelope or a deer is hung up they are adding a fat wether to the flock"—a gain Grinnell computes at $45 per steer and $5 per sheep ("Load" 222).

As with the Boone and Crockett Club's transatlantic network of gentleman hunter interests, the WSGA, especially through the cultural façade of the Cheyenne Club, formed one plank in the formation of an international upper class, undergirded by international finance. It also helped to finesse the transition from informal partnerships between family and friends to full-blown incorporation.[48] Although, in one sense, the Cheyenne Club was on the margins as a distant, recent off-shoot of the long-established eastern club networks, in another sense it was tied into the new realities of monopoly and centralization on an international scale. After the bubble burst in 1886–1887—the perfect storm of drought, savage winter, and an overstocked range which killed hundreds of thousands of cattle—many cattle kings fled eastward to other forms of investment finance. Dick Trimble, for example, ended up as secretary of United States Steel Corporation, a company born out of the white heat of consolidation, monopoly-building, and competition cutting (and site of a titanic struggle between J. P. Morgan and Andrew Carnegie)—on the face of it the antithesis of clubland, but in fact marked by the same deep logic.[49]

Cowboys and Vigilantes

If the Cheyenne Club clothed market culture in one form that was enthusiastically welcomed by Wister that July in 1885, another was revealed to him when he was taken first by train then stagecoach north and west from the club deeper still into Wyoming's cattle land, to the ranch at which he would stay for the next two months. The VR Ranch, just south of the little town of Glenrock, remains a vast, well watered, and breathtakingly beautiful landscape of endless sagebrush flats and rolling hills of rich grass. John Clay described the view from the ranch-house on the eve of Wister's arrival: "As you stepped out of the house there was a pleasant garden, little rills of water bubbling, singing, spreading themselves about the plots of vegetables, and over the lawn. Then away southwards were towering mountains, a deep rift in their side where Deer Creek rushing down a cañon reached the vale and wandered carelessly amid cottonweeds, willows and box elders"; it was "a scene of supreme beauty" (143–44). On this range were spread an estimated five or six thousand cattle.

The manager of this vast enterprise, and Wister's host, was Major Frank Wolcott. A Civil War veteran, former U.S. marshal, and current justice of the peace, Wolcott was another larger-than-life stalwart of the Cheyenne Club. In Clay's description we can recognize the two faces of the clubman, familiar from the likes of Chanler and Lodge, in coarser form: "He was a fire-eater, honest, clean, a rabid Republican with a complete absence of tact, very well educated and when you knew him a most delightful companion. Most people hated him, many feared him, a few loved him" (142). A month before Wister arrived, Wolcott had taken a major financial gamble by greatly expanding his ranch from the proportions that could be supported by investment by himself and a few co-investors.[50] He borrowed $50,000 from the Scottish American Investment Company, then subsequently $30,000 more, to increase his appropriation of the waters of Deer Creek, purchase more pasture, and make improvements on the land.[51] The level of his risk was typical of cattle kings in those years, operating on economies of scale and grabbing as many natural resources as possible. Clearly, the categories that Mitchell posited as opposites in *Wear and Tear*—"borrowed capital" *versus* "a sturdy contest with nature"—were intimately codependent in this western venture. Like so many investor-managers, Wolcott was becoming increasingly immersed in venture capitalism and increasingly subject to boards of directors' obsession with the market.[52]

Here, on the Wyoming plains, was a textbook mass market, controlled by an anglophone elite. Richard Ohmann has schematized the power dynamics of emerging, nineteenth-century mass culture in terms that map onto the power dynamics on the plains in illuminating ways. He argues that a corporate ruling class in America consolidated itself by delegating management of its enterprises to a new "professional-managerial class" that marshaled the swelling industrial working class in the production of mass commodities (118–19). Likewise, on the plains, a cartel of owners raked in profits from the comfort of home and club via middlemen (managers of animal and human resources), disposable contract labor (cowboys), and economies of scale (thousands of cattle roaming the open range). The WSGA systematically sought to trap their labor force as a proletariat. They prevented cowboys from owning cattle or even bidding on unbranded cows with the notorious Maverick Law of 1884, which the Laramie *Daily Boomerang* denounced as "atrocious class legislation" (quoted in H. H. Smith 60). They decreed an end to the tradition of ranch hospitality, by which cowboys "rode the grub line" to get themselves through the winter months when there was neither work nor wages. In 1886, they tried to slash wages, a measure against which cowboys finally organized and went on strike, led by Jack Flagg among others. It was this set of power relations that the frontier club—through Mitchell's prognosis, Wister's fiction, and the clubmen's collective resources—would come to disguise as individualistic heroism, boyish adventure, and a combat between good and evil on the empty frontier.

Whatever Wister knew about the financial transactions, mass-market operations, and labor conditions surrounding him in the ranching West in 1885, he did not record it in his diary.[53] The only moneyed class that he acknowledges in his day-by-day observations is the wrong sort, the corrupt politicians and railroad tycoons—"Tweeds and Jay Goulds"—who have not yet got their hands on the West (7). The easterners with whom he consorts in the West are the right sort. They include the gentlemen of the Cheyenne Club and his clubmates from home. Like Roosevelt in the Dakotas, Wister kept his eastern friends close to him through constant correspondence—his journal records with glee "a good letter from Winty Chanler" among others—and joint travel (7). For the first month, he yearned for the arrival of Jack Mitchell, who eventually joined him on his first hunt in the mountains around the VR ranch. Wister also made some new acquaintances: "Every man, woman and cowboy I see comes from the East—and generally from New England, thank goodness" (5).

What Wister purported to see in the ranching lands, and what he would later fictionalize, was a pre-capitalist, elemental type, part cowboy and part clubman. The cowboys that Wister wrote into his diary were not the seasonal laborers about whom the Cheyenne clubmen grumbled over their 1848 Brandy and Reina Vic cigars and whom the WSGA sought to discipline. Wister's cowboys are a new type arising from a new land. Leaving the train at Rock Creek and traveling the fifty miles to the VR ranch by stagecoach, fortified by "a bottle of fizz" from Trimble, Wister records the scene around him:

> I can't possibly say how extraordinary and beautiful the valleys we've been going through are. They're different from all things I've seen.... It's like what scenery on the moon must be. Then suddenly you come round a turn and down into a green cut where there are horsemen and wagons and hundreds of cattle, and then it's like Genesis. Just across the corduroy bridge are a crowd of cow boys round a fire, with their horses tethered. When you go West you find it's all there every time.[54]

On Wolcott's ranch, he admires the cowboys at the roundup and has the chance to speak to Tom King, the foreman who "says he likes this life and will never go East again." When asked what will happen when he grows old, "he replied that cowboys never lived long enough to get old." (Wister put this sentiment, verbatim, in the mouth of the Virginian in "The Winning of the Biscuit Shooter" which he wrote in the Hunter's Cabin at the Chicago Exposition.) At this point, Wister begins to develop his mythology of the cowboy:

> They don't, I believe. They're a queer episode in the history of this coun-
> try. Purely nomadic, and leaving no race of posterity, for they don't marry.
> I'm told they're without any moral sense whatever. Perhaps they are—but
> I wonder how much less they have than the poor classes in New York?

His portrait of the rancher is framed by the same vision. In Wister's diary, as in John Clay's account, Wolcott comes across as a volatile figure, at times the magnanimous host, at other times sulky and withdrawn. In Wister's telling, the pressure Wolcott faces is not caused by the over-stretching of his resources, the demands of his Scottish backers, or the over-grazing of subarid lands (Wister notes the waters of Deer Creek diminishing daily). Wolcott's problem is a home-steader called Branan, unequivocally named here a "squatter," demeaned as a "damn scoundrel" who "jabbers" and "crawls" and refuses to give up his forty acres (which, Wolcott admits to Wister, is "not much among 5 or 6 thousand, it's their [sic] damn scoundrelism of the scheme that bites me"). The climax comes when Wolcott rides off to confront Branan, gun in hand. Again, Wister writes the conflict beyond the frame of capitalism and monopoly: "In the old Testament Lot and Isaac and Uncle Leban and the rest had times not unlike this—only guns weren't invented."

Over the next six years, as Wister headed towards a writing career, he came to see the West increasingly through Cheyenne Club eyes and the Cheyenne Clubmen became increasingly desperate. Near-drought conditions during the summer of 1886, followed by the severest winter on record, left the plains heaped with the bones of dead cattle and the ranchers devoid of money. Many decamped east-wards, but some cattle kings held on, waging an increasingly fierce battle against small ranchers as a tangible threat that they could blame and attack in ways that they could not the weather or financial markets. It was out of this pressure cooker that the clubmen's violence exploded. From drinking too much and doing "other naughty things"—like kicking a barman and delivering a tongue-lashing—their aggressiveness escalated into murder, culminating in the lynchings of 1889 and 1892 (Clay 245). First, six big cattle ranchers led by Albert Bothwell hanged the settlers Ellen Watson and Jim Averell. Then a force of fifty clubmen and hired guns—the self-styled Johnson County Invaders led by Wolcott and including deBillier and Teschemacher (by that point, club president)—ambushed and murdered the cowboys Nick Ray and Nate Champion.

The Cheyenne Club, where these plans had been hatched, continued to serve as social refuge for the vigilantes. Immediately after the murders, one of the suspects, Dr. Charles B. Penrose (the Boone and Crockett Clubman and Philadelphia friend of Wister and Mitchell) was housed in the club with U.S. Marshal Rankin, who had sprung him from the "damn tough jug" in Douglas with a writ of habeas corpus.[55] Three months later, while his fellow invaders were "ostensibly confined" in Cheyenne awaiting arraignment, they daily returned to the club for business and pleasure.[56] Subsequently, when Rankin refused to accede to their wishes by making "wholesale arrests" of suspected rustlers and murderers, they showily ostracized him (Wister noted that, because Rankin "Showed the white feather," he was now playing solitaire at the Club; Rankin was later exonerated by the Department of Justice when it was discovered that the arrest warrants were void).[57] Finally, the club made it possible for the "invaders" privately to enjoy an uproarious dinner ("a Banquet without regard to expense") to celebrate their release and bid the Texas mercenaries farewell.[58]

What the clubmen could not finesse behind club walls was public opinion. The siege mentality typical of exclusive club culture contributed to their being out of touch; certainly, they blamed the failure of their invasion on their inability to connect with "the people." William C. Irvine (the vigilante who later became state treasurer, then senator) complained that "the people did not understand our intentions"; they "honestly thought we were trying to run the honest settler out of the country."[59] Charles Penrose saw the lack of understanding running in both directions, commenting that the lynchers' plan was made "in ignorance of the real popular feeling."[60] Helena Huntington Smith later judged that "the big outfits of that era had achieved a miracle of unpopularity" (32). Conscious of the power of the press, Penrose harped repeatedly on their misrepresentations of the invasion generally and himself particularly. He dismissed the Wyoming newspapers as "rustler newspapers," fretted from his first panicky telegrams east from jail that "newspaper stories to date are untrue," including their portrait of him as "an aristocratic Englishman" proposing to "testify fully against the cattlemen of Cheyenne who inveigled him into the conspiracy."[61] He also repeatedly fed his brother, Pennsylvania State Senator Boies Penrose, material with which to massage the coverage back east: "if you think that a wrong impression is being circulated about me and that it is worth while to correct it in the papers, do so from the above facts. Say, however, that you have heard them from a friend in Wyoming and not from me."[62] Boies Penrose did that and more, pressing the Secretary of War into service on behalf of the invaders.

The large stockmen's take on events was channeled directly to Wister through his frontier club network. Penrose wrote lengthy accounts to his friends and family in Philadelphia, who passed them on to Wister. He saved them in his scrapbook and became something of a spokesman to the Philadelphia press; within a week of the Johnson County murders, he was being quoted on the efficacy of lynching in the West: "In Montana it happened like a visit from the Destroying

Angel.... This extermination of thieves was most wholesome."[63] As Penrose's material accumulated, he gathered it in a tin box and again gave it to Wister, who judged that it would be best "distilled into capable fiction."[64] Among the clippings, letters, and interviews, familiar tropes recur, from finance—the WSGA "was no closed corporation proposition"—to hunting—Tom Horn, the cattlemen's hired killer, saw "cattle thieves as wolves and coyotes."[65] When Penrose wrote directly to Wister, he may have helped to spark the most famous line in *The Virginian* (now inscribed on Medicine Bow's historic town plaque). In their first confrontation, Wister has Trampas calling the Virginian "you son-of-a—" (in the 1928 edition, Wister revised the wording to "son-of-a-bitch") and the Virginian's "pistol came out" as he responded, "When you call me that, *smile.*" Penrose's letter, sent from his "nominal custody"[66] in the Cheyenne Club and on their letterhead, reads in part:

> ... during the last two months "son of a bitch" has been a favorite expression in this country. Wyoming is in the son of a bitch stage of her civilization and could not get on without it any more than she could without a lariat and a branding iron.[67]

Penrose and Wister had planned to go hunting that summer of 1892, until they were warned off by Richard Repath, their Cheyenne Club friend (and clerk to Wyoming's Supreme Court). He wrote that rustlers were moving out through the western part of Wyoming: "if any of the beggars were to run across you they would consider it a fitting climax to their nefarious deeds to put a shot or two through you."[68] Wister chose to make the 5,000-mile roundtrip to Cinnabar, Montana, for a single afternoon, to tell his guide, George West, in person that he could not make it. It is generally assumed that he was too scared to go into his usual hunting grounds but determined not to act the coward (although William Handley has pieced together an alternative theory to do with a same-sex relationship between the two men that adds yet another dimension to the club culture of secrecy and repression).[69] Certainly Wister's diary is oddly oblique on this strange, aborted trip. When Dick Penrose—Charles's other brother and yet another Boone and Crockett Clubman—sees Wister off at the station, "I explained to him that I had abandoned the idea of spending my summer in the mountains. He appreciated the reasons, I think."[70] It was on that trip that Wister encountered the mountain sheep tethered to a telegraph pole that served as the opening of his 1904 hunting tale, "The Mountain Sheep: His Ways." Dated with unusual precision—the morning of July 10, 1892—the disquisition on the threat of bourgeois tame sheep to aristocratic mountain sheep argues the need to preserve "gentlefolk...in the zoölogical gardens" (183). At this precise moment, Wister's aristocratic friends were being held in Laramie, their safety from local forces in serious question, and the passage can be read as an oblique commentary on their beleaguerement.

Wister began to develop a more direct commentary on events when he returned to the Cheyenne Club in early October 1892 while the clubmen were out on bail, waiting for the next term of court, which ultimately released them. This was his first visit as a published author of a western story ("Hank's Woman" had appeared in *Harper's Weekly*—a journal to which the club subscribed—on August 27, 1892). Over more club meals he was brought up to date by Governor Amos Barber, yet another figure joined to the frontier club network. Barber had graduated from the Medical School of the University of Pennsylvania with Penrose before going west to serve as an army surgeon, then as doctor to the WSGA hospital. When Penrose needed to go west for his health in 1890, Barber introduced him to the Cheyenne Club and helped him to establish himself in that city. By 1892, he was acting state governor and played a crucial role in protecting the invaders. Wister spent a melancholy evening, observing that the club was "Comfortable, and full of departed glory" and hearing from Barber about the desperate straits into which Wolcott had fallen:

> he is at his forlorn decaying ranch. Where his wife has not been for 2 years. He is utterly bankrupt.... Barber seemed to think he realized he had made a failure of his life, then, said that a bullet from a rustler would probably be a welcome solution to Wolcott. This too is melancholy.[71]

Wister was left reflecting on the "tragedy in the air of Wyoming, tragedy over these lonely sage brush plains. But they are very dear to my heart."[72]

The Wyoming *Tribune* claimed that Barber was a main source for Wister's fiction: "His narrative of his experiences, related to Owen Wister, became the basis for the most famous of western novels, 'The Virginian.'"[73] Certainly, during the same visit as this conversation with Barber, an unnamed state reporter drew Wister's attention to the narrative potential of recent events, though in terms that the author found distasteful. Perhaps knowing of Wister's Hasty Pudding compositions, the reporter commented "that the rustler war would make a good comic opera"; "I told him that I did not see anything funny about it."[74] Wister ended up writing something quite different and much cleverer. He never produced a direct fictionalization of the Johnson County War; instead, story-by-story, he began to fold in big-rancher perspectives and selected details from those events. The culmination came in the scenes, characterizations, and values of *The Virginian*. In these ways, his westerns extended the work of the Cheyenne Club and the WSGA. They grafted anglophile rituals onto the western plains, rationalized the cattle barons' violence, disguised the real status of cowboys, shut out "the natives," and developed a *modus operandi* for exploiting cattle, commodities, and people with heroic impunity.

Showdown on Publishers' Row

The other market to which Mitchell introduced Wister was the new world of publishing. Like the cattle industry, it was also a mass market in which frontier club members invested and whose class dynamic they helped to massage. Mass media exploded in the second half of the nineteenth century with the development of faster, cheaper technologies of printing and visual reproduction along with the vastly increased distribution network made possible by the joining of the transcontinental railroad in 1869. The flood of newspapers, dime novels, and cheap books was at once threatening and enabling for the social elite. The new society pages of the New York press, for example, put the aristocrats under the microscope in newly exposing ways; at the same time, the upper classes could manipulate press attention to forge their own public images. New cheap publishers threatened the market share of established firms, who styled themselves "quality" publishers as a claim to distinction; at the same time, cheap publishers created mass audiences that could be annexed in support of elite agendas. When the frontier club entered the fray, they contributed resources—financial and literary—that both paralleled and overlapped with their involvement in the cattle market.

Frontier Club Investments

Grinnell and Roosevelt both invested in publishing first and cattle second, and enjoyed decidedly better returns on the former than the latter. In 1880, Grinnell and his father maneuvered their stock takeover of *Forest and Stream*, and, as editor, Grinnell proceeded to enlarge both the audience base and the advertising revenue of the journal. Presumably it was partly returns on his magazine investment that allowed him to purchase his Wyoming ranch in 1883. Soon after his graduation from Harvard in 1880, Roosevelt entered into a partnership with G. P. Putnam's Sons, one of the most prominent quality publishers, investing at least $20,000. Although he subsequently withdrew his money to sink it in, first, the Teschemacher and deBillier outfit in Wyoming, then his own ranches in Dakota Territory, he sustained a close working relationship with Putnam's. He published extensively with them and maintained an office, in which he wrote his multi-volume *Winning of the West*, "one of the few books which were in large part written, put into print, bound, and sold under the one roof" (Putnam, "Roosevelt" xv). According to George Haven Putnam, the firm's president,

Roosevelt regretted severing his publishing investment: "He scolded me later for not having refused to pay him off. 'The publishing undertaking,' he said, 'was a good investment, but the money that you returned to me went into the prairies and has never come back'" ("Roosevelt" xvi).

Although there is no evidence of Caspar Whitney investing directly in ranching, the funding of his takeover of *Outing* magazine did cycle money between livestock and publishing investment. The group he assembled to finance the magazine brought together upper-class gentlemen and quality publishers. They included his ex-boss, Fletcher Harper, and Robert Bacon, Harvard clubmate of Roosevelt's who had joined Boston bankers Lee, Higginson & Co., as well as investing funds in the Teschemacher & deBillier Cattle Company and the Riverside Land and Cattle Company.[75] Subsequently, Bacon was wooed to a partnership with J. Pierpont Morgan; whether the funds he contributed to Whitney's publishing venture were his own or Morgan's is unclear.[76] Around the same time, Morgan also sank considerable funds in the ailing Harper & Brothers.

The channeling of money back and forth between cattle country and publishers' row went well beyond the frontier club. The figures who loom largest in this connection are "the cautious Scots" Thomas and William Nelson, the great Edinburgh publishers (Clay 6). They invested heavily in the American West and Canada, joining with other Scottish businessmen, lawyers, and titled gentlemen to found the Scottish American Investment Company. Thomas Nelson headed up the board of governors and watched over developments on the range like a hawk. It was he who approved the loan to Frank Wolcott that, when Wolcott defaulted in the devastation of 1886–1887, led to the takeover of the VR ranch by the Scottish Tolland Cattle Company and the demotion of Wolcott to manager. Nelson's arm reached wide across the high plains, especially in Wyoming: the Scottish American Investment Company had interests in several vast enterprises, such as the Swan Land and Cattle Company, the Prairie Cattle Company, and the Cattle Ranch & Land Company. Smaller publisher-ranchers included James Gordon Bennett, publisher of the New York *Herald*, who first went west as a gentleman hunter then was persuaded to invest in ranching by Boone and Crockett Clubman Clarence King. John Brisben Walker, publisher of *Cosmopolitan Magazine*, also invested in ranching.

As well as the overlaps in financing the two spheres, they also shared structural homologies in terms of economics and class dynamics. Both open-range ranching and publishing were mass markets engaging in economies of scale that an anglophone elite aimed to control, while disguising their market interest as cultural superiority. As cattle kings forged transatlantic alliances on the plains to defeat competition from small ranchers, so established, "quality" publishers forged transatlantic alliances to battle the new, cheap publishers. This parallelism also played out in audience formation. While clubs, east and west, subscribed to the quality publishers' magazines and books (the Cheyenne Club, for example, subscribed to *Harper's Weekly*, *Harper's Monthly*, and *Atlantic Monthly*), homesteaders more often bought and read the dime novels and reprint libraries of cheap publishers—which could, of course, be a repackaging of "quality" fiction.[77]

This market differentiation was part of a larger restructuring among the culture industries of the period. The nineteenth century saw a boom-and-bust cycle every ten to twenty years.[78] Lawrence Levine and Paul DiMaggio have argued that the crisis in capitalism and subsequent class conflict led to the hardening of a high-low cultural hierarchy: "in its American version, [it] emerged in the period between 1850 and 1900 out of the efforts of urban elites to build organizational forms that, first, isolated high culture and, second, differentiated it from popular culture" (DiMaggio I, 33). DiMaggio singles out the founding of the Boston Symphony Orchestra in 1881 by Henry Lee Higginson—the same broker and cattle investor who was Wister's former employer and current friend—as a paradigmatic case of the upper class wielding cultural bifurcation to its own benefit. Higginson invested a considerable chunk of his fortune to carve out an exclusive cultural sphere. He monopolized the city's professional musicians; he "purified" concert programming by eliminating popular and amateur elements; and he expunged commercial elements such as the "enormous gilt sign [that traditionally hung] over the piano advertising its manufacturer" (DiMaggio II, 313). His reworking of concert space also trained the audience into a passive decorum, emphasizing the boundary between performers and audience, discouraging movement and noise during the performance, darkening the auditorium, and developing a rhetoric that encouraged middle-class audiences, whose support he needed for the venture to be financially sustainable, to identify with upper-class interests. When Higginson opened a new concert hall in 1900, he commissioned Wister to write and deliver a commemorative poem.

The Frontier Club Western and the Literary Marketplace

To appreciate the degree to which the frontier club western emerged from and supported this cultural stratification, we return once more to Silas Weir Mitchell and Owen Wister. It was Mitchell who helped Wister to achieve public notice for the fruits of his literary effort. He worked through the same family and social networks that, thirty years earlier, had brought his own writing to publishers' notice when the Wister and Furness families had helped him to establish a berth with *The Atlantic Monthly*.[79] Mitchell recommended Wister to Henry Mills Alden, editor at Harper & Brothers, who accepted "Hank's Woman" for *Harper's Weekly*, "How Lin McLean Went East" for *Harper's Monthly*, and went on to publish the vast majority of Wister's westerns in magazine and book form over the next ten years. Mitchell was a seasoned guide to a literary marketplace currently in the same throes as the other communications technologies of the period. A man of immense gentility, Mitchell hated talking about money—his correspondence aches with repression on this topic, as he exerts all his delicacy and circumlocution in reference to financial affairs. Yet he was also a popularizer: his medical treatises targeted a lay audience who bought them up in numerous editions; his fiction also sold briskly, with his best-seller *Hugh Wynne* (1896) eventually selling over half-a-million copies.[80] As his successes accumulated, Mitchell became increasingly preoccupied with marketplace dynamics and the power of the public. He zealously negotiated payment rates with magazine editors and he clipped, for example, "The Manuscript Market" from *The American*, treasuring its advice on playing the market, the publishers, and the public.[81] What Mitchell's example told Wister was that publishing, like cattle investment, involved yet another uncomfortable negotiation between clubman and commerce.

Wister received his entrée to Harper & Brothers Publishers at the very moment when this venerable firm was approaching the white-heat of the battle between quality and mass publishers. Earlier in the nineteenth century, the new, lucrative field of mass publishing was controlled by publishers with both cultural power and cultural cachet. The Harper brothers participated in the self-described "American publishing fraternity," composed of "reputable publishers" who operated according to "trade courtesy rules" ("International" 867). A prominent presence in the exclusive club scene of New York, Boston, and Philadelphia, publishers such as the Harpers, Putnam's, Henry Holt, and J. B. Lippincott (who published much of Mitchell's work) prided themselves on their gentlemanly business practices, brokering cultural deals with each other and their authors in the hallowed precincts of club dining and smoking rooms.[82] As the century wore on, they drew the class line more emphatically, trying to block the new generation of publishers who capitalized on technological and transportation advances to invade the market and used economies of scale to saturate it with cut-price reading material. From 1860, Beadle and Adams undersold the old publishers with dime novels ("A DOLLAR book for a DIME!," their publicity blared); George Munro dominated the market with cheap reprint "libraries" from 1874; and Frank Munsey followed with ten-cent monthly magazines. The challenge for the Harpers—like the Boone and Crockett and Cheyenne clubs—was to claim class and cultural distinction while winning over a mass audience.[83]

The Harpers were party to—at times, spearheaded—several institutional maneuvers designed to oust the cheap competition. First, in 1878, Joseph W. Harper initiated a *volte-face* on international copyright, writing to the secretary of state with a proposed "Harper Treaty" between the United States and Great Britain.[84] In their early days, the Harpers had opposed international copyright, arguing for the gentlemanly practice of voluntary payments to British authors and publishers for early sheets. Although the arrangement, known as "trade courtesy rules," was promoted on ethical grounds, Madeleine Stern notes that in fact it created a monopoly by a small group of established publishers—such as Harper & Brothers, D. Appleton & Co., G. P. Putnam's Sons, Henry Holt, Houghton Mifflin, and Lippincott—"a 'close corporation' whose members had no intention of admitting outsiders into their self-satisfied ranks"—not unlike the exclusive clubs, international bank cartels, and stock grower associations of the same period.[85]

When cheap libraries entered the scene in 1874, reprinting foreign works without recompense and radically lowering prices, the established publishers loudly condemned them as "pirates." John Lovell, one of the cheap library publishers, shot back that "courtesy of the trade" had been invented by established houses only once they had secured their market (quoted in Schurman, "Nineteenth-Century" 84–85). The power struggle is again evocative of that on the plains, where cattle kings, many of whom established their dynasties through the branding of mavericks, subsequently attacked small operators as "rustlers"—also known as "range pirates"—for the same practice.[86] Another library publisher, George Munro, also insisted that he stood for democratic access; he "opined that if 'pirate' was how some contemporaries regarded him, 'posterity' would call him a 'reformer'" (Schurman, "Nineteenth-Century" 85). In the face of this new competition, Harper vigorously lobbied for a system of Anglo-American copyright that would force all publishers to pay foreign royalties.[87]

The fight over international copyright provisions went back and forth over the years, with disputes even among parties ostensibly on the same side. At least two core frontier club members joined the fray. In November 1887, the critic Logan Pearsall Smith mounted an argument in favor of royalty copyright attached to open competition in production and sale and against monopoly copyright. In effect, this was an argument that prioritized cheap books over publishers' interests and George Putnam, among others, mounted a point-by-point refutation in the *New York Evening Post*. From his desk at Putnam's, where he was writing *Winning of the West* (a title that has multiple resonances in this market-driven context), Roosevelt intervened with typically martial rhetoric. In the *North American Review* he expressed his frustration that "when we seemed on the eve of at last winning a victory for honest copyright, Mr. Pearsall Smith should have started in to make what I trust will prove to be an ineffectual diversion in favor of the enemy" ("Remarks" 221). Henry Cabot Lodge took a different rhetorical tack when he rose in the House of Representatives to support the International Copyright Bill on May 2, 1890. "Speaking as one who has followed in a humble way the career of literature," Lodge appealed to patriotic duty towards American authors, to morality and, above all, with a glance at Matthew Arnold, to the impressionability of "our boys and girls, our young men and women":

> We should furnish them with a high order of books, not foreign books, not cheap books … but the best books of all ages, and especially whole-some American books, which will bring them up to love America, which will fill them with American ideas, with reverence and love for American principles of government, and with respect for American society, instead of admiration for systems of government and society wholly alien to their own. ("International" 54, 55–56)

The familiar frontier club slippage between "us" and "America"—already seen in their rhetoric about hunting rights, conservation, and big ranching—was out in full force once more.

Ultimately, the battle was won with the passage of the International Copyright Act of 1891, commonly called "the Chace Act" for the Rhode Island senator who introduced the original bill in 1886. The Chace Act was fashioned, again, in terms of exclusionary alliances. It rested on a series of bilateral agreements, a "reciprocity clause" among a transatlantic club of what Lodge called "civilized nations"—the United States, Great Britain, France, Switzerland, and Belgium—while "registration and deposit formalities" favored English-language books.[88] There was also another uneasy cross-class alliance, with quality publishers secur-ing the "intelligent cooperation" (in Joseph Harper's euphemism) of unionized printers and typographical workers (435).

A second front in the battle against cheap publishers was launched in February 1895, when the literary journal *The Bookman* imitated its English parent by pub-lishing bestseller lists: "Sales of Books During the Month … in order of demand." This was the beginning of what Laura J. Miller calls "powerful marketing tools" that shape book purchasing patterns to this day (286); as Christopher P. Wilson notes, "*being* a best-seller was something which could be advertised" (79). The method by which these first monthly lists were compiled immediately benefited the qual-ity publishers. They were based on reports from "leading booksellers" in eighteen cities, each of which reported its six highest selling titles—which, by 1898, promi-nently included Mitchell's *Hugh Wynne*.[89] The venues and methods on which dime novel and magazine sales most depended—railroad depots, department stores, newsstands, subscriptions, and rural commercial travelers—were excluded, as were reprint libraries, cheap editions, and pocket-sized books. As the lists expanded to include thirty cities in the United States and Canada and became the basis for lists of "leaders" and "national best sellers," cheap publications were increasingly blocked from view (Mott 6). This was another fight over marketplace categories: however shrilly dime novels trumpeted their claim to be "Books for the Million!," the estab-lished publishing industry denied them the classification "best seller." Harper & Brothers, on the other hand, visibly dominated the first bestseller list, with Putnam, Macmillan, Appleton, Holt, and a string of quality publishers following behind.

In addition to these somewhat circuitous strategies and for all their moralistic rhetoric, the Harpers were also capable of getting down and dirty, systematically horning in on the territory they publicly decried. They began their own reprint library, *Franklin Square Library*, which they sustained from 1878 to 1893. Although they paid no royalties on the works that they reprinted in this library, they consistently lost money on it but persevered simply to undercut the profits of their cheap rivals.[90] They also began a dime series, *Harper's Young People*, in 1879 "with the declared purpose of providing an alternative to dime novels" (Howard 72). Soon, other "quality" publishers followed suit: Lydia Cushman Schurman estimates that "in all, the regular trade issued twenty-seven libraries" ("Nineteenth-Century" 86). Along with Henry Holt and Company, Harper & Brothers also slashed their prices, with reductions on Harper's *Library of Select Novels* from 20 to 40 percent.[91] Cheap publisher Frank Munsey initiated the "magazine revolution" by dropping the cover price of monthly magazines to 10 cents and relying on advertising for income, commodifying readers once and for all.[92] The Harpers, too, began to pile on advertising in their periodicals (*Harper's Magazine* went from ten pages of advertisements in 1885 to seventy-five pages in 1890).[93]

When the Harpers took on Wister, they added another gun to their arsenal in the battle against cheap publishers. Precisely because Wister gained his entrée into publishing through the frontier club, he was attuned to the delicate balance between culture and commerce within the ongoing class struggle. He fitted right into the club culture, conducting business with Henry Mills Alden, editor of *Harper's Magazine*, and J. Henry Harper in the intimacy of their club rooms and homes. In the words of J. Henry Harper, "I always thought of you as one of our family of authors."[94] At the same time, Wister understood the necessity for marketing. In his rather mythical account of his first act of authorship in the Philadelphia Club with which this chapter opened, he recognized the need to elbow out dime-novel versions of the West: "Was Alkali Ike in the comic papers the one figure which the jejune American imagination ... could discern in that epic which was being lived at a gallop out in the sage-brush?" And his attitude to the masses on whom his success depended, a mixture of disdain and embarrassment, closely mirrored that of Harpers as well as other aristocratic authors. As he put it in his uneasily jocular, rhyming preface to his second volume with Harpers, *The Jimmyjohn Boss*: "leave the masses, / Read me, and join the small selected classes."

Wister was not the only member of the frontier club to enter into mutually beneficial arrangements with the Harper "family." Caspar Whitney "was an important correspondent for the *Weekly*" (Exman 93). When he left to found the sporting journal *Outing* in 1900—partly as a platform for his fellow Boone and Crockett clubmates—he was bankrolled by Fletcher Harper among others.[95]

Harpers accepted Frederic Remington's first illustration in 1882, brought Wister and him together, and up to 1900 published many of Remington's illustrated magazine writings and six of his books. Theodore Roosevelt, Henry Cabot Lodge, and George Bird Grinnell all made steady contributions to the Harpers' magazine and book publications. In 1913, Grinnell brokered a deal with them to publish a Boone and Crockett volume and reissue all five in a uniform edition. Well into the 1920s, the Harpers continued to approach Grinnell with schemes for profitably issuing new or reprinted work by him.

For all their strategy and authorial talent, however, the Harpers could not beat the marketplace. In 1896, they approached Wall Street's most powerful banker, J. P. Morgan, to bail them out of insolvency. He agreed on the condition that they convert the 79-year-old family firm into a joint-stock company, with him as the controlling shareholder.[96] This arrangement was an uneasy alliance at best. It not only removed control from the Harpers of what has been called "one of the most powerful commercial cultural institutions of the Empire City"—by the 1850s, the largest publishing house in the world (Howard 6). It also immersed the publishers in competitive capitalism with an explicitness and aggressiveness that they had avoided for years. The Harpers agreed.

With Morgan at the helm, however, the fragile balance between commerce and culture at Harper & Brothers could not hold. In December 1899, unable to pay the interest on Morgan's loan, the firm went into receivership. All the Harpers except J. Henry resigned, and Morgan brought in new management from the cheap competition that lionized him as a captain of industry: at first S. S. McClure, doyen of the 10-cent magazine revolution, then Col. George S. Harvey, former editor of Pulitzer's sensationalist *New York World*. The first thing Harvey did when he moved into his Harper's office was to hang a photograph of J. P. Morgan on the wall (perhaps the same portrait that Wister encountered a dozen years earlier in Omaha). Practices became at once more commercial and less effective. First to go were the Harpers' trademark handwritten letters (*Publishers' Weekly* said that "for years it was said that the Harper establishment and the Department of State were the only institutions in America which did not use the typewriter" [quoted in Howard 88]). Harvey replaced them with typewritten form letters, promising "such new methods of vastly greater public-ity for books, that the returns promise increased results for both of us."[97] Yet Wister felt that his work was unappreciated, under-advertised, and poorly pack-aged. In 1901, with *The Virginian* nine-tenths completed, he jumped ship to the Macmillan Company of New York.[98]

The transfer to Macmillan was in many ways a sideways move. The publisher claimed a similar middle-class, quality position to Harper & Brothers, and its president, George Platt Brett, belonged to exclusive clubs on both sides of the Atlantic. But Macmillan was more adept at sustaining the double vision necessary to survival in the new literary marketplace. They understood, for example, that novels sold in quantities unavailable to short story collections, particularly since the onset of bestseller lists. Whereas the Harpers had repeatedly gathered Wister's work into short story volumes and envisaged *The Virginian* in the same terms, Brett from the first talked up the work as a novel. Macmillan was also more attuned to techniques of mass advertising—the key, in Richard Ohmann's analysis, to newly emerging mass culture. They accompanied *The Virginian* with an advertising campaign worthy of their cheap rivals. Wister was both delighted and apprehensive, writing to Brett:

> Last Thursday I was sitting at the extreme back of a railroad car bound for Beverly Farms. In the extreme front somebody opened a newspaper—& I had immediate prolapsis inter. My gracious. I saw THE VIRGINIAN in words so large that many people gave up trying to find seats in the car, thinking they were all occupied—It was only your advertisement.
>
> … I'm getting more & more anxious (as if you didn't know your business!) that you'll get all this money back. It must cost like the devil & all to kick up such a splendid noise. I'm inundated with letters congratulatory & that's all right. But cold hard cash into the publisher's pocket is the other half of my prayer just now.[99]

Macmillan was also more aggressively transatlantic in its reach. Whereas the Harpers vaguely promised Wister "some English publisher," Macmillan had a secure contract with its parent company in London, providing simultaneous publication in the United Kingdom and the far-flung British Dominions.[100] The move from Harper & Brothers also freed Wister to publish pieces in the *Saturday Evening Post*, a more widely distributed, commercially attuned magazine than *Harper's Weekly* and *Monthly*. Finally, Brett knew how to finesse the gap between Wister's cultural aspirations and his audience, gradually persuading the author to disguise his distaste. For a Christmas edition of *The Virginian*, Brett cajoled Wister into adding a few respectful words to his audience: "The book is the best American story that has ever been written and it might not be inadvisable to thank the American public for its very hearty appreciation and for its great good sense and discernment in seeing that fact."[101] With this array of marketing techniques, Macmillan pushed *The Virginian* to the top of the bestseller list—"doing in one week two-thirds of what its three predecessors have done in two, five, and seven years"—and kept it there all year.[102]

As it had on Mitchell, however, the brush with publishing economics left its mark on Wister. As *The Virginian* became more and more successful, it became more closely embroiled in brand-name advertising—the form that Ohmann

argues ushered in niche advertising and the commodified reader. In one advertisement, Underwood's, "The Only Original Deviled Ham," lifted a passage
"From Page 43 of 'THE VIRGINIAN'" in which the narrator describes tins of
ham on sale in Medicine Bow with their trademark "label with the devil and
his horns and hoofs and tail very pronounced." Beneath this passage, the advertising copy splashily declares "Of Course It's UNDERWOOD'S THE ONLY
ORIGINAL DEVILED HAM." When Wister saw the ad, his reaction mingled
disdain and glee. He wrote to Brett: "Is this simply objectionable or simply
splendid? Or is nothing wholly simple in this sad world?"[103]

He became increasingly immersed in the details of commerce. In March
1902, he wrote to George Lorimer, editor of the *Saturday Evening Post*, from the
Charleston Club, suggesting that the publicity for his forthcoming story "With
Malice Aforethought" could also serve as advertising copy for his imminent
novel *The Virginian*, of which it was "the concluding climax." This was a kind of
"double dipping" Lorimer rejected.[104] For periodical publication, Wister came
to prefer *Collier's*, *The Saturday Evening Post*, and *The Ladies' Home Journal* over
Harper's, *Century*, and *Scribner's*, because "the weeklies come along quicker, pay
as well, and have a more intelligent audience" and he began to chase syndica-
tion deals.[105] He paid more and more attention to the details of royalties, sales,
and international copyright agreements—ironically, some of the very issues he
was trying to escape in his flight from banking and law into the West twenty
years earlier. He began to refer to his readers as "buyers" and personally to follow
up every complaint about a bookseller not keeping his work in stock.[106] When,
in 1903, he dramatized *The Virginian* for theater, he became even more directly
embroiled in legal and financial agreements.

The arc of Wister's interventions and of the literary marketplace more generally makes it increasingly clear that cultural stratification, east as west, was a
strategic maneuver under the guise of an aesthetic distinction. Sarah Wadsworth
analyzes the contribution of packaging to shoring up distinctions between "high"
and "low" books (even when the text was the same) throughout the post-bellum
period as well as the success of cheap library publishers in helping to "modern-
ize the book industry and establish a national audience for literature" (109); the
claim to national influence was, of course, another strike against the authority
of the frontier club class. Moreover, the division between quality and cheap
publications upheld by so many cultural commentators and quality publishers
crumbled in the face of pragmatics. In 1912, for example, Macmillan encouraged Wister to approve a sevenpenny edition of *The Virginian* by their London
house: "quite recently the London publishers have been engaged in a race to see
who could publish the cheapest editions of books...they seem to have a feeling (whether justified or not I do not know) that the people who read these
cheap editions are encouraged in a habit of reading, and afterwards buy new and

much more expensive books by these authors."[107] The quality publishers' aim is to displace cheap novels and embrace the entire reading market. It is a more programmatic version of the vision articulated by Grinnell back in December 1888, when he reviewed Roosevelt's *Ranch Life and the Hunting Trail* in a deluxe gift edition as "popular." From S. Weir Mitchell right through the frontier club, the aim was to control commercial society for their own purposes, not eradicate it.

Although Wister's sales flourished under Macmillan, his creativity as an author of westerns did not. Despite his promise to Brett that he would produce an epic western—and despite Brett's repeated cajoling in that direction—Wister published only a few more western stories, many of which he had drafted during his Harper years. He increasingly turned away from the West—to Charleston with *Lady Baltimore* and to Philadelphia with *Romney*—then away from fiction, with a series of increasingly xenophobic publications on international relations. The Harpers, meanwhile, managed to pick up the dropped thread of the genre when they contracted with Zane Grey to publish at least one western novel by him a year, beginning with *The Heritage of the Desert* in 1910. In this immensely acute move, they hitched their wagon to an even greater western star who made the bestseller list with *Riders of the Purple Sage* (1912) and stayed in the top ten from 1915 to 1924.[108]

The Frontier Club vs. Alkali Ike

So what was this cheap story of the West that the frontier club disdained? Who was "Alkali Ike" whose popularity goaded Wister into writing his own western fiction? Specifically, the figure is associated with the Wyoming humor of Bill Nye, sometimes claimed to be modeled on Nye's friend Daniel Bellows, who was a frontier scout and guide. More generically—and presumably the way in which Wister used the name—it came to stand for a range of popular, often comical western figures as they appeared in dime novels, comic books, and silent films. Again, this popular literature joins cowboys with publishers, but the cultural equation runs in the opposite direction: the settlers and cheap publishers are the good guys fighting the cattle kings and quality publishers, who are the villains.

The hunter-turned-cowboy—the figure in whom the frontier club was particularly invested—was well established in dime novel fiction by the late nineteenth century. When Irwin P. Beadle & Co. initiated the dime novel format in 1860, they quickly turned to promoting the heroic hunter, ramping up their advertising techniques and enjoying huge sales with their eighth novel, *Seth Jones; or, The Captives of the Frontier* by Edward S. Ellis, which editor Orville Victor pronounced "the perfect Dime Novel" (quoted in H. N. Smith 93). Ellis, a young school teacher, seems to have modeled Seth Jones on James Fenimore

Cooper's Leatherstocking, creating a hunter who is equally sharp-shooting and involved in a similar capture-chase-rescue sequence of adventures in the wilderness of western New York State, but is more graphically violent and more wisecracking than philosophical. Beadle and Adams paid Ellis to produce dozens more variations on this figure, and western heroes multiplied across the popular print world, in the form of scouts, guides, miners, Indian fighters, and outlaws. Settings gradually moved further and further west, while the action continued to emphasize melodrama, flamboyant disguise, uproarious gender bending, physical derring-do—what Bill Brown has called the "vertiginous" possibilities of representation.[109]

In 1882—ten years before Wister's first published western story—the prolific dime novelist Frederick Whittaker re-shaped the frontier hero into the cowboy, with *Parson Jim, King of the Cowboys; or, The Gentle Shepherd's Big "Clean Out"* in Beadle's Dime Library. The novel revolves around James Arthur, a Harvard man who goes west to Colorado for his health and matures into a true westerner (the signs of his maturation are that, after two years, he could outshoot everyone on the range, "run twenty miles in two hours, turn fifty handsprings successively, and had increased his chest girth by three inches").[110] Arthur discovers that the local cattle barons have formed a Rancher's League to terrorize small settlers and independent cowboys, all the while entertaining themselves profligately in the Rancher's Club of Denver with its "gorgeous, not to say ostentatious furniture and carpets" (25). (There was in fact a Denver Club, which had close ties to the Cheyenne Club.) Arthur challenges the big ranchers politically and physically. First, he is elected to the State Assembly as "the champion of the poor man": "We have all heard a good deal of our cattle kings, simply because they are rich men. They go to Europe and live in wealth, while the cowboys take care of their cattle, and work for a bare pittance" (21, 19). Then, when a "crowd of clubmen" attempt to lynch him, he faces them down with "a revolver in each hand," dropping "a man with every shot out of twelve in as many seconds" (26, 28). In the climactic showdown, Arthur wins a "Whip Duel," egged on by his new Mexican-Scottish-American bride. Ultimately, the range is transformed: "The ranchers, with all their wealth, were only a hundred or so of men, while the Cowboys' League...contained nearly twenty thousand voters, and exercised a great silent force on public opinion" (29).

A similar populism informs Whittaker's subsequent cowboy novels, as well as those of William G. Patten and Prentiss Ingraham, who developed the cowboy hero further. Ingraham was most famous as mythmaker for Bill Cody, and his contribution to the dime novel cowboy was based on a performer in Buffalo Bill's Wild West, Buck Taylor. Ingraham first fictionalized Taylor in 1887 (the same year as the Boone and Crockett Club came into being) in *Buck Taylor, King of the Cowboys; or, The Raiders and the Rangers* in Beadle's Half Dime Library.

In Ingraham's hands, the cowboy's roots in the chivalric tradition become more explicit, and his flamboyance increases: he is richly dressed in bejeweled, quasi-vaquero costume and participates in much showy gun play and other forms of violence, lynching included.[111]

It hardly needs saying: when frontier clubmen developed cowboy fiction, they fastened on many of the same figures, events, and settings as the dime novelists. The differences are in narrative voice, the communication of violence, and the race and class alliances. Over and over again, dime novelists intervene in the action to acknowledge that the battle in which they are participating involves as much commercial calculation as gun-play.[112] In the frontier club western, the narrator is intent on his own maturation and honor, and none of the good guys admits to commercial motive. Violent action is central to both formulas, but dime novels revel in it to such an excess that the effect can be parodic while the frontier club western communicates violence in clinical, coded, and repressed form. Racial codes work differently in the two popularizations of the West. Buck Taylor's flamboyant Mexican costume, as written by Ingraham, is not only toned down by Wister, it is transposed to the villain Trampas, especially in the stage costuming of that character. The love interest of Whittaker's Harvard tenderfoot not only mixes Mexican and Scottish heritage but encourages his mano-a-mano violence for the sake of his honor and reputation, the very attitude that Wister's "old stock" heroine disavows.

Above all, a class line separated how the early dime novelists fictionalized cowboys and cattle barons and how frontier clubmen did. While, in Whittaker's story, a Harvard education fits Jim Arthur to stand up for homesteaders, townspeople, and independent cowboys, Harvard taught Wister to celebrate the "natural aristocracy" of big ranchers and their loyal cowpunchers and to demonize small, independent settlers. In Whittaker's West, the cowboy hero enters government to give democratic voice to the people. In Wister's West, frontier club heroes do essentially what exclusive social organizations did back east: "set standards of behavior in public and private places" and bar undesirables from the orbit of America's emerging aristocracy (Homberger 10). The Virginian is particularly occupied in enforcing codes of behavior, often gun in hand—from his public dressings down of Trampas to lynching, shooting, and miscalling those who do not fit the prototype.

That class distinction was bolstered by marketplace strategies that marked every aspect of the classification of westerns into quality and cheap literature, including their material qualities. Again, the relationship was symbiotic: a work that was packaged cheaply was, ergo, cheap (except when quality publishers opted to appropriate the category for their own purposes). Ten-cent and later five-cent pamphlet dime novels contrasted with the clothbound volumes of frontier club writers, priced around $2.00.[113] Pamphlets were sold through the mail, by traveling salesmen (Wister's "Jew drummers") on railroad and street stalls, in dry goods stores. Books were sold in bookstores and qualified for best-seller lists. The awareness of participating in a class-driven publishing battle is a staple element of frontier club culture, evident in Mitchell's conversations with Wister, Wister's with Walter Furness, and any of the quality editors or publishers with their clubmen authors. The note is sounded from the Boone and Crockett Club's first book, when Roosevelt and Grinnell denounce other hunting books as commercial trash and position their own as both of broad appeal and superior culture.

Frederick Whittaker had already called out such distinctions in a scorching letter to the editor of the *New-York Daily Tribune* in 1884. Best remembered now for his dime novels about the adventures of tramps, factory operatives, and Knights of Labor, Whittaker waded into the public debate with an explicit class mandate, speaking up for dime novelists "to defend the class to which I belong."[114] Skewering the establishment position on cheap books, Whittaker attacked the standard hierarchy that belittled dime novels as corrupting "trash," he reversed the cultural stereotypes being promoted by the press, and he brandished a nationalistic rhetoric that frontier clubmen would later seize for their own purposes. Whittaker argued that "the dime novel is now the only representative of purely American literature that exists on its own merits alone" and that "cheap stories" will be the source of "the regeneration of American literature," partly because they pay a living wage. One of his examples of quality writing for Beadle and Adams was Grinnell's and Roosevelt's favorite author, Mayne Reid. Whittaker also turned the trope of "pirating" back on "the piratical houses, that pose as the 'leaders of the trade,'" and he asserted that cheap publishers exercised more stringent editing than "quality" publishers—naming Scribner's specifically ("Dime" 8).

The threat of cheap books and dime novels never receded for the frontier clubmen. When the literary periodical *The Nation* reviewed the first Boone and Crockett Club book slightingly in 1893, Wister immediately imagined the fate of his own writing at their hands: "There'll be a brief estimate in which I shall be described as aiming for Bret Harte and Kipling and achieving a mild species of dime novels" (F. Wister, *Owen* 194). When Grinnell was approached by Harpers in 1914 about publishing with them "the story of an Indian boy" or "a book of Indian battles," the editor, Ripley Hitchcock, had to assure him: "No, we are not looking for the dime novel sort of thing. All that you write would bear the stamp of historic truth."[115]

History suggests that, while frontier clubmen ultimately lost the range war, they won the publishing war. Not only does their formula remain imprinted on dominant print and movie forms, but very quickly it impacted dime novelists' production. Two years after the publication of *The Virginian*, Edward S. Ellis,

Beadle and Adams's first "find," published *Cowmen and Rustlers: A Story of the Wyoming Cattle Ranges*. With this story Ellis does an ideological about-face, no longer competitor to but now imitator of the frontier club western. The novel is part hunting tale, part sentimental drama, and it explicitly revolves around the Johnson County War. The action takes an eastern family (whose name, Whitney, connects them with the eastern upper classes) from Maine to Powder River, Wyoming, where they become embroiled in the range war. The tale accepts frontier club terms: it defends the "legitimate owners," parallels rustlers with wolves, and admires the big cattlemen as "a force invading a hostile county." History is bluntly rewritten, with the excision of the WSGA lynching and an attempt by the "rustlers" to set fire to besieged cattlemen, before the easterners return to Maine to marry. Soon, more dime and nickel novels, especially as they became pressured by forces of censorship and regulation, would follow the frontier club formula (for more on which, see Chapter Four, this volume). By 1906, Ellis had turned his hand to hagiography of Theodore Roosevelt (Saxton 333).

Conclusion

The argument of this chapter is that the frontier club western served as the hinge between the cattle and publishing industries, among other things. These two spheres shared financial and personnel overlaps as well as structural parallels. Powerful interests on the plains and on publishers' row worked to structure and publicize marketplace competition as a class- and race-based hierarchy setting Anglo gentlemen (cattle barons and quality publishers) who transcended commercial interests above the dregs of society ("squatters" and "pirates") who were consumed by them.

That the two spheres were engaged in the same power plays was evident in the vocabulary of their market strategies. In the 1880s, Harper and Lippincott castigated the cheap competition as "pirates" and the *New York Evening Post* designated cheap publisher George Munro "the eminent pirate."[116] Ten years later, the *Cheyenne Sun* vilified independent cowboy leader Jack Flagg as a "range pirate" while the *New York Times* alluded to "alleged 'rustlers,' or range pirates."[117] When, in 1893, publisher Henry Holt testified in court that "courtesy of the trade" meant an agreement "not to jump another publisher's claim," he again echoed the language of the cattleman (quoted in Tebbel 54). Both industries operated by "book count." The term was used by big-ranch managers presenting steers to investors and prospective buyers (that is, the managers were following numbers on paper, often inaccurate and exaggerated, rather than an actual head count). It was similarly used by publishers advertising sales to their buyers (that is, advertisements cited numbers printed rather than sold).

Three months after *The Virginian*'s first appearance, George Brett explained to Wister that Macmillan was about to take advantage of the "book count" system: "We took our courage in both hands to-day and decided on printing a further edition of twenty-five thousand copies of your book in order that we might advertise to-morrow the 100th thousand."[118]

Returning to the Philadelphia Club one last time, we can see that Wister's staging of the western's creation as an act of individual genius in the bosom of aristocratic culture hid as much as it revealed. The "wild glories" of Wyoming that he dedicated himself to preserve referred not to the unbridled adventures of cowboys but to the unbridled dominance of cattle kings. His opposition to "Alkali Ike in the comic papers" may well have been aesthetic, but it also signaled his commercial alignment with quality publishers battling for dominance in the new, mass literature marketplace. Even the scene's exclusiveness was not as complete as it seems. In order to hold sway in the modern world, the club class needed the support of the very masses whom it despised and who were emerging as competitors in the battle for public opinion and cultural dominance.

What, finally, might we say about the "tea-cups" that the Philadelphia Clubmen also wished "to hell" that night of September 1891? The reference is presumably to the feminized culture against which, Jane Tompkins argues, westerns rebeled.[119] Women were, of course, barred from gentlemen's clubs, so Wister's account serves to confirm the essential masculinity of the genre—born as it was between men in an all-male enclave. Not so. Not only did Wister's first attempt at a western not take place in the Philadelphia Club, and not only was it not titled "Hank's Woman"; it also was not fostered by an all-male fraternity. This was, finally, the largest and most revealing fabrication of Wister's origin myth. How deeply indebted he—and the frontier club as a whole—was to women in forging the western is the subject of the next chapter.

Women in the Frontier Club

In September 1909, Louisa Gulliver Sheldon, member of New York high society, went west with her new husband Charles Sheldon, a rising star of the Boone and Crockett Club.[1] Their destination was Admiralty Island off the coast of Alaska, and their purpose was to stalk and shoot bear. Louisa began the journey by sharing the eight-foot-square sleeping cabin of a launch with four men (her husband, their hunting guide, and the boat's pilot and engineer), then spent four rain-soaked weeks camping in the rough, tramping through rocks, brush, woods, and rivers, shooting a doe and its fawn, and taking shots at bears. When her husband published an account of the trip, he observed that she "remained perfectly cool, even more so than most men would have done when three bears were approaching so closely" (177). Louisa was not by any means the only "hunting spouse" in the wilderness (T. Kelly, "Hunter" 195). Throughout the late nineteenth and early twentieth centuries, wives, daughters, and single women of the eastern establishment went west on big-game hunting expeditions. Some accompanied Boone and Crockett Clubmen, some had guns, and some wrote about their experiences.[2]

You wouldn't know it from the Boone and Crockett Club book series, which labors to erase and suppress the presence of women from the hunting fraternity. Even Sheldon, who could write and photograph his wife as gun-toting hunter, expunged women from the hunting scene in his contributions to the club series. Yet women were deeply involved in the creation of the big-game hunting-tale genre, especially as it morphed into the frontier club western, and they are due both the credit and the responsibility that went with that process. The women who were most closely connected with the core frontier club group are not to be found, like Louisa, rifle in hand posing with their kill. Rather, their influence and contributions lie deeply buried in the material, social, and literary conditions of frontier clubmen's writing. The very nature of women's participation was such that the remaining evidence is skimpy, requiring both piecemeal reconstruction and a degree of informed speculation. Nevertheless, by assembling fragments of biographical, archival, and textual evidence, we can appreciate how many strong women buttressed the frontier club, how much frontier clubmen depended on these women for their creativity and their sense of audience, and the degree to which particular narrative characteristics were shaped under these women's influence.

Women in the frontier club also got something out of the genre for themselves. They did not create a woman-centered western—that work was done by very different women outside the frontier club[3]—but, in ways both direct and indirect, they claimed and protected imaginative space in the West. The payoff can be seen in a figure like Louisa Sheldon. The Sheldons' participation in frontier club ideology post-dated its formative period. (Sheldon rose to vice president of the Boone and Crockett Club and member of its editorial committee after World War I). The physical space that Louisa and her ilk enjoyed as hunting women was partly the legacy of the imaginative space cleared by the frontier club women who came before her. This was an important gain, but it was limited by class and race. The space teased out by white upper-class women for white upper-class women involved a cost that was born by other categories of women in the West. This chapter aims to reverse the forms of exclusion and suppression practiced on frontier clubwomen while recognizing that this was a far different process than the demonization and marginalization inflicted on Indigenous peoples and people of color. The chapter ends by acknowledging that the gains made by clubwomen, as by clubmen, depended on the exploitation of others—a point that is pursued more fully in Chapter Six.

Reconstructing women's contributions to frontier club successes brings a new angle and a new set of questions to "the Wister moment"—that is, to the understanding of Wister's centrality in forging the modern western formula.[4] Perhaps more than any other frontier clubman, Wister benefited from the generations of women who helped to forge his authorial persona and his literary output. Their imprint on his fiction is decisive. Even when Wister created textual ripostes to women, most famously with his character Molly Wood, he worked within the coordinates that they introduced and he was drawn into a gendered negotiation that shaped his fictional scene. Scholars of the western are keen on birthing metaphors to characterize this moment—John Cawelti typically declares that, in 1902, "the modern Western was born"—but they must imagine a kind of male parthenogenesis because women do not figure in the process (*Six-Gun* 95). In this suppression of women's contributions, critics collude with the myth that Wister perpetrated in public. Yet women of the frontier club class deserve, at the very least, midwife status; without them, the popular western as we know it would not have come into existence.

Frontier Club Women and Families

Revisiting the frontier club through its mothers, wives, daughters, confidantes and female mentors reveals another network, undergirding and enabling the more famous group of men. There is no symbolic gathering of these frontier club women—nothing like the Boone and Crockett Club dinner at the Metropolitan Club in Washington, DC, or the Hunter's Cabin at the Chicago World's Fair—by which to introduce them. Women's authority did not cluster and announce itself in that way. Their power lay in the filiations and connections they provided, strengthening the frontier club network biologically and socially, increasing clubmen's cultural cachet, extending their transatlantic reach, and fine-tuning their scripting of the West.

Take, for example, the bond between Owen Wister and Winthrop Chanler, the frontier club friendship most typical of the boyish homosociality celebrated in their writings and central, in Gail Bederman's analysis, to white male power in this period. Long before "Dan" and "Winty" became Harvard clubmates and collaborated as Boone and Crockett Club authors, their links—to each other and to transatlantic high society—were forged by women. In the early 1870s Fanny Kemble, the famous Shakespearean actress, took her daughter, Sarah Butler Wister, and young grandson, Owen, to winter in Rome. From her career on the international circuit, Fanny had a vast European network, including her good friend Margaret Terry, an expatriate American living with her family in an artistic community well connected to Roman high society. The young Owen came daily to the faded but still magnificent Palazzo Odescalchi where the Terrys rented an apartment, to share French lessons with Margaret, familiarly known as Daisy, their eldest child. She took to Wister immediately: "I was charmed but not a little shocked by him, he seemed so emancipated from our unquestioning obedience" (*Roman* 34). A decade later, another attractive member of the eastern establishment, the Terrys' cousin Winthrop Chanler, came visiting. Daisy was even more charmed by him. Over the next two years, as Daisy and Wintie (as she always spelled it) pursued a courtship on one side of the Atlantic, Dan and Winty began a long friendship on the other. Once the Chanlers married, in 1886, they began a peripatetic life together, shuttling back and forth across the Atlantic with their growing family, living sometimes among his family and social set on the American East Coast, sometimes among hers in Rome. Margaret provided her husband with access to international connections, including sporting and big-game hunting opportunities in Europe, some of which figure in Boone and Crockett Club tales.[5] She also operated as a third presence in the bond between Winty and Dan. Wister confided his hopes and fears about marriage to her— "More than I've ever told to any one"—and she encouraged his friendship with her insouciant husband as a steadying influence.[6] Urging Wister to visit them at Rokeby, the Chanler estate, Chanler wrote to him: "my wife likes you Dan! Of all my hitherto produced friends & former playmates she most approves of you."[7] When Wister subsequently married his own cousin—Mary Channing Wister, familiarly known as Molly—Winthrop gleefully took credit for setting the trend.[8] Margaret was also a strong believer in marriage between cousins:

"There is a similarity of fibre, a coincidence of wave lengths, which make for good understanding" (*Roman* 182). The wives reinforced the biological and social circle, redoubling connections within and between family units.

Margaret also, along with many other women, contributed her literary nous to the frontier club. She was a talented writer who, after her husband's death, was persuaded by her children to go public with her work; she published three volumes of memoirs and social sketches. She was also a talented reader. She recognized the quality of her husband's writing, evident in his voluminous letters to her in which he poured out the vivid details of his travels and hunting adventures to his "Dearest Wuffie." Although he would agree to work up this material for publication only within the safe confines of the Boone and Crockett Club books, after his death Margaret also made his work public, publishing a hefty selection of his letters.

Silas Weir Mitchell's place in the frontier club network and his literary productivity were equally shaped by women. His second marriage, to Mary Cadwalader, a member of Philadelphia's old aristocracy, raised Mitchell several rungs up the city's social, economic and cultural hierarchy. He moved into his wife's former home—a grander accommodation than his own—where he "became known for his hosting of literary friends and acquaintances" (Lovering 14). For all his loyalty to the gentlemen's club life, the friends and acquaintances whom Mitchell identified as "unequalled in my memory for all that adds to the social interests of life" were dominated by women: Fanny Kemble and Sarah Butler Wister, again, along with Agnes and Sophie Irwin.[9] Sarah was a literary presence in her own right. She published essays and poetry in the *Atlantic Monthly*, *The North American Review* (of which Lodge was an editor), and other "quality" magazines. Her weekly salon attracted "such persons as Matthew Arnold, William Dean Howells, Henry James"—he modeled several characters on her— "Sydney Lanier, William M. Evarts, and Arthur Stanley, dean of Westminster, not to mention many of the most distinguished families from Philadelphia, Boston, and New York."[10] Mitchell said that he valued the opinion of "cultivated women" over that of male critics. According to Wister, Mitchell called his second wife "his best critic," and Sarah became one of his closest literary advisers.[11] In 1886, she wrote to him: "It is needless, I hope, that I shd. say to you that every line you publish, every important word & act of yrs. is a subject of living interest to me."[12] She commented on drafts of his fiction, and he wrote regularly to her from his camping and fishing trips in Wyoming and northern Quebec, shaping descriptions of outdoor life that appeared in his medical treatises, while they shared their worries about Dan's present health and future prospects. Sarah was related to Mitchell twice over: he was her distant cousin, and Mary Cadwalader Mitchell was her even more distant relative.

The Irwin sisters provided further links among Weir Mitchell, Sarah, Owen, and Molly Wister. Agnes and Sophie Irwin ran Philadelphia's most prestigious girls' school, where Molly was one of the top graduates. Agnes coauthored two books with Sarah Wister: *Worthy Women of Our First Century* and the rather ris-qué novel *Brisée*, which they wrote with Miss Benoni Lockwood and published anonymously in their youth. Agnes also closely protected Owen Wister from infancy onwards; he received his first letter from her at four years of age, a considerably more affectionate communication than anything that survives from his mother: "My dear Dan: I am going to write you a little letter because I hope you may like to get one, and one that you cannot expect. This paper is made for letters to young people, like yourself, and I have tried to choose the colour you would prefer to have a note on."[13] Wister felt equally close to her, saving that letter to the end of his life. In 1894, when Agnes went to Radcliffe College as its first Dean, he was the only non-pupil (and the only man) to contribute to her farewell tribute.[14]

Theodore Roosevelt also solidified his social and political connections with his first marriage, to Alice Lee, a member of the interlocking network of Boston's oldest families. In one direction, Alice's family connected with Lee, Higginson, and Company, Owen Wister's first employers. In another direction, she provided a biological connection to Henry Cabot Lodge, who became Roosevelt's great friend, political ally, and literary collaborator. Through her father, the prominent banker George Cabot Lee, Alice belonged to the Boston blueblood Cabots, famous for protecting their social exclusivity through intermarriage. Henry Cabot Lodge's wife, the beautiful, witty Nannie Lodge (full name Anna Cabot Mills Davis) was also related to her husband through the Cabot line on his mother's side.[15] Nannie, "daughter and sister to Admirals," was not only a valuable political asset for Senator Lodge, "So sharp was she of intellect that her vain husband depended on her to edit his speeches."[16] Anna Cabot, Lodge's mother, has also been identified as "a central force in his life" (E. Thomas 19). When Roosevelt married for a second time, after Alice's death, it was almost as if he had married into his own family network: he reunited with his childhood sweetheart, Edith Carow who was an intimate of his sisters and, although not biologically related, was "as a sister" to him (Morris 319).

The first audience for Roosevelt's hunting tales was also female. In the years between Alice's death and his marriage to Edith, he corresponded at great length about his hunting and ranching adventures in the West with his sisters, Corinne and Anna—especially the latter, known as Bamie. Much of the material in these letters reappears, almost verbatim, in his publications. Some years later, Corinne also worked some of his letters into her publication of her own western adventures—on horseback, at the roundup, and joshing with cowboys on her brother's Elkhorn ranch and camping in Yellowstone Park.[17] For all Roosevelt's shows of intense virility and his belief that "a woman's highest duty was fulfilled in her separate sphere, that of homemaking and childbearing," he depended on the good opinion of "Edie" and other women around him when it came to his writing (Watts 112). These women gravitated to each other. When the Chanlers temporarily moved to Washington, DC, Margaret became part of the social network revolving around Edith Roosevelt and Nannie Lodge; when the Chanlers lived in New York City, Margaret happily accepted an invitation to join a ladies' discussion club that included Anna and Corinne Roosevelt.

Women figured differently, but still prominently, in George Bird Grinnell's and Caspar Whitney's frontier club work. Like Roosevelt, Grinnell had a tutelary deity, but his was very different: Lucy Audubon, the elderly widow of the famous ornithologist. Where Roosevelt named his hunting club after Daniel Boone and Davy Crockett, Grinnell named the first Audubon society "as much for her as for her husband" (Reiger, *Passing* 22). As a boy growing up on the grounds of the former Audubon estate, George attended the small school Lucy—"Grandma Audubon" to the children—ran from her bedroom in order to support her sons and their families, as she had earlier supported her husband (Punke 6). She exposed Grinnell to natural science, encouraged his interest in birds and animals, and taught him "the central creed of his life," the self-denial he would develop into a conservation ethic (Punke 8). Grinnell married late in life, and it was his western writing that brought his wife and him together. Elizabeth Curtis Williams, a young widow and practicing photographer, initiated the relationship after reading his "Last of the Buffalo" in *Scribner's Magazine* in September 1892.[18] After their marriage, she accompanied him on all his trips west, taking photographs as part of their fieldwork with Native peoples and in support of his lobbying for the creation of Glacier National Park. Grinnell may have been paying private tribute to her qualities when he editorialized in *Forest and Stream* that "most men are wholly blind to many things which a woman sees clearly; she possesses certain intuitions which are hers alone" ("Woman" 447).

During his tenure as editor of *Forest and Stream*, Grinnell worked very publicly with women in developing the hunting genre. Andrea Smalley has argued that women were crucial to the efforts of hunter-conservationists to mark off sports hunting as "respectable, family-centered recreation" in contradistinction to subsistence and market hunting and that sporting magazines worked to bring women hunters into "the larger public relations project of hunting reform" (359, 373). During the years in which Grinnell became involved with *Forest and Stream*, it developed its profile as "a ladies' paper" as well as "a gentleman's paper," partly by introducing a "Ladies Department" (Smalley 356). He continued this policy as editor, supporting women's participation in hunting, publishing women's hunting narratives, and appealing to women readers to support the campaign to enforce game laws. Caspar Whitney, as editor of *Outing* from 1900, was in a similar position. Although no direct connection has been established between any of Whitney's three wives (Anna Childs, Cora Adele Chase, and

Florence Canfield) and the hunting genre, he was deeply engaged with wooing women readers, publishing women authors, soliciting sports advertising directed at women, and supporting women's activities in the sports hunting domain.[19]

These sketches suggest, cumulatively, how women provided fundamentally enabling conditions for the frontier club's cultural production, through social, material, and literary support. Women also boosted their husbands' racial confidence. Steeped as they were in eugenics, clubmen believed that marrying their relatives kept their bloodlines pure. (Ironically, Madison Grant, who became a leader of the eugenics movement, was the only one of the group not to marry.) Most of these women were "in the club" of procreation necessary to class and race survival, and several of them paid the price. Alice Roosevelt and Molly Wister died in childbirth. Mary Middleton Elwyn, the first Mrs. Mitchell (mother of Jack and Langdon; "Cousin Mary" to Owen Wister), died after contracting diphtheria from her older son.[20]

The one woman who stood outside this social circle was Eva Caten, who became Eva Remington. She was a small-town, middle-class housewife from upper New York State whose social pretensions were decidedly local. In this sense, she reinforced Frederic Remington's social liminality in the frontier club network. Her husband's dependence on her was, however, close in kind and degree to his upper-class clubmates' reliance on their wives. "Missie," as he called her, provided the refinement and the domestic stability that he lacked but craved; a childless couple, their relationship was in some ways reminiscent of a mother-son dynamic.

If women played such a formative role in the process of frontier club writing, where are they in the final product? On the face of it, the books of the Boone and Crockett Club are singularly devoid of women of the frontier club class. The hunter is always, unquestionably, white and male. Sometimes women are simply absent, as when Grinnell writes in 1933 of his trips to Glacier National Park, with no acknowledgment that his wife had been accompanying him there for many years.[21] Sometimes Indigenous women—in the American West, northeast Africa, and Rhodesia—hover on the edge of the hunting grounds, their eroticized presence emphasizing the need for the gentlemen hunters' purified spaces. Winthrop Chanler develops this trope most fully in his account of hunting mouflon in Sardinia, a scene that maps almost exactly onto the American West as constructed by the Boone and Crockett Club formula. As the four hunters travel to "one of the wildest parts" of the island, they encounter various "natives," one of whom serves them their supper: "one of the loveliest girls it has ever been my good fortune to meet; a pure Arab type, with large melting black eyes full of a burnt glow, and with perfect features. On her lovely cheek was a smudge of black" ("Mouflon" 1, 2, 3–4). She is the last woman they encounter before departing into the space of the hunt proper.

Within the hunting grounds, there are of course magnificent female presences: the noble matriarchs of the animal world. A parade of she-bears, buffalo and elk cows, and one "goat mama" ferociously protect their young, furiously charging hunters when threatened (O. Wister, "White" 49). The Boone and Crockett code discouraged "the killing of the females of any game species save under rigid limitations," although, in practice, the gentlemen hunters sometimes could not resist the trophy-taking nor the telling of it (Roosevelt and Grinnell, *American* 14). What female animals most often usher into the hunting landscape is the family frame. The hunter-writers, so scathingly opposed to authors who indulged in anthropomorphism (Roosevelt decried them as "nature fakers"), came closest to it whenever they described family groups, from seal and elk harems, to "wolf family dynamics," to bands of ewes with their "patriarch" (Allen 156; Rogers 99). The anthropomorphic impulse is clearest in a Boone and Crockett hunting tale, "Big Game in the Rockies," by Archibald Rogers (one of the original twelve men invited by Roosevelt to discuss forming the club). Rogers delivers an extended and bizarre metaphor describing the shooting of two bears: "I opened the ball with the young lady who was sitting down. She dropped her bone, clapped one of her paws to her ribs, and to my happiness waltzed down the snow-bank. As she now seemed to be out of the dance, I turned to her brother ..." (116). In this context, Grinnell's tale of a killing a fawn, which I earlier called clinical, cuts across the family unit in particularly chilling ways. On one hunting trip, he spies a doe and imitates a fawn to turn her towards him. His noise unexpectedly flushes a young deer out of the underbrush: "To decide to kill, if possible, the fawn, required not a moment's thought, for I knew that the does at this season are usually thin, having been nursing their young all summer." He details the course of his bullet through the fawn's body: "The ball had entered the left shoulder just at the right spot and had come out an inch or two in front of the right ham, and the animal had run fifty yards or so before falling. Altogether, the shot was a very satisfactory one ... It took me about three minutes to cut up the fawn" ("Trip" 670).

Meanwhile, in the social world in which the hunter-writers produced their tales, the mothers, wives, and sisters were also providing crucial family frames. June Howard has discussed how the figure of the family enabled old-style publishers to disguise their increasing commodification in the burgeoning marketplace: "In the early twentieth century, the gesture of equating a publishing enterprise and a family evoked powerful fantasies of wholeness" (8). Familial rhetoric was equally central to frontier club dynamics, providing one more shield for authors against the commercial marketplace by imagining production and reception within an organic, traditional network. When these men passed their accounts by their female relatives and mentors, when they read each other's published works aloud to their wives, and when they reported their wives' approbation to each other, they were reinforcing a community to which women were central. Wister's joking image of white goats clustered on a mountainside is redolent of the same structures: "groups, caucuses, families sitting apart over some discourse too intimate for the general public" ("White" 55).

That there is a connection between the animal and human forms of family comes across most clearly in Chanler's contribution to the first Boone and Crockett Club volume. "A Day with the Elk" recounts his elk-hunting adventures in 1890. The essay opens with the all-male party—Chanler, three friends, three packers, and a cook—in camp in northern Colorado. Many years later, Margaret Chanler takes the reader behind the scenes of this trip, revealing that it began when her husband displaced her and their young family from Rome to England, because he wanted to spend summer in the country where he had enjoyed happy schoolboy days at Eton. Margaret, however, found London "sunless and depressing." When, ten days later, "Wintie" ran into a "sporting parson" of his acquaintance in St. James' Restaurant and was invited to join a big-game-shooting expedition to Colorado, he abandoned his wife and children; "He was all on fire to go and I had not the heart to deny him the adventure. I was left in London with two babies...and felt rather stranded" (M. Chanler, *Winthrop* 11; *Roman* 230). She describes spending a dreary period in Yarmouth, after which she made her way back to New York, babies in tow, and reports, in tones that can be read as sardonic or forbearing, "There Wintie met me, having had a glorious time in Colorado" (*Roman* 231).

In this context, it seems telling that Chanler tells the story of his lone stalk entirely in familial terms, stressing the cows and young spike bulls whom his hunting code protects as "sacred" and describing a magnificent bull with a trope at once Roman and familial: "the great-grandfather of all the elk in the State of Colorado...His back was as broad and as yellow as the Tiber in spring.... his wives and children thronging round him so close that I could not shoot for fear of doing useless harm" (62, 68–69). One of his friends succeeds where Chanler failed, stalking and shooting either the same elk or his "full brother...while superintending the luncheons, siestas and gambols of his numerous family" (72). The tale ends with them leaving the elk's body "as a *memento mori* to the valiant bull who succeeded him in the affections of his widows and offspring" (72). The playful tropes suggest both guilty conscience and a degree of anxiety. The fundamental lens through which he—and most frontier clubmen—saw the world was a familial one made possible by women.

As the hunting tale morphed into the western, family remained an organizing narrative principle, now with actual women populating the narrative. Mitchell's medical writings, which recommend "West cures" for neurasthenic men and rest cures for neurasthenic women, were shaped by conventional notions of the Victorian family and gender-appropriate behavior, while his novels included fictionalized portraits of the women in his literary circle, including Sarah Butler Wister.[22] Grinnell's westerns for young readers employ the standard female figures—society mother, ranch wife, girl companion—necessary to the hero's maturation, while the final volume of his series foregrounds the girl shot. While Frederic Remington's visual art of the West excludes women, the central tragedy of his novel *John Ermine of the Yellowstone* (1902) is precisely that the hero is shut out by race and class from the tight network of eligible marriage partners. Remington wrote in a romantic female protagonist (though he pretended that he required Charles Dana Gibson to draw her, lest her illustration dent his macho image).[23] Owen Wister's literary trajectory was most thoroughly enmeshed with female figures, actual and fictional, a process illuminated by the network of women who surrounded and supported him.

The Wister Women

The women around Owen Wister influenced his authorial sensibility in layered ways. They set his horizons in terms of how he saw the West, how he imagined his public, and what he incorporated into his writings. These were strong, accomplished characters. In addition to those already mentioned—Fanny, Sarah, Molly, and Agnes—they included Molly's younger, unmarried sister, Frances, who kept the family together after Molly's death in 1913, and the Wisters' daughter, Fanny Kemble Wister, who kept his legacy alive long after his death in 1938. If it had not been for these women reading, shaping, and contributing to his work, Wister would never have written *The Virginian*, and popular westerns would have evolved in some other direction.

In several senses, Fanny Kemble created the dynamic that ruled her grandson's life from young manhood onwards. Having come from England as the wife of a rich Philadelphian with a southern plantation, Fanny discovered that she could not stomach the slavocracy and withdrew to her own lavish estate on the edge of Philadelphia, sustaining her international career as an actor well into old age. Margaret Chanler saw Wister's thespian talents at Harvard as a direct inheritance from the famous Shakespearean actress: "did not the blood of the great Mrs. Siddons and Fanny Kemble flow in his veins?"; when Wister first began to make a name for himself as an author, he was identified as "the grandson of Fanny Kemble" in an approving notice of his story "Em'ly" in the *New York Tribune*.[24] Fanny used her connections on the international circuit to support Wister's artistic ambitions. On his graduation, she introduced him to Franz Liszt, who auditioned him in Wagner's home in Bayreuth and gave him the nod as a composer: he wrote to Fanny that her grandson had "un talent prononcé" (D. Payne 5). The encouragement set the stage for the young man's plunge into depression, when he caved in to his father's demand that he return to America and follow a career in banking. The tension between the artistic and the commercial, and its gendered dynamics, dogged Wister throughout his career as a popular writer. Fanny died in 1893, just as he was beginning to publish, but she remained a presence in his life—he kept her portrait by Thomas Sully prominently displayed in his front parlor—one of several strong women whom he simultaneously admired, depended on, and resented.

The immediate result of Wister's breakdown, in 1885, was that his cousin Silas Weir Mitchell diagnosed his illness as neurasthenia and prescribed a trip west. It was left to more women—in this case, two of the Irwin sisters—actually to take him there. This is the trip that Wister's daughter, Fanny Kemble Wister, pronounced the formative experience of his life: "going West in 1885 made my father" (*Owen* xix). The Irwin sisters—Agnes, in particular—put their stamp on that experience practically, conceptually, and in its literary realization.

In July 1885, Agnes's sisters, Sophie and Maisie Irwin, accompanied the 25-year-old Wister by train and stagecoach to Wyoming. The three of them lodged at the VR ranch in which the Irwins had financial interests; it seems to have been they who introduced Wister to Frank Wolcott, manager of the ranch, who subsequently became a focal character in Wister's fiction.[25] The sisters also accompanied him on his first hunting and camping trip, occupying a tent, while Wister and Jack Mitchell (Weir Mitchell's son, who followed from Philadelphia to join the party) slept rough. When the weather deteriorated, the sisters invited the men into their tent, discreetly dividing the space by hanging a blanket.[26] When, in subsequent years, Wister returned west to hunt, camp, and gather fictional materials, he regularly corresponded with Agnes Irwin—long letters, in which he tried out tales that later appear in his published writings. The incident of the tenderfoot narrator's lost trunk that opens *The Virginian*, for example, first appears in a letter to Agnes.[27] Descriptions of his adventures hunting big-horn sheep and elk that he first wrote to her appear lightly revised in his Boone and Crockett tales.[28] He depended on her as a manuscript reader for years, and her support was unqualified. Long before he published his bestselling novel, she wrote to him from Cambridge: "Truly the world knows nothing of its greatest men: the [Boston] Transcript makes a pretence of being up in matters literary and has not yet discovered you."[29] A later letter, recounting her attendance gowned and resplendent among the dignitaries at a Harvard commencement, suddenly bursts out in glee: "The Virginian is 'going it,' don't you think so?"[30] Right up to her death, she was commenting on drafts of his unfinished novel *Romney*. He said that her advice "helped to lead me to such standards as I have."[31]

An equally important, though more complex and conflicted, influence was his mother, Sarah Butler Wister.[32] Like her mother, the beautiful, talented, and demanding Sarah found herself in an uncongenial marriage. Owen Jones

Wister, a prominent Philadelphia physician, steered clear of the high literary society to which Sarah's salons were dedicated, did not approve of the arts as a career, and had different ambitions for his son. Throughout his life, their only child was caught between their competing expectations, justifying his academic and artistic performance and ambitions; the evidence is there in his voluminous correspondence, especially with his mother, from the various educational establishments in Europe and America to which he was sent. Sarah was deeply absorbed in his musical and literary development, inquiring closely into his artistic endeavors, from his schoolboy triumphs, his amateur theatricals at Harvard and his success with eminent composers Franz Liszt and Antoine-François Marmontel in Europe to his later adaptation of *The Virginian* for stage and ongoing publications. She never went further west than Chicago with him—to the World's Columbian Exposition in 1893—but she was his constant companion in his thoughts. He wrote to her frequently, sometimes daily, on the western trips that began in 1885, enthusiastically detailing the unfamiliar scenes and types. By 1891 he was emphasizing that his "literary impressions" had transcended their shared European repertoire: having vividly described the Laramie mountains in one letter, he forestalled her response: "You would have said, 'Oh yes! The Dolomites!' But never any Dolomites had such atmosphere and such colour to bask in" (F. Wister, *Owen* 119, 120). He insistently reminded her how much she would hate it all, as if in fear that the strong-minded Sarah might be persuaded westward by his vividness. He also confided his literary ambitions and anxieties, including, in February 1902, a long letter from Charleston explaining his processes and vision for crafting *The Virginian* out of miscellaneous pieces.[33] Sarah proudly boasted that her son had confided his literary progress to her from the first and, in 1905 (when Wister was 45 years old), she pronounced: "The child has fulfilled his promise" ("Early Years" 122).

There was also tension in the relationship. Sarah was famous as an exacting intellect, and she was one of her son's harshest literary critics. It has been speculated, in fact, that Wister's first breakdown and his recurrent bouts of illness throughout his life were partly aggravated by the "mental toll exacted from his demanding, impetuous, and overly sensitive mother," who herself struggled with neurasthenia and depression throughout her life (D. Payne 56). In 1885, as well as having endured the three-way struggle over his artistic and commercial future with his parents and the tedium of the banking life, Wister had also collaborated on his first novel with Mitchell's son Langdon. The eminent critic and friend of Sarah's, William D. Howells, advised Wister to consign it to his bottom drawer: "there was 'too much knowledge of good and evil' in it, and 'a whole fig-tree couldn't cover'—one of the leading ladies in the book for whom I was wholly responsible: Langdon was not guilty of her."[34] In 1902, in response to *The Virginian*'s publication, Sarah sent him a list of four shortcomings, ranging from the novel's structure, to the characterization of its heroine, to the "doubtful morality" of its violence.[35] Wister refuted some of her criticisms at length, rather defensively announcing that "the *next* time I shall write a very big book indeed" (F. Wister, *Owen* 19). He accepted others, following some of her suggestions when he first dramatized and later revised the novel. He ended the play with the shootout she said should have concluded the novel, and he revised descriptions of the heroine's thoughts and reactions in the novel, to make her presence less wooden.

For all this back-and-forth, Wister took pains to conceal Sarah's input. A mother's influence, after all, hardly fitted the vision of heroic individualism that informed Wister's image of his authorial self and his masculine genre. When Wister told how he wrote his first western story, he pretended that it had emerged from a quintessential moment of male intimacy, in the exclusive Philadelphia Club. In fact, several months earlier, he had begun his truly first western story, "The Story of Chalkeye," and confided its progress only to his mother.[36] His repression of Sarah's influence returns most obviously in the two novels that followed *The Virginian*: *Lady Baltimore* (1906), set in Charleston, and his unfinished novel of Philadelphia, *Romney*. In both, the male narrator, Augustus, is guided by his domineering Aunt Carola. The aunt's pride in her southern lineage, her social snobbery, and her imperiousness towards her nephew's composition—"Aunt Carola handed a pen full of ink to me, saying: 'Strike all that out, Augustus....' So I obeyed her"—all resonate with his mother's character and influence (126). Wister's literary dependence on women advisers never ended. Once Agnes and Sarah were dead, he turned to women of a younger generation—such as Anne Mitchell, Jack's wife—for feedback on his work in progress.

Women also loomed strikingly large in the readership of Wister's published work. Men, east and west, repeatedly reported domestic scenes of reading, as they read Wister's magazine and book fiction aloud with their wives.[37] The same message of wifely approval echoed from S. Weir Mitchell a few blocks away from Wister in Philadelphia, to Theodore Roosevelt in the White House, to George West—one of Wister's hunting guides—in Wyoming. This last correspondent wrote of *The Virginian* (for which some speculate he served as model): "Mrs. West says to tell you that she enjoyed it more than any story she ever read because we read it together & *I enjoyed it*, and was sorry when the last chapter was finished."[38] When S. S. McClure, editor of *McClure's Magazine*, sought to flatter Wister into giving him material to publish, he wrote: "Your book did me a world of good personally, and my wife found the same benefit and enjoyment and uplift from it that I did."[39] Sometimes women communicated directly with Wister. Mary Cadwalader Mitchell wrote twice in praise of *The Virginian*, and in response to his next novel, she said, "Thank you for sending me Lady Baltimore for I feel as if I had a part in it."[40] When Wister was invited to the White House a few months after *The Virginian*'s publication, he noted in his diary: "Both men and women not only made polite speeches about it, but asked questions showing they had read it."[41] On another White House visit, Edith Carow Roosevelt monopolized the author with avid questions about the novel's dramatization.[42]

This anecdotal evidence is supported by the responses of leading editors. Edward Bok of the *Ladies' Home Journal* strenuously (although ultimately unsuccessfully) courted Wister for a celebrity profile: "I know there are thousands of women among our readers who would like to know, in the way I proposed, the author of 'The Virginian.'"[43] Wister stressed to George Brett, his editor at Macmillan, that he had shown the first two chapters of *The Virginian* to both sexes and received approbation from both.[44] Richard Slotkin says that bestsellerdom of this period depended on women readers, since they "made up the largest and most reliable readership for literary fiction" (*Gunfighter* 156). As well as their numerical significance, these responses were a great comfort to Wister, who had extremely mixed feelings about the popular audience on whom he increasingly depended. Like many of the eastern establishment, he scorned the marketplace by which he lived, and he feared that his audience was, in the words of his 1900 preface to *The Jimmyjohn Boss*, "a herd of sheep." Being able to envisage at least part of his audience as people of his own class, reading in their traditional family units, relieved his uneasiness about contributing to mass culture. Women readers also helped him to refine his representation of women. Years later, his daughter claimed that women read *The Virginian* to swoon over the hero, but that post-cinematic response was not dominant among this earlier generation, who read in women-centered ways.

In a broader sense, too, women helped Wister to negotiate his identity in the marketplace. These women knew a great deal more about the relationship between private and public than did the sheltered college graduate and clubman. Sarah learned from her mother, Fanny Kemble, who weathered intense public criticism when she flouted convention in divorcing her husband and sustaining a performance career well into old age. When Agnes Irwin left Philadelphia to become first Dean of Radcliffe, she had to sustain a delicate balancing act under intense institutional and public scrutiny. This was the point at which Radcliffe graduated from the "Harvard Annex" to a chartered college, and the development received mixed reviews. Molly Wister, as cofounder of the reformist Civic Club, endured press buffeting for years for this daringly—some thought aggressively—political initiative. With these experiences, the women were well qualified to mentor Wister in how to handle celebrity. He first gave in to Bok's blandishments, agreeing to pose at Saunderstown, his Rhode Island summer home, for photographs—with his two crows, on horseback, with Molly, at work, and so on—to be published in *The Ladies' Home Journal*. After consulting with his womenfolk, he changed his mind—"I resisted the vulgar temptation"—and they helped him to forge a public persona at once manly and modest.[45] A paradigmatic instance occurred when Wister wrote an anti-prohibition operetta, *Watch Your Thirst*, for the Tavern Club in Boston, agreed to its publication, then panicked that what was suitable for the privacy of a gentlemen's club was unfit for public dissemination. Telegramming his editor to stop the presses, he asked an unnamed "midVictorian very orthodox lady" to judge whether the manuscript was indecent. She "read the first act aloud to me, cried 'stuff!,'" laughed him out of his panic and persuaded him to resume publication.[46]

Women continued to shape Wister's persona well beyond his death in 1938. In 1952, for a fiftieth-anniversary exhibition of *The Virginian*, a University of Wyoming librarian, N. Orwin Rush, requested the western journals and diaries that Wister mentions in his book on Theodore Roosevelt. The family had no knowledge of these journals but discovered all fifteen of them in their father's desk, where they had lain for sixty-five years. His daughter, Fanny Kemble Wister, set about editing them for publication. Her introduction to this volume sets the bar high in terms of her father's impact: "Because of him, little boys wear ten-gallon hats and carry toy pistols" (*Owen* 2).

She also protests, with somewhat suspicious insistence, that her editing has removed only superfluous, repetitive, dull material: "The editor conscientiously has omitted nothing concerning Wister that illuminates his character. There are no startling revelations or new discoveries about him. The Journals are never unseemly, and there is nothing to suppress" (28). G. Edward White notes, however, that Fanny excised her father's 1892 journal of his mysterious trip to Montana from her edition (129), and a major question mark hovers over the cutting out of pages from some notebooks; it is unclear whether Wister or his descendants were responsible and why. Even in what survives of the original materials, incrementally, Fanny's excisions create a significant gap. The man who wrote the unedited journals is more gossipy, has more sexualized interested in women and mildly salacious stories, and utters more bigoted statements than the Wister of the published version. The unpublished Wister is also much less alone in the West; in fact, with all the Ivy League and club companions, the encounters with eastern tourists, the numerous letters and conversations, his life in the West sounds considerably more like his life in the East than one could guess from the published accounts. His sister-in-law clearly saw Wister's relationship with the West as deeply familial; she described Wister and Molly as devotees *together* of the West.[47]

Fanny's editing does not transform her father into a macho figure: he is uncertain, often unwell, and his daughter added several of his letters to his mother in which he reflects on his experience. But he is much closer to the stereotypical lone male on the frontier than to the quite social type who emerges in the unedited account. And the edited Wister is much less dependent on women in the West: for example, the account of his first camping trip with the Irwin sisters, including his sharing their cabin, is cut; indeed, his daughter insists that the sisters "returned home before Wister went shooting," which is not how the original tells it (29). Fanny also makes the diaries fit the fiction by whitewashing the western scene. She excises black figures whom Wister encounters, pretending, like his fiction, that African Americans simply did not figure in the West. Again, her editorial remarks buttress that impression. When the family goes to Wyoming with Wister in 1912, they "brought our Negro houseman from home, who attracted the attention of Westerners who had never seen a colored man" (xviii), an unlikely scenario, given the thousands of blacks who went west after the Civil War.

It was also daughter Fanny who, twenty years later again, perspicaciously noted that what Sarah called her biography of her son was, in fact, a diary of her own life; the mother did not seem to notice that she was creating the son out of her own lineaments.[48] Much the same observation could be made of all these Wister women—Fanny Kemble Wister included. A symbiotic process of creation emerges: Owen Wister needed his women to shape not only the myth of the West but the man needed to fit it as much as they needed him as both material support and mythologizer.

Molly Wister

Of all these women, Mary Channing Wister—Molly—was the one whose life as clubwoman, wife, mother, and writer most directly supported and contrasted with her husband's. Molly graduated from the Irwins' school as president of the 1889 class. She immediately embarked on philanthropic and educational work, throwing herself into public life and civic betterment while sustaining domestic and authorial responsibilities in astonishing quantities. She came to be called Philadelphia's "most prominent and best-loved woman"; the mayor said she belonged to "the shining roll of Philadelphia's great women."[49]

That was a less smooth climb than it sounds. Like many women of her class in this period, Molly's entrance into public life involved strategies and evasions far beyond anything her husband experienced. In 1893, she co-founded the women-only Civic Club—"the first 'civic club' proper, in name and purpose"—to give women a greater voice in political affairs in and beyond Philadelphia (Croly 75). They spoke out against municipal corruption, lobbied for improvements in housing, sanitation, transportation, and education, promoted fair employment conditions for domestic servants, investigated discrimination against African Americans, and gradually built influence in public life. They walked a fine line, like so many women's clubs of this era, using, in the words of Anne Ruggles Gere, "the protective coloring of community service" to facilitate women's self-improvement (11).

Compared to groups campaigning for votes for women, the Civic Club was non-confrontational. They chose not to take a position on woman suffrage, recognizing that clarity could exacerbate differences among members as well as hostility from certain public quarters: "The Civic Club has never asked or influenced the opinions of its readers on the suffrage question, although this question attracts the attention of the public more and more. Our constitution and By-Laws do not refer to this subject, and it is to be assumed that members of the Civic Club exercise the same independence of thought on this subject as on religion and politics. Doubtless among our members could be found all varieties of conviction on the fruitful topic of woman suffrage."[50] At the first general meeting in 1894, the president cautioned members that they were arraying themselves "not against any one class of men or any one order of shortcoming, but against the general deficiency which at every turn is felt by those who critically examine into the municipal and intellectual facilities which seem to satisfy the average citizen of Philadelphia."[51] The club established its influence by working along lines traditionally associated with women—housekeeping, childcare, education, recreation—gradually expanding these areas to include municipal politics, immigration policy, and relations between capital and labor.

Nevertheless, for several years, the club endured public ridicule: gentlemen advised against it, and the press showed a "disposition to sneer at the activities of club women."[52] Molly was a prominent target. She functioned in every executive capacity and took on some delicate tasks, such as campaigning to place women on school boards and serving as first vice chairman of the club's Department of Municipal Government, known as the most political wing of the club, with its mandate to serve as a "watchdog committee," observing, investigating, and improving the activities of city government (Toll and Gillam 353). Like her husband, but with very different implications, she identified closely with club life— the first president, Mrs. Cornelius Stevenson, called her "the very soul of the club"—and she was ambitious to move up the hierarchy of women's club organizations.[53] As part of her memorial tribute, another clubmate, Mrs. Mumford, lauded this ambition, as Molly expanded her orbit of influence from the municipal to the state to the national, alongside the growth of the club network:

> she was not to be content with just that little Civic Club of Philadelphia.
> The State soon heard of Mrs. Wister. The State called her; and I remember very well the glint in her dark eyes when she first recognized that her mission was not alone to her own city; that the State had need of just the very ideas that she was standing for here in her own community. And

so she went out into the State Federation, and there became exactly the same leader, the same power, that she had been here. But there she was not to rest, for the whole United States had finally come to see what a wonderful woman we had here amongst us; and the call had come to her from the great Federation of Clubs—from the General Federation of Clubs—that she should take part in the civic work throughout these United States.[54]

For all this support from her community of clubwomen, Molly put up with public and private criticism. When Owen Wister describes the climate in which she worked, he betrays his own reaction too:

> for women to bestir themselves in matters of the public welfare...in Philadelphia was to step rather conspicuously outside of established convention—the things that "a lady could do." It took a number of years for my wife to dispel the cold surprise with which her course was regarded here and there. (*Roosevelt* 58)

Molly also knew how strategic women's claiming of space had to be. Her experience of club space was the opposite of her husband's. Whereas the exclusive Philadelphia and Rittenhouse clubs were confident in their broad-fronted opulence behind which men retreated from modern bustle, the Civic Club was jammed into one or two rooms, constantly moving to find more commodious quarters that would remain affordable to the membership, and always hard up against the soot of the trolley cars and the jangle of neighboring offices. Just as gradually as the club took on political causes, it won a more sociable environment. The Civic Club eventually joined with the College Club and the Agnes Irwin Alumnae Association in a bigger building, which afforded them dining and overnight accommodations as well as meeting space, but they never developed into protective enclaves of the gentlemanly type.

Along with all these civic duties, from her marriage in 1898, Molly also shouldered enormous household responsibilities. In just over eight years, she bore five children, while caring for her own parents, her disabled cousin (known as "Toots"), Sarah Wister in her last long illness, and her own husband during his frequent periods of undiagnosed illness and bed-rest that lasted, in one instance, for an entire year.[55] She also oversaw the house menagerie, much of it the result of Wister's love for animals: two long-haired guinea pigs, a black-and-white Japanese waltzing mouse named Peeshey, cages of finches, canary birds, magpies, a mockingbird, a pet raccoon, a murderous monkey, and Chihuahua dogs. Her daughter's characterization of the household sounds almost nightmarishly cacophonous: "913 Pine Street was too small. There was simply not one room in it away from screaming, often ailing children, and pets who needed attention, and the telephone which rang for Molly with calls from Toots or the Civic Club." Her final comment is telling: "It was no place for an author" (*That* 22).

For Molly—as for so many women—the domestic did not equate with the private. The house to which she moved after her marriage—913 Pine Street— was "a small, four-story house in a block no longer fashionable" in the east end of Philadelphia (F. Wister, *That* 153). They lived on the borders of decaying Society Hill, where the tightly packed row houses were increasingly inhabited by poor African American and immigrant families. The journalist Talcott Williams was her neighbor, and he vividly described how this population pressed in on her on a daily basis:

> Our windows looked across Pine Street between Ninth and Tenth, face to face. The same dusky groups of neglected little children ebbed and flowed about both door-steps. There was for both of us the same strug- gle, often defeated and unavailing, with the visible evils of city streets and alleys. She was the daily friend and defender of her colored friends and neighbors, buffeted by prejudice, beset by temptation and denied the day's fair chance.[56]

He proceeded to describe Molly appearing in court, "testifying for a poor, dark-skinned man" who had fallen victim to municipal corruption: "she seemed the only reality present." Molly's willingness to cross the color line in the domes- tic sphere predated her marriage. As a young woman living with her parents in Germantown, she took advantage of their absence one day to invite to lunch "the entire faculty of a negro school." Over half a century later, her younger sister, the only family member present, was still struck by the momentous memory: "I can shut my eyes and see the long table where at least a dozen colored teachers sat with us."[57] Later, in her capacity as Civic Club officer, Molly lobbied for a colored boys' club and for cooperation with "a League of 75 of the better class of colored women in the 7th Ward."[58]

On top of all this, Molly was involved in authorial work of two kinds—that appearing under her husband's name and that under her own. From before their marriage (when they played together in a piano quartet), she provided literary feedback, steering him away from the melodrama of "Hank's Woman," his first published story, and towards the wistful social comedy—which became inter- mingled with the Boone and Crockett Club tenderfoot rhetoric to forge Wister's trademark tone—of his second, "How Lin McLean Went East."[59] If it had not been for her, it is doubtful whether *The Virginian* would ever have been com- pleted. Invited to attend the Charleston Exposition of 1902 as Pennsylvania's representative, she took Wister with her to write up the novel, which he was struggling to assemble from published and new material. In Charleston, Molly established a working regime by which Wister produced at a pace he never achieved before or since.[60] Throughout their marriage, she continued to support his writing through his frequent spells of despair, illness, and absence, stirring his imagination and cajoling him into production with an insistence that considerably outpaced that of his editor, George Brett of Macmillan. Indeed, at times Brett depended on her exclusively for information about the state of a Wister manuscript.[61] The archives do not reveal how much textual content came from Molly, but it is tempting to speculate whether Wister was reacting to his own experience when he described the impact of Mary Cadwalader Mitchell on her husband's writing: "He called her his best critic, because she could unmercifully condemn. She also, therefore, is ever present in all save his earliest pages."[62] Certainly, Molly's younger sister, Ella, was emphatic that Molly's contribution amounted to collaboration: "From the very beginning of their marriage [Molly] had assisted him in all his work. His great success, 'The Virginian,' novel and play, was as much her writing as his."[63]

Evidence does survive of Molly's input into the theatrical version of *The Virginian*, which led to the novel's reincarnation on film and its continuing influence. After the great success of the novel, Wister and theater producer Kirke LaShelle had worked together on a dramatic adaptation. In 1903, they were on the road with the company, doing tryouts prior to opening on Broadway, and Wister was fretting over numerous theatrical details. Molly targeted his handling of women characters, weighing in with the knowledge she had from her western travels and with a housekeeper's pragmatism:

> In Act 1 [Judge Henry's wife] should wear a plain *old fashioned* black silk suitable for middle aged, prosperous, countrified matron. Take out Mrs. Henry's words "My favorite nook" in 2nd Act. A western woman wouldn't use them. In 2nd Act Mrs. Henry could do far worse than wear costume at present worn by Mrs. Taylor. In 3rd could also do better. Let Mrs. Ogden wear her pretty *pink* dress in 1st Act & buy a nice looking outing costume for 2nd Act—it need not cost a great deal. It can be some light pique with a Gibson shirt waist to save expense of a well made jacket.

She suggested casting changes—"let me beg you to take Mrs. Taylor in Mrs. Henry's place"—and promised to ask around among the clubwomen for suggestions on an alternative lead to Nanette Comstock. She wanted to have the chance to see some actresses in action before the final decision: "If you should have to make a change, please don't let them do anything in haste." She also had advice about the novel's popular "baby-swapping" scene, which they were trying to reproduce on stage, instructing him to search out "some inexpensive woman who has experience with babies" and to send "the ladies of the company to an orphanage for several days running while you are in Buffalo. Let them assist in care of the babies with the permission of the managers. I know this will make a difference."[64]

Wister's major theatrical headache was the revision of Act 3, the "lynching act" in which the heroic Virginian and his posse hang two cattle rustlers. Both LaShelle and his mother wanted Wister to cut the act—his partner considered it too violent for the stage, his mother considered it vulgar—but his own instinct was to make the lynching loom larger, even, in the play than in the novel. Molly seems to have sided with him. When LaShelle was suddenly hospitalized with appendicitis, Wister had the chance to try his version, and he felt that he had got it right.[65] Molly's response suggests that her husband and she had reflected on the revision at length. The letter also speaks volumes about the multiple demands on her energies, as she moved between the labor of childcare and housekeeping and creative support:

> There is so much to write about & at the end of the fourth day on my feet I'm dreadfully tired. I wrote last night about how happy your joyful news of Act 3 made me. I didn't say, couldn't say all I felt about it, but I think you must know. There is a very special happiness when a wish comes true. It would have been good to be together when the act was finished. I have wanted you to succeed in that one act more than in any-thing you have ever attempted since we have been together. No more about it tonight.

One motivation for her enthusiasm was financial. Among her responsibilities was the balancing of household finances, which had reached a critical stage. How carefully even women of this class had to negotiate their authority can be seen in the position of financial dependency from which Molly makes her request: "Babies well. Everything pretty difficult. I must ask for some money at once. I made up my mind not to speak of it again until your act was finished. I will send you a statement of the expenses tomorrow & must beg you to read it. I think I have been *very careful*."[66] At this point, Molly—who was caring for the two-year-old twins and their four-year-old sister—was seven months pregnant with their fourth child.

Unlike Owen Wister—who could write only in the seclusion of his club, an eastern resort, or the West—Molly Wister threaded the many strands of her obligations—domestic oversight and finances, her children, her relatives, her neighbors, the city, her husband's writing, her Civic Club duties—through her daily life at home. Soon, she began also to publish under her own name. In 1907, she initiated, edited, and began to write extensively for the Civic Club

Bulletin which, according to another clubmate, Mrs. Imogen B. Oakley, had an international audience: it "carried the news of civic improvement to women's clubs all over the country, and even to China, Japan, and India."[67] Molly knew the value of public opinion as keenly as any frontier clubman and she used her pen as ardently to seize it. In 1908, she editorialized on "Public Opinion in Our Midst" and advocated for the regulation of "Cheap Amusements"—cheap theaters, moving-picture shows, and penny-arcades—as a sure route to shaping children and immigrants, "the formative and impressionable elements in our population."[68] In 1910, she published a long piece on the need for publicity: "a Press Committee should be constantly informing the public of what the Club has done and hopes to do, or what other clubs are doing elsewhere, as public opinion is the strongest power in American civilization."[69] James A. Butler suggests that these writings directly fed her husband's creative output: "Articles she wrote for the various annual reports of the civic club could be statements of the themes of *Romney*" (xlviii).

For all that Wister relied on women to stoke his artistic confidence and output and to negotiate the gap between club and public spheres, he also seems to have felt threatened by their facility. In numerous book dedications he enthusiastically acknowledged feedback from his clubmates, while he credited the contributions of these women only in the most minimal and coded of ways: one dedication is to "M.C.W.," another, to his mother and father, is to "S.B.W. and O.J.W." His highest praise for "the ladies" who attended Roosevelt's White House *salon*—Mrs. Roosevelt, Mrs. Lodge, Mrs. Chanler—was that "civilized and cultivated as they were," they "did not take the lead; it was the men who set the pace." The ladies "knew how to listen, as well as how to reply" (*Roosevelt* 128). Molly did not quite fit that model, with her predilection for taking the lead in what Mary Ryan calls "the practice of publicness" (199). Wister consistently tried to constrain Molly's public roles. In January 1898, she accepted an invitation to join Philadelphia's Board of Education as the youngest woman member ever. Soon after their marriage, four months later, her husband neatly ended her service by moving her out of the ward she represented. He tried to persuade her to give up her Civic Club work, even contemplating a move to New York City to force the point. Many of his letters to his mother fret about Molly continuing to speak in public and expose herself to lower-class types, but she never surrendered her public duties.

Women's Space in the Frontier Club Western

Owen Wister's fiction is also clearly imprinted with the ongoing negotiations between frontier club women and men. The ways in which the female presence in *The Virginian* disturbs the novel's surface resolutions have been read with considerable critical nuance over the years. Forrest Robinson, for example, has argued that the hero's deep ambivalence to marriage, a motif throughout the novel that surfaces during his honeymoon, dramatizes "key areas of tension in our national culture" (*Having* 52). William Handley analyzes Wister's need to feminize the implied reader in order for the novel to cohere on "both a polemical and an emotional level" (*Marriage* 69). Lee Clark Mitchell has argued that the Virginian's "rhetorical duels" with Molly contribute more to his "dramatic stature" than his physical duel with Trampas (98). The layer that I wish to add concerns the process with which that female presence came into existence. If we read his women characters in the order in which he created them (as opposed to the order and versions in which they were published), they tell the story of Wister's accommodations with the role of women in his social world. Two patterns emerge. First, it takes him half a dozen westerns before he can incorporate a positive image of a woman. Second, once he begins courting Molly Wister, he also begins to draw her into his writing. It may be a sign of Molly's influence and Wister's resentment that her namesake is at once protected in his fictional West and made to accede to patriarchal authority.

Piece by piece, as Wister moved from hunting tales to westerns, women become more prominent and take up more space—textual and physical. In his first, unfinished piece, "The Story of Chalkeye," which Wister annotated as "begun early in 1891," the lack of women is emphasized when the packer teases the lonesome rancher, "Yu' need a woman up here, Chalkeye...Yu'll be forgetting what girls look like hermitting this way" (40). Wister's first published story, "Hank's Woman," whose manuscript is dated December 1891, responds to his own challenge with Willomene, the woman of the title. Willomene, identified variously in the story as German, Swedish, and Dutch (and in the revised version of March 1900, as Austrian) is endowed, in Lin's description, with an animal physicality: "a big wide-faced woman, thick all through, any side yu' looked at her, and she was kind o'dumb-eyed, but fine appearin', with lots of yaller hair." Willomene shows the inevitably negative consequences of a woman entering the western wilderness. A maid suddenly dismissed from her lady's employ, she is stranded in Yellowstone Park, and just as hastily marries the prospector "little black Hank." The couple travel to the prospectors' camp, where their doom unfolds: Hank shoots the crucifix at which Willomene prays daily, she kills him with an axe, then, in attempting to throw his body into Little Death Cañon, plunges to her own death. Other than the framing of the tale—told by Lin McLean, "whom among all cow-punchers I love most," to the eastern tenderfoot narrator—the story is quite unlike Wister's subsequent work. Willomene carries forward the message of the hunting tales: that women (and non-WASP immigrants) do not belong in the wilderness. She also can be read as a direct refutation of the hunting woman: *pace* wide-ranging evidence in the sporting press (including *Outdoor Life, Forest and Stream, Field and Stream,* and *Outing*), this story shows woman to be inept on horseback, unsuited to roughing it, and a mortal threat to men. The fact that the framing tale occurs as part of a hunting narrative, as the two men pause to fish and swim together in boyish camaraderie, underlines the contrast.

In the two short stories that Wister wrote in 1892, "How Lin McLean Went East" (January) and "Balaam and Pedro" (March), women are peripheral. However, in the latter story there is a gratuitously unpleasant portrait of the rancher Balaam's "cold-featured civilized wife, of whom alone he was afraid," who is absent from the ranch, visiting her home in Middletown, Connecticut. For no particular reason of plot or action, we are told that Mrs. Balaam has an antipathy to cowpunchers, to whom she refuses hospitality and "from whom Mrs. Balaam, on a principle somewhat feudal for Wyoming Territory, kept herself totally aloof, even when they fell sick." Much attention has been paid to Balaam's brutal treatment of his horse—Theodore Roosevelt famously persuaded Wister to cut the graphic description of the maiming when he revised the story as a chapter in *The Virginian*—but there is no record of who persuaded him to cut Mrs. Balaam's portrait from the manuscript draft.

Wister's next short story, finished in May 1893 (around the same time as he was writing his first hunting tale for the Boone and Crockett Club), centers the female once more with a sideways species move. "Em'ly" is the story of a hen on "Judge Henny's home-ranche." Wister was developing the character who would become his signature hero, the Virginian, and Em'ly is the first bond between the cowboy and the eastern tenderfoot narrator as they fuss together over her eccentricities. Her oddness manifests itself mainly in her unconventional maternal behavior: what the Virginian calls the "manly-lookin'" hen tries to hatch potatoes, onions, and balls of soap, and adopts and abandons other animals' young, including a litter of red setter puppies. That this is "one of them plumb parables" (as the Virginian says) about civic-minded women is signaled early in the story when the narrator tells his companion that he has named the hen after "an old maid at home who's charitable and belongs to the Cruelty to Animals & she never knows whether she had better cross in front of a street-car or wait." Then he targets bluestocking women specifically, saying of Em'ly, "It was as if she went about this world perpetually scandalized over the doings that fell beneath her notice. Her legs were blue, long, and remarkably stout." The joke is pretty clearly on the traditional maternal qualities of any or all of the formidable women surrounding Wister: the spinster Agnes Irwin, the notoriously unmaternal and intensely intellectual Sarah Butler Wister, and the civic-minded Molly who, at this point, was his spinster-cousin. When the Virginian steps in to help the hen to become a mother, by putting another hen's egg beneath her, the result is traumatic: the egg hatches much too soon, Em'ly is traumatized, and the shock kills her. Yet another female goes down in the manly West.

At last, with "The Bear Creek Barbecue" and "The Winning of the Biscuit Shooter," Wister introduces his genteel eastern woman, who becomes the Virginian's wife in the novel. "The Bear Creek Barbecue" exists in several manuscript and typescript drafts under several titles. The first versions are dated May and June 1893, then Wister revised it as "Concerning Children" in November 1895; it was published in a different version again, as "Where Fancy Was Bred" in *Harper's New Monthly Magazine* of March 1896, then revised once more as a chapter in *The Virginian*. In the first draft of this story the Virginian first meets Miss Wood, "a young woman with delicate lungs from Vermont" who has come west as school-mistress.[70] The central action of the story is a dance at which the Virginian becomes one of a string of suitors whom Miss Wood rebuffs (she has refused nineteen approaches, including from Lin McLean and Judge Henny). Her power is more subtle than that of western women, demonstrated in a cameo of Mrs. Westfall, a rancher's wife, who climbs on a corral gate and harangues the cowboys to show their gratitude to their hosts when her husband takes stage fright: "'Well, friends, ladies and gentlemen,' began Mrs. Westfall, scrambling upon the gate, 'it's a good thing the men aint the only folks in Wyoming Territory'" (23). In revenge against women's high-handedness, the Virginian and Lin play a trick on the gathering by switching around the babies left in an anteroom while their mothers enjoy the dance, then the two cowboys ride off together in happy fellowship.

In "The Winning of the Biscuit Shooter," annotated "July 1st—8th World's Fair. 1893," the courtship between the Virginian and Miss Wood continues to develop to one side of the action that mainly revolves around Lin McLean's wooing of Katie Peck, a "biscuit-shooter" come from Dubuque, Iowa. The eastern narrator reappears in this story, and he makes the west-east contrast plain: "the newcomer was pronounced better company than the school-marm, Miss Wood, a native of Bennington, Vermont. This prim competent lady was fairer to my eastern eyes than the biscuit shooter from Dubuque."[71] Physically, Katie Peck's "brutal efflorescence" represents a return to the vulgarity of Willomene: "She had a broad face, a thick waist, black eyes, white teeth, a big mouth, and her cheeks were a lusty overbearing red. She was the ideal of a prairie woman whom nothing could dismay" (2). Miss Wood, on the other hand, we are told in "The Bear Creek Barbecue," "dressed with New England neatness, and was pretty with New England primness" (8). Both the Virginian and the author protect Miss Wood from too close contact with Katie Peck. Although both are staying in the Taylors' cabin, the Virginian persuades Miss Wood to repair outdoors when the language between Katie and Lin becomes too coarse for her ears and, during the trick "Crow attack," the schoolma'am remains discreetly out of sight—"Miss

Wood did not appear, but I thought I heard her mocking treble laughter coming from somewhere"—whereas Katie and Mrs. Taylor rush out in their nightgowns (15). The narrator is profoundly dubious of Lin's attraction to Katie—"'*Marry* her!' I sang out. 'Marry *her*?'"—and subsequent stories in this sequence prove his point. Katie turns out to be a bigamist who leads Lin a miserable existence until she kills herself with cyanide.

Wister's hierarchization of women in the West is emphatic. The eastern schoolma'am, who the narrator says is "a rare sort to meet in this country," is clearly positioned above and separately from the midwestern biscuit shooter as well as the western girls at the dance who (even more explicitly than Willomene) are animalistic presences. The lines of distinction draw on the same vocabulary as connects the cattle and publishing industries (as discussed in Chapter Two) and demeans "new" immigrants (see Chapter Five, this volume). The Virginian refers to Katie as "that Dubuque stock" dodging Lin's rope, and to his dance partners (compensatory choices after his rebuff from Miss Wood) as "heifers," a description reinforced by the narrative voice that says they follow the Virginian "like the obedient muttons that they were" (3, 22). Miss Wood's ultimate proof of superiority to Katie Peck is, of course, that she outlives the biscuit shooter.

In 1895, Owen Wister began to court his cousin Molly Wister, and he wrote his first portrait of her, "Where Charity Begins" (dated March 1895). This is not a western, but a sketch of the Evening Home for Boys in Philadelphia, where Molly volunteered and where, famously, she pulled off the unlikely performance of Gilbert and Sullivan's *Pinafore* with a group of heretofore sullen urchins. The essay is written with Wister as the first-person narrator accompanying "a young lady in a cloak" and watching her influence on the wayward boys: "To say it was astonishing is pale comment." Molly goes discreetly unnamed, but this is very clearly Wister's first homage in writing to the woman who would become his wife.

Eight months later, Wister drafted a revised version of "The Bear Creek Barbecue" (now titled "Concerning Children"), making several changes to his eastern heroine that changed her from a generic easterner to a version of his wife-to-be. The number of biographical echoes between Molly Wood and Molly Wister has often been discussed. What has gone unnoted is the fact that these echoes begin in a specific way only with this 1895 manuscript. For the first time, Miss Wood carries a first name, and it is Molly. Wister also makes her more nearly share his wife-to-be's upper-class status: she no longer comes west because of illness (which would not explain her need for employment as a schoolma'am), but because of financial pressures at home, a situation that would be elaborated in *The Virginian* as the economic collapse of this family of "gentlefolk" (93). For the first time, Molly Wood is given a distinguished lineage, and it echoes Molly Wister's: Mary Channing Wister was descended from William Ellery, signer of the Declaration of Independence, and William Ellery Channing, founder of the Unitarian faith in America and famous abolitionist; Mary Stark Wood's stock includes the Revolutionary hero General Stark and his heroic wife, after whom she is named and whose cameo accompanies her to the frontier. When Wister revised "The Winning of the Biscuit Shooter" in April 1897, the figure who is again named "Miss Molly Wood" is distanced even further, spatially, from Katie Peck. She now occupies her own cabin and, when the fake attack occurs, she appears, clothed as was the unnamed figure in "Where Charity Begins": "Molly Wood, come from her cabin, very pretty in a hood-&-cloak arrangement. She stood by the fence, laughing, but more at us than with us."[72]

Draft by draft and story by story, the more involved Owen Wister became with Molly Wister—they married in April 1898—the more closely he aligned the two Mollys. Both are independent minded, resourceful, and avid readers. Both are educators: both give music lessons; Molly Wister taught Sunday School and undertook educational reform through the Board of Education and the Civic Club, while Molly Wood takes on the position of schoolma'am in the West. They share physical characteristics—slim and athletic, with clear eyes, a steady gaze, and even the handsome nose over which Molly Wood frets. In the novel as it ultimately appeared, the cumulative effect of the revised pieces and the new bridging sections was, first, to divide women by class more stringently than ever, second, to undermine the authority of even the most respectable, and, third, to position Molly Wood-Wister squarely within both those maneuvers.

The Virginian hardens the line separating women of the lower orders, with their questionable morality, from respectable women of a superior class. On the one side stand figures newly introduced into the novel: a philandering road-house keeper who leaves her blond hair on the Virginian's chest and Cattle Kate who, hanged as a cattle rustler, becomes the butt of cowboy jokes. On the other are western women whom he moves upward in their class affiliation (refining their speech and domestic habits) to form a zone of protection around Molly Wood when she comes west. These characters now echo his network of eastern women: most prominently, Mrs. Henry, the judge's wife, ruling over her salon of eastern visitors and Mrs. Taylor dispensing quiet wisdom from the authority of her domestic security (while Mrs. Westfall fades into motherly discretion).

At the same time, the novel also mounts a sustained challenge to women's maternal authority. From the opening sequence, when the narrator hears the Virginian joshing Uncle Hughey about his marriage plans, through the encounter with Em'ly and the baby-swapping scene, to the verses about a woman's violence against her children that are buried in the Virginian's cowpuncher song, to the exposure of the small-minded respectability of Molly's mother and family back east, western manliness repeatedly wins the upper hand. [73]

In his development of Molly Wood in the novel, Wister continued his argument with his wife by other means. Especially in the chapters that he wrote under his wife's stern regime, in 1901 at their summer home in Saunderstown, Rhode Island, then in early 1902 in Charleston, South Carolina (while she sallied forth to her work at the exposition), he makes the fictional Molly surrender the real Molly's positions one by one. Whereas the fictional Molly begins with the same independence and reform-mindedness as her real-life model, these qualities develop in the opposite direction. Although Molly Wister never declared her position on suffrage for women, Wister must have had his suspicions. Her mother served as president of the Votes for Women League, and one of her close friends in the Civic Club had been jailed for her feminist activism. With Molly Wood, in *The Virginian*, Wister took the opportunity to trenchantly clarify her political stance: like her distinguished ancestor, she was not "a New Woman" (101). While the fictional Molly (like the real one and like Wister's mother) is initially against capital punishment, she becomes unable to defend her position in the face of apologias for western lynching by both Judge Henry and her cowboy lover, who argue that western circumstances demand such measures. For Molly Wood, work outside the home is a temporary response to a crisis whereas for Molly Wister combining work within and beyond the home was a chosen way of life. Whereas, on Molly and Owen's honeymoon in the West, she had upset him by visiting a school and publicly addressing parents and pupils—and, of course, continued to upset him by speaking publicly in Philadelphia—Molly Wood surrenders her western school teacher's position after marriage. The Virginian becomes a public figure of considerable wealth and importance, "able to give his wife all and more than she asked or desired" (503). The climactic riposte comes in the shootout, which Jane Tompkins has read as a blow against "maternal authority," specifically Wister rebelling against his mother (131). Molly Wood forbids the Virginian to engage in a duel with Trampas, on pain of calling off their wedding. He proceeds to kill Trampas, and Molly takes him back; "Thus did her New England conscience battle to the end, and, in the end, capitulate to love" (482).

The stage version of *The Virginian*, which is the bridge to the novel's cinematic influence, further diminishes Molly Wood's authority. When Wister decided to increase attention to the lynching of rustlers, he also multiplied the occasions on which Molly is proved wrong. In the novel, three chapters out of thirty-six address the lynching, and in a couple of key scenes Molly concedes to Judge Henry's and the Virginian's views on violence. In the play, rustling and its violent punishment provide the opening argument, the sustained dramatic structure, the suspense, and the climax. From the first scene onwards, Molly voices her objection to violence only to capitulate to male western mores with insistent repetition, as she is proved wrong by Judge Henry, the Virginian, the other ranchers, and the villains themselves.

The basic disagreement between Molly and Owen revolved around what is now known as "separate spheres" ideology. For him, family represented the limits of a woman's proper role, her private domain. For her, as for Progressive women more generally, family was the moral basis of a woman's claim to public influence; private and public spheres were intimately connected. The campaign literature that she developed to support the election of women to school boards called them "the natural educators of the race. They know the needs of children." A vote for a woman candidate will "bring home and school into closer relation."[74] Her central tactic for seizing public opinion used the home to influence the public sphere. She wrote: "Will not the mothers of growing children place the BULLETIN on their monthly reading lists, and read aloud such articles as they find interesting, giving their children opportunity for free discussion? Public spirit must proceed from the home."[75]

Frontier club women can be understood to have been engaged in a strategy of trade-offs and incremental gains. The sense that Molly was negotiating a space for herself in her husband's fictionalization of the West is reinforced when we look at how Wister's handling of family dynamics and women's position in western space changed over the years. From his early stories that fundamentally eschew women of the eastern establishment, he moved, first in the stories collected as *Lin McLean* and then in his novel *The Virginian*, to make space for them in ways that keep their class and race privileges intact. "Respectable" women enter the fictional West within a zone of protection; at the extreme ends of the social spectrum, the bigamist biscuit shooter who tricks Lin McLean into marriage is contrasted with Molly Wood who is chastely wooed by the Virginian. The distinctions among social levels are precisely the kind of detail on which we see Molly advising Owen in the dramatization of *The Virginian*. Although they are required to accede to violence, they are never directly threatened with it, and they rarely share space with women of doubtful morality.

At the same time, especially in *The Virginian*, the hero asserts male authority over shared space. He arranges separate letter-writing areas for Molly and himself in her cabin and sets up the tent between separate bathing pools on their honeymoon island: "This was his side of the island, he had told her last night; the other was hers, where he had made a place for her to bathe" (490). These scenes speak back to the Irwin sisters dividing up the tent at the outset of Wister's western adventures and to Molly Wister insisting on their honeymoon visit to the mountains. That spatial subordination is confirmed by Molly Wood's entrance into marriage, ending her independence.

Ten years later, Wister wrote a story titled "Where It Was" for a volume of interlinked western stories.[76] Wister and Brett envisaged this book—titled, tellingly enough, *Members of the Family*—as the successor to *The Virginian*.[77] The story revisits the scene of the Wisters' honeymoon in Washington's wild Methow

Valley. Miss Carey, another New England lady come west as schoolma'am (John L. Cobbs calls her "another incarnation of Molly Wood" [92]), gradually becomes attracted to Mr. Edmund, a gentleman store-keeper (based on Wister's Harvard friend-cum-western storekeeper George Waring, who had hosted the honeymooning couple). At one point, in search of teaching space, she and her pupils invade the hero's sitting-room, thereby disturbing his Ivy League sanctuary, "which he had so nicely fixed up with all his college things: mugs, flags, an oar, pictures of his friends, a whole heap of stuff" (255). Despite his initial dismay, Edmund adapts to the invasion, allowing this use of his room until a new schoolhouse is built, at which point the two marry, with no hint that the heroine will surrender her professional position. It's a nice recognition that, when women and men of the eastern establishment met in the wild West, both genders had to negotiate public space anew. Around the same time, Wister was planning his next western—provisionally titled "The Marriages of Scipio"—and requesting that *The Virginian* be reissued with the honeymoon scene on its cover.[78] The imprint of Molly's gentle pressure, her demonstration of the compatibility of public and domestic commitment—visible in private papers for years—was slowly but surely rising to the surface.

Ultimately, Molly's mark on the western remains a "what if?" question. Clearly, she was increasing her influence on her husband's fiction, perhaps he was beginning to share political space with women, and quite possibly she would have ended by writing her own book—her subject might even have been the West, given that she had begun to write of the region in the Civic Club Bulletin. In 1911, her editorial touched on her attachment: "I have been fortunate in seeing the West once more, and I am more than ever impressed with the deep hold which the civic awakening is taking upon our whole country."[79] In 1913, however, a complicated delivery—her sixth child in fourteen years—left Molly dead and the baby, named Sarah Butler Wister, brain damaged, disabled, and mute.

Wister made one more stab at over-writing his wife's identity as clubwoman when, almost immediately, a struggle began over the public image that would be her legacy. At her graveside, Wister said "that his wife had over-used her strength in the service of the people of Philadelphia" and he began a quiet campaign to mark her as a wife and mother *tout court* (F. Wister, *That* 221). Meanwhile, the Civic Club prepared a memorial bulletin in her honor, with encomiums from dignitaries within and beyond the club membership. A detectable fissure runs through the rhetoric, showing that Wister was not alone in his attitudes. Repeatedly, men edge towards praising her for her domestic accomplishments, while women insist on her public roles. The tension rises to the surface when a clubmate from Ohio quotes an editorial "in one of our leading periodicals" on the tragedy of Mrs. Wister's death: "the greater loss just because her service to the city was given as that of a mother of a family. It was because she wanted her children to grow up in a healthful, wholesome community that she felt that it was her duty to help bring about civic improvement there." Molly's Civic Clubmates leap in with a corrective footnote: "Mrs. Wister's philanthropic and civic activities began long before her marriage.—EDITORS."[80]

These memorial publications had a standard format that included a frontispiece of the honored woman. The bulletin in honor of Molly carries such a photograph: the frontispiece shows her dressed in a working suit, in the standard professional pose (Fig. 3.1). At Owen's insistence, however, the frontispiece, alone of the club's memorial pamphlets, carried a second photograph of her surrounded by her five children, all dressed in white. The accompanying caption also sounds as if it came from his pen: *"It is with the sanction and at the desire of her family that the second likeness of the late President of the Civic Club in this memorial number of the Bulletin should be published, in order to symbolize that duty and*

MARY CHANNING WISTER, 1897

Figure 3.1. Mary Channing Wister, 1897 (Civic Club Bulletin *In Memoriam* frontispiece, 1914)

Figure 3.2. Mrs. Owen Wister and Children, 1910 (Civic Club Bulletin *In Memoriam* frontispiece, 1914)

office of woman which always by her words and in her life she placed first and highest" (Fig. 3.2). Finally, if belatedly, Owen Wister managed to contain Molly within his family narrative—and history has done the rest.

Conclusion

A long line of critics—Leslie Fiedler probably remains the most famous—detect in western fiction a distinctively American ritual of male escape from domesticity. Heroes who "light out for the territory"—Rip Van Winkle, Leatherstocking, Huckleberry Finn and, of course, the Virginian—preserve rugged individualism and heroic manhood, freeing these quintessential national characteristics from women's meddling. Yet the women in the frontier club acceded to their husbands' western sojourns (some more happily than others), some accompanying their husbands west, and all enabling them to write up the results. The women shaped and sustained the men as best suited their own strategic purposes. In this sense, the frontier club western is as much a woman's as a man's story.

These women held different attitudes to the West. Margaret Chanler stayed well away after her one experience of frontier California, which she hated, but, as far as her husband went, she "wisely let him have scope to ramble now and then" (L. Thomas 109). Elizabeth Grinnell faithfully accompanied her husband on his field trips and mountain climbs, though she paid a price in chronic vertigo. Corinne, Anna, and Edith Roosevelt seemed to enjoy their trips west with Theodore. Sarah Wister considered the Far West too distant, too rough, and too risky for her son and positively demeaning for respectable women of their class. She excoriated Owen for taking Molly to the wilds of Washington State for their honeymoon: "the propriety of putting yr. bride of less than three months into a one-roomed cabin, I am as much disgusted as ever."[81] Molly loved the West and told her new mother-in-law so in no uncertain terms: "I believe I have never liked anything as much as this new experience" (F. Wister, *That* 145). On her insistence, the honeymooners went camping in the mountains before returning east via Yellowstone Park, and she and their children returned west with Wister several times.

What the women shared was an understanding of the men's need for the West as a boyish game. From Edith Roosevelt in the White House to Eva Remington in the far reaches of New York State, the wives indulged their husbands' regular absences with what Eva called "the boys" (quoted in Samuels, *Frederic* 398). In 1902, Mary Cadwalader Mitchell teased Owen Wister about *The Virginian*: "I am sure you wear your boots & spurs & big hat & put a tent pin in your pocket when you labour to write."[82] Margaret Chanler's analysis was the most uncompromising. She was an accomplished equestrian who took a serious interest in cattle ranching as she encountered it on the big Campagna farms of southern Italy. When Buffalo Bill's Wild West came to Rome in 1888, she took in its full irony: to her unerring eye, Little Annie Oakley was a middle-aged woman, Bill Cody a reeling drunk, and the "howling Indians" devout Catholics (like herself). She understood Theodore Roosevelt's western sojourn as an exit strategy from both personal tragedy and political complication: she said that he "escaped the dilemma by going West and playing cowboy on his ranch for those difficult 'mugwump' years" (*Roman* 194). She was not the only one to notice how quickly he found another wife on his return; his behavior confirmed her sense that both club life and the hunting trail were necessary interludes in men's larger, more mature lives with women. Of her own husband's hunting trip to Colorado in 1889, she observed: "I had not the heart to deny him the adventure" (*Roman* 230).

So we can return to, and trace more closely, the question of where the gain lay for women of the frontier club class. Why Molly Wister apparently aided and abetted her husband in redoubling the capitulation of her fictional alter ego to western men and foregrounding violence in his stage adaptation. Why she lent her efforts to increasing the effectiveness of his women characters without, apparently, trying to change the attitudes he ascribed to them. What—in addition to improved family finances—was in it for her. And why, indeed, all these powerful, spirited women—Agnes Irwin, Margaret Terry Chanler, Mary Cadwalader Mitchell, Edith Carow Roosevelt, Anna Cabot Mills Davis Lodge, among many other women readers (Sarah Butler Wister being the exception)— exhibited such enthusiasm for a fictional portrait that pushed their type to the sidelines and derided their beliefs. Jane Tompkins has argued eloquently that westerns of this period were a means by which men punished women authors for their success, "a reaction against a female-dominated tradition of popular culture" (132). That analysis is persuasive as part of the genre's dynamic, but it is not the end of the story. Reconstructing women's contributions to the dominant western formula makes it read less like the death-knell of female adventure and more like a harbinger of women's increased agency. What they got out of the deal was protected space for women in the western formula, in the hunting West, and in the public sphere more generally, their eastern, upper-class, white privileges intact.

Like the Civic Club members—like clubwomen generally in the period— these women were negotiating space for themselves in terms entirely consistent with their carefully balanced approach to public power. Such women wanted to retain their authority in the home and to preserve class boundaries; their good works were designed to manage the poor, not raise them to states of equal opportunity. The motto of the Civic Club, with which Molly identified so closely, communicates that balance: "to promote by education and active co-operation a higher public spirit and a better social order." So does the characterization of Agnes Irwin offered by Philadelphia essayist Agnes Repplier: "Philadelphia thought her liberal, Radcliffe labeled her as conservative, and both were right" (4).

The cost of this balancing act is explored more fully in Chapter Six, but it should be acknowledged here. We can hear its intimations in the voice of Elizabeth Grinnell. When she wrote about her trips to Montana with her husband many years after his death, she remembered none of the personal discomfort that sometimes amounted to trauma. The point on which she insisted, with an emphasis reminiscent of her husband's, was that "I was the first woman to look on those mountains & glaciers."[83] Given the Aboriginal settlement and hunting patterns in the area, she most certainly was not, but her sweeping removal of prior claimants to western space reminds us that those who were outside the frontier club bore the brunt of its privileges. In a different context, Sherene Razack has mounted a compelling, and devastating, critique of the costs of "savage" or "uncivilized" space—such as the frontier clubmen's West—historically and currently. Razack argues that a central attraction of these zones of boyish adventure is the opportunity they offer for men to enact violence with impunity—particularly sexualized violence against women of color and women in poverty who do not enjoy the respect and protection of the law. Intrinsic to this process is the collusion of white women, such as, in this case, the frontier club women who treated the West as a boy's game free of the rules of social life. In demarcating space for men, women were also protecting their own space from women of other classes and colors. White men's ability to enter, exploit, and leave that savage space, themselves unscathed, shores up white authority, male and female. In the frontier club documents, we see intimations of those power relations. In the tales of hunting and western adventure it is the availability of some women for violent representation that protects other women from its implications.

4

Jim Crow and the Western

"I find now upon sober examination that I distinctly left my heart with
San Antonio, not with anyone unless perhaps Jim Crow."
—Owen Wister, Journal February–March 1893

The frontier clubmen did not always agree—indeed, sometimes quarreled
among themselves—about the politics of post-Reconstruction America. They
had experienced different degrees of intimacy with African Americans—
Roosevelt, Wister, Grinnell, and Chanler were brought up by black servants;
Wister lived for a time in Philadelphia's Seventh Ward, a predominantly black
neighborhood, and campaigned (unsuccessfully) to represent it on the Select
Council. The clubmen held different visions of black political rights: as leading Republicans, Roosevelt and Lodge "were staunch defenders of Lincoln's
legacy toward black Americans," but Lodge is seen by some scholars as more
consistent in his "hardline policy" against southern slavery and disfranchise-
ment (Zimmermann 177; Seelye 3). Wister, on the other hand, disagreed
with Roosevelt's presidential gestures towards black advancement, criticizing
him to his face for inviting Booker T. Washington to the White House and
for appointing Dr. William Crum as the first black collector of the port of
Charleston.[1] At one end of the frontier club spectrum stood Madison Grant,
one of the prominent "hucksters of anti-Negro mythology," at the other his
good friend George Bird Grinnell, the most racially progressive of the group
(Dyer 92).

When it came to mythologizing the West, however, to a man they produced
segregationist stories—not so much arguing the case against African Americans
as pushing them to the margins of the western scene or out of the picture altogether. The only Boone and Crockett hunting tales to acknowledge black presences are those set outside the United States—and then only in subordinated
positions such as the Swahili gun-bearer on William Chanler's East African
hunting trip and the Natives who bodily transport William Lord Smith and his
companion hunter through the waves to the shores of Africa.[2] Even Grinnell

131

drew a clear color line around the hunting and ranching West in his fiction. In his first boys' book, *Jack, the Young Ranchman* (1899), the boy's departure from Manhattan is marked by a fond farewell by his black "Mammy," then he is solicitously helped off the train by the black Pullman porter, at which point he steps into a West overwhelmingly dominated by Anglo-Saxons, briefly touched by some transient American Indians.

Yet the West in which these clubmen spent time was not by any means empty of African American presence. After the Civil War, many formerly enslaved men and women went west to work in a wide range of occupations, including ranch hands, trail hands, and soldiers. According to John Ravage, there were "tens of thousands of African American men, women, and children in the West during the 'cattle kingdom' years from 1860 to1910."[3] Depending on which Far West State is most clearly in focus and whose scholarly figures you trust, as many as one in four cowboys and one in five soldiers in the West may have been African American.[4] In any case, if we gather together the statistics on ranchhands who were Mexican, Mexican-American, Indigenous, Jewish, East European, as well as African American, it seems clear that the Anglo-American cowboy heroized by the frontier club was in the minority.[5]

The process by which black Westerners were displaced by, and even on occasion transformed into, white heroes is largely undocumented—almost by definition, given the impulses towards Anglo-Saxon dominance and the suppression of racial difference motivating these western myth-makers.[6] There are, however, two partially archived stories of racial prestidigitation that left a deep mark on frontier clubmen's careers and their western mythologies: one concerns a private encounter of Wister's, the other a very public display by Roosevelt. Together, these two processes of suppression, transformation, and exclusion suggest how deeply the western formula was motivated and shaped by the blackness it denied. And there was a kicker to this story, when Frederic Remington, from the edges of the frontier club, insisted on making visible—partially, tentatively, but centrally visible—what the others refused to see.

Frontier clubmen's reduction of black figures was not, of course, the end of the story. Wister's intimate encounter with blackness in the ranching West occurred in the private domain, and concerned a figure who seems unrecoverable in the official record (although other black ranchhands of the period did make their voices heard in print, from Nat Love in his 1907 autobiography to the several thousand black cowboys and ex-cowboys interviewed by the Federal Writers' Project in the 1930s).[7] Roosevelt and Remington engaged with black military presences on the public stage, and ultimately these black soldiers refused to disappear. Tracing the subsequent emergence of those we might dub "the black Rough Riders," representationally and actually, exposes a world of popular culture very different from both frontier club productions and the cheap publishing industry. The celebration of black military valor was part of an extended effort to mount a black popular press in these years. The figure popularized by this press represented a black masculinity which, then and more recently, elbowed its way back into the western formula.

Wister: "white for a hundred years"[8]

About halfway through *The Virginian* appears the character who would haunt Wister for the rest of his career. He introduces himself to the Virginian with a flourish worthy of the best popular heroes: "Scipio le Moyne's my name. Yes, you're lookin' for my brass ear-rings. But there ain't no ear-rings on me. I've been white for a hundred years" (162). To the tenderfoot narrator, he confides: "The eldest of us always gets called Scipio. It's French. But us folks have been white for a hundred years" (158).

Although the eastern narrator is the newcomer who works hardest to become intimate with the Virginian, Scipio is the one who most immediately shares his code.[9] From the first meaningful glance, Scipio and the Virginian instinctively understand each other. Scipio explains the tactics of the Virginian's tall tale to the narrator—"this is the show-down. He's played for a show-down here"—and embraces the teller at its climax: "'Rise up, liars, and salute your king!' yelled Scipio. 'Oh, I'm in love with you!' And he threw his arms round the Virginian" (188, 200). The speed with which Scipio enters the cowboy fraternity makes the narrator—who has already expressed his own attraction to the Virginian several times—jealous. "I became dignified. Scipio had evidently been told things by the Virginian"; "I didn't pretend to understand the Virginian; after several years' knowledge of him he remained utterly beyond me. Scipio's experience was not yet three weeks long" (238, 208).

Unlike the other cowboys, however—and unlike Wister's whitewashed western scene generally—Scipio le Moyne carries the marks of African American identity. "Scipio" was a traditional slave name (well known in many quarters, it makes a literary appearance attached to enslaved figures in *Uncle Tom's Cabin*, *House of the Seven Gables*, and *Walden*). "Lemoyne" was one of the most common Creole surnames of the Mississippi Valley.[10] Hence the character's need to insist on the Anglo-Saxon whiteness that Wister and other popularizers of the period promoted as the normative condition in and beyond the United States.[11] How did Wister come to create such a paradoxical figure and what does he suggest about the modern western at its formative moment?

From 1885, when Wister began traveling west, his practice was to surround himself with eastern clubmates of his own, aristocratic class, who had come west as ranchers or hunters. The published version of Wister's western journals and some well-circulated photographs of him—such as on horseback in a deserted Wyoming scene, sporting whiskers, bandana, vest, and cowboy boots—suggest that he was a man alone among the elements on the western plains and in the mountains. In fact, the unpublished journals suggest that he was more often surrounded by eastern company—as in a photograph of the young Wister in the midst of a group of Cheyenne Clubmen (Fig. 4.1), lying unlabeled and misfiled in the Library of Congress archives. Among other effects, this Anglo-American enclave shielded Wister from seeing blacks in the West, even when they clearly provided the labor supporting white privilege and even when, as in this photograph, he stood virtually cheek-by-jowl with an African American man (presumably one of the club's servants). His unpublished journals contain the briefest acknowledgments of a "black porter" here, a "darkey soldier" there on his western travels, but he never develops cross-racial contact into recognition of others' individuality.[12] When Wister moved from private to public writing, his stories at first fleetingly notice some black presence: the ambiguously named "little black Hank" in "Hank's Woman," the black cook ("an old plantation mammy") and black soldiers ("our coal-black escort") in "Pilgrim on the Gila" (242, 259), glimpses of black infantrymen in the Shoshone Agency church in "Lin McLean." His famous novel clears the scene of any such presence, the acknowledgment of

Figure 4.1. Owen Wister at the Cheyenne Club. A young Owen Wister is dead center in the group of clubmen, next to the African American figure—presumably a club servant.

blackness in the West further reduced to the racist ditties, including one about a figure "By de name of Jim Crow," sung by the hero (215).

In February 1893, just after the Boone and Crockett dinner at the Metropolitan Club, however, Wister traveled to the ranching West for the first time by a southern route—from Philadelphia, through Virginia, Tennessee, Mississippi, and Louisiana to Texas. At once, the black presence enters his diary: in Mississippi, "We are in the full warm blaze of the south this morning. The air, the trees, the cotton fields, & the loafing darkeys all prove it."[13] He remained alert to the black presence throughout this trip, including in cowboy country. What remains unmentioned in his diary—although he later comments on the event in the preface to *Red Men and White*—is the massive spectacle lynching of the African American Henry Smith in Paris, Texas, two weeks before his trip began.

Wister's destination was the horse ranch of his Harvard and Philadelphia clubmate, Fitzhugh Savage, Seven Springs Ranch near Brownwood. Much of the account concerns the usual enclave of easterners, as former schoolmates and clubmates of Wister's converge on Savage's ranch. The men hunt, practice target shooting, play polo (during which Wister gets the serious sulks), drink whisky, sing cowpuncher ditties, and generally engage in boyish high jinks. Their conversation ranges from smutty stories to nostalgic reminiscences of their schoolboy magazine: "We talked over St. Paul's school and the days of the Horae Scholasticae . . . and kept the bottle going." One evening they recreate a Harvard dinner: "for a company of people of 30 and upwards, we conducted ourselves like the finest species of undergraduates, and it was most beautiful to see."

Unusually, however, Wister paid attention to Savage's cook and ranchhand, "a negroe weighing 280 pounds, named Homer" (Fig. 4.2), the first and only black figure to be individualized and humanized in Wister's western journals. Wister tells a lengthy story of Homer playing a Mexican card game Cun-can with his "hapless Mexican assistant" in the kitchen while the gentlemen play baccarat in the parlor. The Mexican tries to cheat by branding the deck with spots of wax and sticking cards together at significant discards:

> Homer was instantly aware of it, but said nothing; he simply got the Mexican very drunk and used the wax himself. So on Friday morning when he came with the water for our baths, Groome [another Philadelphia clubmate] & I noticed he looked particularly beaming. We inquired when he had gone to bed, and he said not at all. But that he had no assistant this morning. We were surprised, and Homer told us how the Mexican had become useless through whiskey this morning, and he had chased him off the premises—

Figure 4.2. Homer (as photographed by Owen Wister in 1893)

"how did the game come out, Homer?"

"I beat him, sir."

"How much?"

"Took all he had."

"What time did you quit?"

"Thirteen minutes of eight, sir. Just in time to get ready to cook breakfast." And Homer went roaring out of the room, leaving Groome and me roaring in our beds.

The tale is classic Wister and, notably, Homer speaks without the "darkey" dialect commonly used in the period to depersonalize black figures. Clearly, Wister was entranced, returning to mull over the tale: "I think this picture of Homer and his Mexican assistant...is on the whole a cameo of a pure & clean cut grain." Wister interviewed Homer to make sure that he had the details of Cun-can down. The interview ends with true cowboy laconicism: "Homer says that the Mexican had 188 dollars coming to him and was coming down here this week to play some more—'but he ain't turned up,' said Homer."

Homer continues to figure in the diary, accompanying the group as they travel from ranch to ranch. At one point, Wister photographed him during the round-up, in a set of images that further prove the author's close encounters with cowboys of color, including what appear to be several Mexican-American and African American figures.[14] The final glimpse comes as they ride back, via the town of Brady, to Savage's ranch:

> Homer, rich with wages, and extra pay, and tips, and Mexican spoils, came through Brady town and stopped at the saloon. He came away it is true, overtaking and passing us near home at a thundering speed with a vast grin and roars of hilarity, and for the rest of that day was in no condition of servitude whatever.

Homer here sounds most like a Frederic Remington cowboy, as in his famous "Coming through the Rye" sculpture, uproariously galloping along, pistols aloft, after a night out on the town.

If this trip brought Wister, at least temporarily, alive to the presence of the black Westerner, it also took him to the epicenter of segregation. His route took him through New Orleans where, eight months earlier, Homer Plessy, a light skinned Creole man, had challenged Louisiana Jim Crow laws by sitting in the white section of an intra-state train and whose fight was currently going through the Louisiana courts. The debate about the legalization of Jim Crow was raging; the *Plessy* case would end up, in 1896, at the Supreme Court (as *Plessy v. Ferguson*), whose majority decision legalized the "separate but equal" fiction. The issue was also very much alive in Texas, where railroad segregation had been legalized, challenged, then reinstated. At Fort Worth, Wister noted: "The railroads present a new feature: each car is marked either 'For Whites' or 'For Negroes.'"

As he returned east through Texas, Wister stopped overnight in San Antonio where he selected from a row of hack drivers "an ancient darkey...he told me his name was Jim Crow." Wister hired him for the day, to show him the city sights. The tour made a profound impact on Wister. His 1893 diary ends: "I find now upon sober examination that I distinctly left my heart with San Antonio, not with anyone unless perhaps Jim Crow."

In these places and encounters, I speculate, lie the makings of Scipio le Moyne, the character who becomes sidekick to the eponymous hero in *The Virginian*. The connection can only be speculative because, contrary to Wister's usual practice, there is no record of this character's name or origins in his extant diaries or authorial notes. But the similarities are striking. Both Scipio and Homer bear traditionally black American names, both are cooks as well as ranch hands, and both are tricksters. The tale of Homer duping the Mexican carries the same logic and wit as Scipio turning the tables on innumerable low-lifers and scoundrels: the shell-game shyster whom Scipio robs of his illicit takings in "Extra Dry" (1909); or the hobo in "The Vicious Circle" (1902) who, having robbed Scipio, is tricked into riding back into his arms: "Pie like mother made," Scipio confronts him smilingly.[15] Although Scipio says that he comes from Gallipolice, Ohio, his Creole surname, le Moyne, points to New Orleans where, in Spring 1893, Wister noted, "I walked about Canal Street and noticed the names . . . and today saw the French type of face everywhere."

That Texas trip was the source of several stories—many "spinnings from the same raw material" as Wister put it—that he relocated to Wyoming and later gathered into *The Virginian*.[16] In Texas, he heard of the hen who became Em'ly in the story he wrote up immediately on his return.[17] During one of the elaborate clubmen's dinners, he also heard "'My Looloo,' a cowpuncher's ditty, whose tune was very taking, but the words of which will scarcely bear transcribing" and which the Virginian sings at the opening of "The Bear Creek Barbecue" as first written in May 1893. At another dinner, he heard of the baby-swapping trick that became a key scene in the same story. A further connection between this story and the Texas trip comes when Ben Swinton, the rancher hosting the barbecue, compares his efforts to those in the region that Wister had just visited: "Down in San Saba County, Texas, where we were raised, they did a Barbecue right."

A cluster of details within and beyond "The Bear Creek Barbecue" connects Wister's Texas sojourn with gestures to black cowboys and the introduction of the name Scipio. Miss Wood, who first appears in "Bear Creek," was a product of the Texas trip. Wister later explained that he "found a wife" for the Virginian "in Texas—not any actual school marm; but the type who taught in these schools was apt to be a cut above the mothers of the children she instructed. I decided that when the time came, my Southerner should wed a New England school marm."[18] When Miss Wood first spies the Virginian, she asks her dancing partner, Mr. Taylor, about him, in an exchange that survives in truncated form in the novel. In the first version of the short story, Miss Wood says that she has noticed

> "a man I'm not acquainted with—that black one."
> "He aint black!" exclaimed the literal Mr. Taylor in mirth. "He'd not thank anybody much fer calling him black, I guess. He was raised in Virginia."

This story also contains a character Scip Neil, who never reappears, and whose name could be a conflation of Scipio and Jim Neil, who told Wister the baby-swapping story. The full-blown character Scipio first appears in the short story "The Game and the Nation," dated March 1899. He introduces himself to the eastern narrator in the Black Hills stagecoach on the way to Medora, Dakota (Roosevelt country) with the boast Wister repeats in the novel, that he has been "white for a hundred years." The germ of "The Game and the Nation"—the restaurant rivalry that Wister built into the Virginian's "frog ranch" tall tale in the novel—again was a story he heard on the 1893 Texas trip.

Another link between Scipio and the Texas trip lies in Wister's essay about his experience with polo ponies on Savage's ranch, which he wrote up for Caspar Whitney's magazine *Outing* (published in 1900). In this piece appears the caption "Between the Acts," which is also the title of the chapter in *The Virginian* in which Scipio is introduced. Finally, when he revised "Hank's Woman" in 1900, he had the Virginian connect blackness and Texas once more, saying to the narrator, "Do yu' remember little black Hank? From Texas he claims he is."[19] Cumulatively, these pieces of evidence suggest that the Texas trip on which Wister met Homer gave birth to Scipio.

Even accepting this argument—that Wister whitens a charismatic black man in order to smuggle him into an early story and, ultimately, his bestselling novel, thus in a coded way both drawing on and suppressing western blackness—why draw attention to this maneuver by making Scipio address his racial composition in such loud and insistent terms? One answer derives from the popularity of passing narratives in the period. In the late nineteenth and early twentieth centuries, just as Jim Crow was hardening, stories of those who fooled the color line and undermined its authority proliferated—Frances Ellen Watkins Harper's *Iola Leroy* (1892), Charles Chesnutt's *House Behind the Cedars* (1900), Pauline Hopkins's *Contending Forces* (1900) among them. The phenomenon of passing had breached the very defenses of the clubmen's world: in 1897, Vassar College discovered that it had unknowingly graduated a "colored girl," and the tale was broadcast by the *New York Times*, among other newspapers. The tale was further, and most gleefully, popularized by the breakthrough black musical *In Dahomey*, which hit Broadway in 1902, the same year as *The Virginian* was published. *In Dahomey*'s unruly cast of pan-African characters take back white appropriations of their blackness—co-producer Bert Williams, for example, blacked up his black skin in ridicule of white minstrelsy—and the character Rosetta Lightfoot, played by Ada Overton Walker, celebrated the triumphs of "the Vassar girl."[20] In 1903, when *The Virginian* was dramatized, both plays were on the circuit. A comparison of two scenes from each performance evokes some of their competing vision (Fig. 4.3 and 4.4). The contrast lies not only in the stage presence of all-black and all-white casts but in the way that black figures take over the space of the upper-class drawing room as well as the more demotic street, challenging assumptions of white privilege on several levels. That *In Dahomey* enjoyed considerably more transatlantic popularity than the theatrical version of *The Virginian* is another indication of the power, and threat, of African American cultural production.

Scipio's story speaks back to those unruly narratives of passing, reinstating the reliability and authority of visible whiteness. His name may suggest blackness, but his visible whiteness is authentic—he's been white for a hundred years. The Virginian authorizes Scipio's claim the first time they meet, assuring him: "you're certainly white" (162). Sustaining the western enclave of whiteness

TWO SCENES FROM "IN DAHOMEY,"
THE NEW NEGRO MUSICAL COMEDY AT THE SHAFTESBURY.

A SONG AND DANCE "BROADWAY IN DAHOMEY."

AN ANXIOUS MOMENT FOR THE CZAR OF DIXIE (MR. GEORGE WALKER).
Photographs by Hall, New York.

Figure 4.3. Scenes from *In Dahomey*, Shaftesbury Theatre, in *The Sketch* (May 1903)

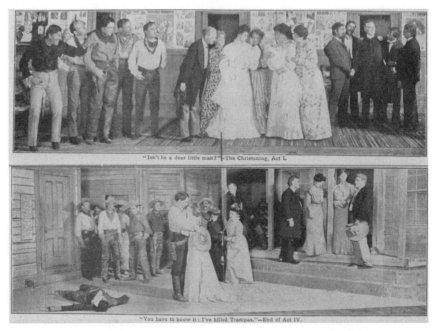

"Isn't he a dear little man?"—The Christening, Act I.

"You have to know it: I've killed Trampas."—End of Act IV.

Figure 4.4. Scenes from the Stage Version of *The Virginian* with Dustin Farnum, in Souvenir Leaflet (c. 1903)

involved not only expunging other racial claims but elbowing out competing popular forms. It is a small but telling moment in the making of the modern western, in the racialized struggle to control the new tools of mass culture, and in the broader, hegemonic establishment of normative whiteness in and beyond the United States.

For the rest of his writing life, Wister was haunted by Scipio-slash-Homer, an absent presence that remained central to his vision of the western. After the success of *The Virginian*, both Wister and George Brett, his editor at Macmillan, turned to Scipio as their next bestselling western hero. Wister planned two novels around him. The first was to be titled *Members of the Family*—in Brett's words "a novel of the type and character of 'The Virginian'"—and the second, in Wister's description, "the sequel—to be probably entitled *The Marriages of Scipio*—will present the roving man of 1878–1895, surviving into the new state of Western things, and not able to adjust himself to them. I grieve to tell you it will be very tragic."[21] Author and editor excitedly puffed Scipio to each other: Brett called him "a personage in whom the public will, I think, delight"; Wister claimed that "I have 'established' Scipio as a popular favorite, &…the whole novel I have planned about him is likely to meet a success if I can write it as I see it."[22]

In the event, and despite constant encouragement and at times daily reminders from Brett, Wister could not write it as he saw it. The attempt turned into a struggle lasting a dozen or more years, as Wister fretted at the challenge through the distractions of competing projects and the periods of pain and depression, including an entire year in which he was bed-ridden with what Brett assumed was neurasthenia, or "nervous troubles," which he himself suffered from and which was, of course, the very condition that had sent Wister west in the first place.[23] Ultimately, author and editor cobbled together some old and new stories featuring Scipio as protagonist or narrator, issued under the title *Members of the Family* and Wister renewed his promises to create, in *The Marriages of Scipio*, a magnum opus, a new, blockbuster western for a new age. As late as 1919, Wister still had Scipio on his mind—hoping for a motion picture of him—but the novel never came to fruition. If you accept my claims about Scipio's racial roots, then the big book touched the biggest racial taboo—miscegenation. Wister couldn't do it, and he never wrote about the West again.

Finally, this is a story of multiple suppressions. When Wister's daughter published his western journals in 1958, she reduced Homer from a character to a single phrase and she expunged most of the brief mentions of African Americans in the West. Meanwhile, Wister's 1893 photographs of Homer lay hidden and undeveloped in his desk. Their survival in that form offers both an apt trope and a true indication of what was valued, and what was acknowledged, in Wister's oeuvre. Until their recent discovery and processing, they existed as nitrate negatives preserving a reversed image—a white Scipio indeed, white for over a hundred years.

Roosevelt's Rough Riders

During the years in which Wister struggled with a private and deeply buried act of whiteface, Roosevelt was engaged in a very public displacement of
blackness, on a much larger—indeed, national and international—scale. His
staging ground was the Spanish-American War, a key moment in the development of U.S. imperialism and the popular western.[24] The war's iconic figure
was Roosevelt's Rough Rider—the Anglo-Saxon gentleman cowboy *par excellence*—who yoked frontier heroism to overseas militarism, in the process justifying American extra-continental expansionism and extending the ideological
reach of the western.[25] The African American military presence in Cuba—and,
subsequently, Puerto Rico and the Philippines—threatened that figure by challenging white superiority on the western frontier and the imperial battlefield. By
tracing how Roosevelt expunged black soldiers *en masse* from a central myth of
American heroism, we can appreciate, again, how deeply the engagement with
blackness was driven into the western's creative fabric.

The Black Rough Riders

African Americans joined the U.S. military in sizeable numbers during the Civil
War. In 1866, Congress created six segregated regiments that were subsequently
reorganized into four units—the 9th and 10th Cavalries and the 24th and 25th
Infantries—constituting around 10 percent of the U.S. army.[26] The "black regiments" were assigned almost exclusively to the West. Despite the harshness of
frontier conditions, military service was often the best option for previously
enslaved men, offering a level of sustenance and dignity not available elsewhere
in American society. The black units acquitted themselves with distinction, winning the title "Buffalo Soldiers" from Cheyenne warriors as testament to their
distinctive physical features and their tremendous strength and endurance.

When America declared war on Spain, the four black regiments were among
the first sent to Cuba.[27] The War Department subsequently authorized additional black volunteer units—known as the "immune regiments" for their supposed resistance to tropical diseases—that saw limited action.[28] The 9th and 10th
Cavalries (Fig. 4.5) fought in General Joseph Wheeler's (dismounted, as it turned
out) cavalry division, alongside several regular white cavalry regiments and the
First United States Volunteer Cavalry—the regiment effectively assembled, led,
and publicized by Theodore Roosevelt, by now a rising political star, and popularly
known as Roosevelt's Rough Riders. Recent decades have seen steadily increasing interest in and scholarship on the Buffalo Soldiers in the American West; that
work makes it possible, now, to consider the impact of their overseas service on
the shaping of U.S. popular print culture at this crucial juncture.[29]

Figure 4.5. 9th Regt. U.S. Cavalry, Camp Wikoff, Montauk Point, Long Island, N.Y., September 1898 (on return from fighting in Cuba)

Black opinion about military involvement varied greatly. Pro-war advocates argued that blacks' participation would reverse increasingly oppressive segregation and white terrorism in the South. The 1880s and 1890s saw an explosion of lynching; in the same year as the Spanish-American War, African American civil rights crusader Ida B. Wells accused the United States of being "a nation of lynchers" (quoted in Gleijeses 186). Some black spokespeople argued that visible demonstrations of black loyalty and national service could only improve their status at home and their opportunities abroad.

Black anti-imperialists argued that "a Jim Crow War" would result in "a Jim Crow empire," rendering populations of color in and beyond the United States more oppressed than ever. They pointed to the war department's continued refusal to commission black officers and, as black troops were transported from the West to the South for embarkation to Cuba, the violent displays of racism by whites unnerved by the presence of armed black men. Far from nurturing cross-racial solidarity, this war brought white Northerners and Southerners into new alignment, healing their Civil War wounds. Black opposition to the war became more widespread in 1899, when America refused independence to the Filipinos who had worked with them to drive the Spanish out of the Philippines. Many blacks sympathized with the Filipino nationalists, especially as they witnessed white American soldiers subjecting the Indigenous people to the extreme violence and racist epithets so familiar at home. At least twenty American soldiers, of various races, defected to the Insurrectos, the most famous being the African American "General" David Fagan who deserted the 24th Infantry in the face of white officers' racism.

Given the violent oppression of black people in post-Reconstruction America and the tense public debates about black involvement in a white man's war, a great deal was riding on the performance of black soldiers in Cuba. The black press, unable to fund professional war correspondents, solicited eyewitness accounts by soldiers on the front. The richer white press also paid attention to black soldiers, mainly because they fought alongside Roosevelt's Rough Riders, the campaign's most famous regiment, which was heralded as carrying America's frontier spirit onto the world stage. It brought together members of the eastern establishment with cowboys, hunters and a segregated troop of American Indians; Roosevelt said, "there are a number of Knickerbocker and Somerset club"—he could have added, and the Boone and Crockett Club—"as well as Harvard and Yale men going as troopers, to be exactly on a level with the cowboys."[30] Some accounts suggested that the African American troops spent considerable time saving these gentlemen volunteers from their own foolhardiness. All agreed that regulars and volunteers, across racial divides, intermingled in battle; there was no chance of sustaining "anything like distinct regimental segregation."[31]

Initially, Roosevelt seized this cross-racial action as the ground of his own political and ideological image-making in the war's aftermath. At "a mass meeting favorable to his candidacy for governor of New York," in New York City, October 14, 1898, he described the assault on San Juan Heights, the climactic action in Cuba, thus:

> We [Rough Riders] struck the Ninth Cavalry and in the first charge, on what we called Kettle Hill, they and we went up absolutely intermingled, so that no one could tell whether it was the Rough Riders or the men of the Ninth who came forward with the greater courage to offer their lives in the service of their country.... That night we took spades and worked at the trenches shoulder to shoulder, white and colored men together...I don't think that any Rough Rider will ever forget the tie that binds us to the Ninth and Tenth Cavalry.... It wasn't because the colored troopers were colored that we admired them...it was because they were brave men, worthy of respect.
>
> And now, in civil life, it should be the same. (Quoted in Washington, Wood, and Williams 51–52)

Black cavalrymen echoed this cross-racial intermingling of identities, declaring: "It's all in the family. We class ourselves *The Colored Rough Riders!*" (quoted in Philips 59).

Six months later, Roosevelt executed a *volte-face* in the middle-class *Scribner's Magazine* which serialized his military memoirs of Cuba. In the April 1899 installment, he reflected on black soldiers: "they are, of course, peculiarly dependent upon their white officers" ("Cavalry" 435). His account of San Juan Hill changed notably:

> None of the white regulars or Rough Riders showed the slightest sign of weakening; but under the strain the colored infantrymen (who had none of their officers) began to get a little uneasy and to drift to the rear.... This I could not allow, as it was depleting my line, so I jumped up, and, walking a few yards to the rear, drew my revolver, halted the retreating soldiers, and called out to them that I appreciated the gallantry with which they had fought and would be sorry to hurt them, but that I should shoot the first man who, on any pretense whatever, went to the rear.... This ended the trouble. (436)

Roosevelt had realized the perils of welcoming black Americans into what Richard Slotkin calls the "mythic space" of the frontier ("Wild West" 34). His first account of battle not only acknowledged black manhood; it had the potential to reverse the post-Reconstruction caste system by proving that blacks could take leadership and equal white valor. By early 1899, Filipino nationalists were playing precisely on this potential. They distributed posters to "The Colored American Soldier," inciting him to join forces with rebel leader Aguinaldo, assert his black manhood, and avenge the blood of Sam Hose, lynched in Georgia. It was crucial that Roosevelt re-segregate black soldiers, relegating them to servile dependency on white authority. He increasingly whitened the Rough Rider image to that end.

Black anger at Roosevelt's reversal simmered for many years. Willard Gatewood characterizes the depth of black hostility to Roosevelt "principally because of his 'slur' upon the performance of Negro troops in Cuba" during the presidential campaign of 1900; "The mere mention of Roosevelt's name brought forth loud protests and hisses at several major gatherings of Negroes in 1900" (Gatewood, "Black" 562). Although black commentators continued to insist on the undying fame of black cavalrymen overseas, those who classed themselves "The Colored Rough Riders"—I here name them the black Rough Riders— faded from mainstream view. Where did they go?

Whitening the Rough Rider

One answer to that question is: deep into the breeding ground of white myth-making. The Spanish-American War was accompanied by—indeed,

Kristin Hoganson has argued it was provoked by—an intensified gendering of political culture that benefited white elite men.[32] Frontier clubmen made a central contribution to that larger discourse with war rhetoric that drew on the same myths of manhood—the same tropes of hunting, sport, whiteness, and youthfulness—as their other writings.

Several members of the frontier club made their voices heard in support of the Spanish-American War; even Grinnell, the least bellicose of the frontier clubmen, briefly proposed to head up a regiment of American Indians to fight in Cuba.[33] Henry Cabot Lodge, chief architect of "the Large Policy" of U.S. expansionism, and generally acknowledged as one of "the fathers of modern American imperialism," extolled his Harvard classmates for their victories on the playing-field that proved the well-spring of "the English-speaking race" as "world-conquerors."[34] He closely followed the press coverage of Roosevelt's adventures in Cuba, clipping the daily newspaper stories.[35] Winthrop Chanler took a small band of irregulars to Cuba—a mixture of patricians and ex-cavalrymen who had been performing in Buffalo Bill's Wild West. He sustained a steady correspondence with Lodge and Roosevelt throughout the war and wrote with boyish enthusiasm from the jumping-off point in Tampa to his long-suffering wife in Rome, "We shall have a bully time with flies & bugs & rain & the war will soon be over," and, once embarked, "Altogether it is lots of fun" (quoted in L. Thomas 252, 254). Caspar Whitney, reporting from the battlefield for *Harper's New Monthly Magazine*, marshaled his stalking and sporting tropes, marginalizing the black troops in his account and heroizing the Rough Riders "in which the man who had hunted big game, who was fond of out-of-door sport, the college athlete, the cow-puncher, and the miner predominated" ("Santiago" 818). There were many clubmen in Cuba fashioning myths of Anglo-Saxon superiority on the battlefield: Richard Harding Davis was Roosevelt's virtual publicist, Stephen Bonsal initially teamed up with Remington to write for the eastern press, and of course the upper-class members of the Rough Rider unit gave their own stories in private correspondence and public interviews. In print as in battle, Roosevelt led the charge. The war was, for him, an extension of his hunting trips: he declared that he was off to hunt "the most dangerous game," man (quoted in E. Thomas 300). On his return, he hung his sword and hat from Cuba over the elk antlers in Sagamore Hill's trophy room.[36] And he most systematically and tenaciously converted the cross-racial scene of combat into an exclusive enclave of white heroism.

Amy Kaplan has explored how Roosevelt's account of storming San Juan Hill implicitly engaged with "black counternarratives" that disputed his version of that action, specifically, and his vision of African American manhood more generally (231). If we tilt Kaplan's analytical lens, to identify stories of black military action as original narratives and war stories circulated by the mainstream press as "white counternarratives," two gains result. First, black rhetorical strategies are given fuller play than if we read them only as rebuttals. Second, we can see how African Americans functioned as the motivating absence in white myth-making, the presence that white counternarratives attempted to appropriate and to expunge from the scene. This operation is part of the larger Africanism identi-fied by Toni Morrison: an "Africanism, deployed as rawness and savagery, that provided the staging ground and arena for the elaboration of the quintessen-tial American identity" (44). Of particular interest here is how such Africanism motivated and shaped the popular western just as the genre was welding national to imperial rhetoric through the figure of war.

If we amalgamate black press accounts, the highlights of the narrative go something as follows. As the American forces advanced towards Santiago, the 10th Cavalry first reversed a Rough Rider retreat, then saved the inexperienced regiment from ambush at Las Guásimas. At El Caney—dubbed Hell Caney for its fierce fighting—black infantrymen led the assault on the Spanish blockhouse, Private Butler of the 25th Infantry seizing the Spanish flag. A black sergeant shouted the decisive charge on San Juan Heights, where 24th Infantrymen and 9th and 10th Cavalrymen took the van, the last two units intermingling with Rough Riders. Sergeant George Berry of the 10th Cavalry planted the colors of his own regiment and the 3rd Cavalry on San Juan Hill. The black press lavished attention on several individuals: six blacks who won the medal of honor; and both Private Horace Bivens (who survived) and Corporal Brown (who did not) for their handling of Hotchkiss guns.[37] Commentators credited black soldiers' frontier experience for teaching them to counter Spanish and, later, Filipino gue-rillas in challenging terrain. For anyone in search of an American hero combin-ing western and military heroism, here was an obvious candidate.

This was the narrative that Roosevelt had to counter. In 1899, Scribner's pub-lished *The Rough Riders* in book form, lightly revised from the *Scribner's Magazine* serial. Critics have analyzed the book's cultural work as a campaign document promoting Roosevelt's political ambitions and as "a microcosm of the progres-sive order" (Slotkin, *Gunfighter* 102). A related challenge was racial. In convert-ing the Cuban battlefield into a space of new imperialism, Roosevelt had both to deny and to draw on African American power. In his writing, he practiced the systematic, rhetorical exclusion that runs through all frontier club productions, from their Boone and Crockett hunting tales, to Wister's fictions of gentlemen cowboys, to the anti-immigration bills promoted by Lodge in Congress.

In *The Rough Riders*, Roosevelt excludes blacks first from the American West, then from the heroic action in Cuba. The frontier from which his Rough Riders draw their virile heroism has only two types, the dominant Anglos and the van-ishing Indians, as in the illustration of two horseback riders, under the caption "East and West": "Captain Woodbury Kane, Promoted for Gallantry in the Fight of July 1st" set against "William Pollock, Pawnee Indian." There are no black cowboys, soldiers, settlers, or even badmen, an astonishing omission, given the visibility of black westerners suggested by the statistics cited at the opening of this chapter and even by Wister's photographs of Texas ranching. Roosevelt's account of Cuba acknowledges the four black regiments, but the most visible African American soldiers are those who behave poorly—as, for example, his story of the cowardly black soldiers, repeated from magazine to book version in the face of participants' protests. The entire power of the 9th Cavalry is diminished in one subordinate, "my colored body-servant, Marshall, the most faithful and loyal of men, himself an old soldier of the Ninth Cavalry" (60); soon, "Faithful Marshall . . . was so sick as to be nearly helpless" (219).

The pressure of that black absence—and of the alternative narratives that Roosevelt cannot admit—makes itself felt on his narration of specific battles. The fight at Las Guásimas was one of the most publicly disputed, with the black press showcasing 10th Cavalrymen's accounts of saving Roosevelt's Rough Riders from a Spanish ambush, into which their inexperience and foolhardiness had led them. Some accounts claimed that the volunteer cavalrymen shot each other by mistake. To seize control of this war narrative, Roosevelt begins it in his most comfortable location: one of the most exclusive gentlemen's clubs. He introduces Brigadier-General Young, the commander at Las Guásimas, as an old acquaintance, first encountered when Roosevelt was president of the Boone and Crockett Club, the linchpin of the frontier club network: "while he was in Washington, he had lunched with me at the Metropolitan Club" (73). This opening enables him to give the battle over entirely to the officer (which is to say the white) class. The engagement becomes "General Young's fight," and the only named participants are commissioned officers and his own non-commissioned Rough Riders (73). It was particularly important to erase black gunners, who, conjoining military heroism and modernity, threatened Anglo-Saxon stereotypes of savage Africanism. The effort to avoid acknowledging who manned the Hotchkiss mountain guns gives rise to awkward circumlocutions: "Young began the fight with his Hotchkiss guns" which, unlike the Spanish armament, shoot themselves: "No sooner had the Hotchkiss one-pounders opened than the Spaniards opened fire in return" (83). More avoidance of black agency accounts for the passive construction with which Roosevelt reports the action at Kettle Hill: "The light battery of Hotchkiss one-pounders, under Lieutenant J. B. Hughes, of the Tenth Cavalry, was handled with conspicuous gallantry" (143).

Roosevelt's key narrative strategy draws on the youthful, naïve perspective so familiar from his and his clubmates' hunting tales. It allows him to represent his men's behavior (which some called foolhardy) as boyish courage and to be so new to battle that he does not know (and therefore does not need to acknowledge) who else is involved. He describes the engagement as exclusively fought by his Rough Riders, with shadowy unraced presences coming and going at the edge of the action. At one point, he says, "I was still very much in the dark as to where the main body of the Spanish forces were, or exactly what lines the battle was following, and was very uncertain what I ought to do; but I knew it could not be wrong to go forward ..." (94); and later, "It is astonishing what a limited area of vision and experience one has in the hurly-burly of a battle" (139). When he finally acknowledges that some newspaper correspondents had reported "with minute inaccuracy, how we had run into an ambush, etc.," that final abbreviation is as close as he can come to naming the possibility that Rough Riders had been saved by black soldiers (108). Boyishness became a very familiar trope of frontier adventure and of America's move into extra-continental expansion, distinguishing American youthful imperialism from Old World, corrupt imperialism. Here the boyish stance, joined with frontier club exclusions, also serves a clear racial purpose.

Rough Rider iconography increasingly attached to whiteness, particularly to Roosevelt in the political sphere. Cartoonists regularly portrayed him in Rough Rider costume, attacking political foes and enemies of the nation. *The Verdict* lampooned his reformist zeal as governor of New York State, for example, with a cartoon of him as wild-eyed Rough Rider, holding the reins of his bucking bronco between his teeth while emptying his six-guns at straw figures labeled "Anarchy" and "Treason" ("Teddy to the Rescue of Republicanism!" October 30, 1899). The next year, when Roosevelt was being courted as William McKinley's running mate, *Puck* showed Rough Rider "Teddy" coyly resisting being drawn into "Vice-Presidential Waters" by four lily-white maidens who represent the four quarters of the nation ("The Struggle for Life," May 16, 1900; Fig. 4.6). When he entered the vice-presidential and presidential races, his campaign paraphernalia—bandanas, pins, leaflets—flaunted his Rough Rider image. The dependence of white political capital on black culture again emerges: his theme tune, "There'll Be a Hot Time in the Old Town Tonight," was a minstrel song heavily associated with the 10th Cavalry in Cuba—yet another debt that remained unacknowledged.[38]

Once Roosevelt entered the White House, the dime publishers Street & Smith took up the Rough Rider image, capitalizing on its central quality of youthfulness and suggesting, again, how closely intertwined were the so-called "quality" and cheap publishing industries. In 1904, as Roosevelt began his second presidential term, they launched a juvenile nickel series titled *Young Rough Riders Weekly* (later, *Rough Rider Weekly*) to compete in the growing market for children's westerns. Ann Laura Stoler has incisively argued "that matters of the intimate are critical sites for the consolidation of colonial power, that management of those domains provides a strong pulse on how relations of empire are exercised" (4). As popular literature marketed to children, *Young Rough Riders Weekly* carried Roosevelt's logic and vision into the intimate spaces of youthful education and desire.[39]

Figure 4.6. Louis Dalrymple, "The Struggle for Life," *Puck* (May 16, 1900)

The first number, *Ted Strong's Rough Riders; or, The Boys of Black Mountain*, introduced the hero, Ted Strong, with distinct echoes of Teddy Roosevelt's career. Ted is returning from military action in Cuba and the Philippines to his Dakota ranch where he gathers around him a gang of upright youth, some from the eastern upper classes, some cowboys of lowly origin, each costumed in "a neatly-fitting khaki uniform such as those worn by the Rough Riders during the Spanish-American War" (N. Taylor, *Young* 1). As well as foregrounding the Rough Rider's youthfulness, the adventure stories develop Roosevelt's appropriation of blackness into a whitened American West with a literalness that exceeds his. In all the cowboys, ranchers, rustlers, and townspeople the boys meet, they encounter one black person: yet another cook, with another Roman name, Pompey. When *King of the Wild West's Haunt; or, Stella's Escape from Sacrifice* (1906; Fig. 4.7) foregrounds a gang of evil blacks, they have been brought from the Caribbean by the dastardly Mexican Don Del Riza. In the West, they are whitened by a mysterious potion: "white negroes" who, in Ted's words, "have lost their only mark of being what God intended them to be—honest negroes"; they are "like white men as to skin, yet savages at heart" (21, 22). The setting

Figure 4.7. Rough Rider Weekly (March 31, 1906)

closes the ideological circle, by taking the young Rough Riders back to the frontier West from which they sprang, a West, like Roosevelt's, at once dependent on, threatened by, and devoid of black men.

The suppression of blackness leaks out through what Toni Morrison dubs "Black surrogacy" (13)—the Black Hills setting; Ted's black mustang, Black Bess; the comic German Rough Rider, Carl Schwartz; and innumerable villains named Black this-and-that. Most insistently, young Rough Rider victories are celebrated with renditions of "There'll Be a Hot Time in the Old Town Tonight," and Ted enters the series as a sergeant—anomalously enough, given that Roosevelt was lieutenant colonel, then colonel. The rank of sergeant had particular meaning for black soldiers, for whom it was the highest rank available in the regular army and from which position several won fame. James Robert Payne argues that "the motif of the heroic Black sergeant at San Juan Hill" functioned as "an Afro-American supplement and corrective to the mainstream American myth of the Rough Riders" (29). In the world of *Rough Rider Weekly*, that final opportunity for elevation is blocked by Ted's white heroism.

Remington: With the Eye of the Mind

The spoiler in this process of suppressing blackness to the point of invisibility— yet again, the one who wasn't quite part of the club—was Frederic Remington. Remington's personal correspondence—which is peppered with racial slurs about a range of non-Anglo peoples—shows him to be as casually and brutally racist as any of the frontier club cohort. Yet he saw and reproduced black figures in terms that the others did not, coming close to positioning them at the heart of western myth-making.

In terms of racial dynamics, Remington's introduction to the West was almost the mirror image of Wister's. Although he had enjoyed a brief vacation in Montana in 1881 then a decidedly mixed experience as a Kansas sheep rancher in 1883, his decisive experience of the heroic West happened in 1886, when he traveled to the Southwest to provide illustrations of the army pursuing Geronimo for *Harper's*. The commission was a triumph for Remington—"an illustrator's plum...his springboard to fame"—and he reported his experience of the army in glowing terms (Samuels, *Frederic* 67). Throughout his career, Remington would continue to structure his landscapes into disciplined formations: the lines and columns in, for example, "The March of Roger's Rangers" on snowshoes through ranks of trees and "The Charge" of cavalrymen in a long line on the empty plain (both 1897) and the defensive circles of "A Cavalrymen's Breakfast on the Plains" (1890) and "The Fight for the Water Hole" (c. 1903). The lifelong patterns suggest that his first artistic encounter with the West trained him to see with a paramilitary eye.

This trip also established a lasting relationship with the 10th Cavalry. He was most intimate with the white Lieutenant Clarke, but he paid significant social and artistic attention to the black troopers, describing them as "charming men with whom to serve" and documenting evidence of their bravery, almost in anticipation of Roosevelt's slurs a decade later: "These little episodes prove the sometimes doubted self-reliance of the negro" ("Scout" 902). He got the idea for his early illustration, "The Rescue of Corporal Scott"—which shows Lieutenant Clarke rescuing one black soldier with the aid of another—from a drinking con- versation with the troop's black sergeant. In 1889, he literally sketched himself into the company: in "Marching in the Desert," he positions himself between the white lieutenant and the black sergeant in a long column of black cavalry- men. His private writings also individualize black soldiers: his journal describes Corporal Scott, for example, as "a fine tall negro soldier" (quoted in Samuels,

Frederic 73). There were both condescension in and limitations to Remington's appreciation of African American contributions—although fascinated with vaqueros, for example, he rarely acknowledged African American cowboys—but his remains, racially, a quite different picture of the West than Wister's or Roosevelt's.[40]

In the frenzied war-mongering against Spain, Remington was as jingoistic as any of the frontier club. From 1896 onwards, in his personal and professional correspondence, he agitated for the war that would test him as war correspondent and expand his nation's reach. He hooked up with the yellow press, commissioned first by Hearst of the New York *Journal* to illustrate Richard Harding Davis's reports on the Cuban revolutionaries in 1897. It was this association that gave rise to the famous telegram: when Remington complained of a lack of action in Cuba, Hearst telegrammed back, "You furnish the pictures and I'll furnish the war." Apocryphal or not, when Remington subsequently invented an image of a Cuban woman being strip-searched by male Spanish officers, he was well on his way to keeping his part of that bargain.

Once the Spanish-American War was declared, Remington went into action with commissions from the Harpers, Hearst's *Journal* and the Chicago *Tribune*. His experience in Cuba was one of the most disillusioning of his life. The mud, disease, and confusion countered all his visions of imperial confrontation. However hard Roosevelt and his retinue worked to promote the "cowboy soldier" image, Remington could see that the unhorsed, sweating, fever-ridden cavalrymen were not the inheritors of the chivalric lineage he had sketched for Wister's "Evolution of the Cowpuncher" three years earlier. The new technologies of war—the shrapnel, the Mauser rifles, the Spaniards' smokeless powder, the dynamite-gun—produced not mano a mano virtuosity but men cowering in the mud. And yet again, Remington was reminded that he didn't fit in: in a quarrel over a mosquito net, Bonsal spurned him as "a self-made man...with parvenu arrogance" (quoted in Samuels, *Frederic* 273). Subsequently, Remington reported being "ostracized by my fellow-correspondents" (clubmen all) and left, literally, out in the mud, without shelter or support, shaking with fever, trailing behind the main action and missing the decisive engagements ("With" 966). He returned home a deflated and defeated man.

Remington had little interest in contributing to the myth-making that rapidly elevated Roosevelt to the war's most popular hero, easing his route to the governorship of New York State. His war writings and illustrations serve to deflate clubmen's claims to glory. Turning the tables on the superior class, he reached for a condescending tone: "I have been amused over Colonel Roosevelt's claims for the worth and efficiency of his Rough Riders. It is such an old soldier trick" ("Colonel" 848). He wrote up the taking of San Juan Hill as a "most glorious feat of arms...considering every condition" but in terms that credit everyone except the volunteer Rough Riders: "San Juan was taken by infantry and dismounted cavalry of the United States regular army" (974). He watched members of his beloved 10th Cavalry cut down at least partly because of the naïve bravado of Roosevelt's Rough Riders, and he mourned the decimation of the 24th Infantry: "A young officer of the Twenty-fourth, who was very much excited, threw his arms about me, and pointing to twenty-five big negro infantrymen sitting near, said, 'That's all—that is all that is left of the Twenty-fourth Infantry,' and the tears ran off his mustache" (974).

However much Remington disapproved of Roosevelt exploiting the war for self-aggrandizement, the rising politician would not be deflected. The Rough Riders seized Remington's imagery in order to cement the connection between frontier and overseas heroism. When they were mustered out at Montauk Point, they presented Roosevelt with Remington's first sculpture, "The Bronco Buster," "the most popular and, not incidentally, probably the most profitable small American bronze sculpture of the nineteenth century" (Shapiro 186). Roosevelt drove home the symbolism, announcing to the assembled troops, "The foundation of the regiment was the 'Bronco Buster,' and we have him here in bronze."[41]

But Roosevelt wanted a more direct endorsement from the best-known artist of the West. When *Scribner's* commissioned him to write up the war, he leaned heavily on Remington to supply an illustration of him in battle. Remington acceded to an extent; as he had not seen this action, he worked—as he titled a later, very different canvas—"with the eye of the mind."[42] He put Roosevelt on horseback with his men rushing valiantly behind him under the caption "Charge of the Rough Riders at San Juan Hill," full knowing that they had attacked Kettle Hill on foot (Fig. 4.8). But Remington's reluctance and revenge are also manifest. His trademark paramilitary order is absent in this scene of disordered rush. Roosevelt is a tiny, indistinct figure well back in the picture's plane, and several of his men are in the process of collapsing under fire. The effect is quite different from Remington's western canvases up to that time, which portray fighting men—often mounted, dashing, and confidently brandishing weapons—well forward in the picture.

Even more mythologically unsettling is the figure in the center of the composition, at dead center of this group of white Rough Riders in their distinctive uniforms: a single black soldier. Alexander Nemerov points out that the "triangular mass" of white soldiers "tapers perfectly to an apex at the black man's head" (90). Yet, in both the oil painting and the black-and-white reproduction that illustrates Roosevelt's account, there is a near *trompe l'oeil* effect. At a distance, the black head in the painted canvas disappears, less strongly contrasted against its background of dark green, almost blue-black trees than the white-skinned figures against the light green grass. Up close, and once you look for the black head, the entire composition seems to revolve around it. The black

Figure 4.8. Frederic Remington, "Charge of the Rough Riders at San Juan Hill"

man is visible and startling to those who want to see him, invisible once more to those who do not.[43]

Black Rough Riders Redux

If we move beyond the frame of the frontier club, the black Rough Rider comes much more fully—indeed, insistently—into view. He was claimed and celebrated in the black popular press, which emerged in this period. African American individuals and communities across the country worked to forge a black popular culture that would take advantage of the newly increased reading audience and the reduced costs of publication while contesting the racist stereotypes promulgated by mainstream presses, both "quality" and cheap. Those representations were part of a long-term legacy that kept black soldiers alive as sources of black pride and of an alternative stream of popular westerns.

Tearing a Piece off the Flag

"we are coming up unrepresented"
—First Sergeant M. W. Sadler,
25th Infantry[44]

One of the many disputed engagements in Cuba occurred at El Caney, when Private Butler of the 25th Infantry led the final rush on the blockhouse and seized the Spanish flag. An officer of the 12th Infantry immediately ordered Butler to surrender the flag to his white superior. Reluctantly obeying, Butler tore a piece off the flag as evidence of his claim in his report to his colonel. The moment is nicely paradigmatic of how immediately blacks were forced into counter-narrative positions that rendered them dependent on the discourse of the dominant class (the flag, the colonel) in staking their own claims. The moment also points to a second answer to the question of where the black Rough Riders went: deep into the arms of black myth-makers.

Although the storming of San Juan Heights is now conventionally associated with white American frontier mythology and Teddy Roosevelt, at the time a barrage of black representations seized this and other battles in Cuba as signs of black heroism. Rayford Logan, dean of African American scholars, remembers: "Many Negro homes had prints of the famous charge of the colored troops up San Juan Hill" (335). The print might have been a color lithograph by the Maryland Lithography Company titled "How the Day Was Won," depicting the charge of the 10th Cavalry up San Juan Hill (Fig. 4.9). Or it could have been the more provocatively captioned lithograph by Kurz & Allison, titled "Charge of the 24th and 25th Colored Infantry and Rescue of Rough Riders at San Juan Hill, July 2nd, 1898." A painting by Fletcher C. Ransom also depicted Troop C, 9th Cavalry charging San Juan Hill. The book illustration from Edward Johnson's

Figure 4.9. "'How the Day Was Won': Charge of the Tenth Cavalry Regiment U.S.A. San Juan Hill; Cuba, July 1st 1898," Maryland Litho. Co.

black history of the Spanish-American War (Fig. 4.10), for all its aesthetic limitations, was in some ways the most politically explosive, because it represented a black soldier in the forbidden epaulettes of an officer.

There was also a barrage of published writings documenting black valor on the battlefield. Bonnie Miller has traced the contribution of the Indianapolis *Freeman*, the first "national illustrated colored newspaper." Between February and April 1899, it ran a series of front-page articles titled "Special War Notes," "featuring portraits of distinguished black servicemen alongside engravings of black regiments in heroic combat in Cuba. This was a rare moment when an African American newspaper, claiming to serve over eighty thousand subscribers, was able to create a visual space in which African American military participation in the war could be recognized and truly celebrated" (150). From eyewitness accounts, Herschel V. Cashin assembled one book, *Under Fire with the Tenth U.S. Cavalry* (1899), and Theophilas Steward, 25th Infantry chaplain, wrote another, *The Colored Regulars in the United States Army* (1904). In his contribution to *A New Negro for a New Century* (1900), Booker T. Washington

Charge on San Juan Hill.

Figure 4.10. Illustration in Edward A. Johnson, *A School History of the Negro Race in America from 1619 to 1890 Combined with The History of the Negro Soldiers in the Spanish-American War, Also a Short Sketch of Liberia* (rev. ed., 1911)

exposed the contradictions in the received account of Cuba when he juxtaposed Roosevelt's earlier and later accounts of San Juan Hill, along with black soldiers' refutations. Many poems and prose chronicles lauded the heroism of black soldiers and excoriated their subsequent neglect by the white establishment. Chroniclers of black heroism in Cuba—from the writings of soldier-poet Charles Frederick White in 1898 to Gail Buckley's history in 2001—position Cuban action within a long catalogue of black military action, beginning with Crispus Attucks in the Boston Massacre of 1770. One 1915 novella nicely turns the tables on Roosevelt. F. Grant Gilmore wrote the famous colonel into *"The Problem": A Military Novel* as the thinly disguised Roswell (which was the name of Roosevelt's grandparents' southern estate).[45] Roosevelt-Roswell's function is to attest to the preeminence of the novel's hero, Sergeant Henderson of the 9th Cavalry, whose prowess in Cuba derives from his service in the American West, where he has won medals for marksmanship. Henderson defeats the Spanish enemy and the Anglo-Saxon officer who attempts to steal his sweetheart. The black hero conjoins the West, military, manhood, and modernity with considerably more success than any white Rough Rider.

As a campaign to change the mainstream image of the black Rough Riders, however, these attempts were contained by their demonstrations of patriotism, which served to shore up the status quo. Cashin's volume, for example, is framed by a foreword by General Wheeler, who recommends Thomas Nelson Page's vision of the "loyal darky" as the model to which African Americans should aspire (xv). Sergeant Presley Holliday of the 10th Cavalry made the futility of this effort clear. Holliday was on San Juan Hill, and he refuted Roosevelt's *Scribner's* article a month later, in the *New York Age*. He ended, however, with resignation: "I could give many other incidents of our men's devotion to duty, of their determination to stay until the death, but what's the use? Colonel Roosevelt has said they shirked, and the reading public will take the Colonel at his word and go on thinking they shirked" (quoted in Washington, Wood, and Williams 60).

The most powerful, potentially radical treatment of the black Rough Riders came at the hands of those who understood the need to change that reading public if they were to change "the imaginary world of what is possible" for African Americans (Kelley 9). In this period, several African American groups and individuals across the country set about creating the apparatus for a distinctively black popular literature by taking ownership of the means of production and distribution. Key figures included Sutton E. Griggs, James Ephraim McGirt, and the Colored Co-operative Publishing Company, founded by Walter Wallace, Jessie Watkins, Harper S. Fortune, and Walter Alexander Johnson, and later joined by Pauline Hopkins.[46] Running through all their efforts as a central source of cultural power and political motivation is the figure of the black soldier in the Spanish-American War.

Sutton Griggs created the Orion Publishing Company in Nashville, Tennessee in 1901 (and, later, the National Public Welfare League in Memphis). Winning a black audience involved the wholesale cooperation of the black community, including endorsements from cultural leaders, attention from the black press, financial contributions, amateur sales agents, and door-to-door canvassing by the author.[47] Meanwhile, his work remained "virtually unknown to white Americans of his time" (Gloster ii). His novels are powerful melodramas of black life, largely set in the post-Reconstruction South, demonstrating the violence of the Anglo-Saxon regime in America. In three of his five novels—*Imperium in Imperio* (1899), *Unfettered* (1902), and *The Hindered Hand* (1905)—the war in Cuba and the Philippines becomes the basis of heroic black solidarity.

In his first novel, a secret black government—the Imperium—follows the liberation struggle in Cuba "with keenest interest, as the Cubans were in a large measure negroes" (201). As well as forging bonds across national divides, black leaders work to erase distinctions of color within their race. On the same morning that the U.S. Congress meets to debate war resolutions against Spain, the Congress of the Imperium meets to consider its president's resolution of war against the United States: "These two congresses on this same day had under consideration questions of vital import to civilization. The proceedings of the Anglo-Saxons have been told to the world in minute detail, but the secret deliberations of the Imperium are herein disclosed for the first time" (203). Bernard Belgrave, the mulatto president, understands black subordination: "They have apparently chosen our race as an empire, and each Anglo-Saxon regards himself as a petty king, and some gang or community of negroes as his subjects" (218).

The Hindered Hand, Griggs's most graphically violent and complexly plotted novel, shows how black military service can reverse that relationship. Three protagonists are veterans of the Spanish-American War: Ensal Ellwood served as chaplain, and Earl Bluefield and Gus Martin as soldiers: "These three were present at the battle of San Juan Hill, and Gus, who was himself notoriously brave, scarcely knew which to admire the more, Ensal's searching words that inspired the men for that world-famous dash or Earl's enthusiastic, infectious daring on the actual scene of conflict" (36–37). Military service stamps their approach to race war. Ensal tries to persuade Americans into racial equality by force of pen, distributing millions of addresses to every home. Earl plans to lead a band of five hundred men to take over a southern state capitol and a U.S. government building ("to make it a national question" [144]). Gus Martin undertakes a standoff against the local citizenry before being murdered by a white mob. Here, overseas militarism is a resource for black militancy, not for conformity to hegemonic notions of patriotism.

Griggs's commitment to African American independence was part of a larger vision of transnational solidarity among people of color. In *Unfettered*, the

Republican Party's refusal to recognize the independence of Filipinos precipitates the narrative's central crisis. Dorlen Warthell, heretofore loyal speechwriter to the traditional party of southern blacks (which was the party of Roosevelt, Lodge, and the majority of the frontier clubmen), denounces the administration and sets about forging a third political alternative. This novel also expands the conventional gender focus, by bringing the heroine, Morlene, centrally into the political debate. Signing herself "The Ardent Expansionist," Morlene becomes the arbiter of Warthell's political analysis: only once she finds his plan for racial equality persuasive does she consent to marry him.

The sense of black military service simmering as a source of black power also runs through the productions of James Ephraim McGirt. McGirt was a poet—of, among other work, *Avenging the Maine* (1899)—who left North Carolina for Philadelphia in 1903 to begin *McGirt's Magazine* and, in 1905, a book publishing business. It is an apt symbolism that McGirt worked from premises just blocks away from Wister's law office in Philadelphia where he did his writing. McGirt advertised his aim to reach a white as well as a black audience, "that they may know great men of our race and what they are doing and saying," and his editorial tone remained respectful of that potential white audience ("I Publish"). Yet the magazine's content promotes an ambitious agenda for black citizens. Editorials, articles, fiction, and poetry advocate a distinctive African American higher education, business, religion, and publishing. The magazine's watchwords are black manhood and black leadership. Every so often, these qualities attach to the figure of the black soldier in the Spanish-American War, and then their militant potential becomes clear.

In McGirt's short story "In Love as in War," which he subsequently reprinted in *The Triumphs of Ephraim* (1907), a black sergeant defeats a white officer twice over. The central love plot takes place in the Philippines, during the service of the 9th and 10th Cavalries. Again, a woman arbitrates. Filipina Princess Quinaldo rebuffs the advances of Lieutenant Vaughn in favor of Sergeant Roberts. When Vaughn tries to assert his superiority by both rank and race—"I am a commissioned officer with authority; moreover, my parents are of the best blood in New Orleans"—the princess tells him in no uncertain terms that she "infinitely prefer[s] the company of this noble hero" (73, 74). Roberts's romantic victory encompasses the larger fight over credit for military victory:

> It will be remembered that when our company was ordered up San Juan Hill, in the famous battle, and the Spanish shell and fire were sweeping us down so rapidly that our captain gave the command "To the rear!" it was "Sarge," who had seen blood and in his rage yelled, "Hell to the rear!" and made a dash up the hill like a wild devil amid the flying shells, leading the company behind him and so startling the Spaniards

that they dropped their guns and were so panic-stricken that they were soon buried in their own trenches, and, in truth, the day was saved by "Sarge." (64–65)

No Roosevelt's Rough Riders, no white men in the van.

Meanwhile, in Boston, the Colored Co-operative Publishing Company began *The Colored American Magazine* in May 1900 and a few months later expanded into book publication. The journal's mandate was more radical and its tone more assertive than McGirt's. It announced itself as a "race journal" whose collective structure kept production and decision-making exclusively in the hands of black stake-holders:

> American citizens of color have long realized that for them there exists no monthly magazine, distinctively devoted to their interests and to the development of Afro-American art and literature…. the Anglo Saxon race fails to sufficiently recognize our efforts, hopes and aspirations.
>
> The Colored American Magazine…aspires to develop and intensify the bonds of that racial brotherhood, which alone can enable a people to assert their racial rights as men, and demand their privileges as citizens.[48]

One of the co-operative's founding principles was "mutual benefit" within the race, a goal that was furthered through several organizational structures quite different from the quality or cheap publishing businesses of white, mainstream America. For an investment of at least $5, readers could join the co-operative and share its dividends; the company employed agents to sell magazine subscriptions and books; and it initiated at least two clubs, the Literary Agents' Business Club and the Colored American Magazine Club. In late 1901, the stock prospectus reiterated its commitment: "The company is first, last and always, a *Race Publishing House*. It has been from the start, and will continue to be, *controlled absolutely by members of the Negro Race*" (quoted in Knight 451).

Given these principles, it is obviously significant that the first issue of *The Colored American Magazine* opens with a frontispiece of black soldiers returning from the Spanish-American war. "Company 'L' of the Sixth Regiment, M. V. M., reviewed at the State House on its return from Cuba" was also offered as a mounted print for 50 cents—perhaps yet another of the prints Rayford Logan remembers seeing in black households. Accompanying the illustration is an article on the action seen by Company L—the only black company in the Massachusetts militia—in Puerto Rico; "it was the first colored organization of volunteers mustered into service, and the only one favored with active service" (Braxton 19). The authorship also showcases the only officer class available to blacks: Lieutenant Braxton holds his rank as a member of a volunteer regiment. In the early years of the magazine, essays and fiction lauding black military service in the Spanish-American War recur regularly, often authored by black volunteer officers. Running in counterpoint is a sustained call for transnational solidarity: one writer criticizes the federal administration for denying self-government to people of color in Puerto Rico, Cuba, and the Philippines; another warns Aguinaldo about U.S. Jim Crowism; and a third links Antonio Maceo, leader of the Cuban rebels, with Crispus Attucks. There is also a sustained critique of America's domestic race politics: one essay lambasts the white American press for minimizing the black contribution to the war; another criticizes President Roosevelt's treatment of black soldiers; and a third skewers anti-imperialists who oppose the subordination of Filipinos abroad but acquiesce in the subordination of African Americans at home. The outlines of a cultural network also emerge: author, editor, and publisher James Ephraim McGirt is featured in one issue of *The Colored American Magazine*, Theophilas Steward, author and 25th Infantry chaplain, is a regular contributor, and other veterans reappear in these pages.

In short, we can see that the black Rough Rider was immersed in a network of racialized culture quite as deeply as Roosevelt's Rough Rider was immersed in the Anglo-Saxon frontier club network. The difference lies in the two figures' meanings and purposes. Seeking to expunge blackness, the white Rough Rider insists on his own youthful innocence as the basis of his imperialist rights. Ironically, this image points up the contrasting manliness of the black Rough Rider. No boyish figure, he is a model of transnational militant resistance, ready to rise in protest against Jim Crow with oppressed peoples of color across the globe and to break down intraracial class, color, and, to an extent, gender divisions at home. The threat of such a figure at such a moment—the motivation for its suppression—was powerful.

"These cats was the original posse"

'Twas I who rescued from the urn
Of death thy fickle soldier chief;
Tis he who gives me in return
Disgrace, dishonor, no relief
—Corporal Charles Fred. White,
"Plea of the Negro Soldier" (1907)

Where the black Rough Riders went representationally and where they could go in actual, material terms were, of course, intimately related. Inasmuch as African Americans' social conditions limited their recognition in the mainstream press, so the repressed representation detailed above enabled a redoubled racism and authoritarian oppression when the soldiers returned to American soil. Ultimately, the black community's one "resource of hope" (as Raymond Williams would call it) was their own memory-making capacity. From this resource came the resurrection of the black Rough Riders.

Edward Van Zile Scott details the "almost daily racial incidents" as black troops returned to Florida, Georgia, and Alabama (28). One of the worst occurred in 1906, in Brownsville, Texas, where three companies of the 25th Infantry were stationed despite warnings about rabid racism. After a night of violence—known as the "Brownsville Raid"—and the murder of one white civilian, 167 soldiers were dishonorably discharged without a public hearing and with the complicity of President Theodore Roosevelt—an act that provoked Corporal White's angry poem, quoted above.[49]

Paradoxically, some black soldiers found relief from Jim Crow through employment in an icon of Anglo-Saxon frontier imperialism: Buffalo Bill's Wild West. Begun in 1883, the show developed from the spectacular demonstration of western skills to reenactments of western history, becoming, in Richard Slotkin's words, "the most important commercial vehicle for the fabrication and transmission of the Myth of the Frontier" in the late nineteenth century (*Gunfighter* 87). In the 1890s, having won an international audience, the show expanded its ideological mandate from frontier nostalgia to global triumph. In 1893, it added a "Congress of Rough Riders of the World," showcasing the name subsequently applied to the First U. S. Volunteer Cavalry—and provoking a public wrangle between Roosevelt and Cody over who popularized the term. As well as the commercial imperative to own the brand, a racial divide ran between the two men's usage. While Roosevelt claimed the term exclusively for his Anglo-Saxon cowboy-clubmen, Cody used it to designate an array of racial and national types: South American gauchos, Mexican vaqueros, Arab Bedouins, Cossack horsemen, French Cuirassiers, along with cowboys, American Indians, and U.S. Cavalrymen. Slotkin analyses the Wild West parade as imperialist display subordinating these international representatives to the triumphant Anglo-Saxonism of their leader, Bill Cody. Louis Warren reads it more inclusively, arguing that the Congress invited a diverse range of Americans (including immigrants from the represented countries) to understand their identities in a national and global framework.

This was the context in which black Rough Riders performed when, in 1899, the show added to its reenactments the charge up San Juan Hill. It featured some members of Roosevelt's Rough Riders, some American Indian scouts, and some 9th and 10th Cavalrymen and 24th Infantrymen.[50] Black veterans performed themselves, bivouacking in Cuba then storming San Juan Hill. While the African Americans were not exactly stars of the event, the program did draw attention to them. Its illustrations of "Scene I.—The Bivouac the Night before the Battle of San Juan Hill" and of "Scene II.—The Rough

Riders' Heroic Charge at San Juan Hill" include black soldiers off-center
within the composition. The accompanying text reads in part: "There is a
frantic yell of admiration and approval as the soldiers—*white, red and black*—
spring from their cowering position of utter helplessness and follow Roosevelt
and the flag."[51] Certainly the black soldiers are subordinated to Roosevelt and
the nation. Only a year after San Juan Hill, however, in the face of frontier
clubmen's accounts of black cowardice, it was unusual for any white-owned
medium to credit black soldiers for playing their part in America's international adventure.[52] Black performers' living conditions were also unusually
integrated within a racial mixture of Native Americans, Mexican-Americans,
white Americans, Cubans, Filipinos, and Europeans.

It did not, however, last. The storming of San Juan Hill served as the show's
culminating spectacle for two years, then was replaced by "The Battle of
Tien-Tsin," a display of American might and international cooperation stem-
ming from China's Boxer Rebellion of 1901, which followed the same performance structure as the Cuban reenactment. In 1902, San Juan Hill returned for
two more seasons, but with a revised program text. With Roosevelt now in the
White House, the spotlight was exclusively on him in this scene. All mention
of black soldiers disappeared; if they were present in the ring, they were tucked
within the designation "U.S. Regulars." If the program was potentially both a
framing device and a mnemonic for the audience, this version gave little encouragement to see or remember the black Rough Riders.

There are those, however, who remember them. This is the final place
that the black Rough Riders went—into black cultural memory, which has
continued to contest the dominant western formula up to the present day.
In the 1900s, the black community in Manhattan's West Fifties renamed
their district San Juan Hill, "a folk tribute to the exploits of Negro soldiers
in the Spanish-American War" (Federal Writers' Project 160). In the 1950s,
Rayford Logan remembered them as a source of racial pride: "Negroes
had little, at the turn of the century, to help sustain our faith in ourselves
except the pride that we took in the 9th and 10th Cavalry, the 24th and 25th
Infantry.... They were our Ralph Bunche, Marian Anderson, Joe Louis and
Jackie Robinson" (335). In the 1980s, the novelist Ralph Ellison remembered them through his father, Lewis Ellison: "having had a father who
fought on San Juan Hill, in the Philippines and in China, I knew ... an arche-
typical American dilemma: How could you treat a Negro as equal in war and
then deny him equality during times of peace?" (xiii). And in the 1990s actor
and screenwriter Sy Richardson remembered them, through his grandfather,
Abe Richardson, who fought with the 10th Cavalry.[53]

It was from this last source that Mario Van Peebles' 1993 film *Posse*—
co-written by Richardson and dedicated to both his grandfathers—erupted,

telling, as the film's poster announces, "The untold story of the wild west." The film opens in Cuba, where the 10th Cavalry is pinned down by enemy fire and by their commander, Colonel Graham who—with his political ambitions and his steadfast refusal to retreat—is a mad, horrifically violent version of Roosevelt. Jesse Lee leads a small group of cavalrymen in resistance, escaping to the United States. They travel west to Freemanville, the all-black town begun by Jesse Lee's father, Reverend King David Lee (based on Richardson's maternal grandfather), who has been lynched by whites. Jesse leads his posse in revenge against the lynchers, ultimately triumphing in a Peckinpahesque hail of bullets and conflagration to establish a new frontier settlement with his Native lover.

This film fulfills much of the black Rough Rider vision of a century earlier. Like many of those works, it places black military service in a lineage of forgotten heroes. The film is framed by the aged Woody Strode who, as John Ford's staple black actor, embodies numerous black Westerners as well as the Buffalo Soldier in Ford's *Sergeant Rutledge* of 1960. The ancient "Storyteller" remembering his youth both signifies on Jack Crabb in *Little Big Man* (1970) and—as in turn-of-the-century accounts—insists on black eyewitnesses challenging the dominant story. He leafs through photographs of forgotten blacks on the frontier: Nat Love, Isom Dart, Cherokee Bill, 9th and 10th Cavalrymen; "People forget their past and they forget the truth. But pictures don't lie.... These cats was the original posse." Like *Rough Rider Weekly*, *Posse* takes a group of Rough Riders back to the West, in a radically different register and with a radically different purpose.

Through Jesse Lee's flashbacks, we learn of the savage lynching of his father and gradually realize that western mythology—the coming of the railroad, the town sheriff, the assault on Indigenous peoples, the justification of lynching—is repeatedly motivated by racism. This film shows how the frontier is literally built on the bodies of black people. Lee's tactics of resistance are reminiscent of Griggs's. His service in Cuba teaches him to forge solidarity of the oppressed—blacks, Native Americans, and one white posse member—and lead them into smashing evil white mobs and conspirators.

The film, of course, goes farther than Griggs could. The violent confrontation only imagined in *Imperium in Imperio* is enacted in the film, and it leads to a resolution unavailable to Griggs's characters. The film usurps white authority, bringing black Rough Riders into mainstream media and seizing the western genre to a degree that no earlier black writer could. In a recognizably John Ford moment, a spokesman for the fearful black townspeople protests to Lee: "These people ain't soldiers and this ain't Cuba." When the townspeople rally to fight on Lee's side, the implication is that Cuba does, after all, have something to say to black American independence, historical and contemporary.

Conclusion

Heather Cox Richardson has argued that, in order to understand the politics of Reconstruction (a period that she extends to 1901), we need to look west. Equally, in order to flesh out the politics of the western, we need to look to Reconstruction. During a period riven with the collapsing and reinstating of racial boundaries, frontier clubmen protected some antebellum southern privileges by removing them to the western plains. In 1886, Roosevelt noted with satisfaction that the big cattlemen constituted "a class whose members were in many respects closely akin to the old Southern planters," a connection his fellow authors reinforced with tales and images of chivalrous southern cowboys on the western plains (*Hunting* 29–30). The displacement of the Old South to the frontier West brought with it, of course, the problem of African American presence, with which Wister, Roosevelt, and Remington wrestled in significantly different ways.

Wister most thoroughly expunged blacks from his West, to a degree that speaks of deeply buried impulses. Immediately after *The Virginian*, despite Brett's urging to write another western, he wrote *Lady Baltimore*, a portrait of Charleston (the city in which he completed *The Virginian*) revolving around another chivalrous southerner. Here there welled up a sustained diatribe against "the modern negro"—the hero bursts out at one point, "if we could only deport the negroes and Newport together to one of our distant islands, how happily our two chief problems would be solved!" (133, 60). Wister uses the novel to justify disenfranchisement and lynching with such insistence that Roosevelt scolded him for it (eighty years later, John L. Cobbs called *Lady Baltimore* "an unabashed outpouring of racist attitudes unmatched in the fiction of any other major American writer of the twentieth century" [107]). Whatever Roosevelt's enthusiasms during his time as a Dakota rancher, it was a mainstay of his perceived presidential commitment to clean government that he was staunchly anti-lynching, whether the victims were blacks in the South or "stock thieves" in the West.[54] Wister, in turn, vehemently criticized Roosevelt's 1903 presidential appointment of Dr. William Crum, an African American, as collector of ports in Charleston—to his face at some length, three years later in *Lady Baltimore*, and, having the final word, in his 1930 biography, long after Roosevelt's death at a point when black rights in America rankled Wister more than ever.

Roosevelt himself vacillated on the recognition of African Americans, caught between conflicting political, personal, and ideological imperatives. He publicly promoted individual black figures—as early as 1884, when Lodge and he nominated the African American John R. Lynch as temporary chairman at the Republican National Convention—but he steadfastly deemed the race as a whole to be inferior. He certainly was not prepared to share equal billing with blacks in western—which came to equal imperial—myth-making, although even on this front political expediency led him to temper his portrait of black cowardice. In 1901, as a vice-presidential nominee concerned about losing black Republican votes, Roosevelt publicly declared that he would be the "last man in the world to say anything against the colored soldiers" (quoted in Dyer 101). Five years later, however, now-President Roosevelt outraged the black community once more by dishonorably discharging an entire battalion of the 25th Infantry stationed in Brownsville, Texas (many of them veterans of the Spanish-American War), on the basis of unproven accusations of violence by white townspeople.

Remington was perennially uncomfortable with the imposition of an Anglo-Saxon template on the racially diverse West. In 1895, while agreeing to illustrate "The Evolution of the Cowpuncher," he tried to persuade Wister to credit Mexicans as the true cowboys: "I never saw an English cow-boy—have seen owners" (quoted in Splete 265). He disapproved of Roosevelt's appropriation of black cavalrymen's valor and was not prepared, in his paintings and writing, to endorse their exclusion from the western scene or the imperial battlefield. He devoted book-length fiction to mixed-race and racially conflicted characters in the West (in *Sundown Leflare* and *John Ermine of the Yellowstone*, which I discuss in Chapter Five), although African Americans did not figure in this mix. It was only in the military sphere that Remington lauded African Americans at length, perhaps because the military hierarchy ensured there could be no threat to white supremacy, no claim to black rugged individualism, from this quarter.

The parallels that G. Edward White traced among Wister, Roosevelt, and Remington over forty years ago seem, more recently, to have hardened into an image of three friends working in concert to mythologize a unified West.[55] Looking at their work through the lens of African American representation, however, magnifies the fissures in both the relationship and the myth. What the triad undoubtedly did share was that they structured their Wests, in different ways and to different degrees, around black figures—absent or present.

The lens of African American representation also makes visible another arena of popularization, a black literary marketplace beyond the boundaries of the frontier club. By unraveling the making of the white Rough Rider image, we can appreciate the power and threat of the black Rough Riders on and beyond the battlefield. They refused to be silenced, and they were championed by their own publicists and cultural producers. The trope of white boyishness that was forged in places of privilege—the English public school system, the American Ivy League campuses, the gentlemen's clubs on both sides of the Atlantic—and that was so central to mainstream western mythologizing, looks quite different in contrast to narratives of black masculinity—less

like innocence and more like weakness. Frontier club narratives shaped the
dominant western formula into a negative image of blackness that ultimately
diminished white masculinity. They were also challenged by black cultural
networks and discourses of valor, independence, and transnational solidarity
that have remained a potent resource for black cultural expression.

Immigrants and Indians

No need to send in the cavalry with guns blazing. Legislation will do just as nicely.

—Thomas King, *The Truth about Stories* (143)

In 1924, in the space of a week, President Calvin Coolidge signed two acts that, could the frontier club have been reassembled, would have set its members to popping champagne corks once more. The National Origins Act and the Indian Citizenship Act were decades in the making, and the frontier clubmen were deeply involved in their generation, through their political activity, their production of cultural and recreational spaces, and their hunting tales-turned-westerns. Together, the two acts legislated the vision—at once exclusionary and assimilationist—of "What 'Americanism' Means" that Theodore Roosevelt articulated thirty years earlier: "We have no room for any people who do not act and vote simply as Americans, and as nothing else" (202). Walter Benn Michaels has said of their complementary effect in removing agency from designated racial groups, "they were both designed to keep people from *becoming* citizens" (31). In other words, this legislation called the shots on who belonged in the nation and on what terms, drawing the line between insiders and outsiders. Federal policy was always in the sights of the frontier clubmen, as hunters, lobbyists, legislators, and tellers of western stories. These two acts took their influence beyond the reaches of game and conservation laws, into the full-blown regulation of American citizenship.

Vanishing Acts

The National Origins Act (also known as the Immigration Act and the Johnson-Reed Act) became law on May 26, 1924. After a series of Exclusion Acts, beginning with the Chinese Exclusion Act in 1882, the National Origins Act definitively entrenched limitations on non-northern European groups and officially removed Natives and African Americans from the polity (the statutes decreed that "inhabitants in continental United States" did not include "the descendants of slave immigrants" or "the descendants of the American aborigines").[1] The act rolled back the vision of the American population to the 1890 census by establishing entrance quotas at 2 percent of national demographics at that moment. This benchmark reduced annual immigration to 150,000 (from approximately one million a year before World War I) and reserved two-thirds of these places for people from northwestern Europe. Using the 1890 census as a baseline for quotas, the anti-immigration lobbyists argued, would "Keep America American" (Garis, quoted in Simon 137).

On June 2, 1924 what has been called "the crowning legislative achievement of the assimilationist epoch" occurred with the signing of the Indian Citizenship Act (Dippie 177). The legislative erasure of Indigenous identities took off in 1887 with the Dawes Allotment Act. This measure sought to break up national and tribal affiliations by forcing Native peoples into individual and nuclear family units, parceling up the commonly held land into allotments of 80 acres (for a single man) or 160 acres (for a family). This vision was implemented in the following decades through a series of laws—including the Curtis Act of 1898, the Lacey Act of 1907, the Sells "Declaration" of 1917, and the Citizenship for World War I Veterans Act of 1919. These acts created irresolvable contradictions among tribal membership, ward status, the lack of voting rights, and national citizenship, leaving Native people "sovereign yet dependent" (Trachtenberg, *Shades* 125). The conferring of citizenship upon Native people perpetuated "an ill-defined politico-legal status for which in the law of human relations there is no precedent" (Wise 339).

The conjunction of these two acts was only the most recent coming together of the "entangled figures" of "the immigrant" and "the Indian" (Trachtenberg, *Shades* xi). As Richard Slotkin has discussed at length, the mainstream media repeatedly substituted the one for the other as a way of demonizing both throughout the second half of the nineteenth century, part of "the grand imaging of the struggle of savagery vs. civilization, or evil vs. good" (*Fatal* 436). Labor militants—often conflated with "new" immigrants—were figured as violent "savages" and "redskins" while Native warriors were shown to threaten the industrial base of civilization, especially through the metaphor of the last stand, widely circulated after the defeat of Custer's 7th Cavalry at the Little Bighorn in 1876.[2] Senator Dawes, in proposing the allotment bill in 1886, equated tribal communalism and Henry George's socialism as threats to American democratic individualism.[3]

Although World War I was a crucial determinant in the passage of both acts in 1924, they also carried an indelible nineteenth-century orientation.[4] One sign of that was the imprint of the 1890 census. It was used as the baseline for National Origins quotas of inclusion and exclusion, and it had been the first census to count Native people. This was another strategy of assimilation, counting them out as distinct Indigenous nations by counting them in as individual Americans.[5] 1890 is also often cited as the year in which the Plains Indians Wars "ended," with the death of Sitting Bull and the Massacre at Wounded Knee—that is, the year in which actual and cultural genocide proceeded by non-military means. And, of course, the 1890 census was the very one that Frederick Jackson Turner had enshrined in his frontier thesis during the Chicago exposition in 1893—an iconic moment in the frontier club's founding and in the western's cultural power.

The frontier club was deeply involved in the generation and circulation of legislative assumptions and categories as they cycled back and forth between Congress and club. It was no coincidence that the Boone and Crockett Club came into being in the same year that the Dawes Act was signed, nor that Senator (at that point, Representative) Dawes had earlier supported the creation of Yellowstone Park, a connection noted in the first Boone and Crockett book.[6] By shrinking reservations and initiating the language of "excess" and "surplus" lands—that is, the unallotted remainder of nations' and tribes' territories—the Dawes Act made possible the Boone and Crockett campaigns to convert these lands into federal big-game and wilderness sanctuaries. Congressman Lacey, who spearheaded the 1907 bill implementing American Indian assimilation, had earlier been elected associate member of the Boone and Crockett Club for successfully introducing legislation enforcing game laws and protecting forest reserves and game refuges. In 1904, Senator Dillingham was simultaneously chairing the Senate Committee on Immigration (the forerunner of the Dillingham Commission) and negotiating with Boone and Crockett Club lobbyists over amending the game laws of Alaska. Congressman Albert Johnson, co-author of the National Origins Act, had been courted by Boone and Crockett Clubmen for several years. He was present, for example, at the 1920 annual dinner where he heard about the latest emergency—"There is nothing so important as this one idea at the present time"—created by the new hordes invading the West, in the form of motorists. The Boone and Crockett Game Preservation Committee reported that game reserves and sanctuaries were threatened by motor cars "enabling hundreds of people to engage in the sport of big game shooting that heretofore never had a chance."[7] Presumably this kind of rhetoric contributed to Johnson's claim "that the immigration restriction movement was really a branch of the conservation movement" (Spiro 207).

In their mutually reinforcing writings, frontier clubmen also brought new meanings and a new sense of crisis to the "cult of the Vanishing American," the long-standing motif that figured Indigenous populations as inevitably doomed to extinction, whether as noble or bloodthirsty savages, and promoted both U.S. and British imperialist expansion.[8] Silas Weir Mitchell was a major player in the expansion of that trope across race and class. From the 1870s, he conjured another "vanishing population: North American white elites" (Simpson, "Powers" 58). The urgency of his medical prognosis derived from the perception that market capitalism was on the brink of destroying upper-class masculinity (individual and collective) and that the antidote lay in the outdoor reinvigoration offered by the West. Yet that West, the Boone and Crockett Club warned repeatedly in their hunting tales, conservation essays, and lobbying resolutions, was also vanishing. Wilderness spaces were being crowded out and superior species rendered extinct by degenerate types—including immigrant settlers and Native hunters. The only way to protect the imperiled remnants of purity, according to the logic of this argument, was to forge legislation and enforce regulations that made these threats vanish through a combination of exclusion and incorporation.

The Boone and Crockett Club continued to perpetuate the same sporting logic and linkages well into the 1920s, as can be seen from two of its campaigns in 1924. One was the formulation of a national recreation policy, enjoined upon President Coolidge by prominent club members—particularly Theodore Roosevelt Jr. and Charles Sheldon. The resolution they formulated again pro-moted a dominant, monolithic model of Americanism. "Good citizenship," they asserted, depended upon forms of outdoor recreation that inculcated "sturdy character" by developing "qualities of self-control, endurance under hard-ship, reliance on self, and cooperation with others in team work."[9] The rheto-ric updated the promise by the previous generation of clubmen, that fair chase hunting would inculcate the ideal "race" qualities listed in the first book of the Boone and Crockett Club: "energy, resolution, manliness, self-reliance, and capacity for hardy self-help" (Roosevelt and Grinnell, American 14–15). Also in 1924, the club expanded the reach of its law enforcement when it succeeded in having the Alaska Game Law passed in the face of resistance by the local Native and non-Native population.[10] As always, these interventions in policy-making were undergirded by forms of narrative, as the club continued to publish its book series and individual members their essays, short stories, and novels.

By 1924, the frontier club was much depleted. Silas Weir Mitchell, Theodore Roosevelt, Henry Cabot Lodge, and Frederic Remington were dead; Winthrop Chanler would die in 1926 and Caspar Whitney in 1929. The Boone and Crockett Club had entered a newly mercantile phase in 1923, when it incorporated in order to receive testamentary bequests—a sign of an aging, wealthy member-ship that wanted to leave portions of its estates to the club. (Yet again, the club sought to disguise its compromise with modern market forms, insisting that the incorporation was "a mere 'shell,'" and "that the active organization still remains the old unincorporated Club.")[11] But Owen Wister, Madison Grant, and George Bird Grinnell were still going strong, carrying forward frontier club movements that were always collective and cumulative in their impact, especially in welding an exclusionary "socio-legal worldview" to "a particular elite understanding of masculinity" (Weiner 81).

Wister, Grant, and Grinnell all participated in the policy developments that issued in the Acts of 1924. They served the causes of immigration restriction and American Indian assimilation through their long-time contributions to advocacy organizations, federal committees, congressmen, and presidents. While the results of these efforts were writ large on the American landscape, cultural and physical, the three men's writings also show that the stakes were very personal. From the beginnings of their writing careers, they had centered their maturation in the West—as first-person narrators in their hunting tales and via first- and third-person surrogates in their westerns. The fiction of lifelong friends Grant and Grinnell makes particularly manifest the intensely private impulses driving policy prescriptions for the nation. All three writers produced stories that naturalized the values and structures informing federal policy. Not only did the action in these stories make certain forms of exclusion and assimilation appear heroic; structurally, they also organized racialized types into zones of purity and degeneration, or security and threat. Their central narrative machinery drew on the stock heroes and villains of the western formula and on the devices first worked up by the Boone and Crockett Club: the enclave and the showdown.

Immigration Restriction

Part of what paved the way for the National Origins Act was the popularization of evolution and eugenics. In the wake of the publication of Charles Darwin's 1859 *On the Origin of Species*, America became, in Richard Hofstadter's words, "*the* Darwinian country" (4–5). When English philosopher Herbert Spencer toured the United States in 1882, arguing the application of biological principles to society, he was so bolstered by the popular press that his books won their largest sales on that side of the Atlantic. (Wister regretted that his first trip west in 1885 meant that he missed a return appearance by Spencer.) The language of evolution permeated wide swaths of public political debate close to frontier clubmen's interests.[12] Frederick Jackson Turner schematized the West as the "record of social evolution" (6), for example, while publishing battles were conducted in evolutionary terms. One signature essay, "The Evolution of Copyright," was by the critic Brander Matthews, who a few years earlier had bolstered the emerging cultural hierarchy by inveighing against the "dreadful damage" wrought by dime novels (quoted in Denning 9). This logic was also used to promote hysteria about "new" immigrants from southern and eastern Europe and Asia and census counts that, since 1870, indicated declining Yankee birthrates and accelerating immigrant populations. The eugenics movement also wielded the biological vocabulary of Social Darwinism. Claiming a pseudoscientific superiority for Anglo-Saxon heredity it quickly took hold within the Anglo-American elite that felt itself threatened by the influx of southern and eastern Europeans. Harvard University, for example, "was a hotbed of eugenics" in the years when Roosevelt, Wister, and Chanler were undergraduates and Lodge a graduate student and briefly an instructor (E. Thomas 43).

From the Harvard club culture arose the most vocal organization to spearhead the resistance to open immigration, the Immigration Restriction League. It was founded in 1894 by three Harvard graduates: Charles Warren, Robert DeCourcy Ward, and Prescott Farnsworth Hall. The league was supported by the same network of "blue-blooded" Boston families as invested in open-range ranching and cultural entrepreneurship. One prominent member was Henry Lee Higginson, Boston's most powerful broker, Wister's erstwhile employer, and a major cattle investor (it presumably reinforced Higginson's prejudices when, in 1888, Thomas Sturgis, WSGA secretary, wrote to him from the high plains blaming the collapse of the Union Cattle Company on "immigrants," a group whom Michael Cimino's *Heaven's Gate* squarely identifies as eastern European [quoted in Gressley 255]). From 1904, the league's main financial support came from Joseph Lee, also part of the banking firm of Lee, Higginson and Company.[13] Henry Cabot Lodge was their mentor and mouthpiece in the Senate and on the United States Immigration Commission. Owen Wister and Madison Grant increasingly entered the league's inner circle: Wister became vice president in 1903, the same year that they successfully campaigned for the first immigration restriction law, and Grant in 1909. Roosevelt further advanced the league's cause when he appointed one of its leaders, Jeremiah W. Jenks, to head the U.S. Immigration Commission in 1907.[14] Roosevelt later became honorary president of another anti-immigration organization, the American Defense Society.

At first, the Immigration Restriction League had an uphill job. In attempting to change immigration policy, it threatened a cornerstone of America's self-image as a democratic refuge for all. The contradiction between the welcome afforded league members' ancestors and the exclusion they were advocating against newcomers was stark. On January 11, 1893, the same day as the Boone and Crockett Club announced its cultural program at its annual dinner, the satirical magazine *Puck* skewered the restrictionists' inconsistency in a cartoon of corpulent dandies—clubmen to a "T" in top hats and frock coats—blocking a poor laborer's access to America's shores (Fig. 5.1). The league had to sustain a persuasive distinction between desirable, north European immigrants and undesirable immigrants from southern and eastern Europe and Asia. It had to distance itself from other anti-immigration groups—the virulently anti-Catholic, the pro-labor—so that it could maintain its class privileges. For those and other reasons, it maintained strong transatlantic links with English immigration

Figure 5.1. Joseph Keppler, "Looking Backward: They Would Close to the New-Comer the Bridge that Carried Them and their Fathers Over" *Puck* (January 11, 1893)

restrictionists who had brought their ideas to America in the early 1880s and continued to lead the way in integrating restrictionist ideology with social sciences and social work.

The Immigration Restriction League, not unlike the Boone and Crockett Club and the Cheyenne Club, was a socially exclusive group—"Probably no more than twelve ever came to a meeting"—ultimately dependent on broad public support for its power (Higham 102). The league's constitution emphasized the need to seize the public sphere: "to issue documents and circulars, hold public meetings, and to arouse public opinion to the necessity of a further exclusion of elements undesirable for citizenship or injurious to our national character" (De C. Ward 639). They responded to Lodge's urgent call for "an intelligent and active public opinion to which Congress will respond" ("Lynch Law" 612). Prescott Hall used the popular *Saturday Evening Post*—which became known as a virulently anti-immigration organ—to claim that the league's existence was proof of "public demand" (Simon 317). Other members capitalized on the league's academic, social, and business networks to place essays in mass magazines and over five hundred daily newspapers, undertake cross-country speaking tours, and issue pamphlets on immigration figures, immigrants' illiteracy, the "Character of Present Immigration," and "Needed Additions to the Excluded Classes" (Higham 102).

Cumulatively, league publications provided "an educational program for the American public" (according to Barbara Solomon, "very much in the pattern of teaching at Harvard College" [106]). One strategy, already seen repeatedly in frontier club constructions of "the popular," was the attempt to harness the support of the emerging middle class for their cause. Their rhetoric attempted to build an alliance with skilled workers, arguing that the interests of organized labor and upper-class Brahmins were identical. The 1895 annual report of the league's executive committee, for example, appealed directly to skilled workers in terms that elided class divisions within a vision of the national good: "the horde of illiterate, unskilled laborers" from abroad was "a menace to the labor as well as the national interests" (Immigration Restriction League).

Whereas some groups argued the anti-immigration case on economic grounds, the league was deeply racialist in its principles. Its rhetoric, like that of "quality" publishers who published league authors, connected directly to the western range. Francis Amasa Walker, economist and director of the 1870 and 1880 censuses, whose increasingly race-based analysis partially inspired the league and who became one of its leading members in the 1890s, paralleled cattle and human breeding to prove Anglo-Saxon superiority: "The climate of the United States has been benign enough to enable us to take the English short-horn and greatly to improve it...to take the English man and to improve him too...so that in rowing, in riding, in shooting, and in boxing, the American of pure English stock is to-day the better animal."[15] Prescott Hall said that the league aimed to prevent interbreeding between "the native American stock" and non-Anglo Saxons who "dilute the Yankee gumption...pollute the Yankee blood."[16] For years, "British, German, and Scandinavian stock, historically free, energetic, progressive" composed the bulk of the American population. Now "Slav, Latin, and Asiatic races, historically down-trodden, atavistic, and stagnant" are flooding the country ("Immigration" 395). The language of "stock," "breeding," and "bloodlines" could equally be used to dehumanize immigrants. Henry Cabot Lodge approvingly quoted one description of Polish immigrants traveling the railroad, packed into "fourth-class cars, like cattle and at live-stock rates" ("Lynch Law" 607). Traveling in steerage across the Atlantic, poor immigrants were in fact treated like animals—penned in holding areas like stock, their bodies poked and prodded for defect and disease—on arrival in America. Scaremongering about floods, waves, and seepage of "aliens" was highly reminiscent both of the cattle barons' fear of saturation on the western plains and of established publishers' fear of market saturation by their cheap competitors.[17]

This is the vocabulary that frontier club westerns echo and extend, from Caspar Whitney "herding up Mexicans" in his Boone and Crockett hunting tale to the Virginian characterizing lower-class western women as "heifers." George Bird Grinnell wrote in *Forest and Stream* in 1888 that "the hunting field is the best training field" for "the survival of the fittest intellectually and morally," whether the wars are against racial others—"Sclav [sic] and Tartar and Latin races are not going to bow themselves politely out of the earth to make

Figure 5.2. Frederic Remington, "The Last Cavalier," *Harper's New Monthly Magazine* (September 1895)

room for us"—or "sectional wars or class wars at home" ("Ethics" 341). In 1895, Wister's "The Evolution of the Cowpuncher" used Social Darwinism to implant Anglo-Saxonism triumphant in the West. The essay argues that the cowboy is the direct and last descendant of the chivalric knight of old England, a heritage distinguishing him from what Wister elsewhere called the "dingy whites"—the Jewish peoples, southern and eastern Europeans, laboring poor—who had also crossed the Atlantic; "No rood of modern ground is more debased and mongrel with its hordes of encroaching alien vermin, that turn our cities to Babels and our citizenship to a hybrid farce, who degrade our commonwealth from a nation into something half pawn-shop, half broker's office" (*Roosevelt* 267; "Evolution" 603–04). Frederic Remington, five of whose paintings illustrated the essay (including "The Last Cavalier," Fig. 5.2), was also rabidly anti-new immigrant, writing to Poultney Bigelow that "Jews—inguns—chinamen—Italians—Huns, the rubish [sic] of the earth I hate" (quoted in Samuels, *Frederic* 177).

 In its final flyer, of June 14, 1924, the Immigration Restriction League saluted the recent passing of the National Origins Act: "those still living of the hand-ful of men who, at the call of Mr. Robert DeC. Ward, first met thirty years ago on May 31, 1894 to form the Immigration Restriction League...have thus at last seen their belief embodied in what promises to be effective and permanent legislation" (quoted in D. King 206). On the floor of the Senate, the celebration reverted once more to the language of bloodlines and breeding: this was a vote to protect "pure, unadulterated Anglo-Saxon stock," "the same stock as that

which originally settled the United States, wrote our Constitution and established our democratic institutions."[18] The senators' vocabulary echoes once
more the genre that most dynamically contributed to their cause: the frontier
club western, especially as it emerged and became popular between the 1890s
and the 1920s "when restrictionist rhetoric and anti-immigrant sentiment
peaked" (D. King 19).

Owen Wister

All Wister's writing trades in ethnic stereotypes that prove Anglo-American
superiority, and his early western stories include caricatures of venal Jewish
drummers and pidgin-English speakers. His first published story—"Hank's
Woman," published in 1892—showed how a recent immigrant failed the test of
the frontier West by having a Catholic European woman and a racially blurred
American—"little black Hank"—enter into a hellish marriage and ultimately
destroy each other over religious differences (821).

As he became increasingly prominent in the Immigration Restriction League,
so his fiction became increasingly explicit in its anti-immigration emphasis. In
1903, the year in which he became the league's vice president, *Philosophy 4:
A Story of Harvard University*, appeared in book form. Set during his years at
Harvard, this whimsical novella of undergraduates on the spree before their
philosophy exam launches a sneering attack on "new" immigrants. The students
are celebrated as "old stock" northwestern European immigrants: "Bertie and
Billy had colonial names" and "belonged to the same club-table" (23, 45). Oscar
Maironi, their tutor of Jewish Italian descent, has parents who "had come over
in the steerage" (36). With his "suave and slightly alien accent," "shiny little cal-
culating eyes," and "patient, Oriental" manner, he provokes distrust and is ultimately bested in the exam by his wholesome, boisterous students (14, 15, 29).
Wister's next novel, *Lady Baltimore* (1906), was a study of Old South manners.
It positions colonials who trace their roots to Elizabethan England as the true
Americans and takes repeated swipes at newly enfranchised African Americans
and the North's "pest of Hebrew and other low immigrants" who make up "our
sullen welter of democracy" (112, 48).

Throughout Wister's westerns, this exclusionary logic and language work in
concert with other frontier club discourse. Since 1891, Henry Cabot Lodge had
been agitating for a literacy test for immigrants, designed to discriminate against
"alien races" (especially Italians, Poles, and Hungarians).[19] This cause was central to the Immigration Restriction League's first nationwide campaign in 1894,
and with Lodge's help they managed to pass the measure through Congress several times, only to have it vetoed by a series of presidents.[20] Their efforts were
redoubled between 1907 and 1911, in response to the Dillingham Commission's

study of immigration patterns (inaugurated by Roosevelt). In the same period, Wister published "The Gift Horse" in the anti-immigration *Saturday Evening Post* (July 18, 1908). Wister was clearly invested in the story. Not only was it "The last story I read in ms. to my mother shortly before her death," but it was annotated with stylistic corrections by his Philadelphia clubmate and Shakespearean scholar Horace Howard Furness—"Uncle Furness"—in his library at Wallingford.[21] The point of this western is the threat of illiteracy. In yet another enclave—the hidden Still Hunt Spring, deep in the Wind River country of Wyoming—the eastern tenderfoot narrator confronts death, rescued at the last moment by the cowboy Scipio. The sides in this confrontation are scrambled, however, in terms of the natural hierarchies promoted by the frontier club western: the narrator is the near-victim, rather than club intimate, of cattle barons, who almost lynch him as a rustler. (Insiders would recognize that the horses have been stolen from the big WSGA ranches, including Wister's home away from home, the VR outfit managed by Wolcott.) The central flaw, it turns out, is the illiteracy of a rustler who, unable to read the narrator's plans, unwittingly lets him ride into a trap. More than his thievery, it is the rustler's illiteracy that, as with "new" immigrants, marks him as alien. The story ends with his hanging, which the narrator accepts as justice.

In a cultural environment thick with mutually reinforcing discourses of privilege and exclusion, the Virginian's violent expulsion of alien types from the pure space of the West can be read as reinforcing and naturalizing these legislative exclusions. The hero himself makes the connection with the immigration debate in a leading joke. In 1896 and 1899, Henry Cabot Lodge campaigned publicly against the railroad barons' pro-immigration stance, charging that they were motivated purely by their greed for cheap labor. In March 1899, Wister has his hero echo the point in his short story "The Game and the Nation" (and, subsequently, in briefer form, in *The Virginian*). In a scene at the railroad, the Virginian misidentifies some immigrant workers:

"There go some more I-talians."

"They're Chinese," said Trampas.

"That's so!" acknowledged the Virginian, with a laugh. "But both come that cheap they kind o' mix in my mind.... Without Chinese and I-talians the company couldn't afford all this hyeh new gradin'," the Southerner continued.[22]

The joke—which the villain Trampas does not follow—is that Italians and Chinese are all one to the immigration restrictionists and, Lodge charged, the railroad capitalists.

The Virginian, the Southern Anglo-American *par excellence*, demonstrates his heroism by dominating alternative presences on the plains. At the novel's center,

Wister underscores the link between his actions and the national good with a series of chapters named "Acts" (which he developed out of "The Game and the Nation"). In the chapter titled "Between the Acts," the Virginian, recently promoted to deputy foreman, pens his mutinous cowboy gang in a railroad car. He declares that he will herd them like steers back to their employer Judge Henry: "Never a calf of them will desert to Rawhide" (166). At various moments he shoots down one cowboy and lynches others who refuse to serve the cattle barons' interests; mocks with racist epithets the Jewish drummers and black Pullman porters, as well as Chinese railroad workers; denigrates American Indians as alternately savages and pathetic dependants; and generally rids the West of unwanted categories. In his first annual presidential message of December 3, 1901, Roosevelt advocated barring "all persons of a low moral tendency or of unsavory reputation" from entrance into America (quoted in Garis 102). Wittingly or not, his words echoed the WSGA which, in the notorious Maverick Law of 1884, excluded "all persons … of a reputation notoriously bad" from owning cattle in Wyoming (quoted in H. H. Smith 62). Whoever ruled on a person's reputation—in one case the immigration board, in the other the WSGA executive—held considerable power. The echoes are multiple when, in pages that Wister wrote a few weeks after Roosevelt's speech, the Virginian hotly defends his own reputation, to the point of gunning down Trampas over Molly's objections: "What men say about my nature is not just merely an outside thing" (475).

The shootout is the climax of this movement. Trampas's racial symbolism—what must be expelled for the secure union of southern and colonial Anglo-Saxons—is finely tuned. On the one hand, he must qualify—by Boone and Crockett Club values—as a worthy opponent for the climactic confrontation, and he is never explicitly identified as non-Anglo (in the way that Jewish or Chinese or Italian figures are). On the other hand, his name and physicality are reminiscent of otherness. His name, which has Hispanic connotations to do with trick, trap, and cheating, appears in Wister's first western story, the unfinished "Chalkeye" of 1891, when reference is made to "Link Trampas." By 1892, in the draft version of the story "Balaam and Pedro," his name—"Sorgy Trampas"— sounds doubly Mexican, and now he is identified with rustling: Shorty, referring to a big rancher, says, "Carew's an Englishman and hires Trampas because he don't know enough not to" (5). This version of his name resurfaces in the 1903 stage version of the novel, in which, as performed by Frank Campeau, he is dressed in a Mexican vaquero outfit, a look more subtly suggested in the novel, in which he has slim black eyebrows, slim black moustache, and a black shirt with a white handkerchief. Wister's racial positioning of the villain proved to be prescient. The Mexican was a liminal, malleable figure within nationalistic U.S. rhetoric of this period; in 1924, the National Origins Act "deemed Mexicans to be white" (Ngai 50).

If we trace a line from Wister's involvement in the Immigration Restriction League to his explicitly xenophobic writings to his western fiction, the connection between the drab documents of the league and the exclusions and ultimatums of the western is clear. While a great deal of frontier club discourse contributed to the whipping up of anti-immigrant sentiment, *The Virginian* most neatly takes what Alan Trachtenberg calls "the discourse of crisis … regarding nationality," displaces it and resolves it with a showdown on main street (*Shades* 118).

Madison Grant

The trope of vanishing—the vanishing frontier, the vanishing Indian, the vanishing American—is a pronounced element of western fiction from at least early-nineteenth-century authors such as James Fenimore Cooper, Catherine Sedgwick, and Lydia Maria Child. The frontier club brought its own sense of class beleaguerment to this trope, yoking it to hunting, conservation, and immigration restriction. Madison Grant was the one who most energetically and explicitly tackled the issue of imperiled purity, by creating enclaves— narrative, organizational, legislative, and physical—for superior species, animal and human.

Madison Grant dedicated himself simultaneously to the Boone and Crockett Club, the Immigration Restriction League, and several eugenics committees (among other bodies), working to forge an organizational web in which these groups supported each other in the push-back against open immigration. Immigration historian John Higham judged: "The man who put the pieces together was Madison Grant, intellectually the most important nativist in recent American history" (155). During the years in which Grant rose through the Boone and Crockett Club, he forged his relationship with the Immigration Restriction League—later, he claimed to be "one of the founders and life members"—becoming its vice president in 1909.[23] He also served as president of the Eugenics Research Association and worked extensively with league founders Robert DeCourcy Ward and Prescott Farnsworth Hall on eugenics committees that advised Congress. When Congressman Albert Johnson was appointed chair of the hearings on the National Origins Bill, Grant courted him assiduously, bringing him to Boone and Crockett Club dinners and sending him his publications. Grant became one of the committee's primary witnesses; Mark Weiner has judged: "Perhaps nowhere in the history of American lawmaking were the arguments of modern eugenics given such an open reception and allowed to exercise such deep influence over the formation of national policy" as by the House Immigration Committee chaired by Johnson (92–93). In turn, Johnson lent his weight to the conservation movement, arguing that new immigrants would harm unregulated natural resources.[24]

Grant's development as a writer proceeded apace with his very active involvement in the Boone and Crockett Club, contributing frequently to club books and quality publishers' periodicals. As hunter and writer, his favorite animal was the moose, what his first article, published in *Century Magazine* (January 1894) titled "The Vanishing Moose," because it represents "a survival of a long past order of nature," "a line of unbroken descent of vast antiquity" ("Canadian" 104; "Distribution" 390).

He moved rapidly from using his hunting tales to prove the urgency of game law enforcement to advocating for game refuges, establishing and writing about the New York Zoölogical Society as a place that would save specimens from across the world from complete extermination. He also argued that Alaska should become a "gigantic preserve" because its species—the giant moose, brown bears, and wolves—were "the very culmination of their respective genera" but needed protection from the locals (including the Native people) who, he claimed, killed the game then blamed visiting sportsmen ("Condition" 369). The rhetoric of disappearing opportunities is redoubled in this essay. Not only is the game vanishing but so is the possibility of refuge: Alaska is "our last chance to preserve and protect rather than to restore" (374). As the urgency increases, so does the range of targets in need of protection, moving beyond animals to the giant sequoias and redwoods in California, "a failing and dying race," and Glacier National Park in Montana, whose establishment fifteen years earlier must be recorded "before it was too late" ("Saving" 186; "Beginnings" 446).

These arguments for protecting animal and natural life served as templates when Grant moved on to human enclaves, in his "bible of scientific racism," *The Passing of the Great Race* in 1916 (Spiro 140). Many influences bore on this work—including Gregor Mendel, William Z. Ripley, and Francis Galton—but the logic, vision, style, and narrative structure all palpably owe something to his Boone and Crockett work. From the preface by Henry Fairfield Osborn, honorary Boone and Crockett Club member and president of the American Museum of Natural History, through the argument about the ancient emergence and contemporary superiority of the Nordic race in Europe and the United States, the basis is insistently biological. History is in heredity, and culture, language, and environment are sentimental myths. Given that "The laws which govern the distribution of the various races of man and their evolution through selection are substantially the same as those controlling the evolution and distribution of the larger mammals," the lessons of hunting and conservation clearly apply (33). In the same way that trophy heads are ranked by dimensions of heads and horns (a process the Boone and Crockett Club began to standardize in 1902, the same year as *The Virginian*'s publication), so racial superiority in humans is proven by the cephalic index (proportions of the skull) and various "unit characters" including—like the moose whose "Jewish" features worried Grant—the nose.

Population control follows the same lines: "indiscriminate breeding" is not the answer to "race suicide" (43). "Public opinion" should follow the lessons of cattle and sheep "stock breeders" (49). First, the herd must be culled: "A rigid system of selection through the elimination of those who are weak or unfit" must be exercised among human populations (46). Bloodlines must be kept pure: "the laws against miscegenation must be greatly extended if the higher races are to be maintained" (56). And racial enclaves must be established, much beyond the methods of Jim Crow segregation: "If the purity of the two races is to be maintained, they cannot continue to live side by side."[25] As ever, the impelling motive is the threat of vanishing: without such measures, "the native American"—by which he means the Anglo-American—"will entirely disappear" (81). One reader who objected to Grant's argument unwittingly made his work sound just like *The Virginian*: "the whole book extols aristocracy and apparently the aristocracy of physical force."[26]

The Immigration Restriction League used Grant's arguments in their representations about "new"—that is, non-Nordic—immigrants to the congressional immigration committee, which (along with several of Grant's Boone and Crockett clubmates, his clubs, and the Zoölogical Society) received a complimentary copy of *The Passing of the Great Race*.[27] The book explicitly connects government policy, national belonging, and club membership: Grant argued that "the European governments took the opportunity to unload upon careless, wealthy, and hospitable America the sweepings of their jails and asylums" and, quoting Gouverneur Morris, said, "Every society from a great nation down to a club has the right of declaring the conditions on which new members should be admitted" (*Passing* 80; quoted in Spiro 196–97). He also worked closely with his friend Charles Benedict Davenport, head of the Eugenics Record Office, to weld this rhetoric to data on heredity.

The Passing of the Great Race was very successful in whipping up eugenic panic more broadly. Although its sales were not massive, they were steady and long-lasting. For several years, it appeared in new editions annually and semi-annually, and it answered the quality publisher's perennial desire to seize the market from a "high culture" position. Scribner's told Grant that it was "one of the most successful books addressed to the thoughtful public published at the same period, in a commercial sense as well as one of the most widely discussed and favourably commented upon."[28] Grant soon found himself in the familiar bind of the frontier clubman who wanted to exert popular influence without being implicated in the mechanisms of commercial production. By 1922, Scribner's was trying to persuade him to compromise with the large reading public that they believed was available for his work: "If we could leave off the appendices the book could be made in a new edition decidedly lower in price and a little less formidable to the popular reader."[29] Also, they wanted to create publicity by profiling him as a personality—similar to the kind with which Wister wrestled earlier in the century. Grant was even more uncomfortable: "You have asked me to do a very embarrassing piece of personal work but here is the result. I don't like to talk about myself and have kept it in relatively small limits."[30] By 1933, when he published *Conquest of the Continent*, which he liked to call "the first history of any nation that has been written in terms of Race," with Scribner's, he turned to an advertising source with which he felt more comfortable: Owen Wister.[31] Wister obliged with an endorsement combining the familiar frontier club blend of nationalism, species hierarchy, and beleaguerment—the last bolstered by a reference to another Scribner's volume that had been subject to what they called "unofficial censorship" four years earlier:

> I have seen no book that tells the great adventure of the United States as does this one. It cuts down to the roots of the grass....
>
>   Over our birth presided Washington, Hamilton, Jefferson, Adams, Franklin, Patrick Henry, and their like. Over our present dangerous illness preside—Who? Where are the Washingtons gone, and why?
>
>   These pages give the answer: We invited cuckoos to lay in our nest.
>
>   The cuckoo newspapers are denying publicity to this book as naturally as Christian Science endeavoured to stifle the true biography of Mary Baker Eddy.[32]

Grant's vision—conjoining the western narrative formula, conservation laws, and immigration policy—devolved directly onto the U.S. landscape, in the form of game reservations and protected stands of California Redwoods. His most culturally visible impact on the natural world came in 1895, when he was the main architect of the New York Zoölogical Society, which he oversaw throughout his life. For Grant, the zoo was dedicated as much to fencing out the hoi polloi of humanity as fencing in the magnificent specimens of animals: "On his deathbed he was still battling to keep the public from bringing cameras into the zoo" (Higham 155). He also saw it as a Boone and Crockett Club project. He persuaded the club to lobby and take initial responsibility for the organization and he drew nine club members (including Roosevelt, Grinnell, Osborn, and W. Austin Wadsworth, club president at that point), as well as Andrew Carnegie, into the board of managers. Grant also hired William T. Hornaday, a big-game hunter and former chief taxidermist at the American Museum of Natural History in Washington, DC, as first director of the New York Zoölogical Park (later, the Bronx Zoo). Hornaday would become an important ally of the Boone and Crockett Clubmen, especially when he co-founded the Bison Society with Roosevelt.[33] However, he was also something of a thorn in their side. He campaigned long and hard for election to the club. Grinnell was privately reluctant, at first because Hornaday's hunting motives were insufficiently gentlemanly

(Grinnell wrote to Roosevelt, "I am a little bit doubtful about Hornaday.... all his hunts have been in a measure professional. That is to say, he has been a taxidermist and hired to go out and collect"), later because of his irascible tendency to offend other allies.[34] He finally achieved associate member status in 1910.

This institution also came to frame frontier club output. Owen Wister recognized as early as 1901: "To see an antelope to-day you must visit a Zoological Garden, or else get out of your Pullman and search far into the wilderness. These destructions, these vanishings, have happened within the lives of men in whose hair no gray has come yet" ("Wilderness" 252). In 1907, Remington struggled to find a model for his sculpture "The Buffalo Horse" (later made into an oil painting). The only way he could find a buffalo to study was to travel to the Bronx Zoo. When we consider how iconic, and how imitated, Remington's vision of the West was, it seems significant that he saw himself "getting my Bronx ideas in to buffalo."[35] Grant's presence long hovered over the Bronx Zoo. Following in the footsteps of Roosevelt who, in 1897, had a species of elk, *Cervus Roosevelti*, named after him, in 1901, a "magnificent" new species of caribou, discovered in Alaska, was named after Grant: *Rangifer granti* (Morris 589; Spiro 25). In 1915, wildlife artist Carl Rungius (whom Grinnell called "beyond question the best animal painter in the country" and who illustrated some later Boone and Crockett volumes) was commissioned to paint a portrait of *Rangifer granti*.[36] Titled "Patriarch of the Herd," it hung for decades in the zoo's administration building.

Another Hank

We would seem to have traveled quite far from western fiction, except that Grant himself sealed the connection. In 1931, he published the strangest western produced by any frontier clubman: *Hank: His Lies and His Yarns* (whose format and title echo Wister's first published story). In some ways discontinuous and fantastical, the work is most legible as Grant's attempt to reach back to the late-nineteenth-century ur-western and revive its first principles of frontier club exclusion.

By 1930, Grant was bed-ridden, crippled with rheumatoid arthritis; Grinnell lamented that his friend had become "rather an invalid, only about 65 years old."[37] Long past hunting and soon unable to participate in government lobbying, Grant had one remaining resource he could contribute to the frontier club project: his writing. In his last essay for the Boone and Crockett Club, "The Vanished Game of Yesterday" (1933), he advocated two strategies of revivification. First, there should be a sustained effort to keep restoring "vanishing species" (8), as had been effected by W. T. Hornaday with bison from the New York Zoölogical Park transplanted to Oklahoma. Second, "There is need of an energetic writer" (3).

These years also saw the rise of B western movies, the singing cowboy, and the sexed up, sensationalized westerns of Zane Grey, Max Brand, and the pulp magazines. Grant's response to what he saw as cultural degeneration was to return to the frontier club tipping point, when the Boone and Crockett Club hunting tale morphed into the cowboy adventure, and to heroize the type whose Nordic purity he lauded in *Passing*: "our Western frontiersmen, who individually were a far finer type than the settlers who followed them" (67). *Hank*, his only work of fiction, consists of twenty-two anecdotes which, as the foreword says, "stretch across the Continent,—from Newfoundland on the east to the Seward Peninsula, Alaska, where the Old World and Asia are in sight. They illustrate a phase of the frontier which is passing" (9). The tales are told by a hunting guide to a gentleman hunter, mostly in the all-male enclave of the campfire in the midst of hunting trips for moose, bear, and antelope. The result reads like a private conversation—men sharing intimacies round a campfire or behind club walls—in which the gentlemanly façade is stripped away.

Hank most often appears as a white hunting guide. At times, he shape shifts into other versions of frontier masculinity, as if Grant were packing in the full range of types he encountered on his western trips, including the transnational Aboriginal in the process of vanishing into the mixed-race figure: "He may be a Yankee from Maine or a French half-breed from Quebec, or a hard-riding cowboy on the plains, or a mountain man from the Cassiars" (9). His tales touch comically on many frontier club motifs, including the fair chase, fossil-hunters, investment schemes, very briefly a genteel eastern woman, and a snobbish English hunter whom he takes down a peg or two. Parable-like, his adventures invariably issue in a naively expressed but deep-seated truth.

Hank's main function is to speak eugenics in the vernacular. Where, for example, *Passing* lauds "*Homo europœus*, the white man par excellence" (150) at length, Hank supports the principle "that all men are equal," as long as Mexicans, Native people, African Americans, Frenchmen and Dutchmen (the last "ain't so bad") are not included: "Hell, no,...I am talking about White Men" (51). His vocabulary seems to include every known racial slur and derogatory term. He echoes Wister, Roosevelt, and Whitney in classifying a "Greaser shepherd" as "vermin" (53), while also, like the Boone and Crockett executive in 1920, worrying away at the definition: "'Vermin,' says Hank, 'is anything you can't eat, so sheep ain't vermin, though they ought to be'" (53). He castigates Jews and Slovaks (the major bête noir of *Passing*) at length. In a period in which the long-standing Chinese Exclusion Act reduced Chinese immigration to zero, the tone ultimately feels cathartic: "I tell you it's an outrage for this damn British empire to allow Chinamen to come over to this country and take a white man's living right out of his mouth. Worse than that, the law makes a fuss whenever white men try to get their rights" (66). The final words of the volume— "women are queer"—sound more like a feeble swipe at the now enfranchised group (114).

The gentleman hunter to whom Hank speaks is simply known as "the Major," a figure whose identifying features so closely echo Grant—he is of the New York upper class and has traversed the same hunting grounds—that Mark Weiner has called the work "his frontier memoir" (84). This was also the pseudonym under which the book was published. In the foreword, "the Major" positions himself as simply the transcriber of Hank's stories—"The undersigned assumes no responsibility for their authenticity"—thereby distancing Grant twice over from their brutality (10). At the same time, Hank validates the Major's credentials as hunter and democrat, distinguishing him, for example, from the English hunter: "Now you are different, Major. Sure, you are too modest like. You've got more education than I have, but you don't rub it in" (50). The only action sequence in which the Major plays the main role is a stalk and anticipated showdown in Nome, Alaska. He is pursued by a miner named Broncho Jim, "awful quick on his feet and with a gun," in revenge for a company the Major now owns having earlier defaulted on his wages (95). Just at the point when the scene is about to climax into a face-off between old and new—or gunslinger and corporate—Wests, it deflects into a comic tale about another miner, Stillwater Bill, winning his girl, Nell, with a trick to do with "scrambled aigs." Echoing Wister's Molly, who "wants a man that is a man" (261), Nell says ecstatically to the Major, "That's what I call a man" (103). Perhaps this is, after all, Grant's Virginian moment—the Virginian of the tall tale and "frawgs' laigs."

The volume preserves racial purity in the West, expelling what *Passing* calls "disharmonic combinations" in the raw racism and sexism that are displaced to Hank's untutored voice (12). His function as anecdotist is to ventriloquize the brutal attitudes that the clubmen could not openly speak, voicing "the prejudices and antipathies of our Colonial ancestors" (9)—the same "Colonial stock" (80) who are heroized in *Passing* and in the fraternal Society of Colonial Wars, which Grant and his brother co-founded and of which Grinnell was a keen member.

Grant approached his long-time editor, Maxwell Perkins at Scribner's, with this manuscript in May 1930. Scribner's had earlier published the transnational hunting travelogue of Grant's colleague William T. Hornaday, *Camp-Fires in the Canadian Rockies* (1906).[38] Perkins (also, more famously, Hemingway's editor) had coached Grant encouragingly through the many editions of *Passing* as well as other projects by him and his protégé, Lothrop Stoddard (whose *The Rising Tide of Color Against White World-Supremacy* Scribner's had published in 1920). Perkins weathered various storms of protest from critics and readers over the ideological leanings of Grant's publications, pleading a big-tent publishing policy that could embrace diverse viewpoints without endorsing them all. The experienced editor could not, however, see any sales prospects in Grant's fictional tales. He immediately recognized their proper placement as the arena in which Grant first began writing—"A sporting magazine might well be delighted to have them."[39] His other suggestion was "a newspaper syndicate," and he offered to put Grant in touch with a syndicate agency. As always, Grant balked at contact with the commercial press: "I would hate to see them syndicated in newspapers."[40] (He did, however, approach the *Saturday Evening Post*, the periodical of choice for eugenics and immigration restriction pieces, which also seems to have turned him down.)

The project was too close to Grant's heart for him to let it go, and ultimately he turned to private publication, funded from his personal resources. He issued an edition that, like club membership, was "limited strictly to one hundred and fifty copies." This was one of the last enclaves Grant would create. He died in 1937, one of the figures least associated with the western but in some ways the one who expressed the motive force of the frontier club in the most uncompromising terms.

American Indian Assimilation

No frontier clubman was as directly involved in the Indian Citizenship Act as was Madison Grant in the National Origins Act, although, as president, Roosevelt engaged with American Indian policy, and Grinnell served as one of his main advisors. Frontier club narratives also made a significant contribution to the broader logic of assimilation. Like the Dawes Act of 1887 and its subsequent implementation acts, allotting tribal lands in severalty, clubmen's hunting tales re-map the landscape, replacing tribal patterns with individualized white presences whose adventures invariably end in acts of ownership, in the form of the trophy heads they carry home. The figure who is "native" to this scene is the white hunter—and his readership. Louis Warren argues that, "emulating Theodore Roosevelt, white middle-class Americans turned to hunting to establish themselves as natives in a country of new immigrants" (Review 621).

Boone and Crockett Clubmen underscored that process by "playing Indian," participating in the long, complex tradition traced by Philip Deloria, by which imaginary, mythologized Indigeneity is absorbed into white group identity while actual Native people are expelled. In the same way that many fraternal societies and other U.S. organizations, from the Revolutionary period onwards, created "insider identities" by drawing on Aboriginal culture, so in the Boone and Crockett Club "some members were given distinguished Native American names such as Pappago, Little Brave, and Running Waters" (Deloria 48; Brinkley 205). The Club's particular ritual of Aboriginal appropriation joined hunting and territorial acquisition. An extended demonstration appeared in the second book of the Boone and Crockett Club. Henry L. Stimson—who would become secretary of war to Presidents Taft, Franklin D. Roosevelt, and Harry Truman, as well as secretary of state to Herbert Hoover—wrote up the ascent of Chief Mountain completed by Dr. Walter B. James and himself with the guidance of "our faithful packer, Fox" and "Piegan Billy" (221). At that time part of the Blackfeet Reservation, Chief Mountain was (and remains) a sacred place to the Blackfeet Nation and was said to have been scaled only once, via its west face, by "a great Flathead warrior, a man watched over by a spirit so mighty that no peril of battle or of the hunt could overcome him" (297). When the Boone and Crockett hunters decide to tackle the east face, Stimson frames their undertaking in recognizable stalk-and-showdown terms: "was it not better to meet our king face to face than to steal on him from behind?" (230) When all but the mixed-race Fox achieve the top, they—white men and Native guide together— become the heirs to the Flathead warrior. They discover the ancient bison skull that he left on the summit—"The old Flathead's pillow!" (235). While reverence (and perhaps the presence of Billy) prevents them from removing it, Stimson manages to appropriate the mountain itself: "for the first time we felt as if our king were really ours," yet another trophy for Boone and Crockett Clubmen (234). When Grinnell received Stimson's submission, he enthused to Roosevelt that it was "capital" and "first class."[41] The following year Grinnell would facilitate surrender of Chief Mountain to the federal government, another iteration of the familiar process of appropriation—from names to rituals to territory.

Other hunting tales and conservation essays confirmed that Native people had become unnatural presences in their own land, by alternately erasing and demonizing their presence. From the first pages of the first volume in the series, the term "reservation" is stripped of its human connotations, recasting sites across the country, from the Adirondacks in New York to the Yosemite Valley in California, as places of game and timber only. Arnold Hague, who, as head of the U.S. Geological Survey mapped the land according to hegemonic coordinates, extended that project in his Boone and Crockett essay. "The Yellowstone Park as a Game Reservation" writes Native people, whose trails crisscrossed the area, out of the scene: "It had been visited only by a few venturesome pioneers, mining prospectors, and fur-hunters" (243). Repeatedly, essays and club resolutions position Native hunters as the greatest threat to the sanctity of the national parks and reserves, arguing that they must be barred from those spaces because of their propensity to slaughter big game and destroy timber indiscriminately. Again, the imaginative and rhetorical appropriations of the Boone and Crockett Club dovetailed absolutely with the federal policy appropriating tribal lands: pre- and post-Dawes, Native peoples' holdings shrank from 138 million to 5 million acres.[42]

As the frontier club western developed, it did not lavish attention on war-whooping savages nor battles between cavalrymen and Indians; that was dime-novel territory. Frontier clubmen dominate the West by assimilating

Native presences into Anglo perspectives. The West that Dr. Silas Weir Mitchell offered up as a resource for upper-class masculinity was quietly emptied out of its Indigenous inhabitants. In the story of his own maturation as hunter in the West, Roosevelt kept Natives hovering, temporally and spatially, on the fringes so that they do not displace his ownership but serve as residual threat, spicing up his account. In *Hunting Trips of a Ranchman*: "There are now no Indians left in my immediate neighborhood, though a small party of harmless Grosventres occasionally passes through; yet it is but six years since the Sioux surprised and killed five men in a log station just south of me ... and, two years ago, when I went down on the prairies toward the Black Hills, there was still danger from Indians" (18–19). Wister wrote stories about selected tribal people on commission by the Harpers early in his career—some of them were collected in his first book, *Red Men and White* (1895)—invariably coming at his subject through the perspectives of white soldiers and his familiar eastern narrator.[43] The closer he came to his cattle-country western, the more tightly he absorbed Native presences into the Anglo voice. In *The Virginian*, they appear twice: the silent "Indian chiefs ... in their show war bonnets and blankets" listening on the edge of the crowd to the Virginian's tall tale and the unseen assailants of the Virginian, made present only through the narrator's and the Virginian's accounts. (In the stage version, where the mechanics called for the attack to happen on-stage, the culprit was changed to Trampas.) As always, narrative and legal strategies developed hand in hand. Later in 1902, Wyoming game laws barred Natives from game reserves.[44]

Once more, the choices made in the frontier club western are thrown into relief by work at its outer reaches. Frederic Remington was no keener than the others on the survival of contemporary Natives as sovereign people with agency. As usual, however, he was blunter in demonstrating the costs of cultural genocide. In three book-length works he put mixed-race and Native figures front and center, in order to dramatize their violent displacement and extinction in the West. The eponymous protagonist of *Sundown Leflare* (1899) is the wittiest figure, "cross-bred, red and white, so he never got mentally in sympathy with either strain of his progenitors" (3). Employed as an interpreter by a first-person narrator lightly reminiscent of Remington (an artist who comments that he does not have the hunters' "purpose, which is 'big game,' close to my heart" [50]), Sundown insists on taking over the storytelling, recounting his own exploits and visions in broken English. *John Ermine of the Yellowstone*, published in the same year as *The Virginian*, speaks back most directly to Wister's novel, exploding its love plot that harmonizes the West, South, and East. Ermine, who comes to occupy the central consciousness of the novel, is a white boy brought up by Absaroke, then retrained for white life by an old mountain man and hermit through the standard hunting rites of passage. Ermine becomes a scout for the cavalry and falls in love with the colonel's daughter, Katherine Searles, after she flirts with him. Proposing to Katherine, Ermine offers to "make a good camp in the mountains" with her (223), exactly the same honeymoon as the Virginian provides for Molly. The difference is that Katherine laughs in Ermine's face. Ultimately, he is killed, shot down for daring to cross class and race lines in his approach to the eastern, upper-class woman. *The Way of an Indian* (1905) completes the end-game, telling the elegiac coming of age, resistance, and death of a Cheyenne warrior.[45]

When the *New York Times* reviewed *John Ermine* enthusiastically—"it is 'The Virginian' with a thousand differences"—the reviewer zeroed in on the passage that most nearly echoes Remington's liminal position in the frontier club. When Katherine rejects Ermine, Captain Lewis of the cavalry, whom Ermine has saved from Sioux attack, sympathetically says that he "felt for him." Ermine shoots back: "I know what you feel for me, Capt. Lewis. You feel that I am an uneducated man, without money, and that I do not wear a white shirt; that I tuck my pants in my leggings, and that I sleep among the Indians. I know that you think I am a dog" ("Remington's"). Again, Remington's words resonate with his private attitude to *The Virginian*, which he had declined to illustrate, considering it "slop," "without truth" and narrated by a type of "thin-chested, cigarette-smoking dude" whom he scorned (quoted in Scharnhorst ix). The frontier club fiction that Remington refused was reinstated in Louis Shipman's dramatization of the novel; for a (somewhat unsuccessful) Broadway run, Shipman changed the ending to a happy wedding of Katherine and Ermine, similar to Molly and the Virginian. In Remington's authorship, however, "playing Indian" leads not to personal fulfillment but to death, and the process of assimilation is not invisible nor romantically vague but melodramatic and violent.

George Bird Grinnell

Choctaw/Cherokee/Irish critic Louis Owens has argued that, in the late nineteenth century, white custodianship of Native peoples manifested itself in American Indian reservations, national parks ("fixed spaces within which the imagination of the dominant culture can play"), and western narratives (73), which together worked to constrain Indigenous nations' mobility and agency. The most powerful boundary setting—"the ultimate hegemony"—lies in fiction: "Whose novel is the West, and who gets to tell the story?" (74). Owens here focuses on Owen Wister, but his analysis is even more illuminating of George Bird Grinnell. It provides an answer to the conundrum of how Grinnell, the most progressive face of the frontier club, could end up helping the U.S. government to perpetrate what Louis Warren calls "a massive 'poaching' of Indian wildlife" and territory (*Hunter's* 126). The key lies in the terms by which Grinnell expanded the club's conservationist mission—in preserving animals, nature, and Native and non-Native peoples, he was also preserving his class's "elite custodial identity"—and in the narrative methods that underpinned this vision (Deloria 82).

Grinnell is always spoken of as self-effacing, someone more interested in building alliances than stealing the show; Madison Grant told him, "You have been altogether too modest all your life."[46] While he was proud of being adopted into the Blackfeet Nation by White Calf, who gave him the name Pi-nut-u-is-tsim-o-kan (Fisher Hat), he acknowledged the limits of his ethnographic insight: "I have reached the shell with two or three tribes, and perhaps have gotten a little way into the white, but way down deep there is the yolk of the egg—the heart of the matter—which I do not penetrate and perhaps no one ever will" (quoted in S. Smith 58). Yet his deeply personal investment in this work led him to closely align policy and the private and to write his personal story on a larger scale across the landscape and in more intimate terms in his western fiction than any other frontier clubman.

Grinnell's campaigns to protect wilderness and wildlife were accompanied by calls for justice for tribes. Under his tenure, a typical *Forest and Stream* editorial page juxtaposed a call for wardens to enforce game laws in the West with "The National Shame," a smaller item on starving nations and tribes in Montana that clearly blamed the "cruel apathy of officials" and called for a congressional investigation (September 4, 1884). Two years later, a longer column titled "A Nation's Honor" recounts a cabinet officer's attempt to remove the Puyallup from their reservation in northwest Washington Territory in "a fair example of the shameful course of fraud and oppression carried on by the Government toward the Indians" (241). He exposed corruption on reservations, lobbied for good governance, increased annuities, and adherence to treaties. He told Blackfeet who approached him for aid in combating a corrupt agent on the Blackfeet Reservation that he would put his writing at their service: "My business is to write. Many thousands hear my words, more people perhaps than live in all Montana" (quoted in S. Smith 60). He pursued this mission both in his magazine campaigns and in his ethnographies of Pawnee, Blackfeet, and Cheyenne, which he aimed at a general audience and which long remained sources of reference.[47] He also developed friendships with particular Native and mixed-race hunters and guides, and he won the trust of many Natives in the West. In 1916, when Grant was publishing *The Passing of the Great Race*, Grinnell was publishing "What We May Learn from the Indian."

He carried that vigilance into the governmental realm when he worked with the Indian Rights Association and the Sequoya League and served as one of Roosevelt's informal advisors on Indian affairs. He alerted the president when action was needed to address corruption or adverse conditions on reservations, especially those of the Northern Cheyenne and Blackfeet; at Roosevelt's request, he acted as negotiator between Sioux and white cattlemen who sought to graze their cattle on tribal lands; and he drafted the relevant parts of Roosevelt's State of the Union messages in 1902 and 1904.[48] He also lobbied vigorously, though ultimately unsuccessfully, to adapt the provisions of the Dawes Act to particular tribal terrains and needs.

But Grinnell also put his stamp on that land in classic frontier club terms. In 1885, as Wister was being introduced to Wyoming, Grinnell was led to the St. Mary Lake country on the Blackfeet Reservation in northwestern Montana. He had been approached by Appekunny (James Willard Schultz), a white man married to a Blackfeet woman, to intercede on behalf of the destitute Blackfeet, and he was guided into the mountains by Appekunny and Otokomi, whom Grinnell described as "a French half-breed" ("To" 382). The area was the traditional hunting grounds of people now identified as Ariskapi Pikuni (Blackfeet), Sqeilo (Salish) and K'tanaxa (Kootenai).[49] This would become his new mecca: the mountains, glaciers, and valleys were even more breath-taking and even less touched by commercial industry than Yellowstone. He returned yearly, doing a little hunting but soon concentrating more on geo-logical exploration and ethnographic fieldwork on the Blackfeet Reservation, gathering information and artifacts.

Frontier clubmen never conceptualized the wilderness they set out to pre-serve as the natural commons (far less the natural right) of Native peoples. Here we can turn to the second object in the Boone and Crockett Club con-stitution: "To promote travel and exploration in the wild and unknown, or but partially known, portions of the country." The unasked question, of course, is "unknown to whom?" Mark Spence has discussed at length how important it was for the late-nineteenth-century conservation lobby to imagine western land as unclaimed, untouched wilderness—to the point of ignoring the Native hunt-ing trails and tepee structures that zigzagged Yellowstone and to the detriment of tribal land-use rights. Grinnell, who refused to stereotype and demonize Native American people, could not resist writing them off the land when it came to his beloved St. Mary's region. His essays about this area literally wrote the Blackfeet out of the park's history: following Blackfeet guides on Indian trails up the mountains, he marveled (with, as Mark Spence comments, no apparent sense of irony) at the "absolutely virgin ground...with no sign of previous pas-sage" (quoted in Spence 78).

Grinnell moved from narrative control of the region to a more literally admin-istrative control when he began to name and map its features. It remained a point of pride with him that he did not initiate the affixing of his own name to the land-scape. He explained that, in 1887, Lieutenant John H. Beacom was reconnoiter-ing the St. Mary's region for cartographic purposes and was helped by him: "The reason I possess a basin and a glacier is because this young man insisted in naming both after me." Grinnell quickly followed suit: "I, having secured these pieces of property, could do no less than sprinkle the names of other members of [the] party over the adjacent territory" (quoted in Diettert 45). Gradually he superimposed his hunter-writer narrative over a huge swath of the Blackfeet Reservation east of the continental divide, the spot to which he returned repeatedly. One mountain, on which his party unsuccessfully blasted away at mountain goats, he called Fusillade Mountain; others he named after Boone and Crockett clubmates who accompanied him on hunting expeditions (Mount Gould, Mount Seward, Mount Stimson, Mount James), after the managing editor of *Forest and Stream* (Reynolds Mountain), and after the then-U.S. president, saying "that is the biggest mountain anywhere around here, and Cleveland is the biggest man in the country" (quoted in Diettert 75). He named other formations after his guides—Mount Jackson and Jackson Glacier after Billy Jackson, a Blackfeet mixed blood, and Appekunny's Mountain (contemporary spelling is Apikuni) after James Willard Schultz—and to others he gave tribal names, including Mount Siyeh and Siyeh Glacier after a Blackfoot chief, and Blackfoot Glacier and Piegan Mountain after the local people.[50] The most prominent and repeated name on the landscape was his own: to Grinnell Glacier and Grinnell Basin he added Grinnell Mountain, Grinnell Lake, Upper Grinnell Lake, Grinnell Point, and Grinnell Falls (more recently, a rock stratum and a lane on the west side of the park have also been named Grinnell).[51] Grinnell wrote these and many more names into the maps he began to sketch from 1887. His influence with the U.S. Geological Survey (whose head was fellow Boone and Crockett Clubman, Arnold Hague) was such that most of his names received imprimatur in the official maps. Their permanence was further secured when first President Harrison, in 1890, then President Roosevelt, in 1906, established boards to regularize geographical names.[52] So the gentleman hunter's narrative became writ large in the official, federally mandated representation of this space.

These names dislodged stories and figures attached to the land by the local Indigenous peoples; Pikuni scholar Darrell Robes Kipp says that his people fully chronicled "the glaciers, lakes, mountains, streams, and trails of the area with long-established Blackfeet names and descriptions" (viii). Take, for example, Mount Stimson and Mount James, which Grinnell named after his Boone and Crockett clubmates from New York who scaled Chief Mountain. Over the years, these names have been switched from one peak to another in the park, so that it has become particularly difficult to recover the relevant Indigenous names. By one account, Mount James was called by the Blackfeet Ah'-kow-to-makan (Double Runner), by another account, Nitáina or Nitai´na Îstûkî (Lone Chief).[53] Mount Stimson has a Kootenai name—variously reported as Aqa¢ku'tła, Qa¢ku'tła, or Kâtsku´ta Ahkowokalet´ (Flint Lodge)—and is referred to by the Blackfeet as Kriszikúmi-Pítaw or Xiszikúmi-Pítaw (the aerie of the Thunder Eagle).[54] All of these names carry stories of human and spiritual significance: Double Runner has been identified as a warrior, Lone Chief as a signer of the Judith Treaty of 1855, and Flint Lodge as a lady of great age, while the Thunder Eagle signifies natural and sacred powers. When Grinnell overwrote such associations with the names of gentlemen hunters and clubmen, he put in process an irony that is particularly acute in the case of Henry Stimson. As Jack Holterman points out, as secretary of war under Franklin Roosevelt and Harry Truman, Stimson "has to share the responsibility for the internment of an estimated 120,000 Japanese Americans and the manufacture and dropping of atomic bombs on Hiroshima and Nagasaki.... There remains a bothersome question about the propriety of such a politically loaded name for a prominent feature in a national park that belongs to people of all political and ethnic persuasions" (194–95).

This rhetorical appropriation of the land through the 1880s and 1890s was soon matched by its material appropriation, with federal ownership of the space cleaving ever more closely to the frontier club template. In 1891, Grinnell began to dream of turning the St. Mary's country into "a National reservation or park," by buying "say 30 × 30 miles from the Piegan indians [sic] at a fair valuation."[55] At the same time, rumors of mineral finds brought increasing numbers of white trespassers onto the mountains, and tribal leaders were approached about surrendering their land, which would become known as the "ceded strip," since it was the remnant of their reservation, much of which they had relinquished in 1887. Having been cheated out of much of the funds from that treaty, by "a series of incompetent and inexperienced agents," the Blackfeet were determined to secure honest negotiators to protect their interests on this occasion (Diettert 62). They requested Grinnell and Charles E. Conrad, a local banker.

Grinnell reluctantly agreed to serve on the government commission that ultimately negotiated these additional land cessions from the Blackfeet and Assiniboine/Gros Ventre reservations in 1895.[56] He wrote to Jack Monroe, one of his Montana hunting guides, that his appointment to the commission was "a good deal to my own disgust, for it is not a job I like a bit."[57] While some tribal representatives believed that Grinnell worked to secure a fair price for them, he was party to convincing them that their way of valuing the land was inappropriate. He was also somewhat in conflict of interest, given that he was actively developing his plans to turn the land into a national park, should the mineral promise not pan out (his skepticism on this front proved to be accurate). In 1894, he had approached the Great Northern Railroad for its support in developing "a public park and pleasure resort, somewhat in the nature of Yellowstone National Park," which it would be in their interests to monopolize. Grinnell's diary entry during the negotiations, as he was arguing the Blackfeet down from their $3 million price, comes close to admitting the conflictedness of his position: "the whole thing is amusing but sickening. See both sides of the game" (quoted in Diettert 66). In the end, White Calf, the tribal chief, reluctantly agreed to a price of $1.5 million along with the continuation of tribal hunting, grazing, fishing, and timber rights. White Calf's language is vividly at odds with the image of Grinnell sprinkling names across the landscape (and with the clubmen's stories of triumphantly conquering its peaks): "Chief Mountain is my head. Now my head is cut off. The mountains have been my last refuge" (quoted in Diettert 69).

Once Congress ratified the treaty to reduce the Blackfeet Reservation, in 1896, Grinnell began his lobbying efforts for a national park in earnest. He fostered links with the senators from Montana (partly by nominating Senator Thomas H. Carter to associate membership of the Boone and Crockett Club), and pressing his Boone and Crockett clubmates and his *Forest and Stream* readership into service as lobbyists. Louis W. Hill of the Great Northern Railroad also became seriously interested in the proposition. Carter introduced his first bill to create the park in December 1907. In the face of much local opposition— the park would mean the end of timber harvesting, hunting, and settlement—he modified the bill and introduced a second version in February 1908, in support of which Grinnell shepherded a resolution by the Boone and Crockett Club.[58] In the end, success came with a third bill that Carter introduced in June 1909— again Boone and Crockett Club members were exhorted to write on its behalf— and was signed into law by President Taft on May 11, 1910. Grinnell wrote to his Boone and Crockett clubmate D. M. Barringer: "Please pat yourself, the Boone and Crockett Club and me on the head, because the Glacier national park bill has been signed by the President."[59]

Grinnell came to claim ownership of the region with increasing confidence, as revealed in his repeated references to "my glacier" and his position as "chief of the St. Mary's country," however jocular (quoted in Diettert 76). Madison Grant, the clubmate who got behind the lobbying for Glacier National Park most energetically, encouraged this sense in Grinnell. After the park came into being, Grant produced a booklet documenting its history to ensure that Grinnell's formative role would not be forgotten. In his standard Boone and Crockett rhetorical move, Grant positioned him as a vanishing type: "Mr. Grinnell, perhaps more than any other living man, represents the now disappearing class of educated easterners who went to the frontier in the buffalo and Indian days and devoted their lives to the welfare of the great West" (*Early* 5). Grant recognized the possessive force of naming, filling two-thirds of the pamphlet with such details. He explained to Grinnell: "In the last analysis, the fact that you named all these natural features is the proof that will be most readily accepted of your identification with the region."[60]

Grant was correct. The 1926 Glacier National Park Report shows Grinnell's continuing dominance, in its attention to his person, in his name on natural formations, and in the names he gave to formations.[61] When President Calvin Coolidge presented Grinnell with the Theodore Roosevelt Distinguished Service Medal in 1925, he called the park "peculiarly your monument" (quoted in Diettert 106). Emerson Hough heralded him as the "father of the park" in the *Saturday Evening Post*, Billy Hofer long referred to "Your Black Foot and other Indians," and another admirer sent him "a slight token of appreciation for having founded this noble mountain wonderland for us."[62]

Those familiar emphases on possessive individualism ushered in the inevitable exclusions. First the government reneged on the land use agreement built into the cession, then the Glacier National Park Act of 1910, the courts decreed, definitively "extinguished all Blackfeet claims to the mountains on the western boundary of their reservation" (Spence 72). The Great Northern Railroad, which trademarked the park with its logo and images, branded the members of diverse Indigenous nations whom it employed as entertainers at Glacier Park Hotel under the homogenous title "Glacier Indians" in its advertising. The National Park Service was also eager to employ Blackfeet as part of their tourist apparatus, but pressed charges against any who exercised their traditional right to hunt the back country.

Soon Grinnell suffered the familiar frontier club reaction of feeling himself to be both beleaguered and excluded. The Great Northern Railroad monopoly he had facilitated produced crowds of tourists traveling to the park and kept prices high in their many hotels. The National Park Service laid down rules and regulations against which Grinnell rebelled. In July 1923, when he was told that visitors could only travel by saddle horse with a guide, he went to the top, winning "a letter of exception" from the acting director of the National Park Service. "Without such protection I do not care to go into the park," Grinnell threatened, in language strongly reminiscent of eastern club culture.[63] Even with these special provisions, the new conditions meant "my practical expulsion from the region" (quoted in Diettert 104-05).

Jack the Young Frontier Clubman

In February 1908, Senator Thomas H. Carter of Montana introduced his second bill to establish Glacier National Park. In support, Grinnell sat down and wrote a children's book. *Jack the Young Explorer* was the sixth in a series that eventually grew to seven volumes, all revolving around the boy Jack Danvers, a wealthy New Yorker who travels west every summer during the late 1870s and early 1880s. Even more than the standard hegemonic operation of the western novel as identified by Owens, Grinnell's series reinforces white custodianship over animals, nature, and Indigenous peoples. Characters often voice his advocacy on the enforcement of game laws, protection for Yellowstone National Park, justice for Native peoples, conservation of timber,

and the like. As with so much children's literature of the era, the novels massage cultural contradictions, in this case between gentlemen hunters and
Native rights, revealing the dependency of the mythic space of conservation
on the historic time of American Indian assimilation. The series also exposes
the deeply personal investments that connected the emerging western formula with government policy. If Glacier National Park represents one very
public demonstration of Grinnell's private hunter-writer story, his Jack books
represent another.

Grinnell began his cycle of western novels in 1899 as an entertainment for his
young nieces and nephews, making up the stories out of his own western adventures. His brother, Morton, showed the first manuscript to Frederick A. Stokes,
a quality children's publisher who belonged to the Ivy League network: "All the
firm members were Yale graduates"—as, of course, was Grinnell (Tebbel 375).
Stokes offered to publish it and continued to press for new volumes with the
same cast of characters. As always with frontier club authors, Grinnell was concerned that his work should be positioned appropriately in the literary marketplace, keeping a close eye on the first volume's production: "the cover is rather
brilliant, but should attract the class that we want to reach."[64] Stokes clearly found
the Jack books a going concern: in 1907, in sending along one royalty report, he
told Grinnell, "the new book ought to result in even better returns for you for the
coming year," and he lobbied strongly for Grinnell to produce an eighth volume
in 1918, "especially if you could bring him up to date as participating in the military activities in which every young American of the right sort is taking part."[65]
Grinnell declined, although he later commented wistfully, "I have sometimes
thought that it would have been better if I had kept on grinding out those books
up to the present time. They seemed to please small boys."[66] Grinnell continued
to receive enthusiastic letters from readers for many years, often asking him for
practical advice about going west.

The books aspire to a tremendous amount of cultural work. The stories are
replete with Grinnell's knowledge, experiences, desires, and friends. He strongly
works the pedagogical dimension, drawing on paleontology, ornithology, ethnography, tribal stories, natural and human history, along with practical advice
on big-game hunting, trapping, shooting, roping, cattle ranching, bronco breaking, horse-packing, and camping. He writes himself into the western scene as
two characters, a wealthy easterner and a rugged westerner, who fulfill the identity for which he strove, described by his friend Hamlin Garland admiringly as
"a singular mixture of the old Manhattan and the old borderman" (quoted in
Hagan 139). Jack's Uncle Will Sturgis—Grinnell seems to borrow the name of
the secretary to the Cheyenne Club, William Sturgis—is an ornithologist who
owns a ranch in Wyoming, in the same location as Grinnell's ranch, returning
east every winter to live with the Danvers in the same district of Manhattan as

Grinnell made his adult home. The identification is so close that in two volumes he slips into referring to the character as "Uncle George." Hugh Johnson is of an older generation. Originally from Kentucky, he has long lived as a mountain man, trapper, cavalry scout and, now in his 50s (the decade Grinnell had just reached when he wrote the first volume), ranch-hand on Sturgis's Swiftwater ranch. Johnson's experiences are the young Grinnell's: he has guarded the railroad and hunted buffalo with the Pawnee under the command of Major Frank North, worked on the ranch of Luther North and Bill Cody, and accompanied General Custer on his Black Hills and Yellowstone expeditions, and he and Jack re-live several encounters with Sioux that Grinnell recorded in his memoirs. The central boy, Jack Danvers, could be named after Jack Audubon (who was named after his grandfather, John James Audubon), the childhood friend with whom Grinnell first hunted (years later, he remembered himself hunting with "a light double-barrel gun" given him by his own Uncle Will while Jack "was privileged by his father to carry his grandfather's gun").[67] Or the reference could be to Jack Nicholson, his fellow Yale graduate with whom he went west and shared hair-raising adventures on their first fossil-gathering expedition. Out of this mesh of memories, Grinnell creates another closed circle in which Sturgis and Johnson receive the unfailing admiration of Jack and of each other, and Jack depends particularly on Johnson, his faithful companion, for his western education, adventures, and achievements. Grinnell was so personally invested in this confluence of memory and wish fulfillment that he had the series read to him as he lay bed-ridden in his final illness.[68]

If the series was Grinnell's idealized version of the past, it was also his prescription for the future; the moral and practical lessons are, after all, directed at the young. And he used the books to negotiate his ongoing relationship with the West. Unlike Remington, whose narrator in *Sundown Leflare* declares of his account, "Neither sundown nor the agent will ever read it" (56), Grinnell sent his Jack books west to two of his hunting guides, both of whom were written into the stories as friends of Hugh Johnson: Jack Monroe and Billy Hofer. Johnson voices many of these guides' attitudes and sayings, as well as those of Grinnell's friend Charley Reynolds who died at the Little Bighorn (a signature saying of both Johnson and Reynolds is "You can't prove it by me"). Grinnell sent his first Jack book to Monroe, quite nervously asking for his opinion of "my youngest infant, the boy's book"; "I cannot imagine that you will find it very exciting."[69] Whatever Monroe responded, Grinnell sounded more relaxed and jocular with the second volume: "I have sent you copy of the book, 'Jack Among the Indians' which is offered for criticism. If you had paid more attention to the manners of the Indians in old times, and had given less attention to amusing yourself at the drunkenness of old Weaver at the old agency, I should regard you as a better critic."[70] Clearly, Grinnell envisaged a broader audience than eastern boys:

"What a great thing it would be if all innocent big game hunters would think that their success depended on reading this book."[71] Hofer encouraged him in this attitude, admiring the books as a resource for hunters. When asked by an eastern hunter for information about the small mammals of Colorado and Yellowstone, he reported, "I told him to get your Jack book 'Jack the Trapper.'"[72]

The first volume in the series—which was also Grinnell's first stab at a western—was *Jack the Young Ranchman* (1899). Its premise echoes the writings and experience of Mitchell, Roosevelt, and Wister. Jack is a sickly 14-year-old whose doctor prescribes a trip west to bring him to healthy manhood, a directive that takes him from his Manhattan mansion complete with black servants to his uncle's Wyoming ranch. Partly because of the pedagogical imperative, there is a great deal more detail afforded ranch work than in any of Wister's western fiction. At the same time, Grinnell struggles to develop adventurous action in this scene, falling back repeatedly on his Boone and Crockett style of narrative (sometimes literally importing chunks of his previously published hunting tales). The action is replete with the killing of animals, accompanied by the familiar Boone and Crockett Club code delivered by Hugh: no wastage, no greediness, and give animals a fair chance. When Grinnell makes the transition from animal to human kill, in *Jack in the Rockies* (1904), his showdown is even more explicitly patterned on the hunt narrative than Wister's. After having been charged by bears, elk, and a lion, Jack and Hugh are now charged by Jack Dowling, a rustler on horseback. The scene unfolds:

> The man came on; his horse was a great powerful beast and had been ridden hard, for it was covered with dust and foam. When he got within a hundred yards, Hugh dismounted, and stepping out in front of his horse, raised his rifle to his shoulder, and pointed it at the man. The man paid no attention to the motion, save to put his hand behind him and jerk from his holster a six-shooter. He called out something as he came on, but they could not distinguish what he said.
>
> "Hands up!" Hugh called; but the man paid no attention, and the distance between the party and the rider grew smaller.
>
> "Hands up!" Hugh shouted again, and then a third time; and still the man came on. Hugh fired, and the horse plunged forward on his knees throwing the rider far before him. It was Dowling.
>
> He struck on his head and hands and slid a little way along the earth, and then springing to his feet, with his left hand he pulled another six-shooter from his belt; but as he raised it, Hugh's rifle sounded again, and the man fell.
>
> "Look out for him, boys! Don't go near him; he's like a grizzly bear; likely to be playing possum." (268)

In his final book in the series, *Jack the Young Cowboy* (1913), Grinnell rings his own changes on what were by this point well entrenched elements of the frontier club formula. The novel, the most fully focused of the series on cattle range adventures, opens with Bess Powell, the young daughter from a neighboring ranch, shooting dead another suspected rustler who threatens her mother and herself. The rustler hies from just south of Buffalo, Wyoming, the territory of the Johnson County War, which postdates the action of the novel but would be a talismanic reference for some readers. Jack then averts a threatened lynching of the rustler's companion by seeing him off to the railroad. Later in the action, one of the Swiftwater Ranch cowhands, Jack Manson, converts a showdown with bad guy Claib Wood from six-shooters to fisticuffs then, at the closing dance, shakes hands with him. Grinnell emphasized that he wrote his stories for his nieces as well as his nephews. His reworking of the formulaic gunplay and lynching here may have been a gesture to the female members of his audience, writing them into the action in a way that none of the other frontier clubmen did.

In policy terms, the most suggestive feature of the story cycle is Grinnell's handling of the Native presence. Despite Mrs. Danvers's repeated worry that Jack is off to the land of "cowboys and Indians and wild animals," in fact Grinnell rarely brings cowboys and Indians together (*Jack the Young Ranchman* 5). His ranching scene is not quite as whitewashed as Wister's, in that there is some enthusiasm for the Mexican vaqueros, but the Indian is certainly vanishing. Aboriginal skills are present through Hugh's teachings—how to track animals, tan hides—and the injustices that have been done them are exposed repeatedly in Hugh's tales of massacres by U.S. cavalrymen. Their physical presence in the ranching West, however, has diminished to remains and relics. In the first novel, Jack stumbles upon a cave containing implements and pottery, along with the shrouded remains of a body. Grinnell uses the occasion to preach the message of cultural respect once more: to Jack, who is itching to take the bundle off to an eastern museum, Hugh says, "how would you like it if some day some fellow was to come along to the place where your great-great-grand-father had been buried, and should talk of carrying off his bones for a curiosity?" (292–95). But Grinnell upholds the basic myth of the vanishing Indian within the space of the frontier club western.

The avenue to a different space—the space of the Indigene—is opened by John Monroe, an old friend and hunting companion whom Hugh describes as "a Piegan half-breed, raised in Canada among the Crees and Frenchmen" (94). The character seems to be closely based on Grinnell's "great friend" of the same name.[73] John Monroe was son of Hugh Monroe (no relative to Jack Monroe), the first white man to settle in the St. Mary region with his Blackfeet wife. Before Grinnell wrote Monroe into his fiction, he wrote him into the landscape: in 1892, he reported that the "shoulder above the lake under 'my glacier, we have called Monroe Peak.'"[74]

Close to the end of the first Jack book, "John Monroe, Half Breed," as the chapter title calls him, emerges out of the snow at Swiftwater Ranch: "'Well, seh,' he said, 'my glad my get here'" (93). In a mixture of English, French, Piegan, and sign-language Monroe tells of the happenings in his country in Montana, where Natives and buffalo survive. Hugh is convinced that "It's like old times yet up north after all," while "the more Jack heard of their talk, the more eager he became to see something of this strange life, which seemed to him so much more wild, and so much more natural than even the life on the ranch" (97, 272).

This is the space to which Grinnell takes Jack in his second novel, *Jack among the Indians* (1900), a sequel that he itched to write and considered superior to his first effort.[75] After a few brisk chapters that bring Jack west to the ranch and join him with Hugh, the two set off northward, to a land where "they would probably not see a white face again," where "old-time Indians and old-time Indian ways" predominate (36, 56). Much is made of this rite of passage. First, Jack, bathing naked and unarmed—"He had never before felt so utterly helpless"—is surrounded by a group of armed Piegans, led by a Black Indian, who, luckily for him, turn out to be friendly (62). Then they must dodge hostiles—Sioux or Cheyenne—and, almost immediately after surviving that ordeal, Jack finds himself naked and vulnerable once more, caught in a quicksand, "the boy's white skin shining above the muddy water" (112). Safety comes when they arrive in the Piegan camp. Jack makes friends with a Piegan boy Joe, who, a later volume reveals, is a survivor of the infamous Baker Massacre of 1870, when Colonel Baker and his troops gunned down a peaceful Piegan village, the majority of them women and children. Jack saves a young Piegan girl from drowning, counts coup on an enemy Assiniboine, and becomes adopted into the Piegan tribe under the name White Warrior. With these standard "playing Indian" moves, Grinnell was teaching the next generation of white Americans to appropriate Native skills and identities, as were children's woodcraft and boy scouts movements in the same period.[76]

The other component of that dynamic is the assimilation that Grinnell works upon the next generation of Native Americans. In the final movement of *Jack among the Indians*, Jack and Joe discover a bag of gold which, it emerges, belongs to Baptiste Lajeunesse, an old, mixed-race mountain man who is now mentally incapable. The boys, under Hugh's guidance, put the money in the bank under their joint authority, the monthly interest to be meted out to Lajeunesse. Once more the frontier club author negotiates the new financial order of turn-of-the-century America, folding the Native into the dominant white system in protection of a mixed-race ward. In a time when American Indians were legal wards of the nation, this transfer of power and collective responsibility to a cross-cultural couple of teenagers—"Jack and Joe sat together on the back seat not saying much, but holding fast each other's hands"—was Grinnell's utopian vision of assimilation (301).[77]

In 1908, with *Jack the Young Explorer*, the novel written as a lobbying tool for the creation of Glacier National Park, Grinnell adhered more closely to the real-life workings of assimilation. On this trip, Jack travels by train directly to Montana, meeting up there with Hugh and Joe, and riding first to "The Blackfoot Agency" then on to the mountains and glaciers of the St. Mary's River region. The trio retrace Grinnell's steps from the 1880s—"By Northern Pacific Railroad to Helena, thence to Fort Benton, 116 miles by stage; from that point to old Piegan Agency on Badger Creek, 90 mls by wagon; and from there horses."[78] They also replay his battles when they hear the story of the "starving time" in 1883–1884 when six hundred Piegan died from government neglect—the emergency that first brought Grinnell to the region when he was alerted to it by James Schultz.[79] For two chapters, Grinnell grapples with the challenges of reservation life, condemning corruption but accepting the need for assimilation and regretting the hunting culture that ill fits Native peoples for modern life. These passages also echo the letters he had been sending to the Piegan for years. In the same year in which he wrote his first Jack book, for example, he sent a series of letters to Little Plume, Brocky, Mountain Chief, Jack Weasel, and Joe Calf Robe, scolding them for laziness, encouraging them to learn agricultural methods, and exhorting them to make all the men on the reservation plant gardens. To Joe Calf Robe, he wrote:

> There is one man on the Piegan reservation that you may all look up to because he works hard and earns money, and is getting to be just like a white man, that is Cut Bank John (Takes Gun in the Night). I should like to have all the Piegans imitate him.[80]

Hugh finally voices a resigned inevitability—"They've got to learn the lesson of steady, continued effort, and it's going to be mighty hard to teach them that"— then the three leave the historical, contradictory space of the reservation for the mythic pureness of what would become Glacier National Park (57). It is another neat sleight-of-hand by a frontier clubman, especially significant given the constitutive role played by works of imagination for young people: Jack sweeps off with his hunting party, leaving the Piegan, who have just been deemed unfitted by their hunting life, struggling to farm in his wake.

In this section—the bulk of the book, filled with the familiar hunting and camping adventures—Grinnell again stamps his claim on these lands as unknown and unpeopled. Repeatedly, Hugh insists that Natives did not travel the mountains, that their land stopped at the plains, and Joe concurs with his fear of the mountains and glaciers—on which, in climbing, they again follow Grinnell's footsteps—and his repeated desire to return to the familiar plains. Indeed, throughout these adventures, the white Hugh acts as guide to the Piegan Joe, a direct reversal of the means by which Grinnell first encountered these mountains and glaciers. It is Hugh who knows the names of mountains and lakes, strenuously advocating that they be named after Native figures. In detail after detail, the novel replays and reshapes Grinnell's private experiences into evidence of the need for white custodianship.

Here we can see Grinnell both assuaging his own conscience—his plans for the park are not robbing the Blackfeet of their land—and propagandizing on behalf of the 1908 bill. His emphasis here is strikingly different from his first writing about the region, over twenty years earlier, when he reported: "The Kootanays know these mountains well and are familiar with the best game locations. They are true mountain Indians, at home as much afoot among the rocks as on the plains in a saddle. We are almost entire strangers and have everything to learn for ourselves."[81] In contrast, his epilogue to the novel, titled "To-day," insists once more on the "unknown" status of the land around the head of the St. Mary's River and Swift Current, grappling uneasily with the evidence of previous travel: "ancient but long-disused trails ran up the rivers…it was hard to say whether they were Indian hunting trails, or merely paths worn by the buffalo and the elk" (306). He tells the story of Senator Thomas H. Carter of Montana introducing a bill establishing Glacier National Park "to include territory visited and seen by Hugh and Jack" (307). "If the measure shall become law, this most beautiful country, with its wonderful glaciers, its rushing rivers, its broad forests and its abundant game supply"—all of which have just figured in the novel—"may remain forever as a pleasure resort and playground for the benefit of the whole people of the United States" (307–08). In yoking Jack's adventures to the "whole people," Grinnell reaches once again for the classic lobbying rhetoric of the Boone and Crockett Club.

The fissures in the series, especially as they devolve on the separation of spaces, also speak strongly to the policy environment. Whatever Grinnell's complex of motives in helping Native people to assimilate, he needed them to be absorbed into white society if he was to carve out his beloved wilderness—specifically Glacier National Park, more generally the enclaves of conservation—for federal control. His series in effect separates off cowboys from Indians. The volumes set in the ranching West, which bookend the series, are dominated by whites, with some Mexican presence, and Indians as vanishing types represented by their remains and relics. The volumes set in the mountain and coastal wilderness of the United States and Canada are devoid of cowboys, paying considerable attention to a range of tribal people and their practices, as well as embracing a much more multicultural landscape, which includes Chinese, African Americans, and the Black Indian, Hezekiah Alexander (who has escaped from slavery in the South).

The only figures to cross between these two spaces are Hugh and Jack. The old mountain man is himself a vanishing species, "one of the old kind," who professes himself at the end of his adventures in the final volume (*Jack among the Indians* 34). The young boy turns nineteen in the final volume, on the cusp of manhood and well equipped to face the future. Jack is the ideal American: now a Yale student, he has matured as ranchman, cowboy, hunter, canoeman, trapper, and explorer, combining the best of the East and the West. In other words, he has become the ideal frontier clubman.

Conclusion

Both the National Origins Act and the Indian Citizenship Act imposed long-term limitations on national belonging. Mae M. Ngai argues that the immigration restriction codified in the 1924 Act—which was not reversed until 1965—instated fundamental racial assumptions and categories leading directly to present-day "nation-state territoriality based on border control and deportation policy" (13). The Indian Citizenship Act similarly reverberates in the contemporary dishonoring and denial of Indigenous identity and identification. Kuna/Rappahannock theater artist Monique Mojica protests the "imaginary lines in the sand drawn by white men" (her argument targets U.S. and Canadian federal regimes) and elaborates the richness of the "relationship among world Indigenous people that is outside of the boundaries of nation-states or ports of entry."[82]

Frontier clubmen drew those lines across the political, physical, and popular print landscapes. By reconnecting their efforts across these spheres, we can see the deep structural links and common ideological baggage of cultural forms that might otherwise seem benign or trivial. In 1895, for example, the trio of Wister, Grant, and Grinnell were engaged in cognate activities when Wister published "The Evolution of the Cowpuncher" to enshrine the Anglo cowboy as the true American, Grant created the New York Zoo to preserve superior species, and Grinnell helped to bargain the Blackfeet Nation out of their tribal land to found a national park. Each involved setting aside, making vanish, those defined as inferior and non-American. In terms of continuing impact, Grinnell's contribution is the most discomfiting for those of us who continue to benefit from frontier club initiatives. It may seem quite easy to distance ourselves, now, from Grant and Wister, who bare the brutal eugenics at the heart of the frontier club western. Grinnell, however, speaks more closely to modern ears.

Several years after the establishment of Glacier National Park, Grinnell began to massage the story of his ongoing relationship with it. Having been approached by historian L. O. Vaught, Grinnell entered into an extensive correspondence in which he mulled over and reshaped his legacy in accordance with changing times. He claimed that he had come to terms with the loss of his exclusive access:

> I began to go through the feeling of resentment against the intrusion
> of tourists into the west a good many years ago, but it is a profitless

feeling, for it causes one discomfort and can do no good. So far as the actual Glacier Park goes, I reasoned long about that twenty years back. It was a question between having the mountains, the game and the fish destroyed by a lot of vandals, or trying to get the Government to take the region over as a park. After the vandals had got through with it, it would be no good to any of us, while if made a park, and protected, it would give a great number of people a deal of pleasure. I made up my mind that my small feelings and the feelings of the small number of people who felt as I did ought to be sacrificed for the good of the public, as they have been.[83]

Calling himself an "average tourist" (as, three decades earlier, Roosevelt had insisted he was an "average" rancher), he emphasized that "the national parks are for the average man."[84] By 1922, he contemplated writing a new history of the park: "If such a little history were written, why would it not be useful to the public to demonstrate by figures, which perhaps you could furnish, that 'a summer in Glacier Park is within the means of the man of modest income'? People do not know how to go to work to travel in the park in an economical way, and it would be a public service if they could be taught how to do so."[85]

Year by year, during the same period in which the assimilation and exclusion bills were presented, debated, and revised in Congress (and during which Grinnell objected to and won exemption for himself from park regulations), he reworked the story and meanings of the park. In familiar frontier club fashion, he kicked over the traces of power, refiguring it as sacrifice by a white elite. Tremendous privilege and assumption of ownership remain palpable in this making of democratic spaces (as in the making of popular narratives). A "small number of people" (reminiscent of the Cheyenne Club's "us" and the Immigration Restriction League's "handful of men") had the power to define "vandals" (as they defined "rustlers" and "vermin"), to leverage the government, and to decide what was good for a strictly delimited notion of "the public." This is the double-edged legacy still imprinted on such spaces.

6

Outside the Frontier Club

In the papers of Owen Wister, among the correspondence with his clubmates, family, publishers, and assorted fans, lies a letter from Princess Chinquilla, the "Only United States Reservation Indian in Vaudeville," dated November 4, 1904 (Fig. 6.1). It stands out among the sombre letterheads and formal calling cards, a gaudy bright pink and dark green concoction, with half of the slick paper taken up by portraits of Princess Chinquilla and Ed Newell, her assistant "Cowboy Juggler," and scenes of their "Strong Novelty Act." The letter is a bid for a piece of the marketplace that Wister and his ilk control: "I saw the Virginian, and I was thoroughly convinced who ever wrote it understood western life perfectly. Now I am in want of a play, under what conditions will you write a play around me." Chinquilla knows how to pitch her proposal, claiming uniqueness—"there has never been anything written to my knowledge with an Indian girl star part"—popular taste— "the public want her with lots of romance"—and cultural superiority—"I have never been with any [of] the cheap price shows & always play the best Vaudeville shows."[1] There is no evidence that Wister ever replied to Chinquilla, and he certainly did not write a play for her. Tracing how her letter ended up in his papers, however, provides a glimpse into the corners of the popular print marketplace which the frontier clubmen—among other forces—most thoroughly obscured: that is, the multiracial competition in popularizing the West.

Scholarly and creative work of the last few decades has recovered much of the West's cultural diversity at the turn of the century, in terms of racialized populations and forms of cultural expression. There has also been considerable incisive analysis of the power and purposes of cultural stereotyping, as promulgated by the dominant western formula. What remains much more fragmentary is the record of marginalized cultures as agents in the making of the popular print West—whether by "popular" we mean large sales, adherence to successful formulas, publication in mass circulation organs, or accessibility by price and style to the broadest possible audience. The high-low cultural binary that took hold in the late nineteenth century, with considerable help from the frontier club network, obscured the variety of stories, styles, and publishing paradigms that

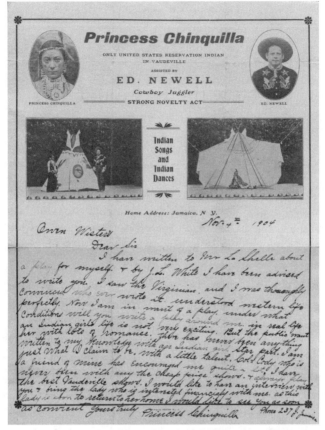

Figure 6.1. Letter from Princess Chinquilla to Owen Wister, November 4, 1904

were in circulation. Richard Slotkin has thoroughly mapped the binary, but also underlying consensus, between progressive and populist ideologies that forged the dominant mass-culture mythologies of the West in this period, and he has plumbed how "the language of racial difference" (specifically "the principle of Anglo-Saxon superiority") grounded that consensus.[2] Princess Chinquilla's letter reminds us of the voices beyond those coordinates, working outside the framework of "Anglo-Saxon superiority" and popularizing the West according to very different interests. The fact of seeking popular reach put these voices into conversation with dominant, capitalist forms of production, but they introduce perspectives and modes of communication that differ in important ways from the models of "quality" and "cheap" westerns. Particularly when these voices are among those that the frontier club most sought to rein in—Native peoples, African Americans, white women, non-elite white men—their stories range far from the tenets of heroic individualism and white masculinity and disrupt the homogeneity imposed by the formulas of the enclave and the showdown.

Of all the "unexpected places" in which such voices might be found, I begin with some of what hides in plain sight in the clubmen's own archives.[3] *Pace* frontier clubmen's caricaturing and disappearing of non-Anglo presences in their western writings, contenders from those cultural groups are to be found surprisingly often in the interstices of their network, cheek by jowl with clubmen in the publications, cultural spaces, and government debates they sought to dominate. The popularization of the West was also happening more broadly, in ways and places that are excluded from the prevailing literary history of the western. As a preliminary read on this diverse output, I revisit the dominant history's high point of 1902, when *The Virginian* appeared, to consider some other popular versions of the West in circulation that year. This exercise puts back into play not only competing stories, characters, and styles but different modes of production and cultural networks. These findings contribute to the ongoing recovery of popular print histories. They are fragmentary and partial; even so, they enrich our sense of the cultural landscape outside the frontier club and illuminate how the frontier club looked from the outside.

Princess Chinquilla

Outside the frontier club, recovering people's stories gets a lot murkier. There is a lack of paper trail: less likelihood of personal fonds being institutionally preserved, of memoirs and biographies being published, of official records being available. In this sense, Princess Chinquilla is the perfect point person. Her case emphasizes the larger cultural implications of speaking to or back to the frontier club within the spaces it dominated. As a figure being recovered from social, cultural, and literary historical margins, her story is slippery to the core. Not only does it wend in and out of larger cultural spheres, exceeding the neat confines of "print" in its strictest definition; it also cracks open questions of identity and community to the point of radical undecidability.

There are at least two ways to tell Princess Chinquilla's story. The first version is based on what she seems to have said about her own history. In 1878, as members of the Cheyenne Nation fled north from Indian Territory, escaping their incarceration in the arid southwest for their lands around the Yellowstone, the infant Chinquilla was "lost" somewhere between Oklahoma and Montana Territory.[4] She was taken east by white people and became one of the first generation of American Indians educated at the Carlisle Indian School, Pennsylvania, one of the primary institutions of enforced assimilation, which opened in 1879. In the mid-1890s, she began a robust vaudeville career, playing banjo with Newell and, later also Dufree ("the Chinquilla Trio"), through the turn of the century at New York City houses such as Proctor's Twenty-Third Street Theater, the American

Theater, and Hurtig & Seamon's. Various versions of her act began to appear on the national vaudeville circuit. By late 1905, she was headlining the tour of M. B. Curtis's American Novelty Company—"A !Phenomenal! Aggregation"—from the West Coast across to Australia and New Zealand, singing, dancing, playing the banjo, and giving press interviews in buckskin dress, moccasins, and wampum as "the only Indian woman on the stage."[5]

Chinquilla had entered into a form of cultural entrepreneurship that was not only antithetical to but in competition with the frontier club. According to Robert C. Allen, "high-class vaudeville"—with which Chinquilla affiliated herself in her letter to Wister—"was the most important and most popular form of theatrical entertainment in the United States at the turn of the century" (62). An especially powerful draw for women and recent (that is, "new," non-English-speaking) immigrants, vaudeville's power as a mass form made the frontier club class nervous. Molly Wister joined in a wider debate initiated by the Woman's Municipal League when she editorialized at length in the Civic Club Bulletin about an investigation into the "cheap amusements of Manhattan Island," lobbying for legislation to regulate them on the urgent grounds that "the bulk of the patronage of these cheap amusements is from children and immigrants, 'the formative and impressionable elements in our population.'"[6] New York City was also Chinquilla's main stomping ground.

Among other innovations vaudeville houses brought to mass entertainment, they served as the main exhibition space for the newest sensation: moving pictures, which Molly Wister noted were rapidly superseding penny-arcades as the "most reprehensible" form of cheap amusements.[7] These short one-reelers, which ran continuously between live vaudeville acts such as Chinquilla's, provoked another competition over market share. As with the print marketplace, the contenders were international, but they were also much more visibly multiracial, in terms of producers and casts, a fact that is of particular pertinence to the development of the film western. The earliest moving pictures, in the 1890s, featured Indigenous people and sweeping western landscapes, and "Indian and Western" films as a narrative cinematic genre emerged in the early 1900s as a main plank in the efforts of U.S. companies to supplant the French Pathé's dominance with distinctively "American" fare (Abel 138). William Handley has calculated that, during the silent-film era, Indigenous figures appeared in "300-800 pictures, as characters, extras, actors, and themes" ("Vanishing" 44). These westerns worked much more with dime novel sensationalism and the vocabulary of melodrama (with the introduction of text cards) than with the genteel violence favored by the frontier club. At this stage, the film genre was much less dominated by Anglo-American men. Native and Jewish Americans were prominent as producers, and western films were as likely to revolve around Native, Mexican, and white women characters.[8]

The highest profile Natives in the emerging film industry were James Young Deer and Lillian Red Wing, the Winnebago couple who rose to prominence in the New York Motion Picture Company before being lured away by Pathé. The films Young Deer directed and in which Red Wing and he starred took on racism and discrimination, and nicely turned the tables on dominant assumptions by dramatizing the possibility for accommodation between Native and white Americans only if it happened on tribal terms.[9] Around 1913, with the onset of multi-reel movies, Young Deer began to lose artistic control, and his work was displaced by the "epic" westerns of the non-Native Thomas Ince which used non-Native actors for major Native roles and relegated Natives to alternately threatening and pathetic crowds of extras, a shift that a delegation of Native actors went to Washington, DC to protest.[10] By this point, Young Deer and Red Wing had retreated to the New York City community of American Indians. The usefulness of cinema to Native people had been established, however. In 1920, Chinquilla herself appeared as part of an "Indian movie program" in New York City.

Chinquilla did not challenge stereotypes in the ways that Young Deer and Red Wing did, but she did insert herself into dominant white narratives as an authentically Indigenous voice. She said that, at Carlisle Indian School, she had been introduced to the Leatherstocking Tales of James Fenimore Cooper, who wrote "beautiful stories" but was "wrong in his ideas of the red-face" (New Zealand *Freelance*). Her purpose as a performer was, not unlike the frontier club's, to challenge "the five cent, novel notion" of the North American Indian with her traditional songs, stories, and dress. She also became a cultural producer in her own right. In 1900, she and her vaudeville partner A. B. Newell (whom she later married) opened an Indian Craft Museum in Queens—"Specimens of almost all the native hand work are on view from New York to New Zealand" (Chinquilla, *Old* 16). It also functioned as a meeting place for Native people, and it came to house a printing press from which, in time, Chinquilla issued a number of her own histories in pamphlet form. In May 1902, the same month as *The Virginian's* publication, she won the endorsement of one of the gatekeepers of the popular West, Bill Cody, when he was in New York City. (Indeed, according to her obituary, she appeared for a time in his Wild West Show.) His letter of introduction reads:

> This will serve to introduce Chinquilla, who is a full blooded Indian and a real Princess of the Cheyenne nation.
> Princess Chinquilla is a lady honourable, deserving and capable and any favors shown her will be appreciated by
> Very sincerely yours,
> Wm. Cody
> "Buffalo Bill"

In late October 1904, "Chinquilla's Indian Company" appeared at the Grand Opera House in Manhattan in the same week that *The Virginian*, with Dustin Farnum, was playing at the Broadway Theatre in Brooklyn; the shows were advertised cheek-by-jowl in the *New York Times* of 23 October. The next week, she wrote the letter that survives among Wister's personal papers, asking that he write a play about her. The terms of her approach were entirely consistent with her other attempts to infiltrate dominant mythologies of the West as a corrective Indigenous presence.

The second version of Princess Chinquilla's story goes something like this: Chinquilla was no Indian. A white imposter, of unknown origins and parentage, she capitalized on a touristic, primitivist interest in Native people to make a living. This view emerges from the papers of white historians. In the early twentieth century, the most recognized ethnographer and historian of the Cheyennes was George Bird Grinnell. In 1915, he published *The Fighting Cheyennes*, which covered their 1878 trek from Oklahoma, among other events, and in 1923, his two-volume ethnography, *The Cheyenne Indians: Their History and Ways of Life*, which included photographs by his wife Elizabeth. Grinnell's and Chinquilla's worlds overlapped. Both lived in New York City, and both travelled west to Cheyenne reservations at the turn of the century. Grinnell and his wife undertook extensive fieldwork in both of the reservations with which Chinquilla identified: the Tongue River Reservation in Montana (which some of the Cheyenne reached on their trek from Indian Territory) and the Cantonment Reservation in Oklahoma (to which some of them were returned). Chinquilla also visited these reservations in search of "her people" (from the Tongue River Reservation, she was directed to Oklahoma, where apparently she found a brother).[11] Both had a relationship with the Reverend Rodolphe Petter, the Mennonite missionary on the Tongue River Reservation. He acted as informant and linguistic adviser to Grinnell, and he and his wife gave Chinquilla hospitality and advice on searching for her family.

Yet Chinquilla is nowhere to be found in Grinnell's published and private papers. Whether by birth or by impersonation, she belonged to a generation of Indigenous peoples—urban and commercial—whom Grinnell quite literally did not recognize. For him, the Cheyenne and other nations existed in what Philip Deloria calls the "ethnographic present" (106). Although Grinnell would fight for better conditions for them, he saw them—as did his friend the photographer Edward Curtis—as, in Deloria's words, "always temporally outside of modernity," figures who belonged to an earlier stage of evolution than himself and who are, by definition, vanishing. The younger generation of Native peoples did not interest him; he felt himself better informed on "Indian matters"—by which he meant traditional practices—than them (quoted in Diettert 108). An assertive, commercially astute entertainer such as Chinquilla simply did not fit his frame of reference.

In the mid-twentieth century, Grinnell's mantle was taken up by the non-Native Nebraska writer Mari Sandoz. She endorsed his work—"the finest body of material on any American tribe was his writings on the Cheyenne Indians"—and herself produced several heavily researched works about the Native peoples on the Great Plains. Among them was *Cheyenne Autumn* (1953), her novelistic history of the 1878 trek. Unlike Grinnell, Sandoz did address Chinquilla's case, but only to challenge her authenticity. Although, in 1954, Mrs. Petter, by now a widow, vouched for Chinquilla and said that Blackhorse on the Tongue River Reservation "adopted her, believing her story to be true," Sandoz was skeptical.[12] She had never met Chinquilla, basing her assessment on booklets Chinquilla self-published in the 1930s: *Natives of N. America* (1932), *A Speech by Red Jacket* (1935), and *The Old Indian's Almanac* (1938). Sandoz did not believe Chinquilla's representation of her lineage: she "says she is the daughter of Lone Star, the head chief of the Cheyenne nation in the early fifties. This I doubt. There was never a head chief of the Cheyenne nation, and in the fifties the Cheyennes were already separated into Northern and Southern Divisions." Even more damning is the image of herself that Chinquilla published as frontispiece to one of the booklets: "The photograph of her in Indian regalia is very-unIndian. She probably had some Indian blood but not very much, or it didn't show through the make-up.... Black Horse may have been taken in by Chinquilla but I'm harder to please."[13]

Sandoz does not address the ways in which Chinquilla's pamphlets make a bid to position her as a chronicler of Native history. Her publications cover some of the same ground as Grinnell and Sandoz. *Natives of N. America* includes discussion of contemporary conditions at the Blackfeet Agency, the Lame Deer Agency, and the Crow Agency in Montana, and on the Cantonment Reservation in Oklahoma. Her annual *Old Indian's Almanac* documents "land cessions, treaties, etc., and the various quarrels and dissimulations that have been taking place between the N.A. Indians and the U.S. Gov't." The 1937 edition of the almanac suggests her ambition in the quotations that bookend the pamphlet. It opens with General Crook, stating, "The American Indian commands respect for his rights only so long as he inspires terror for his rifle" under a photograph of a Sioux warrior, and ends with an unattributed paraphrase of Walt Whitman: "this is no book, who touches this touches Men." The advertisements—which include one by the Reverend Rodolphe Petter for his translation of the New Testament into the Cheyenne language—tell their own story. While the text focuses on the West, the advertising provides a strong sense of the commercial, urban presence of American Indians: New York City has Indian Exhibits, Indian Merchandise, Indian Jewelry, Indian Baskets, Motion Pictures and Radio programs ("Indian Features A Speciality"), teachers of Indian dances, a Winnebago bead expert, and a Navajo silver worker. Sandoz dismisses this popular print output: "There are ten or a dozen of these accounts, most of them I'm convinced, spurious."[14]

One way of resolving the discrepancy between these two versions of Chinquilla's story would be to say that white guardians of Cheyenne history were jealously protecting their territory, including their role in defining and authenticating "Indianness." There was, however, another disbeliever in Chinquilla's status as Native: Zitkala-Ša (also known as Red Bird and as Gertrude Simmons Bonnin), the famous Yankton Sioux writer, performer, and activist.[15] In the 1920s, Chinquilla developed some prominence as a public and political figure in New York. She lobbied successfully for American Indian Day "as a tribute to the 12,000 young men of the red race who fought during the World War" and presided over various ceremonies on that date each year, and she became involved in expositions organized by society women (including Eleanor Roosevelt).[16] In late 1926, she also co-founded an American Indian Club in Manhattan with Red Fox St. James, one of the leaders of the American Indian Association. This was the point at which she fell out of favor with Bonnin, who had been heavily involved in the first pan-Indian organization, the Society for American Indians, and had recently founded the National Council of American Indians. Although Bonnin had earlier approached Chinquilla to join the NCAI, her association with Red Fox St. James, whose claims to be part Blackfoot Bonnin and others considered fraudulent, made her doubt Chinquilla's identity as a Cheyenne. She secretly set another NCAI member to investigate Chinquilla's claims and they came to the conclusion that she, too, was a "faker."[17] Among the evidence was Chinquilla's appearance, which, like Sandoz, Bonnin distrusted as "not natural": "Her pictures in Indian dress are not right; and . . . I believe she 'painted' her face all over with some kind of stuff, attempting to copy the 'Indian complexion'" (quoted in Carpenter 148). The quotation marks here suggest that, simultaneously, Bonnin was wary of such an essentializing notion as "Indian complexion" and was using it to judge Chinquilla (Carpenter 149).

Cari Carpenter has explored Bonnin's secret investigation of Chinquilla at length, partly for what it suggests about the pressure brought by the Indian Citizenship Act of 1924 on Native people's sense of their own and each other's identities, breeding suspicion and tension. In an era when federal policy was regulating the definition of who was and was not "American" (including who did and did not qualify for "Indian citizenship"), the pressures on not just the definition of Indian but the performance of "public Indianness" were profound (139). The fight was carried on more publicly in the journal of the American Indian Association, *Indian Tepee*, where St. James tore into Native critics of the American Indian Club, which Chinquilla and he had just founded: "There is no unity among our people of the Red Race; there is overmuch jealousy and tale bearing; everyone would be the Big Chief or some kind of a princess; each is jealous of the publicity his neighbor gets, and so on and so on, worlds without end" (2). Native identity was entangled in a web of stereotypes and expectations fostered by mainstream popular culture, ethnography, and government policy. The fissuring of Native solidarity seems profound.

I would argue that the irresolvable question of Chinquilla's racial makeup, at least on the evidence which I have managed to unearth, is another frontier club effect.[18] Her case provides a glimpse into the impact of the white establishment on Indigenous community-building: from her avowed experience of residential school to her attempt to enter the popular western marketplace to her cultural activism under the shadow of the Indian Citizenship Act. Whichever way we interpret the fragmentary evidence, Chinquilla exposes the cost of frontier club dominance. If she was non-Native, she was participating in an act of self-invention that Laura Browder argues is central to American identity—and which the frontier clubmen finessed, reinventing and reinvigorating themselves in the West for their status and profit in the East. That Chinquilla remained on a different social and economic plane shows how class, race, and gender hierarchies marked this process too. If she was Cheyenne, she belongs to the tradition probed by Dakota historian Philip Deloria:

> In the early twentieth century, Indian people participated in the making of Indian Others as never before. Yet the fact that native people turned to playing Indian—miming Indianness back at Americans in order to redefine it—indicates how little cultural capital Indian people possessed at the time. Such exercises were fraught not only with ambiguity, but with danger. Mimetic imitations could alter political, cultural, and personal identities in unanticipated ways. (125)

Chinquilla, whose story slips in and out of dominant structures at several levels, continued to shadow the frontier club intermittently for the rest of her career. In 1928 her political activities touched on theirs when she stumped for Herbert Hoover's presidential campaign. Hoover belonged to the same circle as the remaining frontier club members: Grinnell took over from him as president of the National Parks Association in 1925, Madison Grant was his friend, and Boone and Crockett Club stalwart Henry Stimson (of climbing Chief Mountain fame) became his secretary of state. This was the first year in which American Indians had the right to vote in a presidential election, and Chinquilla's role was controversial. When she tried to harness an American Indian Day celebration to a political speech for the Republicans, the speaker was drowned out by hecklers. Chinquilla was unrepentant, showing more than a touch of anti-immigrant prejudice herself: "I don't care. They can boo and hiss all they want to. New York isn't an American city anyway. We Indians are all Republicans and I don't care who knows it" ("Politics"). In 1938, Chinquilla, Wister, Grinnell (and Bonnin) all died.

Cheek by Jowl

Other resistant figures, Native and non-Native, lurked within and were partially obscured by the frontier club network, raising their voices and circulating their writings in cultural spaces the clubmen sought to dominate. In every case, recovering these presences is again beset by slipperiness of various orders.

We can, for example, revisit the World's Columbian Exposition of 1893, a key moment in the cultural program of the Boone and Crockett Club and the consolidation of the frontier club western. This site is often remembered as staging an opposition between serious and commercial versions of the West: on one side, the eastern establishment plus Frederick Jackson Turner; on the other, Bill Cody.[19] Buffalo Bill's Wild West—the antithesis of the Hunter's Cabin in scale, spectacle, and commercialism—raked in as big attendance as the Exposition from its position just outside the gates (so massive was the show, in fact, that many people only went to it, mistaking it for the Exposition proper). Robert V. Hine's description of the extravaganza, as "the dime-novel western come to life" (293), lines up the show with the popular genre by which frontier club writers perennially felt themselves threatened. George Bird Grinnell had already put distance between the frontier club West and Bill Cody's Wild West in a blistering *Forest and Stream* editorial. When the show came to Madison Square Garden in 1887, its star turn was "Custer's Last Stand" (with Cody as Custer). Grinnell lambasted the reenactment—"the uproarious mimicries of the deaths of our Generals killed in battle by Indians"—as "an outrage on decency" pandering to "depraved taste" (privately, Grinnell was more pithy, writing to his friend Luther North that it was "disgusting" [quoted in J. Mitchell 86]). As ever, the rhetoric disguised the closeness between these two spheres of cultural production. Grinnell had worked closely with Cody, not just on his early expeditions west when Cody served as scout to the fossil- and game-hunting parties but also in his introduction to ranching on the spread co-owned by Cody and Luther North. Cody had fostered his ties with aristocrats out west, from his service on Grand Duke Alexis's hunt of 1872 onwards, and he remained friends with some of them, including Roosevelt's friend William Moncreiff, of the Scottish Moncreiffs of that Ilk; when Cody and Roosevelt quarreled over the origins of the term "rough rider," this was more a quarrel between acquaintances than strangers. Also, of course, the Wild West show remained one of the domains through which Roosevelt built his popular image, in the reenactments of the charge at San Juan Hill starring some of the volunteers from his regiment.

Another voice at the Fair triangulated that apparent cultural binary, disrupting the smooth flow of frontier triumphalism emanating from both frontier club and commercial productions. Four months after the Boone and Crockett dinner, on Chicago Day (October 9), Simon Pokagon (Potawatomi) seized the attention of the record-setting crowds circulating just south of the Hunter's Cabin. Pokagon spoke as Potawatomi chief of the nation on whose land the fair was located. He had been invited to speak only after he had very publicly protested the lack of Native representation at the exposition. There is considerable scholarly disagreement over exactly what Pokagon said and with what authority he spoke. Skeptics call him a "charlatan" for his claims to an outmoded status as tribal chief and question whether he solo-authored his publications (a question which could just as fittingly be asked, but rarely is, of frontier club authors).[20] They accuse him of performing "the white man's kind of Indian" with an accommodationist speech, the text of which was reproduced in his bilingual novel, *O-gî-mäw-kwe Mit-i-gwä-kî, Queen of the Woods* published posthumously in 1899. Others, however, have lauded him as a voice of courageous resistance who flouted the paternalism of white authorities, and there is some uncertainty as to the accuracy of the published transcription.[21] A present-day member of the Potawatomi tribe attests to continuing "mixed feelings" about Pokagon within the community (quoted in Berliner 76).

What is indisputable is that, before and after his speech, Pokagon also circulated at the fair an illustrated birchbark booklet, first titled *The Red Man's Greeting*, later retitled *The Red Man's Rebuke*, published by C. H. Engle of Hartford, Michigan.[22] This work unambiguously challenged the international display of American triumphalism:

> In behalf of my people, the American Indians, I hereby declare to you,
> the pale-faced race that has usurped our lands and homes, that we have
> no spirit to celebrate with you the great Columbian Fair.... (1)

The text skewers the main tenets of the eastern establishment. Addressing demeaning stereotypes—"You say of us that we are treacherous, vindictive, and cruel"—Pokagon turns the trope of vermin back on white settlers, whom he styles as carrion crows, wolves, and "ravens that were soon to pluck out our eyes, and the eyes of our children" (7, 2). Among other depredations, Pokagon specifies the wanton slaughter of wild life, including buffalo, moose, deer, and elk—the very species that Boone and Crockett Clubmen were targeting as trophy heads and accusing Native peoples of decimating. He exposes the self-interestedness at the heart of Social Darwinism: "in answer to our complaints we are told the triumphal march of the Eastern race westward is by the unalterable decree of nature, termed by them 'the survival of the fittest'" (12–13). In narrating white settlers' destruction and exploitation, Pokagon reversed both Turner's thesis of westward-moving progress and Cody's staging of white violence as necessary retaliation to savage Indian attack.[23] He even takes on the rhetoric of immigration restrictionists: "as the United States has now decreed, 'No Chinaman shall land upon our shores,' so we then felt that no such barbarians as they, should land on *ours*" (3). Pokagon's subsequent injunctions to "retain the names our fathers gave" to the American landscape again speak back to frontier club practice (quoted in Berliner 83).

If Pokagon reframed ideological terms, he also reshaped material form into what his publisher called a "little unique rustic book" (quoted in C. Walker 210). The author opens by drawing attention to the book's traditional materials: "My object in publishing the 'Red Men's Greeting' on the bark of the white birch tree, is out of loyalty to my own people, and gratitude to the Great Spirit, who in his wisdom provided for our use for untold generations, this most remarkable tree with manifold bark used by us instead of paper, being of greater value to us as it could not be injured by sun or water." Jonathan Berliner details its physicality: "Small enough to fit in an open hand, these booklets were printed on both sides of thin birch-bark pages and bound together with ribbon. Because the grain on the pages is lighter than the printed text, the words appear to be behind the grain of the wood. The visual effect is three-dimensional, as though the words were emanating from within the bark" (73). What Pokagon sold at and beyond the fair was his own version of the mass-produced pocket book, an inventive combination of Indigenous and Euro-American technologies that brought together the traditional and the touristic and, again, triangulated the binary of "quality" and "cheap" publishing. In Berliner's analysis, Pokagon capitalized on the hybrid positioning of his people to create "a material resolution to a rhetorical problem for Native Americans of the late nineteenth and early twentieth centuries" (73).

If we pursue the line of Native naysayers to frontier club ideologies, another cluster of voices emerges around the Dawes Allotment Act of 1887, which shrank Native land tenure and facilitated the founding of the Boone and Crockett Club later that year. Jason Edward Black has tracked the production of "Native antiallotment discourse" in all the modes in which frontier clubmen operated: published commentaries, public speeches, and petitions and memorials to Congress. Black lists, among others, Piute Sarah Winnemucca, Shoshone Gibson Jack, Nez Perce Young Joseph, Otoe Mitchel Deroin, Omaha Thomas Sloane, Shoshone Washakie (whom Wister knew), as well as Zitkala-Ša and Pokagon (192ff.). In the realm of popular print, one of the earliest and most intriguing interventions was made by S. Alice Callahan, a part-Muskogee (Creek) novelist and teacher, who published her only known work at age 23 and died young. *Wynema: Child of the Forest* appeared in 1891 and is currently identified as the earliest novel published by a woman of American Indian descent. Set in the Muskogee Nation (in what would later become Oklahoma), Dakota, and, fleetingly, the South, the novel follows the codes of sentimental romance in much of its action and character relations. At various points in the action, Callahan employs the voices of her Muskogee, Sioux, and white characters to critique the federal government for passing the Dawes Act as well as the military for the very recent massacre at Wounded Knee in 1890, and Buffalo Bill's Wild West for its exploitation of Native—especially Sioux—people. The novel has been roundly criticized by Muskogee Creek and Cherokee scholar Craig Womack, for its caricaturing and minimizing of Creek voices, its misrepresentation of Creek culture, and its general lack of artistry, and he questions to what extent Callahan, while "biologically Creek," was "culturally Creek" (118). In terms of plotting the popularization of the West beyond the frontier club, what remains important are not only the targets of Callahan's attack but the ways in which she uses popular genres to circulate a non-dominant perspective on the condition of Native Americans. She injects the codes of domestic sentimentalism into western adventure—conjoining two genres that Jane Tompkins argued are antithetical—and she folds newspaper material into the narrative dynamic, with characters quoting and debating racist press accounts and angry rebuttals by Native contributors.

Or we can look to another domain of frontier club cultural authority: the "quality" magazines. From 1900, Zitkala-Ša entered the genteel literary marketplace, publishing tales from her side of the frontier line in middle-class magazines. In 1901, she appeared cheek-by-jowl with frontier club writers in *Harper's Monthly*. In the February issue, Grinnell and Remington published their visions of American Indians: Grinnell with "The Girl Who Was the Ring," his sentimental version of a Pawnee tale, and Remington with a short story, "Natchez's Pass," a violent tale of the Apache, ending with the observation, "What I wonder at is why highly cultivated people in America seem to side with savages as against their own soldiers" (443). In the next issue, Zitkala-Ša "Of the Sioux Tribe, of Dakota" weighed in with a very different vision of Native life (illustrated by Remington, a further indication of how closely these visions abutted on each other). "The Soft-Hearted Sioux" is a short story told from the first-person perspective of a Sioux man whose ability to function tribally is destroyed by his education in a residential school. Starving and deprived of traditional hunting skills, he is driven to butcher a white man's cow for his dying father—yet another demonstration of the consequences of forced assimilation and the back-story to "rustling" on the plains. When "the paleface" attacks him and grabs the meat, the Sioux narrator kills him in a delusional frenzy. The story ends with his removal to the gallows. Taos Pueblo scholar P. Jane Hafen has addressed the "turbulent cultural waters" Bonnin navigated in engaging with establishment organs as "part of the complex mediation that Native peoples frequently reconcile in order to survive in the modern era" (xx). The fact that this story was criticized by officials at the Carlisle Indian School, who objected that in writing it "she injures herself and harms the educational work in progress for the race from which she sprang," suggests that, at the very least, her writing

disturbed the course of assimilation (quoted in Bernardin 216). Bonnin proceeded to develop a high-profile career as teacher, activist, editor, and author of
many genres, including autobiography, political writings, folktales, fiction, and
opera, yet she died in destitution.

In addition to these Native writers and performers, African American voices
of resistance clustered around the frontier club. We have already seen, in Chapter
Four, black soldiers, historians, journalists, novelists, and publishers contesting
Theodore Roosevelt's Rough Rider myths of the Spanish-American War. The
black cowboy Nat Love also made his move on dominant western mythologies,
with *The Life and Adventures of Nat Love, Better Known in the Cattle Country as
"Deadwood Dick."* Like the authors of slave narratives, he insisted on the title
page that this "true history" was "By Himself." He claimed back the term "rough
rider" for himself as a cowboy and asserted his right, as winner of the 1876 roping contest in Deadwood, Dakota, to the title which Beadle and Adams would
assign to a fictional white outlaw the next year and which would be claimed by
various other white men. Love states, "Right there the assembled crowd named
me Deadwood Dick."[24]

Several white women authors spoke directly back to Owen Wister. Nina
Baym has excavated a cluster of western women novelists whose works play-
fully reference *The Virginian*. The prolific writer of westerns B. M. Bower makes a
dig at the schoolteacher-cowboy romance when her cowboy "Weary's romance
with a schoolteacher is overshadowed by his love for his horse Glory" in *The
Lonesome Trail and Other Stories* (1904) (Baym 185). Mary Austin, in her novel
The Ford (1917), speaks back to Wister's ridiculing of the "New Woman" when
her New Woman character performs the West in "the key of Owen Wister and
the Sunday Supplements" (242). Margaret Turnbull, in *The Close-Up* (issued by
Wister's erstwhile publishers, Harper & Brothers, in 1918) also quietly critiques
Wister's representation of masculinity when her female character is led astray
by seeing western men through "the illustrations in *The Virginian*" (193). Two
years before the publication of *The Virginian*, Mary Stickney explicitly disavows
the shootout; a local rancher in *Brown of Lost River: A Story of the West* (1900)
says, "the sentiment in favour of dying with one's boots on is rather out of date
in Wyoming" (12). And Wister's status as father of the western was challenged
by suffragist Emma Ghent Curtis, newspaper editor Mollie E. Moore Davis, and
journalist Florence Finch Kelly, who published vigorous cowboy novels in 1889,
1899, and 1900, respectively.

When George Bird Grinnell was closely pressed by competition, his strategy
seemed to be to laugh it off. This was his approach to Mary Roberts Rinehart,
bestselling author of mystery novels and other popular genres, who wrote about
her travels and camping adventures in Glacier National Park. Grinnell wrote to
the historian L. O. Vaught:

Mrs. Rinehart's writing about the mountains is, of course, somewhat comic and should not be taken seriously. She sees things from her point of view, swallows everything that is told her whole, and later turns it out for popular consumption. If the checks she gets are as large as supposed, the writing certainly helps her, and it really doesn't harm anyone. It is up to us to smile over it, rather than to "get mad."[25]

Rinehart's western novel *Lost Ecstasy* (1927) got its own back on frontier club mythology. Her heroine regrets marrying a cowboy: "Take a cowboy off a horse and what was he? A field hand!" (203).

Grinnell took a similarly dismissive approach to Appekunny or James Willard Schultz, whom he had first published in *Forest and Stream* in 1883, with "Life among the Blackfeet," and whose publications he continued to endorse into the twentieth century. Of Schultz's 1907 book, *My Life as an Indian*, Grinnell wrote, "Such an intimate revelation of the domestic life of the Indians has never before been written" (although he hated the title, which had been changed from the work's first serialization in *Forest and Stream*).[26] Schultz, who was married to the Blackfeet Nät-ah´-ki, had alerted Grinnell to the starvation and mistreatment on the reservation, acted as his guide in the St. Mary's Lake area, and continued to supply him with material for his ethnographies. Their co-dependent relationship turned into something more competitive when, in 1915, with sponsorship from Louis Hill of the Great Northern Railroad, Schultz mounted his own campaign to rename various mountains and lakes in Glacier National Park after some of the local Blackfeet.[27] Grinnell dismissed Schultz's petition as "comic but sad," accusing him of favoring his friends, "old coffee coolers" and "regular scrubs."[28] He increasingly denigrated Schultz in private as a drunk and a fantasist, while at the same time continuing to use his information for his own ethnographies and to publish his material in *Forest and Stream* (although under a pseudonym, at Grinnell's insistence; he told a Boone and Crockett clubmate, "I would not allow his name to the stuff, because his reputation is so villainous").[29]

Schultz is another figure beyond the frontier club who evades clear characterization. He barely figures in Madison Grant's history of the park, and is absent in any recognizable form in Grinnell's Jack books (although Vaught's account makes him sound very like a model for Jack Danvers in Grinnell's *Jack among the Indians*: "Within three moons after his arrival Schultz had an Indian name: Appekunny—Scabby Robe—, had gone on the war path, stolen a horse and killed a Cree, so could count two coups, had gotten himself a Piegan woman and had a lodge of his own.")[30] Schultz's stories of the Blackfeet Nation continue to have some credibility among the Blackfeet: Darrell Robes Kipp, executive director of the Piegan Institute in Browning, Montana, attests: "While some purists scoff at the way he romanticized our tribal history, most of us rejoice in his recollections," giving him "high marks for storytelling and for keeping memories alive" (vii). Shari Huhndorf is more skeptical, observing that "his use of Native America as a playground or tourist destination of sorts, a means of escaping confining 'civilized occupations,' betrays a privilege predicated on white dominance" (21). In any case, Schultz's stories adhere to quite different narrative paradigms than the frontier club's. In *My Life as an Indian*, his hunting adventures do not follow the rituals of heroic individualism; he hunts with his wife, as do most men in this account. He also represents cattle raising as a joint undertaking, and marriage and family generally play a much more central role in this narrative of the West.

In *Blackfeet Tales of Glacier National Park* (1916), Schultz mounts an extended diatribe against white naming practices in the area, with a pointed dig at the eastern establishment. He quotes Takes-Gun-Ahead: "Who are these white men, James, and Vorhis, for whom the mountains were named? Were they great warriors, or presidents, or wise men?" When Schultz responds that he has never heard of them, "'Huh!' he exclaimed. And 'Huh!' all the others, even the women, echoed" (99). Like Grinnell, Schultz urged his readership to petition Congress, but his aim was to reverse frontier club effects by replacing the names on the official maps with Indigenous names. When that campaign failed, he published his own map, the result of his work with Pikuni and Kutenai to erase white names and restore their ancestral names to the park's topography. *Signposts of Adventure* (1926) lists over 300 names and many of the stories they carry with them. If a degree of self-interest is evident—the council allows the place names honoring Schultz (as Appekunny) to stand—there is also considerably more respect shown Grinnell than Grinnell afforded Schultz: the council "emphatically decided" to retain Grinnell's name on the glacier, lake, and mountain as tribute to his friendship and support for the Pikuni.[31]

These are just some of the voices that spoke back to frontier club dominance. As much as they were contained by the cultural power of the eastern establishment, they also pressed closely on it, making the clubmen's position seem that much more defensive. This was not a level playing field. These voices spoke from positions of considerably less security and power, beyond the insider networks which supported clubmen's cultural output with a combination of social status, financial investment, access to "quality" publishing, and government influence. Pursuing even a few of such voices suggests both the vigor with which they resisted the complete domination of the frontier club western and the complicated and contradictory impact of these efforts on their own cultural milieux. They call to mind, too, the diverse Native peoples, Hispanics, African Americans, Jewish Americans, East European immigrants, and non-elite Anglo-Americans—the guides, cowboys, vaqueros, Pullman porters, railroad workers, traveling salesmen, women entrepreneurs, and club staff—on whom the clubmen depended for their western stories and knowledge. This rich, multiracial culture resourced the frontier club western while falling beyond the pale of its representation.

Rewriting 1902

Not all popular western writers hewed this closely to frontier club networks of power. Another way of moving beyond the enclave is to return to 1902, the year that saw the publication of *The Virginian* (and Remington's *John Ermine*), with a focus on some of the voices co-opted or occluded by Wister's novel: white women, African Americans, and Native peoples. If we look for these voices within the popular print marketplace, we find not only diverse stories and narrative forms, but a range of publishing paradigms. The further away from the club network we move, the more the story about the West changes. Power and community configure differently, both as they are represented in fiction and as they are formed in its methods of production and circulation. I will limn the coordinates of just three works from 1902 as a preliminary indication of how this difference might look.

The question of how a white woman might fictionalize the Johnson County War of 1892 was answered in summer 1902, a month or so after the appearance of *The Virginian*, when Frances McElrath published *The Rustler: A Tale of Love and War in Wyoming* with Funk and Wagnalls (illustrated by Edwin Willard Deming, who also illustrated Grinnell's Jack books). This New York publisher was part of the "quality" echelon, but not in the first rank of "the industry's leaders," defined in 1900 as Harper, Macmillan, Putnam, Scribner, Appleton, Century, Houghton, and Dodd, Mead—most of whom had close relationships with frontier club writers (Tebbel 123). Indeed, a few years earlier Funk and Wagnalls had become embroiled in a court case in which it was accused of egregiously flouting the "courtesy of the trade" protocols that held this group together (Tebbel 53–55). McElrath seems similarly liminal in her social situation compared to the upper-class clubmen. Little is known about her beyond the fact that her father was a writer and editor, that she was advertised as having spent time on western ranches and army outposts, and that this was her only novel.[32]

Its scenario is very similar to *The Virginian*'s. An upper-class eastern woman, Hazel Clifford, comes west to Montana then Wyoming as a result of her family's failing fortunes, takes up teaching, and becomes romantically entangled with a cowboy-foreman of lowly origin, Jim. The action in this case, however, is told from the woman's perspective and what it reveals is that power on the plains is thoroughly class ridden and driven by historically contingent social structures, rather than by the kind of innate morality preached by Wister.

Hazel is engaged to Horace Carew, an easterner of her own class who follows her west as manager on a big ranch, yet she toys with Jim's affections—as

Remington's Katherine toys with John Ermine (and as Wister's narrator fears at one moment Molly might be toying with the Virginian). Her raising Jim's romantic expectations only to humiliate him causes him to turn rustler, and he is eventually shot down. In dramatizing the making of a rustler, McElrath cites economic as well as romantic motives. Although she does not go as far as Helena Huntington Smith would sixty years later in showing how thoroughly the big cattlemen stacked the deck against independent cowboys, she does have Jim say that the cattle company does not allow "their men" to run their own cattle and that his methods are as "straight" as the big ranchers' (44, 70). The point is confirmed by the narrative voice, which shows the larger historical role of the rustler in "the evolution of the *rancher*" and that Jim "had the principles of a thorough business man" (73, 153). The novel also shows the appetite of "Eastern capitalists" for violence: Horace "was beginning to feel that he should personally enjoy the work of extermination of the rustler band" and advocates that they "form a vigilante committee and shoot or lynch" every one of them—a characterization very much at odds with the ostensible reluctance of Wister's Judge Henry (58, 87). At the same time, Hazel's behavior as a "social actress" shows the performative basis of class distinction (40). Jim's assessment of Horace rings true: "he's her kind, and it's all because he's got education and fine clothes, and he's got those things because he's got money" (60).

And yet, the gulf of class—"the impassible barrier of natural difference"— remains, strong enough to destroy the cowboy who dares to breach it (80). Jim kidnaps Hazel to the Hole-in-the-Wall, a hidden valley where he leads a society of rustlers and their families. Here, McElrath creates an enclave that serves not to preserve white masculinity but to bring the white woman to the realization of her responsibility and power. Hazel begins to understand the causes of Jim's actions, and when he is shot by a posse, she removes him to the further sanctuary of Black Gulch, where they share a spiritual awakening and where she stands guard with a gun to allow him to die peacefully. The fate of Jim—the model for whom, Victoria Lamont hypothesizes, was the cowboy leader Jack Flagg— challenges the myth of democratic mobility ("Introduction" xii–xiii). The fate of Hazel—who ends by releasing her fiancé and devoting herself to a single life of teaching—challenges the marriage plot. With more pathos than heroism, and no climactic shootout, *The Rustler* probes the costs of inequity in the West.

In April 1902, an advertisement appeared in the *Colored American Magazine* for its upcoming "Grand Anniversary Number." This was the journal produced by the Colored Co-operative Publishing Company whose first number honored black soldiers returning from Cuba and Puerto Rico (as discussed in Chapter Four). It was now entering its third year as an enterprise that was very different in its economic organization and its commitment to the black community from both "quality" and "cheap" publications: "The company is first, last and always, a *Race Publishing House*. It has been from the start, and will continue to be, *controlled absolutely by members of the Negro Race*" (quoted in Knight 451). The star publication announced for the forthcoming number was *Winona* by Pauline E. Hopkins, "a popular serial to run for six months…a thrilling story filled with incidents of heroism for which many Negroes have been noted in our past history." Hopkins had moved from a performance career in Boston's black "entertainment culture" to publishing fiction and non-fiction—including, eventually, four novels, a monograph, over thirty articles, and several public speeches—developing a strong voice as a black activist, anti-lynching protestor, and public intellectual.[33] She joined the Colored Co-operative Publishing Company a few months after its inception, eventually becoming the magazine's most prolific contributor, literary editor, then editor in chief; she remains the best known of the writers associated with this experiment. It was consistent with the publishing company's aim to produce entertaining work that eschewed demeaning racial caricatures that Hopkins's magazine fiction signified on "the elements of suspense, action, adventure, complex plotting, multiple and false identities, and the use of disguise" (Carby, *Reconstructing* 145).

Part One of *Winona: A Tale of Negro Life in the South and Southwest* appeared in May 1902, the same month as *The Virginian*. Hopkins's novel has been read as playing with both the dime novel and western genres, especially (in Nicole Tonkovich's argument) for the way in which the black heroine cross-dresses to save the white male who will become her husband.[34] The novel begins in James Fenimore Cooper frontier country, the mid-nineteenth-century wilderness of northern New York State. In a utopian island community just beyond the national boundary—a very different enclave again—peacefully cohabit white, black, Native, and mixed-race figures of different genders and generations. From the opening paragraph, Hopkins is considerably more revisionist than McElrath in insisting on the positive effects of bringing difference together.

> Many strange tales of romantic happenings in this mixed community of
> Anglo-Saxons, Indians and Negroes might be told similar to the one I
> am about to relate, and the world stand aghast and try in vain to find the
> dividing line supposed to be a natural barrier between the whites and
> the dark-skinned race. No; social intercourse may be long in coming,
> but its advent is sure; the mischief is already done. (287)

In flouting the erection of the color line, Hopkins also flouts the notion of the frontier line. In this, she anticipates Houston Baker's denunciation of establishment thinking seventy years later: "When the black American reads Frederick Jackson Turner's *The Frontier in American History*, he feels no regret over the end of the Western frontier. To black America, *frontier* is an alien word; for, in essence, all frontiers established by the white psyche have been closed to the black man" (2).

The novel revolves around the eponymous mixed-race heroine, who bears a Sioux name. She is the daughter of an aristocratic European-gone-Indian and his African American wife, who died soon after Winona's birth. The present action is precipitated by the murder of her father, White Eagle, and the forcible removal of Winona and her African American adopted brother, Judah, from their island to a Missouri plantation, under the terms of the recently passed Fugitive Slave Act. The melodramatic adventure shows how intimately the western movement was intertwined with North-South relations, especially in terms of the extension of slavery, a dynamic that the frontier club western disguises in its insistence on the East-West axis as the foundation of the nation. Here, the action insistently moves back and forth between frontier and plantation, and the characters' heritage is a mixture of both regions. One compelling scene shows Judah demonstrating his manly credentials by breaking a bucking bronco by means of the whip, then almost immediately himself being seized and whipped brutally by the white overseer intent on breaking his spirit. The violent assertion of manliness in both cases—the one so paradigmatic of frontier stories, the other of southern slave tales—is pointedly similar.[35]

Racially, the novel repudiates the frontier club vision of white gentility and racial purity. The white Southerners, "garbed in hunter's dress," murder White Eagle and kidnap Winona and Judah back to their plantation where they further demean them (294). They reveal their full brutality when they lead a hellish mob of pro-slavery men in the near-lynching of the Englishman Warren Maxwell, come to save the captives: "their faces distorted like demons with evil passions," howling "the angry, inarticulate cries of thousands of wild beasts in infuriated pursuit of their prey," the lynchers reveal "the brute latent in every human being" (367, 368). The narrative voice could be speaking directly back to any of the apologists for the Johnson County Invaders, Judge Henry included: "They who speak or think lightly of a mob have never heard its voice nor seen its horrible work" (368). It is the white supremacists who lose, morally and actually, in this adventure story. Ultimately, the novel ends in a romantic union which celebrates cross-race solidarity and critiques America. Winona abandons the United States as a place where justice is unavailable to black people, heading to England with her husband-to-be, the aristocratic Maxwell, where she is worshipped as "the last beautiful representative of an ancient family" (435). Judah goes with them, entering the service of the Queen: "His daring bravery and matchless courage brought its own reward; he was knighted; had honors and wealth heaped upon him, and finally married into one of the best families of the realm" (435). If we imagine this story speaking to the black community that the *Colored American Magazine* worked to foster, its denouement—however utopian and inaccurate in terms of English prejudice—is stirring: "American caste prejudice could not touch them in their home beyond the sea" (435).

Beyond the orbit of east coast publishing—over one-and-a-half thousand miles west into the Creek Nation, Indian Territory—emerged perhaps the most inventive popular writer of the West in this period. In early 1902, Alexander Lawrence Posey, a mixed-race Creek writer, purchased the weekly newspaper *Indian Journal* in Eufaula, Creek Nation, and began to publish the Fus Fixico letters on 24 October. The best known American Indian humorist before Will Rogers, Posey published seventy-two Fus Fixico letters, in various weekly and monthly newspapers, from 1902 to 1908, when he drowned at age 34. Posey adopted the persona of a "Creek full-blood" writing in "Creek English dialect" to himself, as newspaper editor (Posey xiv; Littlefield 8). Over time, Fus Fixico receded to the sidelines, reporting the conversations among his Creek friends, particularly the dialogue between Hotgun and Tookpafka Micco and the responses of Wolf Warrior and Kono Harjo. His focus also expanded from his own domestic affairs to the politics of the Creek Nation.

The impetus for the Fus Fixico letters was the local impact of federal policies, some of which we have already encountered from the frontier club perspective. The Curtis Act of 1898, part of the legislation introduced to implement the Dawes Allotment Act, was of particular concern to the Creek Nation. Initially, nations in Indian Territory were exempt from allotment, but their rights crumbled in the face of the demand to open up their land to non-Native settlement and resource extraction. The Curtis Act brought the Dawes Commission to the Creek Nation, shifting the balance of power, threatening the dissolution of Indigenous government, and introducing a host of additional problems, all of which Fus Fixico took on. Daniel Littlefield summarizes the list of issues addressed in the letters: "the impact of federal policy on the Indian nations ... statehood for Indian Territory, allotment policy, condition of the conservative Indians, bureaucratic ineptness, fraud and other forms of corruption, politicians and political ambition, and capitalism" (20). The letters also provide insight into the different interests and tensions created within the Creek Nation. Politically, the nation was fissured into "progressive" members who advocated compliance with allotment policy as the best way forward, and the "conservative" Snake faction which resisted the move away from traditional forms of government and land tenure. Racially, fractures ran among the full-blood Creek, the mixed-race people, and the blacks, a sizable population in this previously slaveholding nation. Racism against African Americans increased under the pressure of the federal presence, partly because of the suspicion that the Republican Party in power preferred blacks over Natives.[36]

Posey has been described as belonging to the progressive camp, and he actually worked for the Dawes commission in 1904, enrolling Creeks for land allotments.[37]

His letters, however, resist incorporation into dominant white systems. They draw on a rich tradition of Native humor and create an inventive language, which plays back to structures of dominance and fosters Indigenous community. Posey criticized white writers' "cigar store Indian dialect stories"—a characterization which could be aptly applied to some of the representations of Native speech by Wister, Grinnell, Roosevelt, and Remington—and he developed a rich linguistic play (Littlefield 17). Its elements include "coined words, slang, western expressions, Latin phrases, puns and other plays on words, literary allusions, and understatement," in a style that another Creek writer, Charles Gibson, called "este charte" or "'red man' English" (Littlefield 10, 17). Craig Womack, who is so critical of S. Alice Callahan, calls the Fus Fixico letters "perhaps one of the strongest expressions of Native literary nationalism" (132).

Fus Fixico deflates the nationalistic piety about "surplus lands" that developed around the Dawes allotment rhetoric (and that also contributed to the enabling conditions of the Boone and Crockett Club): "surplus land what the white man was had his eye on long time. They is lots a good land like that and Injins ought a grab it theyselves 'stead a letting government sell it cheap for spot cash like storekeeper that think he was going get busted" (71). He also seizes back the power of naming in, for example, his satirizing of U.S. imperialism that was justified by the "More Money doctrine" (Monroe Doctrine), including the violent overthrow of "Aggy'll Not Do of Fullabeans" (independence leader Emilio Aguinaldo of the Philippines) and "Lilly Suky Annie of Howareyou" (Queen Lydia Kamakeha Liliuokalani of Hawai'i) (83). In terms of rewriting 1902, Fus Fixico spoke back to two assimilationist edicts issued that year: the directive from the Commissioner of Indian Affairs to school officials to cut the long hair of Native children (a violation searingly represented from the child's perspective by Zitkala-Ša) and the regulation from the secretary of the interior that each member of a Native family should be given the same name.[38] Posey exposes this hypocrisy by playing the power of naming back against itself; as Womack says, "names of characters are little caricatures of their personalities" (136). In typical deadpan style, Fus Fixico explains federal policy: "Big Man say Injin name like Sitting Bull or Tecumseh was too hard to remember and don't sound civilized like General Cussed Her or old Grand Pa Harry's Son" (George Armstrong Custer and William Henry Harrison, Indian fighters both) (87).

The Fus Fixico letters became so popular across the country that the national press tried to woo Posey into syndicating them and expanding their range of reference from the Creek Nation to the American nation. He was courted by, among others, the newspapers that circulated in the frontier club milieu: the *Philadelphia Ledger*, the *New York Times*, and the *Boston Transcript*. Posey resisted such overtures, working within a discourse of the popular which is rooted in the local and in Creek conventions of teasing and wordplay.[39]

Womack surmises that Posey's primary political commitment was to a Creek audience, "alerting that audience to the disaster of statehood in hopes that the population of the nation might be roused and dissolution of tribal government might be thwarted" (140).

The Fus Fixico letters are, of course, very different from the narrative arc of the frontier club western novel. But, structurally, they are not so different from the kinds of conversations among men, often around a campfire, which loom large in the Boone and Crockett Club hunting tales, Madison Grant's *Hank*, George Bird Grinnell's *Jack* series, and even in long stretches of Wister's *The Virginian*, as well as many of his short stories. A major distinction between Posey's conversation circle—again, it could be understood as another kind of enclave—and the frontier club's is that the Creek group dispenses with the mediating voice of an eastern narrator. This western community may be subject to eastern power, but it is self-sufficient in its cultural voice, its political priorities, and its humor.

The frontier clubman who was most directly the butt of Fus Fixico's jokes was the one who most directly impacted Creek fortunes: the strutting, at times shrill-voiced Roosevelt, here known as "President Rooster Feather." Fus Fixico welds his personae as Rough Rider and big-game hunter together in one image: "Newspaper say he was hired a train and ride in front on the cowcatcher so he could see good and maybe so scare all the game off with his teeth and spectacles, like when he was made a bad break at Spaniards on his bronco" (82–83). A more coded dig concerns Alice M. Robertson, the Creek schoolteacher to whom Roosevelt gives the last word in his Scribner's volume, *The Rough Riders*, as testament to the admiration shown to him by Native volunteers in his unit. To the community in the Fus Fixico letters, she is "Alice M. Lobbysome," a thoroughly political figure who enjoys Roosevelt as her benefactor and cow-tows to him with various surreal actions: "Alice M. Lobbysome she go and buy the platform the President stood on for a souvenir. Maybe so she was made a bedstead out of it and distribute the sawdust and shavings among the full-bloods to look at" (204–05).

In 1905, Roosevelt made a whistlestop train trip through Indian Territory on his way to hunt in Oklahoma and Colorado, and Posey went to town on the relationship between his big-game hunting and his politics—a familiar frontier club connection, but revisioned in notably unflattering terms. Roosevelt made brief speeches along the route enjoining the Creek to single statehood with Oklahoma, a position to which Posey was opposed because of the inequities he foresaw ensuing from what would be essentially annexation for the Creek Nation. In Hotgun's satirical assessment, "the Great White Father from Washington…showing his teeth and shaking the Big Stick before the multitude up to Muskogee" has his eye much more firmly on his hunting trip than on the particularities of the Creek situation. He quotes from Roosevelt's speech at Muskogee as a model of talking in generalities without listening—"You all ought to had statehood and let Oklahoma show you how to run it"—and ends with him rushing off: "But I didn't had time to talk any more, 'cause I couldn't stop here but two minutes and I have been here put near five. So long" (203, 204). Roosevelt wrote up the ensuing hunts in two long *Scribner's* articles ("A Colorado Bear Hunt" and "A Wolf Hunt in Oklahoma"), which work familiar themes: he recounts his past glories stalking and shooting bears, revels in the cowboy fellowship of hunting coyote on horseback, and provides an authoritative throng of natural history details. Posey disposes of Roosevelt's adventures as speedily as Roosevelt disposed of his speech to the Creek, with something of a suggestion that the hunter had been toying with his Creek audience as he would proceed to toy with his prey:

> Then Hotgun he go on and say, "Well, so the next stop the Great White Father make was out in Oklahoma in a big pasture, where they was lots of cayotes [sic]. He was got after one a horseback and crowd it over the prairies till he was get good results and captured it alive. He was had lots of fun with it before he was run it down. The President was a great hunter and was kill big game well as a cayote or jackrabbit. So he was go on to the Rocky Mountains to beard the bear and lion in they den."
>
> And Tookpafka Micco he say, "Well, so this time the Lord better help the grizzly." (205)

Indeed. Roosevelt's final count in "A Colorado Bear Hunt" is eight grizzlies and nine black bears by still-hunting with rifle, along with another nine black bears hunted with hounds.

From the Fus Fixico perspective, winning the West means not what it does in Roosevelt's four-volume history of that name—conquest by white Americans—but independence for the Creek Nation. In 1905, Hotgun looks forward to a vote which will "pile up a staggerin' majority for separate state hood November the seventh. That be a big day in the winnin' a the west...all Injuns be constituents instead a wards a the big man at Washington" (227). As with Pauline Hopkins's stirring denouement, the further away western writing moved from the frontier club enclave, the more powerful became the sense of community between speaker and listeners and of solidarity building.

These three voices gesture to the burgeoning of popular western publications by writers outside the frontier club in 1902. Some appeared in organs of the eastern establishment, including Mary Hallock Foote's *The Desert and the Sown* with Houghton Mifflin and Zitkala-Ša's "Why I Am a Pagan" in the *Atlantic Monthly*. Some were published by outfits on the outer reaches of the "quality" class: for example, Charles Eastman's *Indian Boyhood* with McClure, Phillips, and Zitkala-Ša's "A Warrior's Daughter" in *Everybody's Magazine*.

Others—such as Sutton Griggs's *Unfettered*, and the broadside corrido about Gregorio Cortez's 1901 adventures—circulated well beyond east coast networks. This is a more complicated, less singular vision of 1902 as a moment in the popularization of the West than "the Wister moment."[40] This thicker, more diverse version of 1902 points to a larger, paradigm-shifting body of cultural production across the turn-of-the-century period.

Conclusion

In seeking to loosen the grip of the frontier club on the dominant vision of the popular western, there is a risk of yoking other works to my framework, re-colonizing their vision within the project of expanding "the popular." All the works discussed in this chapter were created within and contributed to their own cultural communities and lineages.[41] In the case of McElrath, Hopkins, and Posey, we might name these culturally specific contexts as proto-feminism, African American collectivity, and Creek oral tradition, respectively—in other words, as various forms of independence, equality, and cultural sovereignty. The works are written, to different degrees, in what Womack calls "code talk" (153), which is not fully legible from the perspective of this study or from my own cultural position. At the same time, the alternatives and resistances that they can be understood to offer to the master narrative of the frontier club western are too important to ignore.

Outside the frontier club, the West was popularized in myriad, inventive ways. Some writers counted the cost of frontier mythology by dramatizing its class, gender, and race implications. Some took on the larger networks of power that supported and were supported by the dominant western formula: from cattle kings to Congress, from oppressive laws to assimilationist institutions. Some dramatized violence in graphic terms, some rang the changes on tropes of sentimentalism and gentility, and some eschewed both in favor of wordplay and humor. All were engaged in making space for presences, individual and collective, that were pushed to the margins of the frontier club story.

These stories also offer a vision of possibilities before the formula calcified into the coordinates which remain so familiar. A number of these authors—including Simon Pokagon, Pauline Hopkins, Alexander Posey, and Mollie E. Moore Davis—have been discussed as unruly and genre-bending.[42] Perhaps we can take a lead from Paul DiMaggio's point about nineteenth-century culture before the high-low binary took hold: "The promiscuous combination of genres that later would be considered incompatible was not uncommon" (34). It's not so much that these myriad voices challenged the frontier club formula as that they reveled in the heterogeneity, porous lines of difference, and inventive combinations that made up the popular West before the patterns of purification—the enclave, lynch law, and shootout—took hold. Like the frontier club network, these partially recovered voices were connected symbiotically with larger social and political communities. They remind us of how powerful popular print culture can be in promoting survival, solidarity, and sovereignty.

Frontier Club Fingerprints

Conclusion

In *Cheyenne Autumn* (1964), John Ford's film that was "suggested by" Mari Sandoz's historical account of the same name, the Cheyenne are shown on their long trek north from Indian Territory across fifteen hundred miles of desert, scrub, and mountain towards Yellowstone country.[1] As the long line on foot and horseback trudges through Ford's signature setting of Monument Valley, the vast mitten rock formations rising on either side of them and symbolizing the challenge before them, the DVD voiceover by Joseph McBride comments that Ford simply had the actors go round and round Monument Valley in circles, shooting them from different angles to simulate the historic journey. It's a nice symbol of the legacy of the frontier club: the myriad connections, stories, and cultural strategies I've traced in this book concentrated in an illusory image of movement through an apparently vast but actually enclosed space. During the past century-and-a-bit, generations of westerns have continued to revolve around the figures, settings, and ritualistic action consolidated by this group of clubmen.

This is not to reduce the entire genre to the frontier club formula. Popular westerns, in print and on film, have developed a rich vocabulary of intertextuality, stylistic innovation, political commentary, and revisionist jokes.[2] Some reach back to early-nineteenth-century frontier models: the hero-plus-sidekick (think the Lone Ranger and Tonto), for example, traces a direct line to Leatherstocking and Chinchagchook. Other elements (the quest, the knight of the plains) reach back much further than that: the prolific pulp novelist Frederick Faust (who most frequently published as Max Brand) consciously drew on mythic archetypes for his wandering heroes as did his more contemporary heir Louis L'Amour. Still other features borrow from different western genres: the stagecoach attack, for example, owes much to the Wild West show spectacle, which in turn drew on dime-novel melodrama. It has often been noted that western movies, especially, have demonstrated remarkable versatility in responding to changing social and political conditions while sustaining the genre's recognizable coordinates. Yet, within this array, these coordinates remain marked by the ideological baggage the clubmen brought to the genre when they introduced and adapted elements in response to their historical moment. Movies make this legacy particularly visible. By revisiting some of the stock features of movie westerns—from star vehicles to low-budget shoot-'em-ups—we can witness the frontier club's enduring fingerprints.

One sign of persistent influence is the perennial filming of *The Virginian* which reinforces the ideological emphases of Wister and his network through the decades. The work made the transition from stage to screen just at the moment when Indigenous producers and actors were being pushed aside in the developing movie industry. The ascendancy of the non-Native star Dustin Farnum points up the causal connection. In 1914, he starred in *The Squaw Man* and *The Virginian*, both directed by Cecil B. DeMille and produced by Jesse L. Lasky. *The Squaw Man*, adapted from Edwin Milton Royle's 1905 play of the same title, has been identified as beginning the removal of Winnebago actor Lillian Red Wing specifically, and Native figures more generally, into more marginal positions in the industry. Red Wing, who had been playing powerful, independent figures, especially in conjunction with Winnebago actor and director James Young Deer, in this film performed the self-sacrificing Indian maiden who kills herself so that the white English hero (played by Farnum) will not be contaminated by her blood and can return to his pure English love (played by Winifred Kingston). Red Wing's diminished role also played out in the press, with DeMille and Farnum characterizing her as a naïve "Indian girl," even though, as Andrew Brodie Smith points out, "she had more moviemaking experience than both men combined" (98). Later the same year Farnum, who had made his mark as the hero of *The Virginian* on Broadway, was chosen to perform the role on film, and Winifred Kingston reprised her role as an upper-class white woman, in this case Molly Wood. The machinery of Wister's plot further reduced the opportunities for Native figures, who make the most fleeting of appearances in the 1914 film. A huge success, the movie was said to have launched Lasky and DeMille on their Hollywood careers. With the rise of the studio system, Native actors were increasingly marginalized as extras in large crowd scenes, demonstrating yet again the benefits to men and women of belonging to the racial club and the costs borne by others.

The Virginian was revived throughout what are generally marked as the three main periods of the western—the silent era, the classic era, and the revisionist (or "anti-western") era—with its fundamental formula unchanged. After a second silent version, in 1923, it became the first major talkie western in 1929 with Gary Cooper as the Virginian and Mary Brian as Molly. Cooper's acting—the combination of gee-shucks boyishness, laconicism, and restrained violence—closely embodied the frontier club model of the gentleman hunter-turned-cowboy.

He became one of the iconic actors of the classic western period, redoubling the focus on this version of the dominant white male hero. The model was again repeated in the 1946 remake with Joel McCrea and Barbara Britton (the film's success is said to have strengthened McCrea's resolve to make his career in westerns) and in the television series that ran under that title from 1962 to 1970, with James Drury in the eponymous role. The television version was only loosely related to the novel, but it does stand as testament to the trademark power of the name and the sustained focus on the righteous "horseman of the plains" (in Wister's phrase) throughout the period. The most notable change, the making over of Trampas (played by Doug McClure) into the blonde, amiable sidekick of the Virginian, was not in fact inconsistent with frontier club investments, since it whitened the racial dynamic further, while the role of Molly Wood (played by Pippa Scott) was proportionately diminished.

The absence of a remake in the 1970s, R. Barton Palmer has argued, is linked to the fact that the most vigorous revisioning of the western took off in this decade (with such works as Arthur Penn's *Little Big Man* of 1970 and Robert Altman's *Buffalo Bill and the Indians*, 1976). The fundamental conservatism of Wister's model resisted this kind of makeover. Only in 2000 did a new version appear on Turner Network Television as part of media mogul Ted Turner's commitment to producing "conservative Americana films" (Palmer 233). The film was directed by Bill Pulman, who also played the title role, and Diane Ladd was cast as Molly. The most obvious gesture to revisionism and a more liberal age is the casting of prominent Aboriginal actors Gary Farmer (Cayuga) and Billy Merasty (Cree) in small roles that were added by Larry Gross, the teleplay writer. Ultimately, however, their inclusion does not dislodge the reaffirmation of white male power, the inevitability of female submissiveness, and the justification of extra-legal violence—indeed, the film's poster boasts "Times Change, Heroes Remain the Same." To date, *The Virginian* continues to function as the standard-bearer of frontier club values, extending their dramatization into new media and shifting political contexts.

The legacy of the frontier club western is also more generally dispersed throughout movie history. Take, first, the gentleman cowboy hero. Early in 2011, in celebration of the newest western success, the Coen brothers' remake of *True Grit*, film historian Philip French published his all-time "10 best screen cowboys."[3] What is most remarkable about the list—from Gary Cooper, John Wayne, and Jimmy Stewart to Clint Eastwood, Jeff Bridges, and even Woody from the *Toy Story* trilogy—is their racial homogeneity. (Paul Newman, number seven on the list, confirms the WASP hegemony in the western when he is quoted as identifying as Jewish "because it's more of a challenge"—whether to the genre or to his own success is left vague). Not only does this roll-call uphold the Boone and Crockett Club principle—that the white man has the racial right to bear the gun—but the acting style of the men on the list also typically hews to the frontier club laconicism of the gentleman hunter-turned-cowboy, often following the arc from jocular self-deprecation to stoic killing. They live out the prescription laid down by Theodore Roosevelt and George Bird Grinnell in *American Big-Game Hunting*, the first book of the Boone and Crockett Club, in 1893: they "possess energy, resolution, manliness, self-reliance, and capacity for hardy self-help" (14–15). The reaffirmation of this heroic type has at least two effects. It reinforces the marginalization of black, Jewish, East European, Hispanic, and Native cowboys, who, collectively, constituted the majority of ranch-hands in the West, setting up a racial challenge to which revisionist westerns repeatedly rise. Mel Brooks's *Blazing Saddles* (1974), for example, famously combines white racist townspeople, a black sheriff, and a Yiddish-speaking Jewish-Sioux chief; much more than a joke is at issue here, given the ways in which we have seen the mutual reinforcement of the formula western and federal policies of discrimination, immigration restriction, and forced assimilation in the frontier club era. Second, this embodiment of rugged individualism creates—indeed, depends on—an image of helpless community, craven townspeople or fearful homesteaders whom westerns repeatedly represent as incapable of collective action. Such scenes make the clubmen's point, that the populace at large is perennially in need of a strong leader. In the protracted discussion of lobbying tactics, clubmen strategized over how best to constitute and persuade "the people" and "the public" to support their elitist causes— whether the cause was conservation or immigration restriction, winning the range war, seizing the book market, or creating national parks—how best, in other words, to effect hegemony.

The space mastered by the white laconic hero is recognizably the enclave so assiduously cleared by the clubmen for "superior species," animal and human. The cinematic effect is most powerful in John Ford's signature use of Monument Valley in the classic era. In *The Searchers* (1956), a typical scene shows the Comanche closing in from both sides of the desert valley on the white posse whose mission is to recover their white captives. As the Native warriors emerge over the brow of the hill—a shot repeated innumerable times in the western— they become the invaders of their own land, the threat to the pure space of Monument Valley, a frontier club sleight of hand to a "T." Of this scene, the filmmaker Peter Bogdanovich said, "this is a kind of magical shot here of Monument Valley, with the dust over on the left, looks like something out of the Bible or something." The echo of Wister's line about the Wyoming landscape—"a space out of which Noah and Adam might have come straight from Genesis"—could hardly be closer.[4] (While Bogdanovich's echo was presumably unintended, Ford did cite the visual art of Frederic Remington as a major influence on his cinematography.)[5]

Especially as that spatial trope became translated into innumerable B westerns, landscape increasingly proves Native people's unfitness. Not only do "redskins" repeatedly infiltrate the pure space of white heroism, but they're also bad sportsmen. Instead of gentlemanly one-on-one stalking, whooping hordes sweep down on small bands of settlers or defenseless families or trail cowboys around campfires. A typical low-budget western from the same year as *The Searchers*—and a particularly relevant example in this context—was *Daniel Boone, Trail Blazer* (1956), with "former Tarzan" Bruce Bennett in the title role and Lon Chaney in redface as the Shawnee leader Blackfish. The film opens in 1775 in the wilderness of Kentucky, where a swarm of savages ambush a small band of white hunters. Throughout the action the honor code and mano-a-mano courage of Daniel Boone contrast vividly with the duplicitous methods of the Shawnee, who sneak through the foliage in vast numbers, encircling the sleeping men and torturing hostages; later, they swoop down on the settlement from all sides, attempting to starve out then burn out the families. It is a melodramatic and explicitly racialized playing out of the frontier club distinction between the gentleman hunter and the game butchers, poachers, and "savages" who trick their prey with jack-lighting, crusting, and water traps, and destroy big-game stocks with "indiscriminate slaughter." The effect of the contrast is familiar too, hammering home the narrative of white beleaguerement.

The climactic ritual of the stalk and shootout also remains remarkably dominant, from the Boone and Crockett Club's veneration of the principles laid down in Theodore Van Dyke's *Still-Hunter* through their transference from big-game hunting to man-hunting to their reappearance as the culminating showdown between white men in the western. The classic choreography appeared in Fred Zinnemann's *High Noon* (1952), which orients the entire action of the film towards the final suspenseful walkdown, the clock ticking down to noon (in *The Virginian* it was sundown). In the final frames of the film, Marshal Will Kane (Gary Cooper— who had played the Virginian twenty-three years earlier) stalks the four henchmen through the back alleys of Hadleyville before shooting it out on the deserted main street with convicted murderer Frank Miller (Ian MacDonald). The motif of the showdown is resilient, from John Wayne stalking the streets of Lordsburg in *Stagecoach* (1939)—where the use of rifles makes the sequence particularly reminiscent of the Boone and Crockett Club version—to Clint Eastwood's (and, later, Charles Bronson's) repeat one-against-three trick in Sergio Leone's spaghetti westerns of the 1960s. Even in George Stevens's *Shane* (1953), where the political sympathies for farmers and against big cattlemen reverse the ideological alliances of the frontier club, the gender politics stay in place: the climactic shoot-out between Shane (Alan Ladd) and the hired gunslinger Wilson (Jack Palance) removes the power of resolution from the community of settlers or the family unit. Even Clint Eastwood's *Unforgiven* (1992), which seems dedicated to stripping away romantic conventions, climaxes in the standard scene of "frontier justice." In all these cases, what the shootout demonstrates is the importance of the code ("the sportsman's code" become "the code of the West"). It is what justifies the violent domination of one man over another. As the point is reiterated through the decades from the Virginian to the Man with No Name, it becomes increasingly clear that the code is about style. It is one manifestation of the "heroic act with no larger purpose beyond itself" that Jackson Lears argues grew from the need for "manly testing" by "the educated and affluent" in the turn-of-the century period (138).

As well as demonstrating the stalk-and-shootout, craven townspeople, and the stoic gentleman hero, *High Noon* also highlights the perennial function of the good woman. As has often been noted, Amy Fowler (played by Grace Kelly) is tested in almost exactly the same fashion as Molly Wood. Both women's wedding ceremonies abut on a gun duel between hero and villain—in Amy's case, her husband insists on proceeding with the showdown immediately after their wedding, in Molly's case, just before. The women attempt to prevent the violence with the same ultimatum: Amy declares, "I won't be here when it's over," echoing Molly's assertion that "there can be no to-morrow for you and me" (475). Despite Amy's principles as a Quaker (a religion to which one side of Molly Wister's family also adhered), ultimately she "capitulates to love" even more actively than her precursor. Amy joins in the shooting to save her man, before reuniting with him at the end of the movie. The unfeasibility of the pacifist position on the frontier is reiterated by generations of female film characters playing out the ritual of resistance and surrender to violence. The scenes echo all the way back to Silas Weir Mitchell's proper Philadelphia and his heroines who scoff at the gentleman's code of honor. In *Stagecoach*, Dallas begs the Ringo Kid to give up on his pointless revenge; Marion Starrett lectures her husband Joe on his "silly kind of pride" in *Shane*; Mrs. Low ridicules Hondo's sense of honor as male vanity in *Hondo* (1953); even Louisa in Marlon Brando's anti-western *One-Eyed Jacks* (1961) begs the hardened killer Rio to forget the betrayal he intends to avenge with his gun. In every case, male violence is represented as unavoidable, and the women end up in the men's arms.

The least imitated feature of the frontier club western is the one with which I began: the righteous lynching scene. From the first, the justification of lynching was a labored exercise—from Wister's protracted defense of vigilantism in the West, via Judge Henry, to his stubborn shoehorning of it into his stage adaptation. (DeMille, too, is on record as struggling with the lynching scene in the first film version.)[6] I have argued that lynch law represents the ultimate stakes in the frontier club sleight of hand. Specifically, it involves justifying extra-legal violence by converting the perpetrators into the beleaguered and mob violence into individual restraint. More generally, it relates to the methods and rhetoric by which a long list of peoples—Native Americans, African Americans, Hispanics, "new" immigrants, independent cowboys, homesteaders—were violently removed of their human rights on the pretext that they represented a threat to the public or national good. Lynch law also skirts uncomfortably close to the racial dynamics—that is, the terrorizing of African Americans—that the frontier club also labored to disguise.

It may be for these reasons that, beyond the remakes of *The Virginian*, lynching is most often evoked to trouble western conventions. One of the most powerful strikes against lynch law occurs in William A. Wellman's *The Ox-Bow Incident* (1943), which is based on Walter Van Tilburg Clark's 1940 novel of the same title. It is often read as an anti-McCarthyite western, in which mob hysteria about supposed rustlers leads to the hanging of three innocent men, one of them Hispanic. Black westerns often evoke the noose as the ultimate sign of the hegemonic terrorism they challenge. In John Ford's *Sergeant Rutledge* (1960), Woody Strode stars as the 9th Cavalryman wrongly accused of raping and murdering a white woman. At one moment, just after Rutledge has entered the courtroom and announced his name and rank, a mob of angry white men erupts at the back of the room, brandishing a coiled rope towards a ceiling beam. In the frame of the shot, Strode's head is immediately replaced by the coil of the rope and the yelling red-faced men, one of whom mimes a hanging. Mario Van Peebles' angry *Posse* (1993) opens with a cameo by Strode as Storyteller and proceeds methodically to expose the many forms of racism on which western settlement was built. Its hero is haunted and driven by the lynching and burning of his preacher father, which recurs traumatically throughout the film. Even in the spoof western (sometimes called steampunk for its use of nineteenth-century technological fantasy) *Wild Wild West* (1999), black gunslinger James West (Will Smith) finds himself with his head through a noose, pleading with a bloated, drunken mob of rich white people to spare him for touching a white woman (whom, the joke is, he had mistaken for his white male sidekick). Whenever African American perspectives operate within the frame of the western, the myth of what Richard Slotkin names and probes as "the aristocracy of violence" is exploded (*Gunfighter* 156 ff.).

The more these stock features are repeated, the more formulaic they become, the more tightly they bind the histories out of which they were made. As these various examples show, those associations can serve to reinforce or invert power structures. The image of Monument Valley in *Cheyenne Autumn* is again an apt illustration of historical containment, the more telling because it occurs within a work intended to honor the Cheyenne. Not only is much of the action restricted to one area, but the Cheyenne leaders Little Wolf, Dull Knife, and Red Shirt are trapped in the bodies of Mexican and Italian American actors. This is also one of the Ford films that most strongly evokes Frederic Remington canvases in the snaking lines of Cheyenne and of the cavalry pursuing them, the dust-laden charges and tiny figures in the desert panoramas, the campfire and tipi circles. Indeed, it is almost impossible to view these scenes without seeing Remington's vision framed by Ford's, as the two white representations reinforce each other. And, of course, at least in one version of Princess Chinquilla's story, it was this history she was denied and into which she attempted to re-insert herself.

History also bubbles to the surface at unexpected moments, suggesting how much the frontier club is part of the deep memory of the genre. Take John Ford's *My Darling Clementine* (1946), his re-telling of the gunfight at the O.K. Corral. Henry Fonda makes over the sheriff Wyatt Earp into a gentlemanly Virginian fig- ure and Cathy Downs plays eastern schoolma'am Clementine Carter as a genteel yet spirited Molly Wood type—again, as in Wister's novel, the community dance scene is key to their burgeoning relationship. In the film, the Hispanic presence comes in Chihuahua, the sultry saloon girl played by Linda Darnell. She is a gorgeous, vivacious figure, her physicality contrasting with the rather pinched features and contained demeanor of Clementine. In one scene, Chihuahua tries to distract Earp from his poker game with a seductive rendering of a cowboy song. As she arranges her shawl and sways her hips—"Ten thousand cattle gone astray, left my range and wandered away"—she smirks at her saloon audience and moves in more closely on her quarry—"and the sons of guns I'm here to say have left me dead broke, dead broke today"—at which point she contemptu- ously tosses a coin in his ashtray and stalks off to the bar.[7]

If you spend enough time in the frontier club archives, this moment is rich with multiple, somewhat contradictory resonances. Although Wister does not appear in the film credits, he was the author of "Ten Thousand Cattle Straying (Dead Broke)," lyrics and music, which he composed for "Sorgy Trampas" in the stage version of *The Virginian*. In one version of the script, Trampas sings "Ten thousand cattle straying, / They quit my range and travelled ..." as he walks in on big ranchers planning their vigilante action.[8] In another version, the lynching act in Horse Thief Pass opens with Trampas singing "Ten thousand cattle stray- ing" and the other rustlers providing the chorus "Dead broke!"[9] The first echo that can be heard, then, is from one wily Hispanic to another, as both Trampas and Chihuahua incriminate themselves in voicing these lyrics—and both are killed off in their respective scripts.

A different association is carried in the memory of Wister's daughter Fanny Kemble Wister, who fondly remembers the song as part of her father's repertoire on the grand piano in Butler Place, the estate house into which the family moved after Sarah Butler Wister's death. She describes her father moving back and forth among "the light operas of Offenbach ... in beautiful French," the words and music of "Ten Thousand Cattle," and "an air from a burlesque of *Don Giovanni* that my father wrote for the Tavern Club of Boston," effortlessly demonstrating the full range of cultural expression that the clubmen sought to master (*Owen* xii–xiii).

Fanny's recollection resituates the frontier club cowboy in his originating cultural environment and reminds us of the privileged female lives—worlds distant from Chihuahua by race and class—which subtended it.

The archive even brings to this quintessentially heterosexual filmic moment resonances of frontier club homosociality. One letter from Winthrop Chanler to Wister—"Omar dear Dan'l"—requests "Send me the words of the Dogga-Doghie Song. I have got the time and am anxious to make my début at the Metropolitan Opera House in the role of a Texas Cowpuncher."[10] With his typical boyish face-tiousness Chanler exhibits once more the clubmen's investment in manipulating the high-low cultural binary. In this echo, however, also lies the possibility of resistance: the cultural line that can be crossed from one direction can also be breached from another. I choose to read Chihuahua in this moment, shadowed as she is by Wister, Trampas, and his club fellows, as the Latina who makes a strike against the Anglo frontier club class, seizing their power for her own ends. With the song, she marks and mocks Earp as the gentleman cowboy (whose cattle have in fact been stolen) and revels in her own seductive powers "in gam-bling halls"—Wister wrote "hells"—"delaying." (To her lover, the considerably more degenerate and less Anglo Doc Holliday, played by Italian American actor Victor Mature, she sings "Under A Broad Sombrero": "Oh the first kiss is always the sweetest … ".)

At the outset of this project, I had a strong sense of the lineaments of the for-mula western. I went into the archives with two very practical questions: how did we end up with this version as the dominant formula and what other possibilities had it elbowed aside? In something of a follow-the-money exercise, I began to find conjunctions, patterns, and overlaps ranging widely across the turn-of-the-century cultural, political, and social landscapes. But I also discovered fissures within the network and challenges from outside it. I end with Chihuahua's song as one last ambiguous, partially buried challenge, using Wister's words against him and his class, echoing his famous "son-of-a—" line, and giving voice to one among many marginalized figures who takes back her image and her story of the West from the clubmen's control: "And it's 'sons-of-guns' is what I say. They've rustled my pile, my pile away."

NOTES

Frontmatter

1. Fiedler 138. Margaret Reid has reaffirmed as recently as 2004: "Even now, critics acknowledge that this novel 'is the template on which every Western since has been cut'" (136).

Introduction

1. For more on what Kimmel calls "fraternal orders" (171) of the period, see Bederman, Townsend. On the English clubs on which many exclusive U.S. clubs were modeled, see Milne-Smith.
2. See Reiger, *American*; Trefethen.
3. The hidden story about Caspar Whitney—which will further illuminate class dynamics within the frontier club—awaits the publication of Tara Kathleen Kelly's dissertation. For one of many instances of Roosevelt and Grinnell disdaining "vulgar" sporting tales, see Morison 636.
4. Many scholars, including Slotkin and Watts, say that Remington was a Boone and Crockett Club member, but his name appears on none of their membership lists, nor did he contribute to any of their volumes.
5. On European and eastern investment in the open-range West, see Clay; Gressley; Nicholas; Olson; Szasz; Woods.
6. Letter, Wm. Sturgis to F. O. deBillier, June 10, 1880 (CC, Box 195, Folder 1).
7. The most recent estimate of cattle deaths is from Schofield.
8. On Cheyenne Club, see Clay; Patterson; Spring, *The Cheyenne Club* and "The Cheyenne Club," ts. (CC, Box 195, Folder 9).
9. Details of big ranchers and violence on the plains are drawn from Clay; Hufsmith; M. S. Johnson; Mercer; O'Neal; Patterson; Penrose, *The Rustler Business*; Penrose, ms., "The Johnson County War: The Narrative of Charles Bingham Penrose" (1914; CBP, Folder 11); and H. H. Smith.
10. Letter, William C. Irvine to Charles B. Penrose, February 22, 1914 (CBP, Folder 10).
11. A photograph of the cup resides in the Photographs of Johnson County War, CC Records, Folder W994-jcw.
12. See M. S. Johnson for a selection of excerpts from various perspectives.
13. For an extensive discussion of Flagg, see Nicholas 1–32.
14. Owen Wister's Notebook, July–August 1885, 4 (OWPLC, Box 1).
15. Owen Wister's Diary, Wyoming, October–November 1889, 3 (OWPLC, Box 1).
16. "Maj. Frank Wolcott, alias the Jack of Spades" (1886) (HC).
17. See Carrigan; Cole and Parker.
18. See William C. Irvine to Charles B. Penrose, November 21, 1913 (CBP, Folder 7). Richard Slotkin explicitly likens WSGA intimidation to the tactics of the Ku Klux Klan in the

Reconstruction South in his larger discussion of the ideological work of *The Virginian* (*Gunfighter* 174–83).

19. "Plot of The Virginian" (OWPLC, Box 66).
20. Slotkin notes that "Trampas" denotes "treason" from the Spanish, as well as "tramp" and makes the connection with Jack Flagg (*Gunfighter* 179, 695). Saxton also notes: "The name, combined with the adjectives *sullen* and *tricky*, would certainly have suggested to readers at the turn of the century—whether they understood Spanish or not—the notion of *mestizo* or *halfbreed*" (341).
21. These quotations are from the typescript of *The Virginian*, Act III, Lynching Version, 4–5 (OWPLC, Box 65).
22. "Plot of The Virginian" (OWPLC, Box 66).
23. Movies of *The Virginian* appeared in 1914, 1923, 1929, 1946, and 2000, along with the NBC weekly television show of the same title, which ran from 1962 to 1971.
24. See Schubert, "Suggs"; M. S. Johnson 73–76.

Chapter 1

1. C-SPAN claimed: "The American Writer II Walter Lippmann program [in 2002] is the first time the Club has opened its doors to cameras in its 139-year history" http://www.american-writers.org/places/lippmann.asp (accessed February 14, 2010).
2. T. Roosevelt, "Boone" 267. The club also wielded influence over federal policy governing forest reserves, migratory birds, the enforcement of game laws, and the creation of national parks, wildlife sanctuaries, and the New York Zoölogical Society.
3. See Brinkley 205–06; Punke 135.
4. Trefethen, *Crusade* 22; Bolotin and Laing vii; Cox Richardson says 21 million (276).
5. The committee on the Chicago Exhibit to Theodore Roosevelt, March 20, 1893 (BCC).
6. Trefethen says that, from March 4, 1909, the club rented space on the ninth floor of the Engineering Society Building, 29 West 39th St. NYC, where it held "monthly smokers" (*Crusade* 21).
7. Owen Wister's Diary, Journal of Journies (World's Fair, Wyoming, Yellowstone, Arizona, San Francisco, Portland), June 14–December 31, 1893 (OWPLC, Box 1).
8. Ibid.
9. Letter, Charles Deering to Theodore Roosevelt, August 8, 1893 (BCC).
10. T. Roosevelt, "Boone" 267. (They were also the names of his southern grandparents' coach horses and, as Shari Huhndorf points out, of "two notorious Indian killers" [68]).
11. See Cutright 45.
12. O. Wister, *Roosevelt* 27; Slotkin, *Gunfighter* 36; Morris 258. For more details concerning Roosevelt's time in the West, see Hagedorn, Di Silvestro.
13. T. Roosevelt, *Hunting Trips* 11; Morris 792n10. Di Silvestro calculates that "Roosevelt resided in Dakota Territory for about 360 days between 1883 and 1887" (n.p.).
14. Grinnell, "Memoirs, November 26th, 1915," 17 (GBGP, Series II, Other Papers: Memoirs 1915, Folder 214).
15. Grinnell, "Memoirs, November 26th, 1915," 19 (GBGP, Series II, Other Papers: Memoirs 1915, Folder 214).
16. See Stiles 535, 538.
17. Grinnell, "From Notebooks of Black Hills Expedition—Introduction" (GBGP, Series II, Other Papers, Writings: Drafts N.D., Folder 225).
18. See Cutright 5.
19. Grinnell, "Memoirs" 40–41 (GBGP, Series II, Other Papers: Memoirs 1915, Folder 214).
20. See Smalley 360.
21. Letter, George Bird Grinnell to Father and Mother, August 3, 1870 (GBGP, Series II, Correspondence: Grinnell Family 1870, Folder 84).
22. Roosevelt wrote to Grinnell, "I don't disagree with you about the killing at the end of a hunt. I find that the older I grow the less I care for the actual killing—although, on the other hand, I think we want to beware of getting into the merely sentimental stage" (Letter, Theodore

Roosevelt to George Bird Grinnell, August 27, 1897, GBGC, Box 7, Folder Grinnell-T. Roosevelt Letters 1897).

23. Letter, George Bird Grinnell to Billy Hofer, March 20, 1930 (GBGP, Series II, Correspondence: Hofer, T.E. (Billy) 1905–1915, Folder 90).

24. See D. Payne (39) on this detail and his biography generally as the fullest source on Wister's life.

25. This quotation is from page 38 of the truncated version published in 1984. For the full-length original story, see "The Story of Chalkeye," ts. (OWP, Folder 18).

26. See Homberger 242.

27. Letter, Winthrop Chanler to Owen Wister, July 3, 1885 (OWPLC, Box 15).

28. Morison 464. In contrast, the night that Roosevelt won election to the Porcellian Club "was one of those rare occasions on which he drank too much" (Townsend 259).

29. Letter, Winthrop Chanler to Owen Wister, October 1, 1895 (OWPLC, Box 15).

30. Quoted in O. Wister, *Roosevelt* 35; M. Chanler, *Winthrop* 158.

31. Owen Wister's Diary Wyoming October–November 1889 (OWPLC, Box 1).

32. See A. Taylor 73–96.

33. Letter, Winthrop Chanler to Owen Wister, September 14, 1895 (OWPLC, Box 15).

34. Ibid.

35. Letter, Theodore Roosevelt to George Bird Grinnell, January 13, 1894 (BCC).

36. See Spiro xv.

37. See Spiro 117.

38. In the Boone and Crockett Club Records, Lodge is sometimes listed as a full member, sometimes as an associate; the latter seems more likely.

39. M. Chanler, *Winthrop* 133. Lodge wrote, "I owe my membership in the club not to being a big game hunter but simply on account of my interest in some of the questions of forest and game preservation which have come before congress" (Letter, Henry Cabot Lodge to Grant LaFarge, March 7, 1901, BCC).

40. As with so much about Whitney, including his birthdates (which roam from 1861 to 1865— see T. Kelly, "Hunter" 134), the date of his club membership is unclear. On January 19, 1893, in *Forest and Stream*, Grinnell refers to him as an "invited guest" at the Boone and Crockett Club dinner, and by 1894 Whitney appears on a handwritten list of members in the Boone and Crockett Club Records. However, Whitney wrote to Wister "as a fellow member of the Boone and Crockett Club" in a letter dated January 16, 1893, appealing for aid in his plan to enlarge his Department of Amateur Sport in *Harper's Weekly* (Letter, Caspar Whitney to Owen Wister, January 16, 1893; OWPLC, Box 38). A 1925 club listing states that he became a member in 1891. It is very unlikely that Grinnell made a mistake in publicly naming him a guest in 1893; it's more likely that Whitney misdated a letter of January 16, 1894 and that, in the subsequent club record, he stretched his credentials, as he seemed wont to do.

41. Whitney, editorial, *Outing* 36.1 (April 1900): 96.

42. Caspar Whitney, "A Brief Plea for Club Expansion" (BCC).

43. Letter, Charles Stewart Davison to "My dear sir" [La Farge] n.d. [1901] (BCC).

44. Whitney, *Outing* 35.6 (March 1900): 623.

45. Letter, George Bird Grinnell to Caspar Whitney, October 18, 1900 (GBGP, Series I, Letterbooks, Personal, 1900 June 22–1901 Dec 17); Letter, Caspar Whitney to Owen Wister, August 21, 1903 (OWPLC, Box 31).

46. Letter, Madison Grant to George Bird Grinnell, March 25, 1929 (BCC).

47. I borrow this term from Tatum, who calls Remington an "outlier figure" in his discussion of the canvas of the same name (77).

48. See Tatum on the "hunter-artist's" distinctive treatment of the hunting scene (64, 29–72). See, for example, Remington's perfunctory attention to conservation in "Policing the Yellowstone," where his main interest is in his expedition with the cavalrymen.

49. See Samuels, *Frederic* 92, 239. Buckland discusses Remington's "mildly satiric" representation of hunting, including a trip with three young Harvard men (62–63).

50. See the reconstruction of his studio in the Frederic Remington Art Museum.

51. Owen Wister's Diary, Journal of Journies (World's Fair, Wyoming, Yellowstone, Arizona, San Francisco, Portland) June 14–December 31, 1893 (OWPLC, Box 1), 20.

52. Vorpahl, *My* 70, for quotation, and see 47–53 for further details.

53. Frederic Remington Diary, Saturday, December 19, 1908 (FRAM).

54. Letter, W. A. Wadsworth to Madison Grant, Christmas 1903 (BCC); Letter, W. A. Wadsworth to Mr. Sec'ty [Madison Grant], January 17, 1904 (BCC).

55. The Boone and Crockett Club has continued to sponsor publications—for a recent example, see Rattenbury.

56. The first four volumes were published by Forest and Stream Publishing House; once Grinnell sold the firm, other houses—Harpers, Yale, Derrydale—stepped in. At first, Roosevelt and Grinnell co-edited; once Roosevelt entered the White House, Grinnell continued as editor, alone and with others, throughout the life of the series.

57. On April 14, 1913, Grinnell and Grant signed a memorandum of agreement on behalf of the Boone and Crockett Club with Harper & Brothers (BCC).

58. See Cartmell.

59. Letter, Madison Grant to Wadsworth, June 8, 1904 (BCC).

60. Letter, Henry F. Osborn to Madison Grant, September 14, 1904 (BCC).

61. Letter, George Bird Grinnell to Henry F. Osborn, June 1, 1904 (BCC).

62. Letter, George Bird Grinnell to Executive Committee of Boone & Crockett Club, June 4, 1903 (BCC).

63. Letter, George Bird Grinnell to Theodore Roosevelt, September 12, 1892 (GBGP, Series I, Letterbooks: Personal 1892 Apr 7–1892 Dec 23, Box 2, Folder 6,).

64. Owen Wister's Diary, Journal of Journies (World's Fair, Wyoming, Yellowstone, Arizona, San Francisco, Portland) June 14–December 31, 1893 (OWPLC, Box 1).

65. See Brinkley 260–62; Nye and Hoem.

66. Letter, Arthur Erwin Brown to C. Grant LaFarge, February 22, 1901 (BCC).

67. On Whitney, see T. Kelly, "Hunter" 156; O. Wister, "The Evolution of the Cow-Puncher" 603–04.

68. Frederic C. Walcott reported, "The destruction of all Vermin is admittedly dangerous, as tending to upset 'nature balance.' Muskrat, skunk, fox as also the pelts of other Vermin are high in price which also complicates the general question. Skunk are being largely exterminated because of the high price prevailing, meanwhile they probably do more good than harm. The entire subject deserves careful consideration." (Minutes of the Meeting of the Executive Committee of the Boone and Crockett Club held at the house of George Bird Grinnell, the President, 238 East 15th Street, NYC, 4 pm, Wed Jan 7, 1920; BCC).

69. See multiple essays in volumes two and three of the Boone and Crockett Club book series.

70. Low, "Labrador." Grinnell did not agree with this claim: "We sometimes think and speak of the Indian as an improvident savage, but in his control of the game supply he showed a wisdom which it has taken his white successors generations to acquire. Had we followed his ways from the beginning, the story of American big game would have been quite different" ("American Game Protection" 211).

71. *Shane* also echoes the finer shadings of racialized distinction with which Wister worked when he named his white villain Trampas, so evoking non-Anglo associations. In *Shane*, when two "white" American actors face off, the blond, Anglo Alan Ladd contrasts with the dark-haired Jack Palance, whose facial physiognomy suggests his Ukrainian heritage.

72. This summary applies to the manuscript composed at the World's Fair, which differs from the version of the story published in 1893. (See "The Winning of the Biscuit Shooter," OWPLC, Box 62).

73. Letter, George Bird Grinnell to Ripley Hitchcock, April 10, 1896 (GBGP, Series I, Letterbooks: Personal 1894 Mar 30–1896 June 22, Box 3, Folder 7).

74. Letter, George Bird Grinnell to Emerson Hough, March 18, 1901 (GBGP, Series I, Letterbooks: Personal 1900 June 22–1901 Dec 17, Folder 11).

75. Hough, *Getting* 154. On Hough's biography, see also Wylder.

76. O. Wister, "Preface—A Best Seller" (1928) (OWPLC, Box 62).

77. Whitney, editorial, *Outing* 36.3 (June 1900): 315.

78. Letter, Caspar Whitney to Owen Wister, July 16, 1902 (OWPLC, Box 31).

79. Wylder, *Emerson Hough* (1981) 33, 35, 68.

80. See Bold, *Selling* 73.

81. Letter, T. E. Hofer to George Bird Grinnell, April 20, 1922 (GBGP, Series II, Correspondence: Hofer, T.E. (Billy) 1916–1926 Folder 91).

82. Letter, T. E. Hofer to George Bird Grinnell, May 13, 1923 (GBGP, Series II, Correspondence: Hofer, T. E. (Billy) 1916–1926 Folder 91). Remington's diary also reveals that he had an antipathy to Hough.

83. See Jacoby 2, 33.

84. Morris 384; see T. Roosevelt, "Boone" 267.

85. Simpson, "Immaculate" 79. Simpson's focus is on William T. Hornaday, who appears briefly in Chapter Five.

86. Harrison, "Ibex" 319; Harrison, "Shooting" 346–47; Elliott Roosevelt, "Hunting" 112.

87. William Chanler 24. See also Haraway.

88. Minutes of the Meeting of the Executive Committee held at The University Club, NY, on the 16th of July, 1902 (BCC).

Chapter 2

1. See Warner 125–57.

2. See Hodos.

3. Baltzell 154; see also D. Payne 11.

4. This was according to his younger colleague, pioneering neurosurgeon Harvey Cushing (quoted in Earnest 177).

5. See Homberger 197.

6. Homberger 171; Item #6 "People," 228 (SWM, Series 7.1, Box 16).

7. Item #6 "People," 228 (SWM, Series 7.1, Box 16).

8. For an extended, nuanced analysis of how the meaning of hunting (in practice and in narrative form) changed under pressures of the Second Industrial Revolution, absorbing notions of manhood and character previously attached to the workplace, see T. Kelly, "Hunter" 11–54.

9. See L. Thomas 121, 190.

10. Item #6 "People," 233 (SWM, Series 7.1, Box 16).

11. On selling out in ten days, see Earnest 80 (but his number of editions is inaccurate). In 2004, AltaMira Press reprinted the 1887 edition, with a new introduction by Michael S. Kimmel.

12. See Dalton 37.

13. Letter, George Bird Grinnell to Theodore Roosevelt, January 8, 1895 (GBGP, Series I, Letterbooks, Folder 7, Personal 1894 Mar 30–1896 June 22, Box 3); Letter, George Bird Grinnell to Capt. L. N. North, September 5, 1894 (GBGP, Series I, Letterbooks, Folder 7, Personal 1894 Mar 30–1896 June 22, Box 3).

14. S. Weir Mitchell, Item#7 Travel journal–Yellowstone Park, Wyoming, 1879 July 3–27 (SWM, Series 5, Box 12 Travel Journals and Diaries, 1851–1912); Owen Wister's Notebook July–August 1885 (OWPLC, Box 1).

15. Owen Wister's Notebook July–August 1885 (OWPLC, Box 1).

16. See Earnest 130.

17. From 1902, Mitchell was a trustee of the Carnegie Institution (Lovering 131; Earnest 174).

18. The pragmatic woman figures repeatedly in subsequent western fiction and movies: see, for example, Marian Starrett in Jack Shaefer's *Shane* (1949) who argues to her husband and Shane that, to avoid a gunfight, "I can take being insulted just as much as you can" (234). In the film of the same name, she echoes Molly Wood even more closely, exhorting her husband to move the family elsewhere to escape the villainous cattle king and his hired gun. Additional examples are cited in the Conclusion, this volume.

19. Item #5 An Adventure on Fifth Avenue, ts. (SWM, Series 7.4, Box 17 Miscellaneous Writing); Will identifies Wister's handwriting (314, endnote 36).

20. Letter, Langdon E. Mitchell to Owen Wister, June 19, 1906 (OWPLC, Box 3).

21. See Strouse 142, 248–49; Baltzell 91, 12.

22. Baltzell talks of robber barons' determined assault on clubdom; J. P. Morgan led the pack with his election to nineteen exclusive clubs (340). James A. Butler, in his notes to *Romney*,

identifies two other models for Jupiter: George Roberts, president of the Pennsylvania Railroad, and George Baer, president of the Reading Railroad (202).

23. Slotkin, *Gunfighter* 18; see also Robbins 61–82.

24. Cannadine 430; see also Spring 19.

25. See G. E. White 127; Morison 126–27.

26. Reiger, *Passing* 150–51; Glen Barrett, "Stock Raising in the Shirley Basin, Wyoming," *Journal of the West* (GBGC, Box 3, Folder: Grinnell's Ranch). Gressley states that Grinnell also "pre-empted a ranch near Lander, Wyoming," in 1886, but I have been unable to confirm this information (67).

27. See Gressley 67.

28. Gressley 163–64, 254–57.

29. See Gressley 219, 73.

30. See D. Payne 276.

31. Owen Wister's Notebook July–August 1885 (OWPLC, Box 1).

32. See Clay 71.

33. See Gressley 60.

34. Owen Wister's Notebook July–August 1885 (OWPLC, Box 1).

35. Letter, Wm. Sturgis to F. O. deBillier, June 10, 1880 (CC, Box 195, Folder 1).

36. Letter, Wm. Sturgis to H. G. Balch, June 10, 1880 (CC, Box 195, Folder 1); Letter, Wm. Sturgis to Dan'l G. Bacon, June 10, 1880 (CC, Box 195, Folder 1).

37. Letter, Wm. Sturgis to Clarence King, June 12, 1880 (CC, Box 195, Folder 1).

38. Letter, Wm. Sturgis to S. F. Emmons, June 12, 1880 (CC, Box 95, Folder 1).

39. "The Johnson County War: The Narrative of Dr. Charles Bingham Penrose" (CBP, Box 1, Folder 11), 3.

40. See Olson 72; Woods 2.

41. See Cannadine 430.

42. See Atherton, 65, 232–33; Gressley 68; "Hermann Oelrichs."

43. Cheyenne Club Minute Book 1880–1888 (CC, Box 196).

44. Order to Mep Park & Tilford, NYC, August 10, 1881 (CC, Box 195, Folder 1).

45. See Spring 6; Gressley 68–69.

46. See Spring 10, 17.

47. Letter, William Sturgis to Harry Oelrichs, September 21, 1882 (CC, Folder 2).

48. For the classic analysis of how incorporation and violence went hand-in-hand in this period, see Trachtenberg, *Incorporation*.

49. See Clay 71.

50. Clay says "the assistance of a friend" (142); Spring refers to "several foreign capitalists" (23).

51. O'Neal says the VR Ranch was established by Wolcott "using his own savings and working with a Scottish syndicate, the Tolland company" (3).

52. See Gressley 130.

53. By the November 1893 draft of "Em'ly," he does mention that the judge is on a steady 20 percent.

54. Owen Wister's Notebook July–August 1885 (OWPLC, Box 1).

55. Letter, Charles Penrose to Boies Penrose, Cheyenne, April 17, 1892 (CBP, Box 1, Folder 2).

56. "The Johnson County War: The Narrative of Dr. Charles Bingham Penrose" (CBP, Box 1, Folder 11), 54.

57. "Marshall Rankin Removed"; Wister Notebook, Western Trip No. 7, Washington, October-November 1892 (OWPLC, Box 1); H. H. Smith 262.

58. Letter, William C. Irvine to Charles B. Penrose, February 22, 1914 (CBP, Folder 10).

59. Letter, William C. Irvine to Charles B. Penrose, November 21, 1913 (CBP, Box 1, Folder 7).

60. "The Johnson County War: The Narrative of Dr. Charles Bingham Penrose" (CBP, Box 1, Folder 11), 38.

61. Letter, Charles B. Penrose to Owen Wister, May 11, 1892 (CBP, Box 1, Folder 3); Telegram, Charles B. Penrose to Hon. Boies Penrose, April 16, 1892 (CBP, Box 1, Folder 1); "Disclaims Being A Bandit," New York newspaper?, April 16, 1892 (CBP, Box 1, Folder 6).

62. Letter, Charles B. Penrose to Boies Penrose, April 18, 1892 (CBP, Box 1, folder 3).

63. Letter, Charles B. Penrose to Owen Wister, May 11, 1892 (CBP, Box 1, Folder 3); *Philadelphia Times*, April 24, 1892, quoted in "The Johnson County War: The Narrative of Dr. Charles Bingham Penrose" (CBP, Box 1, Folder 11), 15.

64. Letter, Owen Wister to Boies Penrose [son of Charles B. Penrose], February 22, 1936 (CBP, Box 1, Folder 16).

65. "The Johnson County War: The Narrative of Dr. Charles Bingham Penrose" (CBP, Box 1, Folder 11), 21; Letter, William C. Irvine to Charles B. Penrose, February 22, 1914 (CBP, Box 1, Folder 10).

66. "The Johnson County War: The Narrative of Dr. Charles Bingham Penrose" (CBP, Box 1, Folder 11), 44.

67. Letter, Charles B. Penrose to Owen Wister, May 11, 1892 (CBP, Box 1, Folder 3).

68. Letter, R.H. Repath to Charles B. Penrose, June 9, 1892 (CBP, Box 1, Folder 4).

69. See Handley, *Marriage* 79–82.

70. Owen Wister's Diary, Cinnabar and Return, July 6–July 14, 1892 (OWPLC, Box 1).

71. Wister Notebook, Western Trip No. 7, Washington, October–November 1892 (OWPLC, Box 1).

72. Ibid.

73. "Dr. Amos W. Barber, who was youngest governor of Wyoming, is Called" Wyoming *Tribune*, Cheyenne, May 19, 1915 (CBP, Box 1, Folder 13, Box 1).

74. Wister Notebook, Western Trip No. 7, Washington, October–November 1892 (OWPLC, Box 1).

75. See Strouse 335–36.

76. See The Outing Publishing Company, form letter announcement, February 19, 1900 (OWPLC, Box 31); Gressley 275.

77. CC, Box 195, Folder 2, Subscription Records, June 7, 1882; see also Spring 6.

78. See Strouse 24; Eric Love references "the cycle of economic growth and collapse that occurred in every decade between 1870 and World War 1" (2).

79. Mitchell writes that he wrote "The Case of George Dedlow" for amusement, loaned it to Mrs. Caspar Wister, who gave it to her father, Rev. Dr. Furness, to read, and he sent it to Rev. Edward E. Hale, then editor of the *Atlantic*, who published it and sent a check for about $80—all much to Mitchell's "surprise and amusement" (174). (SWM, Item #4 Autobiography, Series 7.1, Box 16).

80. See Earnest 139.

81. See Lovering 32; "The Manuscript Market," *The American* (July 10, 1886).

82. Garvey refers to "famously clubby" publishers, including Harper, Scribner, Holt, and Putnam ("Ambivalent" 175).

83. In her subtle study of literary market segmentation and its role in building collective and national identities, Wadsworth notes "the problem that Henry James faced as a high-toned writer with mass-market aspirations" (2); given the connections between James and Sarah and Owen Wister, this is a particularly suggestive parallel. Radway also explores what she nicely calls "the ongoing fission of cultural production" (128) between "literary" and "commercial" or "circulating" books between 1870 and 1920, and how traditional anxieties about this new book culture shaped the study of literature within universities, as they professionalized in this period.

84. Harper 424–26; see also Exman 51–52.

85. Stern 263; see also Schurman, "Nineteenth-Century" 84.

86. "The Hired Texan Murderers"; see also multiple issues of the *Cheyenne Sun* in 1892, including its characterization of Jack Flagg as a "range pirate" (quoted in Nicholas 27–28).

87. See Schurman, "Effect" 98; Wilson traces this history, succinctly noting: "the bill of 1891 would be the culmination of certain major publishers' long-term quest for market hegemony" (65).

88. Lodge, "International" 56; see also Law and Morita 212.

89. "Sales" 72; see also Hart 203.

90. See Schurman, "Nineteenth-Century" 86.

91. Ibid. 85.

92. See Ohmann; Garvey, *Adman*.

93. See Ohmann 26.

94. Letter, J. Henry Harper to Owen Wister, November 12, 1901 (OWPLC, Box 22).

95. See "Outing."
96. See Exman 173.
97. Letter, George S. Harvey to Owen Wister, April 27, 1900 (OWPLC, Box 22).
98. Several members of the frontier club apparently jumped with him. Remington went from *Sundown Leflare* with Harper's in 1899 to *John Ermine* with Macmillan in 1902. Whitney—whom Wister called "your editor Caspar Whitney"—coauthored a book with Wister and Grinnell for Macmillan (Letter, Owen Wister to George Brett, April 2, 1903, MCR, Box 106). By August 1903, Fletcher Harper was off the *Outing* letterhead.
99. Letter, Owen Wister to George Brett, July 2, [1902] (MCR, Box 107).
100. Letter, Harper & Brothers for E. W. F. to Owen Wister, May 2, 1895 (OWPLC, Box 22). See James 176; Morgan 164; Wilson 76–77.
101. Letter, George Brett to Owen Wister, April 7, 1911 (MCR, Box 106). By 1928, when Macmillan issued a uniform edition of Wister's works, he had learned to cloak his desire to "scorn the wicked rabble" in Latin; this edition of *The Virginian* carries a revised dedication to Roosevelt that quotes Horace: "malignum spernere vulgus."
102. Letter, Owen Wister to George Brett, June 5, 1902 (MCR, Box 106). *The Virginian* appears as #1 for 1902 and #5 for 1903 in Hackett and Burke 66, 67.
103. Letter, Owen Wister to George Brett, September 19, [no year] (MCR, Box 106).
104. Letter, Owen Wister to George Lorimer, March 16, 1902: "Since you're going to announce With Malice Aforethought, I venture to suggest your using some phrase in connection with your announcement like this:… this story forms the concluding climax in Mr. Wister's forthcoming novel …." On March 28, 1902, Wister writes Lorimer: "I perfectly understand the difficulty of advertising it as a piece of a novel. It was just a passing hope that you might find some way to reconcile the two, but there is no way, I see" (WFP, Correspondence of Owen Wister).
105. Letter, Owen Wister to George Brett, July 26, [no year] (MCR, Box 107); Letter, [George Brett] to Owen Wister, September 17, 1923 (MCR, Box 107).
106. Letter, Owen Wister to George Brett, November 25, 1907 (MCR, Box 106).
107. Letter, [George Brett] to Owen Wister, September 19, 1912 (MCR, Box 106).
108. See Hart 218–19; Bold, *Selling* 76.
109. Brown 38. On the "ruses of representation" in dime novels, see Denning 3 and *passim*; on dime novels contesting normative gender conventions and genteel patriarchy, see Worden 18, 23; for more on dime novel westerns, see Bold, *Selling* 1–36; for the symbiotic relationships between dime novels, imperialism, and anti-imperialism, see Streeby; for the movement from Seth Jones to *The Virginian*, see Saxton 332–44.
110. Whittaker 9; see also D. Jones 101–02.
111. For more details, see D. Jones 101–09.
112. See Bold, *Selling* 18–33.
113. According to one method of computing the equivalence, 10 cents in 1860 is equal to approximately $2 today. However, a laborer's daily wage in the mid-nineteenth century was approximately 75 cents for an adult working a 10–12 hour day (equal to approximately $15/day in today's currency) and 30–40 cents for a child (equal to approximately $6–8/day today). A dime novel or mass magazine would cost an adult worker less than one-seventh of one day's wage, whereas a $2 book would cost almost 3 days' wages.
114. Whittaker, "Dime" 8; for more on Whittaker, see Denning.
115. Letter, Ripley Hitchcock to George Bird Grinnell, January 31, 1914 (GBGP, Series II Correspondence: Harper and Brothers 1910–1923, Box 27, Folder 87).
116. Harper 447; Lippincott 867; "International Copyright" 173 (quoted in Schurman, "Nineteenth-Century" 84, 86, 89).
117. "The Hired Texan Murderers"; Cheyenne *Sun* (quoted in Nicholas 27–28).
118. Letter, George Brett to Owen Wister, August 28, 1902 (OWPLC, Box 28). Wister responded to this tactic with apprehensive excitement: "In both hands! Angels and ministers of Grace but you're hitting the iron while it's hot! Well—so long as some new planet of popularity does not swim into the welkin, let it ring loudly" (Letter, Owen Wister to George Brett, August 29, 1902, MCR, Box 106).
119. See Tompkins 37–39, *passim*.

Chapter 3

1. At that point, Sheldon was serving on the Boone and Crockett Club executive committee alongside Winthrop Chanler (having taken over from Owen Wister). Later, he was a member of the editorial committee, and something of a keeper of the flame in collecting the hunting books (see T. Kelly, "Hunter"). See also Harris and Sandler, 46–48; Carmony and Brown.
2. See Czech; T. Kelly; Stange. Tara Kelly notes that Henry Fairfield Osborn, honorary member of the Club, went hunting with his daughter; Carl Akeley, associate member, with his wife; in 1899, cattle king Dall De Weese wrote to his friend Theodore Roosevelt about his hunt with his wife ("Hunter" 188–219).
3. See Baym; Bube; Halverson; Lamont; Yates.
4. See Dorst 44 and *passim* for this phrase, whose meanings he pursues in a somewhat different direction than my argument.
5. See, for example, Winthrop Chanler, "Mouflon in Sardinia."
6. Wednesday, October 16 [1895], Journal & Notes, 1895 (OWPLC, Box 89, Notebooks, 1893, 1895, 1900 folder).
7. Letter, Winthrop Chanler to Owen Wister, January 12, [1889] (OWPLC, Box 15).
8. Letter, Winthrop Chanler to Owen Wister, April 1898 (OWPLC, Box 15).
9. "People" (SWM, Series 7.1, Box 16).
10. D. Payne 11. Leon Edel describes the relationship between Henry James and Sarah Wister— James greatly admired her, though he found her "not easy"—and identifies her influence on "Madame de Mauves," Mrs. Rushbrook in "The Solution," and Christina Light in *Roderick Hudson* (116, 122, 123, 179). James's attraction to "the women of Wister's family"—Fanny Kemble and Sarah Wister—eventually issued in a literary friendship with Owen Wister (Vorpahl, "Henry" 302).
11. Owen Wister, "S. Weir Mitchell, Man of Letters," ms. (1914), 138 (OWPLC, Box 58); Letter, S. Weir Mitchell to Sarah Butler Wister, June 23, 1898 (SWM, Series 4.3, Box 9).
12. Letter, Sarah B. Wister to Silas Weir Mitchell, December 29, 1886 (SWM, Item#18, Box 9).
13. Letter, Agnes Irwin to Master Owen Wister, June 25, 1865 (OWPLC, Box 24).
14. See Repplier 61.
15. See Garraty 30–31; and E. Thomas 49.
16. M. Chanler, *Roman* 193; Zimmerman 78. Zimmerman points out that Henry Cabot Lodge's memoirs "burbled about her father," Rear Admiral Charles H. Davis, for five full pages and barely mentioned Nannie (157).
17. Robinson 135–54.
18. See Diettert 80.
19. Several women appear in advertisements—for fishing reels, bicycles and tires, golf, and "the Kodak Girl" (June 1901).
20. Letter, Owen Wister to Silas Weir Mitchell, May 4 [1898] (SWM, Series 4.3, Box 9).
21. See Grinnell, "Preface."
22. Tuttle, "Rewriting" *passim*; Will 294, 302, 303, 309, 310.
23. See Samuels, *Frederic* 335.
24. M. Chanler, *Roman* 35; "Literary Notes," *New York Tribune* (October 9, 1893), 8; see also O. Wister, "Preface."
25. See Sarah's reference to "the Irwins' ranch" (Letter, Sarah Butler Wister to Owen Wister, September 30, 1898, OWPLC, Box 10); also D. Payne 83.
26. Owen Wister's Notebook July–August 1885 (OWPLC, Box 1).
27. Letter, Owen Wister to Agnes Irwin, June 8, 1891 (OWPLC, Box 24).
28. Letter, Owen Wister to Agnes Irwin, August 21 [1888?] (OWPLC, Box 24).
29. Letter, Agnes Irwin to Owen Wister, July 3, 1899 (OWPLC, Box 24).
30. Letter, Agnes Irwin to Owen Wister, July 13, 1902 (OWPLC, Box 24).
31. Owen Wister, "Note on Agnes Irwin" (OWPLC, Box 50).
32. Indeed, Jane Tompkins has mounted a psychological interpretation of *The Virginian* that argues that the novel is centrally an act of rebellion against his mother (131–55).
33. See F. Wister, *Owen* 14–15.
34. "Preface—Thirty years after" (OWPLC, Box 62).

35. Letter, Owen Wister to Sarah Butler Wister, July 5, 1902 (quoted in F. Wister, *Owen* 17).
36. See F. Wister, *That* 17; and F. Wister, *Owen* 114. The full manuscript of "The Story of Chalkeye" is in OWP, Folder 18.
37. For the larger landscape of reading as a family pastime, from antebellum times onwards, see Brodhead.
38. Letter, George B. West to Owen Wister, September 14, 1902 (OWPLC, Box 38).
39. Letter, S. S. McClure to Owen Wister, December 26, 1902 (OWPLC, Box 27).
40. Letter, Mary C. Mitchell to Owen Wister, July 8, 1902, August 4, 1902, April 8 [1906] (OWPLC, Box 3).
41. "Visit to White House" Jan 8–12, 1902 [sic; in fact 1903] (OWPLC, Box 61).
42. See D. Payne 221.
43. Letter, Edward Bok to Owen Wister, July 7, 1903 (OWPLC, Box 26).
44. Letter, Owen Wister to George Brett, December 31, 1901 (MCR, Box 106).
45. Owen Wister emendation on letter, Edward Bok to Owen Wister, July 7, 1903 (OWPLC, Box 26).
46. Letter, Owen Wister to George Brett, April 24, 1923 (MCR, Box 107).
47. Ella Wister Haines, "Reminiscences of a Victorian Child" (September 1953; HSP), 54.
48. See F. Wister, Preface to *That*.
49. F. Wister, *Owen* 20; Tribute by Mayor of Philadelphia, Rudolph Blankenburg in The Civic Club Bulletin "In Memoriam Mrs. Owen Wister" 8.1 (May 1914), 3 (CCP).
50. The Civic Club Bulletin 3.6 (February 1910), 2 (CCP).
51. Address by Mrs. Cornelius Stevenson, General Meeting, Civic Club, College of Physicians, November 3, 1894 (The Civic Club of Philadelphia Annual Reports 1894–1902, 3; CCP).
52. Quoted from the Reading, PA *Telegram* of 2 October 1907 (Civic Club Bulletin 1.3 [November 1907], 8; CCP).
53. The Civic Club Bulletin "In Memoriam Mrs. Owen Wister" 8.1 (May 1914), 6–8 (CCP).
54. The Civic Club Bulletin "In Memoriam Mrs. Owen Wister" 8.1 (May 1914), 13 (CCP).
55. Letter, Molly Wister to Silas Weir Mitchell, Sunday (SWM, Series 4.4, Box 10).
56. Talcott Williams, Tribute, The Civic Club Bulletin "In Memoriam Mrs. Owen Wister" 8.1 (May 1914), 30–31 (CCP).
57. Ella Wister Haines, "Reminiscences of a Victorian Child" (September 1953; HSP), 52.
58. Minutes of Civic Club, November 27, 1911; Board of Directors Minutes, January 26 1907–April 9, 1913 (CCP). It would be over a decade before her husband joined her efforts, and then only briefly. In 1907, incensed at the latest outrage by the Philadelphia Republican machine, he published "Keystone Crime." Subsequently, the reformist City Party (which had links to the Civic Club) persuaded him to campaign as a select councilman in Ward 7, the predominantly African American ward in which the Wisters lived. In Wister's own words, he gamely "made speeches in stinking halls amid rank tobacco smoke to dirty n[—]s and dingy whites" (*Roosevelt* 267). Unsuccessful in this venture, he soon reverted to a much more reactionary position.
59. See D. Payne 132.
60. See D. Payne 195; Wister wrote, "It took the whole of a winter, passed most delightfully and industriously in Charleston, South Carolina, where I frequently spent nine hours a day at this work" ("Preface—A Best Seller" (1928); OWPLC, Box 62).
61. See letter, George P. Brett to Mary C. Wister, August 6, 1910 (MCR, Box 106, Folder Owen Wister 1907–1910).
62. Owen Wister, "S. Weir Mitchell, Man of Letters" Ms. (1914), 138 (OWPLC, Box 58).
63. Ella Wister Haines, "Reminiscences of a Victorian Child" (September 1953; HSP), 54. In a more postmodern vein, Melody Graulich has conducted a playful reading of *The Virginian* in which she imagines how the novel would read if it were written by Molly Wister.
64. These quotations are from two undated letters (circumstantial evidence places them in late 1903) from Molly Channing Wister to Owen Wister (OWPLC, Box 3).
65. In the preface to the 1928 edition of *The Virginian*, Wister says: "The only act in which he [La Shelle] had no hand was the third" ("Preface—A Best Seller" (1928); OWPLC, Box 62).
66. Letter, Molly Channing Wister to Owen Wister, December 2, 1903 (OWPLC, Box 3). Fanny Kemble Wister deleted that final paragraph when she edited the letter for publication in *That I May Tell You*.

67. Mrs. Imogen B. Oakley, "Mary Channing Wister, Daughter of William Rotch and Mary Eustis Wister, wife of Owen Wister," The Civic Club Bulletin "In Memoriam Mrs. Owen Wister" 8.1 (May 1914), 28 (CCP).
68. Civic Club Bulletin (December 1908), 28 (CCP).
69. "State Civics Department," Civic Club Bulletin 4.22 (October 1910), 10 (CCP).
70. Ts. "The Bear Creek Barbecue" (OWPLC, Box 51), 7.
71. Ms. "The Winning of the Biscuit Shooter" [1893] (OWPLC, Box 62), 1–2.
72. Ts. "The Winning of the Biscuit Shooter" [1897] (OWPLC, Box 62), 19.
73. See Townsend 271 on the Virginian's song.
74. The Civic Club of Philadelphia, Notices & Invitations, March 15, 1894–December 15, 1903 (CCP).
75. Civic Club Bulletin, 2.4 (December 1908), 1 (CCP).
76. "Where It Was" was first published in The Saturday Evening Post, April 22, 1911.
77. Letter, George P. Brett to Owen Wister, February 8, 1911; Letter, Owen Wister to George P. Brett, February 17, 1911 (MCR, Box 106, Owen Wister 1911–1915 folder).
78. Letter, Owen Wister to George P. Brett, April 8, 1911; Letter, Owen Wister to George P. Brett, April 26, 1911 (MCR, Box 106, Owen Wister 1911–1915 folder).
79. State Civics Department, Civic Club Bulletin 5.2 (October 1911), n.p. (CCP).
80. Civic Club Bulletin "In Memoriam Mrs. Owen Wister" 8.1 (May 1914), 43 (CCP).
81. Letter, Sarah Butler Wister to Owen Wister, September 30, 1898 (OWPLC, Box 10).
82. Letter, Mary C. Mitchell to Owen Wister, July 8, 1902 (OWPLC, Box 3).
83. Letter, Elizabeth Grinnell to Mr Pither[?],November 16, 1956 (GBGC, Box 4, Folder Research "Memories"—GBG).

Chapter 4

1. "After Four Years: A Square Deal for Every Man," The Saturday Evening Post, March 4, 1905, 1–2; Wister noted: "I managed respectfully (I hope) to tell him he made a mistake in appointing Crum the negro as Collector of the Port in Charleston" ("Visit to White House" Jan 8–12, 1902, OWPLC, Box 61).
2. See William Chanler 19; W. L. Smith 81.
3. Ravage 151–53. See also Billington and Hardaway; Durham and Jones; Glasrud; Hardaway; M. K. Johnson; Katz; Massey; Savage; and Q. Taylor.
4. These figures are cited by Porter (159) and Buckley (111). Hardaway says there were "several thousand" African American cowboys ("African" 27); Durham and Jones say "more than 5,000" black cowboys went up the trail from Texas in the postbellum years (3). Barr summarizes the disputed figures for African American cowboys in post-bellum Texas, concluding that 8,700 is the most accurate count (xv). Ravage says that there were "tens of thousands of African American men, women, and children in the West during the 'cattle kingdom' years from 1860 to 1910" (151–53).
5. As early as 1886, in Hunting Trips of a Ranchman, Roosevelt implicitly acknowledges and counters ethnic diversity among cowboys: "They are mostly of native birth, and although there are among them wild spirits from every land, yet the latter soon become undistinguishable from their American companions, for these plainsmen are far from being so heterogeneous a people as is commonly supposed" (6).
6. Allmendinger touches on the process of whitening (of, for example, Jim Beckwourth). Clark argues, in a different but complementary vein, that African Americans are transformed into horses in the western of this and later periods.
7. See Baker.
8. For an important essay that riffs off this quotation in another direction, see Owens.
9. The Black Hills to Medora stagecoach in which Scipio first introduces himself to the narrator also connects the scene with Theodore Roosevelt's ranching adventures near Medora and with Buffalo Bill's Wild West, to which the stagecoach was retired (see Hagedorn 209–14).
10. For more ways in which The Virginian parallels the race relations of Uncle Tom's Cabin, see Clark 158–59, 170–71. In Toni Morrison's Paradise, the African American Morgan family,

which prides itself on its pure blooded, "8-rock" status, traces its surname to "Moyne .... Or Le Moyne or something" (192). On "Lemoyne" as a Creole surname, see McDermott (30).

11. On the turn-of-the-century connection between "normality" and heterosexual white racial dominance, see Carter.

12. See journals for July, August, September 1888, Wyoming, and October–November 1889, Wyoming (OWPLC, Box 1).

13. Owen Wister's Notebook, Texas, February–March 1893 (OWPLC, Box 1).

14. I owe thanks to Rick Walters, photographic technician at the American Heritage Center, University of Wyoming, for drawing my attention to these recently processed photographs.

15. O. Wister, "The Vicious Circle" 87. ("Extra Dry" was first published in *The Saturday Evening Post* in 1909; "The Vicious Circle" was first published in *The Saturday Evening Post* in 1902, then, revised as "Spit-Cat Creek," in *Members of the Family*).

16. Untitled [or last two pages of "Preface—Thirty-three years after"?] (OWPLC, Box 62).

17. Wister noted: "She was a real hen, she did everything I have told about her, and she actually lived in Texas, where I did not meet her because she was dead already. It was her sorrowing owner who told me her tragic story. All that I did was to mix her up with the Virginian, with whom I had lived night and day on the closest terms while pondering the equally tragic story of Pedro the pony" (6); and he referred in the same document to "Em'ly, written in April 1893, after the Texas visit" (11) ("Preface—A Best Seller" [1928]; OWPLC, Box 62).

18. Untitled [or last two pages of "Preface—Thirty-three years after"?] (OWPLC, Box 62).

19. This quotation is from the version of "Hank's Woman" in *The Jimmyjohn Boss* (257). The original ms. of "Hank's Woman" (December 1891) is in OWPLC, Box 53. Years later, Wister wrote a story about a black man's pony that ends up on a polo ranch and is talked about in eastern clubs ("Little Old Scaffold," November 24, 1927, ms.; OWPLC, Box 56. The story was published in revised form in *When West Was West*).

20. See Brooks 207–80; Chude-Sokei 161–206.

21. Letter, George P. Brett to Frederick Macmillan, September 12, 1907 (MCR, Box 106); Letter, Owen Wister to George P. Brett, April 8, 1911 (MCR, Box 106).

22. Letter, George P. Brett to Owen Wister, April 11, 1911 (MCR, Box 106); Letter, Owen Wister to George P. Brett, June 22, 1911 (MCR, Box 106).

23. Letter, George P. Brett to Molly Wister, April 22, 1909 (MCR, Box 106).

24. Some scholars now refer to the "Spanish-Cuban-American War" and "Invasion of the Philippines" as more accurately naming the politics of the war.

25. These connections are explored by, among others, G. E. White (149–70) and Bederman (170–215).

26. See Leonard 40–42.

27. My characterization of the black military in Cuba, Puerto Rico, and the Philippines draws on Buckley; Fletcher; Gatewood, "Black," "Indiana," "*Smoked*"; Schubert, "Buffalo"; and Scott.

28. Eventually, black volunteer regiments consisted of the 7th through 10th, 48th and 49th Volunteer Infantry, as well as Company L of the 6th Massachusetts Volunteer Militia.

29. For a recent account of the pre-Spanish-American War formation of the black regiments, see Leonard. For a survey of scholarship on the Buffalo Soldiers from the Civil Rights period onwards, see Leckie with Leckie.

30. Morison 823. Leonard Wood commanded the regiment until he was promoted to general, at which point Roosevelt became the regiment's colonel. All along, he had served as their prime motivator and publicist. On the composition of the Rough Rider regiment, see Jones; Samuels, *Teddy*; E. Thomas; Westermeier.

31. Gianakos examined around 300 works of fiction, concluding that there was an "almost universally favorable image of Negroes in the contemporaneous popular literature of the Spanish-American War" (36). The comment about "segregation" is from Vivian 163.

32. See Hoganson (especially 118–32) and B. Miller (especially 19–54).

33. See Hagan 44.

34. E. Thomas 385; Zimmerman 8; Lodge, "Speech" 293.

35. See E. Thomas 348.

36. See ibid. 406.

37. This summary draws on Cashin; Gianakos; Pullen; Steward; Thweatt; Washington, Wood, and Williams; and Young.

38. "There'll be a Hot Time in the Old Town Tonight" was written by Theodore Metz, first sung by the McIntyre and Heath Minstrels, first recorded by ragtime musician Lew Spencer, then taken up by the 10th Cavalry band in Cuba (Buckley 147; Washington, Wood, and Williams 37).

39. For more on *The Young Rough Riders Weekly* and the symbolism of youth in the Spanish-American War generally and Roosevelt's role specifically, see Bold "The Rough Riders" (332–38).

40. Ravage reads the focal cowboy in Remington's painting "The Stampede" (1909) as African American (51).

41. Quoted in G. E. White 169. In later life, Remington became proud of his association with the unit. On Sunday, December 13, 1908, he noted: "going in towne to Rough Riders dinner to Gen'l Leonard Wood at Union League club—myself only man not R.R. present. 25 in all. I made a speech praising Gen'l Wood. Off wagon. Slept at Manhattan." Remington died on 26 December 1909. Two days later, Eva recorded his funeral at Canton, noting: "A large wreath from the Rough Riders Assoc." (Remington Diary, FRAM).

42. Vorpahl also used this phrase as the subtitle to his book, *Frederic Remington and the West*, with quite different implications to my usage in this chapter.

43. For different readings of the meanings of this nearly invisible figure, see B. Miller 172–73; Nemerov, *Frederic* 87–94; and Seelye 299, 300.

44. Quoted in Washington, Wood, and Williams 62.

45. See Dyer 93.

46. For more on the details of the Colored Co-operative Publishing company, see Knight.

47. For more details on Griggs's publishing efforts, see Coleman, Knight.

48. "Editorial," *The Colored American Magazine* (May 1900): 60.

49. J. Payne 22. Only in 1972—with Dorsie W. Willis the sole surviving infantryman—was the injustice corrected. For segregation and racism against volunteer regiments, see Fletcher 51.

50. My research on black Rough Riders in Buffalo Bill's Wild West is a work in progress. Many questions about their participation in the show are as yet unanswered. Indeed, Warren points out that African American presence in the Wild West is, in several senses, a black hole in recorded U.S. history.

51. "Resplendent Realism of Glorious War," *Buffalo Bill's Wild West and Congress of Rough Riders of the World: Historical Sketches and Programme* (1899), 32–34 (WFC, WH 72, Box 2; and PWFC, MS 6, Series I: D, Box OS1).

52. Compare Bonnie Miller's analysis of the ways in which Buffalo Bill's Wild West at once displayed and contained Cuban insurgents on leave, drawing attention to their wounded bodies, which both heroized them and prevented them from threatening the white "rescue narrative" (26).

53. See Keller 29ff.; McGregor.

54. Richardson 229.

55. See, for example, Watts 145–61.

Chapter 5

1. Ngai 26. On the role of popular culture in enabling the Chinese Exclusion Act, see Moon.

2. See Slotkin, *Fatal* 433–98.

3. See Trachtenberg, *Shades* 38.

4. Michaels treats the Johnson-Reed Act as a new nativism—"nativist modernism" (2, *passim*)—distinct from what has gone before in terms of collective identities.

5. See Hodes 248ff.

6. See Roosevelt and Grinnell, *American* 241.

7. Minutes of the Annual Meeting and Dinner of the Boone and Crockett Club held at the University Club in the City of New York, at 7:30 PM on Thursday, December 30th, 1920 (BCC).

8. Dippie 21; see also Brantlinger.

9. This was the first resolution adopted by the General Resolutions Committee, chaired by Sheldon (Grinnell, "National" 478).

10. Earlier, Senator Dillingham, in attempting to repeal the Alaska game laws, had expressed his concern to "do justice to the bona fide residents of Alaska, particularly the native population" (Letter, W.P. Dillingham, US Senate, Committee on Immigration, to Hon. John H. Mitchell, Senate, April 4, 1904; BCC).

11. Report of Sub-Committee on Incorporation, December 24, 1923, by W. Redmond Cross, E. Hubert Litchfield, Henry G. Gray; see also Certificate of Incorporation, 1923 (BCC).

12. See Bender 6–7.

13. See Solomon 123, 126.

14. See Slotkin, *Gunfighter* 190. Another Boone and Crockett Cubman in the Immigration Restriction League was Charles Stewart Davison, who co-edited two anti-immigration books with Grant. Publisher Henry Holt was a vice president of the IRL.

15. Walker 642–43; see also Ngai 30. A Wyoming cattleman echoed this trope when he nick-named the Cheyenne Clubmen "Herefords" after the broad white shirt fronts of their formal evening wear (Woods 147).

16. Hall to the editor, *Boston Journal*, June 30, 1894.

17. For an account of how the language of Americanization and immigration restriction was propagated by individuals and agencies in the West, producing a "racial frontier," some thought-provoking echoes of eastern establishment rhetoric (especially by Dr. Grace Raymond Hebard in Wyoming), and solid support for the National Origins Act by western congressmen, see Van Nuys (9 and *passim*, 135–44, 184).

18. Senator Ellison DuRant Smith, April 9, 1924, *Congressional Record*, 68th Cong., 1st sess., 1924, 65, 5962; Garis 203.

19. See Higham 101.

20. Ngai 19. Congress passed a literacy test four times from the 1890s onwards, but it was vetoed by Presidents Cleveland, Taft, and Wilson, before finally being enacted in 1917.

21. See annotated copy of "The Gift Horse" in OWPLC, Box 53.

22. Handwritten note on the verso of "The Game and the Nation" March 1899 (OWPLC, Box 53).

23. Letter, Madison Grant to Maxwell Perkins, April 9, 1934 (ACS, Author Files I, Box 67, Folder Madison Grant, Subfolder 1).

24. See Spiro 207.

25. 79. Grant further defends the methods of eugenics: "Race feeling may be called prejudice by those whose careers are cramped by it, but it is a natural antipathy which serves to maintain the purity of type. The unfortunate fact that nearly all species of men interbreed freely leaves us no choice in the matter. Either the races must be kept apart by artificial devices of this sort, or else they ultimately amalgamate, and in the offspring the more generalized or lower type prevails" (193).

26. Letter, (Miss) Margaret R. Bradshaw, 542 East 79th St., NYC, to Scribner's, June 3, 1918 (ACS, Author Files I, Box 67, Folder Madison Grant, Subfolder 2).

27. When it was published in the UK, Grant requested that complimentary copies go to H. G. Wells and John Galsworthy, among others.

28. 3,750 copies of *Passing* were printed on October 1, 1916; 2,000 on December 8, 1916; and a new edition of 1,525 on March 29, 1917 (Letter, [Maxwell Perkins?] to Madison Grant, July 10, 1918; ACS, Author Files I, Box 67, Folder Madison Grant, Subfolder 2). By February 1924, *Passing* had sold about 14,500 copies in all and printed 15,700 in all; by December 1927, 17,360 had been printed and 16,766 sold (Letter [Maxwell Perkins] to Madison Grant, February 27, 1924 and December 21, 1927; ACS, Author Files I, Box 67, Folder Madison Grant, Subfolder 3).

29. Letter, [Maxwell Perkins? Mr. Scribner?] to Madison Grant, February 3, 1922 (ACS, Author Files I, Box 67, Folder Madison Grant, Subfolder 2).

30. Letter, Madison Grant to Maxwell Perkins, February 15, 1922 (ACS, Author Files I, Box 67, Folder Madison Grant, Subfolder 2).

31. Memorandum from R. V. Coleman regarding Grant's *Conquest of the Continent*, June 16, 1933, (ACS, Author Files I, Box 67, Folder Madison Grant, Subfolder 3).

32. Undated ts. enclosed with letter [Maxwell Perkins] to Madison Grant, November 4, 1933 (ACS, Author Files I, Box 67, Folder Madison Grant, Subfolder 3).

33. For information on Hornaday, in addition to extended analysis of the race and class meanings of his sport, taxidermy, conservation, zoo-keeping, and writing, see Simpson "Immaculate," and "Powers."

34. Letter, George Bird Grinnell to Theodore Roosevelt, May 28, 1894 (GBGP, Series I, Letterbooks: Personal 1894 Mar 30–1896 June 22, Box 3, Folder 7).

35. Tuesday, September 17, 1907, Frederic Remington Diary (FRAM).

36. Letter, George Bird Grinnell to Caspar Whitney, May 16, 1901 (GBGP, Series I, Letterbooks: Personal, 1900 June 22–1901 December 17, Folder 11).

37. Letter, George Bird Grinnell to T. E. (Billy) Hofer, May 2, 1930 (GBGP, Series II, Correspondence: Hofer, T. E. (Billy) 1927–1933, N.D. Folder 92).

38. See Simpson, "Powers."

39. Letter, [Maxwell E. Perkins] to Madison Grant, May 19, 1930 (ACS, Author Files I, Box 67, Folder Madison Grant, Subfolder 1).

40. Letter, Madison Grant to Maxwell Perkins, May 29, 1930 (ACS, Author Files I, Box 67, Folder Madison Grant, Subfolder 1).

41. Letter, George Bird Grinnell to Theodore Roosevelt, July 23, 1894; Letter, George Bird Grinnell to Theodore Roosevelt, March 28, 1895 (GBGP, Series I, Letterbooks: Personal 1894 Mar 30–1896 June 22, Box 3, Folder 7).

42. See Schimmel 175.

43. Similarly, Daniel Worden points out that Wister's captioning of his 1891 photograph of "Shoshone Ladies Lunching" makes them "legible only through the genteel discourse of white, middle-class culture" (102); see also Tuttle, "Indigenous" 95.

44. Minutes of the annual Meeting of the Boone & Crockett Club, held at Washington, January 24, 1903 (BCC).

45. Remington had produced at least a draft of this work by 1900, although it was not serialized until 1905, then published in book form in 1906 (see Samuels, *Collected* 625–26).

46. Letter, Madison Grant to George Bird Grinnell, May 26, 1910 (BCC).

47. See Hagan 40.

48. See Hagan 143, 144, 141.

49. Throughout, I am using a mixture of Indigenous names, partly according to Grinnell's turn-of-the-century practice, and partly in accordance with current usage. The names here come from an August 2010 exhibition at the University of Montana, Missoula, on the Great Northern Railway.

50. "Notes on names of Physical Features in the Northeast Portion of Glacier National Park," November 20, 1928 (GBGP, Series II, Subject Files Glacier National Park 1928, Folder 169).

51. His name also lived on in the families of his hunting guides on the Blackfeet agency. Joe Kipp, a mixed-race outfitter and guide, called his son George Grinnell Kipp; J. B. Monroe, a white guide married to a Blackfeet woman, called his son Grinnell Monroe.

52. Letter, D[?] L Chapman, Asst Sect, US Dept of the Interior, Office of the Sec, to L. O. Vaught, July 19, 1945 (LOV, Box 6, Folder 4).

53. See Schultz, *Blackfeet* 99; Holterman 110; Schultz, *Signposts* 76. Although Grinnell ultimately became dismissive of Schultz (see Chapter Six, this volume), contemporary Blackfeet scholar Darrell Robes Kipp and cultural advisor Earnest Heavy Runner credit much of his information as accurate (see Kipp, "Introduction"; comments by Earnest Heavy Runner at Blackfeet Heritage Center, Browning, August 2011).

54. See Holterman 195; Schultz, *Signposts* 212.

55. Quoted in Diettert 57; Grinnell, Untitled Notes, August 3, 1928, 4 (GBGP, Series II, Subject Files: Glacier National Park 1928, Folder 169). Grinnell often referred to the Blackfeet Nation as the Piegan—as was common among white writers of the period—and I have followed his usage when representing his work.

56. The commission was comprised of Grinnell, William C. Pollock, a lawyer connected with the Indian service, and Walter M. Clements of Georgia.

57. Letter, George Bird Grinnell to J. B. Monroe, July 22, 1895 (GBGP, Series I, Letterbooks: Personal 1894 Mar 30–1896 June 22, Box 3, Folder 7).

58. Carter said that he was "very glad to be fortified with this resolution" (Letter, Thomas H. Carter, US Senate, Ctt on Organization, Conduct and Expenditures of the Executive Departments, to Madison Grant, April 4, 1908; BCC).

59. R14, CAS, George Bird Grinnell to D. M. Barringer, May 17, 1910 (GBGC, Box 2, Folder Research: Boone & Crockett Club 2–37).

60. Letter, Madison Grant to George Bird Grinnell, December 11, 1917 (GBGP, Series II: Correspondence Box 27). The history was issued as a pamphlet by the Department of the Interior in 1919—it was Grant's idea to have the pamphlet available in Glacier National Park—then he revised it for *Hunting and Conservation* (Letter, Madison Grant to George Bird Grinnell, November 15, 1922; GBGP, Series II, Correspondence: Grant, Madison 1898–1931, N. D. Folder 81). Grant discouraged researcher L. O. Vaught from using Indigenous place names (Letter, Madison Grant to L. O. Vaught, March 10, 1931; LOV, Box 6, Folder 4).

61. Report of the Park Naturalist, Glacier National Park 1926, by Morton J. Elrod (GBGP, Series II, Subject Files: Glacier National Park 1921–1927, Folder 168).

62. Hough quoted in Letter, James McLaughlin, Inspector, Office of Indian Affairs, Department of the Interior, June 16, 1915 (GBGP, Series II Subject Files: Glacier National Park 1911–1920, Folder 167); Letter, T. E. Hofer to George Bird Grinnell, March 25, 1930 (GBGP, Series II, Correspondence: Hofer, T. E. (Billy) 1927–1933, N.D., Folder 92); Letter, Inez L. Ponshe to George Bird Grinnell, August 29, 1927 (GBGP, Series II Subject Files: Glacier National Park 1921–1927, Folder 168).

63. Quoted in Diettert 104; Letter, Arno B. Cammarer, Acting Director, National Park Service, Department of the Interior, to George Bird Grinnell July 18, 1923; Note, Arno B. Cammarer, Acting Director, National Park Service, Department of the Interior, to the Superintendent, Assistant Superintendent, and Rangers of Glacier National Park, July 26, 1923 (GBGP, Series II, Subject Files: Glacier National Park 1921–1927, Folder 168).

64. Letter, George Bird Grinnell to Frederick A. Stokes, September 5, 1899 (GBGP, Series I, Letterbooks: Personal 1898 Dec 14–1900 June 22, Folder 10).

65. Letter, F. A. Stokes to George Bird Grinnell, April 3, 1907; Letter, F. A. Stokes to George Bird Grinnell, February 28, 1918 (GBGP, Series II, Correspondence: Frederick A. Stokes Company 1907, 1912, 1918, Box 27, Folder 79).

66. Undated, untitled typescript (GBGP, Series II, Other Papers: Writings: Drafts 1928, N.D., Folder 223).

67. Grinnell, "Memoirs, November 26th, 1915," 29, 30 (GBGP, Series II, Other Papers: Memoirs 1915, Folder 214).

68. See Punke 229.

69. Letter, George Bird Grinnell to J. B. Monroe, January 10, 1900 (GBGP, Series I, Letterbooks: Personal 1898 Dec 14–1900 Jun 22, Box 2, Folder 10).

70. Letter, George Bird Grinnell to J. B. Monroe, April 29, 1901 (GBGP, Series I, Letterbooks: Personal 1900 Jun 22–1901 Dec 17, Folder 11).

71. Letter, George Bird Grinnell to J. B. Monroe, January 10, 1900 (GBGP, Series I, Letterbooks: Personal 1898 Dec 14–1900 Jun 22, Box 2, Folder 10).

72. Letter, T. E. Hofer to George Bird Grinnell, May 9, 1923 (GBGP, Series II, Correspondence: Hofer, T. E. (Billy) 1905–1915, Folder 90).

73. In 1919, Grinnell wrote that John, the son of Hugh Monroe (sometimes spelled Munroe) "was my great friend, has been dead for a good many years" (Letter, George Bird Grinnell to L. O. Vaught, April 10, 1919; LOV, Box 6).

74. R3, CAS, George Bird Grinnell to H.L. Stimson, August 19, 1892 (GBGC, Research 1892 1–10, Box 1).

75. Letter, George Bird Grinnell to Frederick A. Stokes, June 1, 1900 (GBGP, Series I, Letterbooks: Personal 1898 Dec 14–1900 June 22, Folder 10); Letter, George Bird Grinnell to Frederick A. Stokes, October 3, 1900 (GBGP, Series I, Letterbooks: Personal 1900 June 22–1901 Dec 17, Folder 11).

76. See Deloria 95–109.

77. Deloria talks of early boys' outdoor camps also involving "banking exercises" (108).

78. Grant, *Early History of Glacier National Park Montana* (Washington, DC: Government Printing Office, 1919), pamphlet (GNP Library).

79. See also Lewis Sabo, "When Wagon Trails were Dim," *The Pacific Northwesterner* [newsletter] 28.2 (Spring 1984), 23–31 (GNP Library).

80. Letter, George Bird Grinnell to Joe Calf Robe, March 17, 1899 (GBGP, Series I, Letterbooks: Personal, 1898 December 14–1900 June 22).
81. Quoted in L. O. Vaught, ms. on Glacier National Park, 240 (GNP Library).
82. Mojica 35, 36. This vision is opposite and resistant to the white elite networks' management of the transnational as "fiefdom" discussed by Simpson, "Powers" (71).
83. Letter, George Bird Grinnell to L. O. Vaught, March 13, 1917 (LOV, Box 6).
84. Letter, George Bird Grinnell to L. O. Vaught, November 4, 1915 (LOV, Box 6, Folder 5); Letter, George Bird Grinnell to L. O. Vaught, January 24,1921 (LOV, Box 6, Folder 5).
85. Letter, George Bird Grinnell to L. O. Vaught, October 17, 1922 (LOV, Box 6, Folder 5).

Chapter 6

1. Letter, Princess Chinquilla to Owen Wister, November 4, 1904 (OWPLC, Box 78).
2. Slotkin, *Gunfighter* 155, 161; the larger argument is elaborated at 125–55.
3. I use this phrase after Deloria, *Indians*; and Gardner.
4. Letter, Mrs. Rodolophe Petter [to Dudley White] Lame Deer, January 8, 1954 (MSC).
5. New Zealand *Freelance*, September 19, 1905. I have reconstructed Chinquilla's stage career from the following sources: "'Chinquilla' at the Novelty"; "The Curtis Novelty Co."; "Midsummer Play Bills"; "Mrs. Mary Newell, Leader of Indians"; New Zealand *Observer*; "Some Vaudeville Headliners"; "The Sunday Concerts"; "Sunday Concerts."
6. The Civic Club Bulletin 2.4 (December 1908) (CCP). For John Collier's article on the investigation, published in April 1908, see Abel 73–77. Two years later, in another editorial, Molly Wister worried, "Who censors the vaudeville exhibits in Philadelphia's political clubs, and various questionable resorts?" (The Civic Club Bulletin 4. 2 [October 1910], CCP).
7. Civic Club Bulletin 2. 4 (December 1908) (CCP).
8. See A. B. Smith 5.
9. See A. B. Smith 95.
10. On March 11, 1911, "*Moving Picture World* reported the visit to Washington, DC, of a group of Native Americans to complain about their filmic representation. The delegation charged that 'moving picture promoters in order to get thrilling pictures of the Indians have used white men costumed as Indians in depicting scenes that are not true pictures of the Indian and are in fact grossly libelous'; and urged congressional action to regulate moving pictures. In an implicit defense of the representation of Native Americans in the early film Western, the editor of the same issue of *Moving Picture World* published a letter apparently from a Native American reader in Rochester, New York. Although the reader attacked Westerns for their exaggeration of the fighting prowess of White protagonists (such as five pioneers chasing away twelve Indians), he praised the majority of films for their accurate portrayal of Native American life" (Griffiths 91).
11. Letter, Mrs. Rodolophe Petter [to Dudley White] Lame Deer, January 8, 1954 (MSC). See also Chinquilla, *Natives* No. 2. "Tribes of the Plains," for her account of one trip to these and other agencies.
12. Letter, Mrs. Rodolophe Petter [to Dudley White] Lame Deer, January 8, 1954 (MSC).
13. Letter [Mari Sandoz] to Dudley White, March 18, 1954 (MSC).
14. Letter, Mari Sandoz to Mr. [Dudley] White, February 13, 1954 (MSC).
15. As Hafen, Carpenter, and other scholars do, I here follow Zitkala-Ša's own usage: she signed her Lakota name to her creative works but generally used "Gertrude Bonnin" in her correspondence and political organizing.
16. "Real and Make-Believe Indians Join in Park Ceremony in Honor of Red Veterans"; "Professional Women to Hold Exposition."
17. See Carpenter 139, 145.
18. Many unknowns and confusions remain in terms of Princess Chinquilla's history. Was she married to Ernest L. Barbour, another vaudeville performer, before Newell (see "Barbour-Chinquilla")? Was she a high-wire artist with Buffalo Bill's Wild West (see "Mrs. Mary Newell")? What name did she use prior to her adoption of her stage name and to her married name, Mrs. Mary Newell?

19. Richard White calls Turner and Cody "the two master narrators of American westering" (7).
20. See Martin; Berliner 75–76.
21. See Dippie 203–05; Hoxie 29–35; C. Walker 209–20.
22. For details of the birchbark book, including this sequence of its titles, see C. Walker 209–10. Berliner puts the titles in the opposite sequence (73).
23. See R. White 27.
24. Love 45, 93; see also Katz, *The Black West* 150–52; Allmendinger 66–68.
25. Letter, George Bird Grinnell to L. O. Vaught, March 13, 1917 (LOV, Box 6, Folder 5).
26. Grinnell, "Editorial Note"; Letter, George Bird Grinnell to L. O. Vaught, February 19, 1917 (LOV, Box 6, Folder 4).
27. See Holterman 23–24.
28. Letter, George Bird Grinnell to C. Hart Merriam, June 6, 1916; Letter, George Bird Grinnell to Robert S. Yard, April 26, 1916 (GBGC, Box 3, Folder Schultz); quoted in Diettert 101.
29. Letter, George Bird Grinnell to George Gould, January 5, 1906 (GBGC, Box 3, Folder Schultz).
30. L.O. Vaught, unpublished ms. on Glacier National Park, 229 (GNP Library).
31. Schultz, *Signposts* (35). L. O. Vaught may provide the most accurate sense of the entangled naming practices and histories: while emphasizing Hugh Monroe as the original white presence in the St. Mary Lake region, knowing and naming the terrain, Vaught credits Schultz with various "firsts" and refers to "the Grinnell-Schultz names" (Vaught ms. on Glacier National Park, 206, 258; GNP Library).
32. See Lamont, "Introduction" ix; Lamont, "Bovine."
33. See L. Brown 139ff., 2–3, 317.
34. Tonkovich develops this analysis most fully and positively. Elizabeth Ammons argues, in contrast, that *Winona* "is trapped into profound self-contradiction by its generic participation in the western" (216).
35. See M. K. Johnson for a comparison of this scene with how western conventions make meaning for Nat Love and the Virginian (123–27).
36. See Littlefield, "Introduction" 56.
37. Womack insists that this positioning of Posey, and the binary of progressives vs. conservatives within the Creek Nation more generally, radically simplifies a complex situation.
38. See Posey 88–89. *Harper's Weekly* supported the first edict, the writer Hamlin Garland the second. Zitkala-Ša's searing account, "The Cutting of My Long Hair," first appeared as one section of "The School Days of an Indian Girl" in *Atlantic Monthly*, 1900, then was reprinted in *American Indian Stories* (1921).
39. Littlefield, "Introduction" 40–41, 42; see also Kosmider on humor and teasing as survival strategies (85, 88).
40. John Dorst formulated this insightful phrase for different purposes than mine (44 and *passim*).
41. See, for example, M. K. Johnson's convincing reading of Nat Love's *Life and Adventures* in relationship to Booker T. Washington's *Up From Slavery* (98–117).
42. Berliner says that Pokagon's work "offers an intriguing blend of hybridity and cultural particularity" (75). Ammons says of Hopkins: "the diversity of Hopkins's literary production and in particular the volatile, unstable, long fiction that she wrote as a consciously political, marginalized, experimental author stand as crucially important paradigms" (214). Womack celebrates "Posey's mixed-genre approach" (171). I discuss Mollie E. Moore Davis's *The Wire-Cutters* as "intriguingly bifurcated along its geographical axis. The southern action is told with dime-novel melodrama—replete with sensational action, disguised identities, and uncanny coincidences— while the western events and characters are invested with considerably more historical verisimilitude" (Bold, "Westerns" 329).

Conclusion

1. Sandoz considered Ford's film a travesty of her 1953 work.
2. Among the numerous studies of the western, John G. Cawelti's *The Six-Gun Mystique Sequel* is distinctive for its overview of popular western fiction, film, and television (57–126).

3. *The Observer*, February 6, 2011. The full list is Gary Cooper, John Wayne, Jimmy Stewart, Henry Fonda, Randolph Scott, Gregory Peck, Paul Newman, Clint Eastwood, Jeff Bridges, and Woody.
4. William Handley traces the western's staging of Monument Valley as typologically Biblical well before Ford: see his analysis of the 1925 movie *The Vanishing American*, whose screen scenario describes Monument Valley: it "must look today as it looked in the time of Christ" (51).
5. Ford also cited the influence of Charlie Russell; Lee Clark Mitchell also detects the influence of Albert Bierstadt—another Boone and Crockett Clubman—and Bret Harte on Ford (93).
6. See D. Payne 284.
7. Eventually Earp drags her out of the saloon, she slaps him, and he dumps her in the water trough, threatening to run her back to the "Apache reservation" where she belongs, a phrase that evokes the Virginian's ostensible confusion between "Chinese and I-talians"—"both come that cheap they kind o' mix in my mind."
8. O. Wister, "A Play in Four Acts," ts. (OWPLC, Box 65).
9. O. Wister, Playscript of *The Virginian*, pencil ms. (OWPLC, BOX 65).
10. Letter, Winthrop Chanler to Owen Wister, January 30, 1894 (OWPLC, Box 15).

WORKS CITED

Archives and Special Collections

Boone and Crockett Club Records (Mss 738), Archives & Special Collections, Mansfield Library, The University of Montana-Missoula. (Cited as BCC.)

Cheyenne Club Records, 1880–1947, Wyoming Stock Growers Association Records, 1858–1987, Accession Number 14, Series VIII, American Heritage Center, University of Wyoming. (Cited as CC.)

Civic Club of Philadelphia Records, Historical Society of Pennsylvania, Philadelphia. (Cited as CCP.)

William Frederick Cody/Buffalo Bill Papers, 1870–1992, Western History Collection, Denver Public Library. (Cited as WFC.)

The Papers of William F. Cody, McCracken Research Library, Buffalo Bill Historical Center, Cody, Wyoming. (Cited as PWFC.)

J. M. Fox Collection, Pennsylvania Historical Society, Philadelphia. (Cited as JMF.)

George Bird Grinnell Collection (Mss 204), Archives & Special Collections, Mansfield Library, The University of Montana-Missoula. (Cited as GBGC.)

George Bird Grinnell Papers, Manuscripts and Archives, Yale University Library. (Cited as GBGP.)

Glacier National Park Archives, Glacier National Park, Montana. (Cited as GNP Archives.)

Glacier National Park Library, Glacier National Park, Montana. (Cited as GNP Library.)

Hebard Collection, American Heritage Center, University of Wyoming, Laramie. (Cited as HC.)

The Historical Society of Pennsylvania, Philadelphia. (Cited as HSP.)

Macmillan Company Records, New York Public Library Manuscripts and Archives Division, New York. (Cited as MCR.)

S. Weir Mitchell Papers, College of Physicians, Philadelphia. (Cited as SWM.)

Charles B. Penrose Papers, 1892–1936, Accession Number 9626, American Heritage Center, University of Wyoming, Laramie. (Cited as CBP.)

Frederic Remington Diary, Frederic Remington Art Museum, Ogdensburg, NY (Cited as FRAM.)

Mari Sandoz Collection (Part 4), University of Nebraska-Lincoln, Archives and Special Collections. (Cited as MSC.)

Archives of Charles Scribner's Sons, C0101, Princeton University Library, Manuscripts Division. (Cited as ACS.)

The L. O. Vaught Papers, 1897–1955, Glacier National Park Archives, Montana. (Cited as LOV.)

Owen Wister Papers, 1829–1966, Manuscript Division, Library of Congress, Washington, DC. (Cited as OWPLC.)

Owen Wister Papers, ca. 1866–1982, Accession Number 00290, American Heritage Center, University of Wyoming, Laramie. (Cited as OWP.)

Special Collections, Howard University, Washington, DC.
Wister Family Papers, La Salle University Special Collections, http://www.lasalle.edu/library/speccoll/wister.php, accessed December 2010. (Cited as WFP.)

Publications

Abel, Richard. *The Red Rooster Scare: Making Cinema American, 1900–1910.* Berkeley: University of California Press, 1999.

Allen, Henry T. "Wolf-Hunting in Russia." Roosevelt and Grinnell, *Hunting,* 151–86.

Allen, Robert C. "'A Decided Sensation': Cinema, Vaudeville, and Burlesque." *On the Edge of Your Seat: Popular Theater and Film in Early Twentieth-Century American Art.* Ed. Patricia McDonnell. New Haven, CT: Yale University Press, 2002. 61–89.

Allmendinger, Blake. *Imagining the African American West.* Lincoln: University of Nebraska Press, 2005.

Ammons, Elizabeth. "Afterword: *Winona,* Bakhtin, and Hopkins in the Twenty-First Century." *The Unruly Voice: Rediscovering Pauline Elizabeth Hopkins.* Ed. John Cullen Gruesser. Urbana: University of Illinois Press, 1996. 211–19.

Anderson, Geo. S. "Protection of the Yellowstone Park." Roosevelt and Grinnell, *Hunting,* 377–402.

"Appendix A: Policies." Grinnell and Sheldon, *Hunting and Conservation,* 492–511.

Atherton, Lewis. *The Cattle Kings.* 1961. Lincoln: University of Nebraska Press, 1972.

Austin, Mary. *The Ford.* Boston: Houghton, Mifflin, 1917.

Baker, Jr., Houston. *Long Black Song: Essays in Black American Literature and Culture.* Charlottesville: University Press of Virginia, 1972.

Baker, T. Lindsay. "Remembrances: Black Cowboy Life in Texas." Massey, *Black Cowboys,* 23–37.

Baltzell, E. Digby. *Philadelphia Gentlemen: The Making of a National Upper Class.* Glencoe, IL: The Free Press, 1958.

Bank, Rosemarie K. "Representing History: Performing the Columbian Exposition." *Theatre Journal* 54.4 (2002): 589–606.

"Barbour-Chinquilla." *The New York Dramatic Mirror,* May 13, 1905: 16.

Barr, Alwyn. "Preface." Massey, *Black Cowboys,* ix–xix.

Barringer, Daniel Moreau. "Dog Sledging in the North." Roosevelt and Grinnell, *Hunting,* 123–50.
———. "In the Old Rockies." Grinnell, *Hunting,* 295–313.

Baym, Nina. *Women Writers of the American West, 1833–1927.* Urbana: University of Illinois Press, 2011.

Beard, George M. "Neurasthenia, or Nervous Exhaustion." *Boston Medical and Surgical Journal* 3.13 (April 29, 1869): 217–21.

Bederman, Gail. *Manliness and Civilization: A Cultural History of Gender and Race in the United States, 1880–1917.* Chicago: University of Chicago Press, 1995.

Bender, Daniel E. *American Abyss: Savagery and Civilization in the Age of Industry.* Ithaca, NY: Cornell University Press, 2009.

Berliner, Jonathan. "Written in the Birch Bark: The Linguistic-Material Worldmaking of Simon Pokagon." *PMLA* 125.1 (January 2010): 73–91.

Bernardin, Susan. "The Lessons of a Sentimental Education: Zitkala-Ša's Autobiographical Narratives." *Western American Literature* 32.3 (1997): 212–38.

Billington, Monroe Lee, and Roger D. Hardaway, eds. *African Americans on the Western Frontier.* Niwot: University Press of Colorado, 1998.

Billington, Ray Allen. *Land of Savagery, Land of Promise: The European Image of the American Frontier.* New York: W. W. Norton, 1981.

Black, Jason Edward. "Remembrances of Removal: Native Resistance to Allotment and the Unmasking of Paternal Benevolence." *Southern Communication Journal* 72.2 (April–June 2007): 185–203.

Bold, Christine. "Exclusion Acts: How Popular Westerns Brokered the Atlantic Diaspora." *American Exceptionalisms.* Ed. Sylvia Söderlind and James Taylor Carson. Albany: SUNY Press, 2011. 93–123.

————. "The Rough Riders at Home and Abroad: Cody, Roosevelt, Remington, and the Imperialist Hero." *The Canadian Review of American Studies* 18.3 (Fall 1987): 321–50.

————. "'Rough Riders of the World': The Frontier Club and the Atlantic Diaspora." *Americas' Worlds and the World's Americas/Les mondes des Amériques et les Amériques du monde*. Ed. Amaryll Chanady et al. Ottawa: University of Ottawa/Legas, 2006, 369–78.

————. *Selling the Wild West: Popular Western Fiction, 1860 to1960*. Bloomington: Indiana University Press, 1987.

————. "Westerns." Bold, *US*, 317–36.

————. "Where Did the Black Rough Riders Go?" *War*. Ed. Michael H. Epp. Special issue, *Canadian Review of American Studies* 39.3 (2009): 273–97.

Bold, Christine, ed. *US Popular Print Culture 1860–1920*. The Oxford History of Popular Print Culture. Vol. 6. Oxford: Oxford University Press, 2011.

Bolotin, Norman, and Christine Laing. *The World's Columbian Exposition: The Chicago World's Fair of 1893*. Urbana: University of Illinois Press, 2002.

"Books on Big Game." Grinnell and Roosevelt, *Trail and Camp-Fire*, 321–35.

Bower, B. M. *The Lonesome Trail and Other Stories*. New York: G. W. Dillingham, 1904.

Branch, Douglas E. *The Cowboy and His Interpreters*. New York: Appleton, 1926.

Brantlinger, Patrick. *Dark Vanishings: Discourse on the Extinction of Primitive Races, 1800–1930*. Ithaca, NY: Cornell University Press, 2003.

Braxton, Lieut. "Company 'L' in the Spanish-American War." *The Colored American Magazine* 1.1 (May 1900): 19–25.

Brinkley, Douglas. *The Wilderness Warrior: Theodore Roosevelt and the Crusade for America*. New York: HarperCollins, 2009.

Brodhead, Richard. *Cultures of Letters: Scenes of Reading and Writing in Nineteenth-Century America*. Chicago: The University of Chicago Press, 1993.

Brooks, Daphne A. *Bodies in Dissent: Spectacular Performances of Race and Freedom, 1850–1910*. Durham, NC: Duke University Press, 2006.

Browder, Laura. *Slippery Characters: Ethnic Impersonators and American Identities*. Chapel Hill: University of North Carolina Press, 2000.

Brown, Bill, ed. *Reading the West: An Anthology of Dime Westerns*. Boston: Bedford/St. Martin's, 1997.

Brown, Lois. *Pauline Elizabeth Hopkins: Black Daughter of the Revolution*. Chapel Hill: University of North Carolina Press, 2008.

Bube, June Johnson. "From Sensational Dime Novel to Feminist Western: Adapting Genre, Transforming Gender." *Change in the American West: Exploring the Human Dimension*. Ed. Stephen Tchudi. Reno: University of Nevada Press, 1996. 64–86.

Buckland, Roscoe L. *Frederic Remington: The Writer*. Twayne's United States Authors Series 716. New York: Twayne Publishers, 2000.

Buckley, Gail. *American Patriots: The Story of Blacks in the Military from the Revolution to Desert Storm*. New York: Random House, 2002.

Butler, James A. "Introduction." *Romney and Other New Works about Philadelphia*. By Owen Wister. Ed. James A. Butler. University Park: Pennsylvania State University Press, 2001. xxiii–lvi.

Callahan, S. Alice. *Wynema: A Child of the Forest*. Ed. and introduction by A. Lavonne Brown Ruoff. 1891. Lincoln: University of Nebraska Press, 1997.

Cannadine, David. *The Decline and Fall of the British Aristocracy*. New Haven, CT: Yale University Press, 1990.

Carby, Hazel V. Introduction. *The Magazine Novels of Pauline Hopkins*. New York: Oxford University Press, 1988. xxix–l.

————. *Reconstructing Womanhood: The Emergence of the Afro-American Woman Novelist*. New York: Oxford University Press, 1987.

Carmony, Neil B., and David E. Brown, eds. *The Wilderness of the Southwest: Charles Sheldon's Quest for Desert Bighorn Sheep and Adventures with the Havasupai and Seri Indians*. Salt Lake City: University of Utah Press, 1993.

Carpenter, Cari. "Detecting Indianness: Gertrude Bonnin's Investigation of Native American Identity." *Wicazo Sa Review* 20.1 (2005): 139–59.

Carrigan, William D. *The Making of a Lynching Culture: Violence and Vigilantism in Central Texas, 1836–1916*. Urbana: University of Illinois Press, 2004.

Carter, Julian B. *The Heart of Whiteness: Normal Sexuality and Race in America, 1880–1940*. Durham, NC: Duke University Press, 2007.

Cartmill, Matt. *A View to a Death in the Morning: Hunting and Nature through History*. Cambridge, MA: Harvard University Press, 1993.

Cashin, Herschel V., et al. *Under Fire with the Tenth U.S. Cavalry*. New York: F. Tennyson Neely, 1899.

Cawelti, John G. *Adventure, Mystery, and Romance*. Chicago: University of Chicago Press, 1976.

———. *The Six-Gun Mystique*. Bowling Green, OH: Bowling Green University Popular Press, 1971.

———. *The Six-Gun Mystique Sequel*. Bowling Green, OH: Bowling Green State University Popular Press, 1999.

Chanler, Margaret Terry. *Autumn in the Valley*. Boston: Little, Brown, and Company, 1936.

———. *Memory Makes Music*. New York: Stephen-Paul Publishers, 1948.

———. *Roman Spring: Memoirs*. Boston: Little, Brown, and Company, 1934.

Chanler, Margaret Terry, coll. *Winthrop Chanler's Letters*. New York: privately printed, 1951.

Chanler, William A. "Hunting in East Africa." Roosevelt and Grinnell, *Hunting*, 13–54.

Chanler, Winthrop. "A Day with the Elk." Roosevelt and Grinnell, *American*, 61–72.

———. "Mouflon in Sardinia." Grinnell and Sheldon, *Hunting and Conservation*, 1–28.

Chesnutt, Charles W. *The House Behind the Cedars*. Boston: Houghton Mifflin, 1900.

"'Chinquilla' at the Novelty." Los Angeles *Herald*, November 21, 1905: 8.

Chinquilla (Cheyenne Nation). *Natives of N. America*. Lame Deer, MT: Printed by Chinquilla, 1932.

Chinquilla (Cheyenne Nation), comp. *The Old Indian's Almanac*. Jamaica, NY: Printed at the Indian Craft Museum, 1937.

Chude-Sokei, Louis. *The Last "Darky": Bert Williams, Black-on-Black Minstrelsy, and the African Diaspora*. Durham, NC: Duke University Press, 2006.

Clark, J. J. "The Slave Whisperer Rides the Frontier: Horseface Minstrelsy in the Western." *Animals and Agency: An Interdisciplinary Exploration*. Ed. Sarah E. McFarland and Ryan Hediger. Leiden, Netherlands: Brill, 2009. 157–80.

Clay, John. "The Cheyenne Club: Recollections of An Organization Once Famous in Connection with the Development of the Western Cattle Trade." *The Breeder's Gazette* 70 (1916): 1182–83.

———. *My Life on the Range*. Chicago: privately printed, 1924.

Cobbs, John L. *Owen Wister*. Twayne's United States Authors Series 475. Boston: Twayne, 1984.

Cole, Stephanie, and Alison M. Parker, eds. *Beyond Black and White: Race, Ethnicity, and Gender in the U.S. South and Southwest*. Walter Prescott Webb Memorial Lectures Series. College Station: Texas A&M University Press, 2004.

Coleman, Finnie D. *Sutton E. Griggs and the Struggle against White Supremacy*. Knoxville: The University of Tennessee Press, 2007.

"Colored Girl at Vassar." *The New York Times*, August 16, 1897.

Croly, Mrs. J. C. *The History of the Woman's Club Movement in America*. New York: Henry G. Allen & Co., 1898.

Curtis, Emma Ghent. *The Administratrix*. New York: John B. Alden, 1889.

"The Curtis Novelty Co." New Zealand *Evening Post*, August 23, 1905.

Cutright, Paul Russell. *Theodore Roosevelt: The Making of a Conservationist*. Urbana: University of Illinois Press, 1985.

Czech, Kenneth P. *With Rifle and Petticoat: Women as Big-Game Hunters 1880–1940*. Lanham, MD: The Derrydale Press, 2002.

Dalton, Kathleen. *Theodore Roosevelt: A Strenuous Life*. New York: Alfred A. Knopf, 2002.

Davis, Mollie E. Moore. *The Wire-Cutters*, 1899. Introduction by Lou Halsell Rodenberger. College Station: Texas A&M University Press, 1997.

Davis, Richard Harding. *The Cuban and Porto Rican Campaigns*. 1898. Freeport, NY: Books for Libraries Press, 1970.

De C. Ward, Robert. "An Immigration Restriction League." *The Century: A Popular Quarterly* 49.4 (February 1895): 639.

Deloria, Philip J. *Indians in Unexpected Places*. Lawrence: University Press of Kansas, 2004.

————. *Playing Indian*. New Haven, CT: Yale University Press, 1998.

Denning, Michael. *Mechanic Accents: Dime Novels and Working-class Culture in America*. 1987. 2nd ed. London: Verso, 1998.

Devereux, W.B. "Photographing Wild Game." Roosevelt and Grinnell, *American*, 299–318.

Diettert, Gerald A. *Grinnell's Glacier: George Bird Grinnell and Glacier National Park*. Foreword by Jerry De Santo. Missoula, MT: Mountain Press Publishing Company, 1992.

DiMaggio, Paul. "Cultural Entrepreneurship in Nineteenth-Century Boston: The Creation of an Organizational Base for High Culture in America." *Media, Culture and Society 4* (1982): 33–50.

————. "Cultural Entrepreneurship in Nineteenth-Century Boston, Part II: The Classification and Framing of American Art." *Media, Culture and Society 4* (1982): 303–22.

Dippie, Brian W. *The Vanishing American: White Attitudes and U.S. Indian Policy*. Middletown, CT: Wesleyan University Press, 1982.

Di Silvestro, Roger L. *Theodore Roosevelt in the Badlands: A Young Politician's Quest for Recovery in the American West*. New York: Walker & Co., 2011.

Dorst, John. *Looking West*. Philadelphia: University of Pennsylvania Press, 1999.

Durham, Philip, and Everett L. Jones. *The Negro Cowboys*. New York: Dodd, Mead, 1965.

Dyer, Thomas G. *Theodore Roosevelt and the Idea of Race*. Baton Rouge: Louisiana State University Press, 1980.

Earnest, Ernest. *S. Weir Mitchell: Novelist and Physician*. Philadelphia: University of Pennsylvania Press, 1950.

Eco, Umberto. *Travels in Hyperreality*. Trans. William Weaver. London: Pan-Picador, 1987.

Edel, Leon. *Henry James: The Conquest of London: 1870–1883*. London: Rupert Hart-Davis, 1962.

"Editorial and Publisher's Announcements." *The Colored American Magazine* (May 1900): 60.

Ellis, Edward S. *Cowmen and Rustlers: A Story of the Wyoming Cattle Ranges*. N.p.: n.pub.: 1904.

————. *From the Ranch to the White House: Life of Theodore Roosevelt*. New York: Hurst & Company, 1906.

————. *Seth Jones; or, The Captives of the Frontier*. Beadle's Dime Novels 8. New York: Irwin P. Beadle & Co., 1860.

Ellison, Ralph. Introduction. *Invisible Man*. New York: Vintage Books-Random House, 1995. vii–xxiii.

Etulain, Richard W. *Owen Wister*. Boise: Boise State College, 1973.

Evans, Max. "Afterword." *The Virginian: A Horseman of the Plains*. New York: New American Library/Signet, 2002.

Evans, Robley. *George Bird Grinnell*. Boise State University Western Writers Series No. 122. Idaho: Boise State University, 1996.

Exman, Eugene. *The House of Harper: One Hundred and Fifty Years of Publishing*. New York: Harper & Row, 1967.

Federal Writers' Project. *The WPA Guide to New York City*. 1939. New York: Pantheon Books, 1982.

Fiedler, Leslie A. *The Return of the Vanishing American*. London: Cape, 1968.

Fletcher, Marvin. "The Black Volunteers in the Spanish-American War." *Military Affairs 38.2* (April 1974): 48–53.

"The Game Preservation Committee." Grinnell, *Hunting*, 421–32.

"The Game of the West." Review of *Hunting Trips of a Ranchman*. *New York Times*, July 13, 1885. 3.

Gardner, Eric. *Unexpected Places: Relocating Nineteenth-Century African American Literature*. Jackson: University Press of Mississippi, 2009.

Garis, Roy L. *Immigration Restriction: A Study of the Opposition to and Regulation of Immigration into the United States*. New York: Macmillan, 1927.

Garraty, John A. *Henry Cabot Lodge: A Biography*. New York: Alfred A. Knopf, 1965.

Garvey, Ellen Gruber. *The Adman in the Parlor: Magazines and the Gendering of Consumer Culture, 1880s to 1910s*. New York: Oxford University Press, 1996.

————. "Ambivalent Advertising: Books, Prestige, and the Circulation of Publicity." *Print in Motion: The Expansion of Publishing and Reading in the United States, 1880-1940*. Ed. Carl F.

Kaestle and Janice A. Radway. *A History of the Book in America*. Vol. 4. Chapel Hill: University of North Carolina Press, 2009. 170–89.

Gatewood, Willard B., Jr. "Black Americans and the Quest for Empire, 1898–1903." *The Journal of Southern History* 38.4 (1972): 545–66.

———. "Indiana Negroes and the Spanish American War." *Indiana Magazine of History* 69.2 (1973): 115–39.

———. *"Smoked Yankees" and the Struggle for Empire: Letters from Negro Soldiers, 1898–1902.* Urbana: University of Illinois Press, 1971.

Gere, Anne Ruggles. *Intimate Practices: Literacy and Cultural Work in U.S. Women's Clubs, 1880–1920.* Urbana: University of Illinois Press, 1997.

Gianakos, Perry E. "The Spanish-American War and the Double Paradox of the Negro American." *Phylon* 26.1 (1965): 34–49.

Gilman, Charlotte Perkins. "The Yellow Wall-paper." *The New England Magazine* 5 (January 1892): 647–56.

Gilmore, F. Grant. *"The Problem": A Military Novel.* College Park, MD: McGrath Pub. Co., 1915.

Glasrud, Bruce A., and Laurie Champion, eds. *The African American West: A Century of Short Stories.* Boulder: University Press of Colorado, 2000.

Glasrud, Bruce A., and James Smallwood, eds. *The African American Experience in Texas: An Anthology.* Lubbock: Texas Tech University Press, 2007.

Gleijeses, Piero. "African Americans and the War against Spain." *North Carolina Historical Review* 73.2 (1996): 184–214.

Gloster, Hugh M. Introduction. *Imperium in Imperio: A Study of the Negro Race Problem.* Sutton E. Griggs. 1899. New York: Arno Press and New York Times, 1969. i–vi.

Goetzmann, William H. *Exploration and Empire: The Explorer and the Scientist in the Winning of the American West.* New York: History Book Club, 1993.

Goldsby, Jacqueline. *A Spectacular Secret: Lynching in American Life and Literature.* Chicago: University of Chicago Press, 2006.

Grant, Madison. "A Canadian Moose Hunt." Roosevelt and Grinnell, *Hunting,* 84–106.

———. "The Condition of Wild Life in Alaska." Grinnell, *Hunting,* 367–92.

———. "Distribution of the Moose." Grinnell, *American,* 374–90.

———. *Early History of Glacier National Park Montana.* Washington, DC: Government Printing Office, 1919.

———. ["The Major"] *Hank, His Lies and His Yarns.* New York: 1931.

———. "The Origin of the New York Zoölogical Society." Grinnell and Roosevelt, *Trail and Camp-Fire,* 313–20.

———. *The Passing of the Great Race; or, the Racial Basis of European History.* New York: Charles Scribner's Sons, 1916.

Graulich, Melody. "What If Wister Were a Woman?" Graulich and Tatum, *Reading* The Virginian, 198–212.

Graulich, Melody, and Stephen Tatum, eds. *Reading* The Virginian *in the New West.* Lincoln: University of Nebraska Press, 2003.

Gressley, Gene M. *Bankers and Cattlemen.* Lincoln: University of Nebraska Press, 1966.

Grey, Zane. *The Heritage of the Desert.* New York: Harpers & Brothers, 1910.

———. *The Last of the Plainsmen.* London: Hodder & Stoughton, 1908.

———. *The Rainbow Trail: A Romance.* New York: Harper & Brothers, 1915.

———. *Riders of the Purple Sage: A Novel.* New York: Harper & Brothers, 1912.

Griffiths, Alison. "Science and Spectacle: Native American Representation in Early Cinema." *Dressing in Feathers: The Construction of the Indian in American Popular Culture.* Ed. S. Elizabeth Bird. Boulder, CO: Westview Press, 1996. 79–95.

Griggs, Sutton E. *The Hindered Hand; or, The Reign of the Repressionist.* 1905. New York: AMS Press, 1969.

———. *Imperium in Imperio: A Study of the Negro Race Problem.* 1899. New York: Arno Press and New York Times, 1969.

———. *Unfettered.* 1902. New York: AMS Press, 1971.

Grinnell, George Bird. "American Game Protection." Grinnell and Sheldon, *Hunting and Conservation,* 201–57.

————. "The Bison." Whitney, Grinnell, and Wister, *Musk-Ox*, 107–66.

————. "The Boone and Crockett Club." *Forest and Stream 31.26* (January 17, 1889), 513.

————. "The Boone and Crockett Club." *Forest and Stream 40.3* (January 19, 1893), 49.

————. "Brief History of the Boone and Crockett Club." 1910. Reprinted in Grinnell, *Hunting*, 435–91.

————. [Ornis]. "Buffalo Hunt with Pawnees." *Forest and Stream 1.20* (December 25, 1873), 305–06.

————. *By Cheyenne Campfires*. Photos. Elizabeth C. Grinnell. New Haven, CT: Yale University Press, 1926.

————. *The Cheyenne Indians: Their History and Ways of Life*. 1923. 2 Vols. Introduction by Mari Sandoz. Photos. Elizabeth C. Grinnell and Mrs. F. E. Tuell. New York: Cooper Square Publishers, 1962.

————. [Ornis]. "A Day with the Sage Grouse." *Forest and Stream 1.13* (November 6, 1873), 196.

————. "Editorial Note." Schultz, *My Life as an Indian*, n.p.

————. "The Ethics of Hunting." *Forest and Stream 31.18* (November 22, 1888), 341.

————. *The Fighting Cheyennes*. 1915. Norman: University of Oklahoma Press, 1956.

————. "Game Protection in Wyoming." *Forest and Stream 15.22* (December 30, 1880), 423.

————. "The Girl Who Was the Ring." *Harper's Monthly Magazine* 102 (February 1901): 425–30.

————. [Ornis]. "The Green River Country." *Forest and Stream 1.14* (November 13, 1873), 212.

————. "Importing Foreign Birds." *Forest and Stream 23.19* (December 4, 1884), 361.

————. "Introduction." *The Works of Theodore Roosevelt*. National edition. Volume 1. New York: Charles Scribner's Sons, 1926. xiii–xxv.

————. *Jack among the Indians; or, A Boy's Summer on the Buffalo Plains*. New York: Frederick A. Stokes Company, 1900.

————. *Jack in the Rockies; or, A Boy's Adventures with a Pack Train*. New York: Frederick A. Stokes Company, 1904.

————. *Jack the Young Canoeman: An Eastern Boy's Voyage in a Chinook Canoe*. New York: Frederick A. Stokes Company, 1906.

————. *Jack the Young Cowboy: An Eastern Boy's Experience on a Western Round-up*. New York: Frederick A. Stokes Company, 1913.

————. *Jack the Young Explorer: A Boy's Experiences in the Unknown Northwest*. New York: Frederick A. Stokes Company, 1908.

————. *Jack, The Young Ranchman; or, A Boy's Adventures in the Rockies*. New York: Frederick A. Stokes Company, 1899.

————. *Jack the Young Trapper: An Eastern Boy's Fur Hunting in the Rocky Mountains*. New York: Frederick A. Stokes Company, 1907.

————. [Yo]. "A Load of Meat." *Forest and Stream 21.12* (October 18, 1883), 222–23.

————. "The National Recreation Conference 1924." Grinnell and Sheldon, *Hunting and Conservation*, 471–91.

————. "A Nation's Honor." *Forest and Stream 26.18* (April 22, 1886), 241.

————. "New Publications." *Forest and Stream 24.23* (July 2, 1885), 451.

————. "The Park Monopolists Checked." *Forest and Stream 19.24* (January 11, 1883), 461.

————. "Preface." Grinnell and K. Roosevelt et al., *Hunting Trails*, vii–xi.

————. [Yo]. "To the Walled-In Lakes." *Forest and Stream 25.20* (December 10, 1885), 382–83– 26.8 (March 18, 1886), 142.

————. [Yo]. "A Trip to North Park. (Fourth Paper.)" *Forest and Stream 13.8* (September 25, 1879), 670–71.

————. "What We May Learn from the Indian." *Forest and Stream 86.3* (March 1916), 845–46.

————. "Woman in the Field." *Forest and Stream 72.12* (March 20, 1909), 447.

Grinnell, George Bird, ed. *American Big Game in Its Haunts: The Book of the Boone and Crockett Club*. New York: Forest and Stream Publishing Company, 1904.

————. *Hunting at High Altitudes: The Book of the Boone and Crockett Club*. New York: Harper & Brothers, 1913.

Grinnell, George Bird, Kermit Roosevelt, W. Redmond Cross, and Prentiss N. Gray, eds. *Hunting Trails on Three Continents: A Book of the Boone and Crockett Club*. New York: Windward House, 1933.

Grinnell, George Bird, and Theodore Roosevelt, eds. *Trail and Camp-Fire: The Book of the Boone and Crockett Club*. New York: Forest and Stream Publishing Company, 1897.

Grinnell, George Bird, and Charles Sheldon, eds. *Hunting and Conservation: The Book of the Boone and Crockett Club*. New Haven, CT: Yale University Press, 1925.

Guterl, Matthew Pratt. *The Color of Race in America, 1900–1940*. Cambridge, MA: Harvard University Press, 2001.

Hackett, Alice Payne, and James Henry Burke. *80 Years of Best Sellers 1895–1975*. New York: R. R. Bowker, 1977.

Hafen, P. Jane. "Introduction." Zitkala-Ša, *Dreams*, xiii–xxiv.

Hagan, William T. *Theodore Roosevelt and Six Friends of the Indian*. Norman: University of Oklahoma Press, 1997.

Hagedorn, Hermann. *Roosevelt in the Bad Lands*. Boston: Houghton Mifflin, 1930.

Hague, Arnold. "The Yellowstone Park as a Game Reservation." Roosevelt and Grinnell, *American*, 240–70.

Hall, Jacquelyn Dowd. "'The Mind That Burns in Each Body': Women, Rape, and Racial Violence." *Powers of Desire: The Politics of Sexuality*. Ed. Ann Snitow, Christine Stansell, and Sharon Thompson. New York: Monthly Review Press, 1983. 328–49.

———. *Revolt Against Chivalry: Jesse Daniel Ames and the Women's Campaign Against Lynching*. New York: Columbia University Press, 1979.

Hall, Prescott F. "Immigration and the Educational Test." *The North American Review 165* (October 1897): 393–402.

———. Letter to the editor. *Boston Journal* June 30, 1894.

Halverson, Cathryn. *Maverick Autobiographies: Women Writers and the American West 1900–1936*. Madison: The University of Wisconsin Press, 2004.

Handley, William R. *Marriage, Violence, and the Nation in the American Literary West*. Cambridge: Cambridge University Press, 2002.

———. "*The Vanishing American (1925)*." *America First: Naming the Nation in US Film*. Ed. Mandy Merck. London: Routledge, 2007. 44–64.

Haraway, Donna. "Teddy Bear Patriarchy: Taxidermy in the Garden of Eden, New York City, 1908–1936." 1984/85. Kaplan and Pease, *Cultures*, 237–91.

Hardaway, Roger D. "African American Cowboys on the Western Frontier." *Negro History Bulletin* 64.1–4 (Jan.–Dec. 2001): 27–32.

———. *A Narrative Bibliography of the African American Frontier: Blacks in the Rocky Mountain West, 1535–1912*. Lewiston, NY: The Edwin Mellen Press, 1995.

Harper, Frances Ellen Watkins. *Iola Leroy; or, Shadows Uplifted*. 1892. New York: AMS Press, 1971.

Harper, J. Henry. *The House of Harper: A Century of Publishing in Franklin Square*. New York: Harper & Brothers, 1912.

Harris III, Charles H., and Louis R. Sadler. *The Archaeologist Was A Spy: Sylvanus G. Morley and the Office of Naval Intelligence*. Albuquerque: University of New Mexico Press, 2003.

Harris III, Edward Day. "Preserving a Vision of the American West: The Life of George Bird Grinnell." PhD Dissertation, University of Texas, Austin, 1995.

Harrison, Jr., George L. "Ibex Shooting in the Thian Shan Mountains." Grinnell, *Hunting*, 314–43.

———. "A Shooting Trip in Northwestern Rhodesia." Grinnell, *Hunting*, 344–66.

Hart, James D. *The Popular Book: A History of America's Literary Taste*. New York: Oxford University Press, 1950.

Herman, Daniel Justin. *Hunting and the American Imagination*. Washington, DC: Smithsonian Institution Press, 2001.

———. "Hunting Democracy." *Montana: The Magazine of Western History 44.3* (Autumn 2005): 22–33.

"Hermann Oelrichs Dies on a Liner at Sea." *New York Times*, September 4, 1906.

Hertzberg, Hazel W. *The Search for an American Indian Identity: Modern Pan-Indian Movements*. Syracuse, NY: Syracuse University Press, 1971.

Higham, John. *Strangers in the Land: Patterns of American Nativism 1860–1925*. 2nd ed. New Brunswick, NJ: Rutgers University Press, 2002.

Hine, Robert V. *The American West: An Interpretive History*. 2nd ed. Boston: Little, Brown, 1984.

"The Hired Texan Murderers." *New York Times*, August 21, 1892.

Hodes, Martha. "Fractions and Fictions in the United States Census of 1890." *Haunted by Empire: Geographies of Intimacy in North American History*. Ed. Ann Laura Stoler. Durham, NC: Duke University Press, 2006. 240–70.

Hodos, Jerome. "The 1876 Centennial in Philadelphia: Elite Networks and Political Culture." *Social Capital in the City: Community and Civic Life in Philadelphia*. Ed. Richardson Dilworth. Philadelphia: Temple University Press, 2006. 19–39.

Hofstadter, Richard. *Social Darwinism in American Thought*. Rev. ed. Boston: Beacon Press, 1955.

Hoganson, Kristin. *Fighting for American Manhood: How Gender Politics Provoked the Spanish-American and Philippine-American Wars*. New Haven, CT: Yale University Press, 1998.

Holterman, Jack. *Place Names of Glacier National Park*. 3rd ed. Helena, MT: Riverbend Publishing, 2006.

Homberger, Eric. *Mrs. Astor's New York: Money and Social Power in a Gilded Age*. New Haven, CT: Yale University Press, 2002.

Hopkins, Pauline. *Contending Forces: A Romance Illustrative of Negro Life North and South*. 1900. Carbondale: Southern Illinois University Press, 1978.

———. *Winona: A Tale of Negro Life in the South and Southwest*. 1902. *The Magazine Novels of Pauline Hopkins*. Introduction by Hazel V. Carby. New York: Oxford University Press, 1988. 285–437.

Hough, Emerson. "The Account of Howell's Capture." *Forest and Stream* 42.18 (May 5, 1894): 377–78.

———. *The Covered Wagon*. New York: Appleton, 1922.

———. *Getting A Wrong Start: A Truthful Autobiography*. New York: The Macmillan Company, 1915.

———. *The Girl at the Halfway House: A Story of the Plains*. New York: Appleton, 1900.

———. *Heart's Desire: The Story of a Contented Town, Certain Peculiar Citizens and Two Fortunate Lovers*. New York: Macmillan, 1905.

———. *North of 36*. New York: Appleton, 1923.

———. *The Story of the Cowboy*. The Story of the West Series. Ed. Ripley Hitchcock. New York: Appleton, 1897.

Howard, June. *Publishing the Family*. Durham, NC: Duke University Press, 2001.

Hoxie, Frederick E., ed. and intro. *Talking Back to Civilization: Indian Voices from the Progressive Era*. Boston: Bedford/St. Martin's, 2001.

Hufsmith, George W. *The Wyoming Lynching of Cattle Kate, 1889*. Glendo, WY: High Plains Press, 1993.

Huhndorf, Shari M. *Going Native: Indians in the American Cultural Imagination*. Ithaca, NY: Cornell University Press, 2001.

Immigration Restriction League. *Annual Report of the Executive Committee of the Immigration Restriction League for 1895*. Boston, 1895.

"Indian Movie Program in New York." *Educational Film Magazine* 3.2 (February 1920): 9.

Indian Tepee: A Journal Devoted to the Red Race of North and South America 9.1 (1927).

Ingraham, Prentiss. *Buck Taylor, King of the Cowboys; or, The Raiders and the Rangers*. Beadle's Half Dime Library 497. New York: Beadle & Adams, 1887.

"International Copyright: The Copyright Controversy." *Publishers' Weekly*, December 9, 1882: 866–69.

"International Copyright." *Publishers' Weekly*, February 10, 1883: 173.

Jacoby, Karl. *Crimes against Nature: Squatters, Poachers, Thieves, and the Hidden History of American Conservation*. Berkeley: University of California Press, 2001.

James, Elizabeth. "Letters from America: The Bretts and the Macmillan Company of New York." *Macmillan: A Publishing Tradition*. Ed. Elizabeth James. Houndmills, UK: Palgrave, 2002. 170–91.

Johnson, Edward A. *A School History of the Negro Race in America from 1619 to 1890 Combined with the History of the Negro Soldiers in the Spanish-American War, also a Short Sketch of Liberia*. Rev. ed. 1911. New York: AMS Press, 1969.

Johnson, Marilynn S. *Violence in the West: The Johnson County Range War and the Ludlow Massacre: A Brief History with Documents.* New York: New Bedford/St. Martins, 2008.

Johnson, Michael K. *Black Masculinity and the Frontier Myth in American Literature.* Norman: University of Oklahoma Press, 2002.

Jones, Darryl. *The Dime Novel Western.* Bowling Green, OH: Bowling Green University Popular Press, 1978.

Jones, Virgil Carrington. *Roosevelt's Rough Riders.* Garden City, NY: Doubleday, 1971.

Kaplan, Amy. "Black and Blue on San Juan Hill." Kaplan and Pease, *Cultures,* 219–36.

Kaplan, Amy, and Donald Pease, eds. *Cultures of United States Imperialism.* Durham, NC: Duke University Press, 1994.

Kasson, Joy S. *Buffalo Bill's Wild West: Celebrity, Memory, and Popular History.* New York: Hill and Wang, 2000.

Katz, William Loren. *Black Indians: A Hidden Heritage.* 1986. New York: Simon & Schuster/ Aladdin Paperbacks, 1997.

———. *The Black West.* 4th ed. New York: Touchstone Books, 1996.

Kavaler, Lucy. *The Astors: A Family Chronicle of Pomp and Power.* New York: Dodd, Mead & Co., 1966.

Keller, Alexandra. "Generic Subversion as Counterhistory: Mario Van Peebles's *Posse.*" *Westerns: Films through History.* Ed. Janet Walder. New York: Routledge, 2001. 27–46.

Kelley, Robin D. G. *Race Rebels: Culture, Politics, and the Black Working Class.* New York: The Free Press, 1996.

Kelly, Florence Finch. *With Hoops of Steel.* New York: Grosset and Dunlap, 1900.

Kelly, Tara Kathleen. "The Hunter Elite: Americans, Wilderness, and the Rise of the Big-Game Hunt." PhD Dissertation, Johns Hopkins University, 2006.

———. "The Still-Hunter and the Temptation Goats: Reconsidering the Meaning of the Hunt in American Culture, 1880–1914." *Journal of Sport History* 35.2 (Summer 2008): 285–301.

Kimmel, Michael. *Manhood in America: A Cultural History* New York: Free Press, 1996.

King, Desmond. *Making Americans: Immigration, Race, and the Origins of the Diverse Democracy.* Cambridge, MA: Harvard University Press, 2000.

King, Thomas. *The Truth about Stories: A Native Narrative.* Toronto, ON: House of Anansi Press, 2003.

Kipp, Darrell Robes. "Introduction." Schultz, *Blackfeet,* vi–ix.

Knight, Alisha R. "'To have the benefit of some special machinery': African American Book Publishing and Bookselling, 1900–1920." Bold, *US,* 437–56.

Kosmider, Alexia. *Tricky Tribal Discourse: The Poetry, Short Stories, and Fus Fixico Letters of Creek Writer Alex Posey.* Moscow: University of Idaho Press, 1998.

Kristofferson, Kris. Interview. *Enough Rope with Andrew Denton.* ABC television. July 25, 2005. http://www.abc.net.au/tv/enoughrope/transcripts/s1422317.htm. Accessed May 7, 2011.

"La Follette Lashes Morgan in Senate." *New York Times,* April 13, 1910.

Lamont, Victoria. "The Bovine Object of Ideology: History, Gender, and the Origins of the Classic Western." *Western American Literature* 35.4 (Winter 2001): 373–402.

———. "Cattle Branding and the Traffic in Women in Early 20th Century Westerns by Women." *Legacy: A Journal of American Women Writers* 22.1 (2005): 30–46.

———. "Introduction." McElrath, *The Rustler,* ix–xx.

Law, Graham, and Norimasa Morita. "Internationalizing the Popular Print Marketplace." Bold, *US,* 211–29.

Lears, T. J. Jackson. *No Place of Grace: Antimodernism and the Transformation of American Culture.* Chicago: The University of Chicago Press, 1981.

Leckie, William H., with Shirley A. Leckie. *The Buffalo Soldiers: A Narrative of the Black Cavalry in the West.* Rev. ed. Norman: University of Oklahoma Press, 2003.

Leonard, Elizabeth D. *Men of Color to Arms!: Black Soldiers, Indian Wars, and the Quest for Equality.* New York: W.W. Norton, 2010.

Levine, Lawrence W. *Highbrow/Lowbrow: The Emergence of Cultural Hierarchy in America.* New York: Basic Books, 1988.

Lewis, Michael, ed. *American Wilderness: A New History.* Oxford: Oxford University Press, 2007.

Lippincott, J. B. & Co. Untitled. *The Critic*, December 2, 1882. Reprinted in "International Copyright: The Copyright Controversy." 866–69.

"Literary Notes," *New York Tribune* (October 9, 1893), 8.

Littlefield, Daniel F. Jr. "Introduction." Posey, *The Fus Fixico Letters*, 1–48.

Lodge, Henry Cabot. "International Copyright." May 2, 1890. Lodge, *Speeches*, 49–56.

———. "Lynch Law and Unrestricted Immigration." *The North American Review 152.414* (May 1891): 602–12.

———. "The Restriction of Immigration." March 16, 1896. Lodge, *Speeches*, 243–66.

———. "Speech at the Alumni Dinner, Harvard Commencement." June 1896. Lodge, *Speeches*, 289–94.

———. *Speeches and Addresses, 1884–1909*. Boston: Houghton Mifflin, 1909.

Logan, Rayford W. *The Betrayal of the Negro from Rutherford B. Hayes to Woodrow Wilson*. New ed. New York: Da Capo Press, 1997.

Love, Eric T. *Race over Empire: Racism and U.S. Imperialism, 1865–1900*. Chapel Hill: University of North Carolina Press, 2004.

Love, Nat. *The Life and Adventures of Nat Love, Better Known in the Cattle Country as "Deadwood Dick."* 1907. Introduction by Brackette F. Williams. Lincoln: University of Nebraska Press, 1995.

Lovering, Joseph. *S. Weir Mitchell*. Twayne's United States Authors Series 183. New York: Twayne, 1971.

Low, A. P. "The Labrador Peninsula." Grinnell and Roosevelt, *Trail and Camp-Fire*, 15–50.

Markovitz, Jonathan. *Legacies of Lynching: Racial Violence and Memory*. Minneapolis: University of Minnesota Press, 2004.

"Marshall Rankin Removed." *New York Times*, September 19, 1892.

Martin, Lawrence T. "Simon Pokagon: Charlatan or Authentic Spokesman for the 19th-Century Anishinaabeg?" *Papers of the Twenty-Ninth Algonquian Conference*. Ed. David H. Pentland and Lisa Philips Valentine. Winnipeg: University of Manitoba, 1999. 182–91.

Massey, Sara R., ed. *Black Cowboys of Texas*. College Station: Texas A&M University Press, 2000.

Matthews, Brander. "The Evolution of Copyright." *Political Science Quarterly 5.4* (December 1890): 583–602.

McDermott, John Francis. "French Surnames in the Mississippi Valley." *American Speech 9.1* (February 1934): 28–30.

McElrath, Frances. *The Rustler: A Tale of Love and War in Wyoming*. 1902. Introduction by Victoria Lamont. Lincoln: University of Nebraska Press, 2002.

McGirt, James E. "I Publish this Magazine." *McGirt's Magazine* (August 1903): n.p.

———. "In Love as in War." *The Triumphs of Ephraim*. 1907. Freeport, NY: Books for Libraries Press, 1972. 63–76.

McGregor, Alex. "Cowboyz 'n' the Hood." *Time Out*, November 17, 1993: 18.

Mercer, A. S. *The Banditti of the Plains; or, the Cattlemen's Invasion of Wyoming in 1892 (The Crowning Infamy of the Ages)*. Foreword by William H. Kittrell. 1894. Norman: University of Oklahoma Press, 1954.

Micale, Mark S. "Medical and Literary Discourses of Trauma in the Age of the American Civil War." *Neurology and Literature, 1860–1920*. Ed. Anne Stiles. Basingstoke, Hampshire: Palgrave Macmillan, 2007. 184–206.

———. *Hysterical Men: The Hidden History of Male Nervous Illness*. Cambridge, MA: Harvard University Press, 2008.

Michaels, Walter Benn. *Our America: Nativism, Modernism, and Pluralism*. Durham, NC: Duke University Press, 1995.

"Midsummer Play Bills." *New York Times*, August 1, 1897.

Milne-Smith, Amy. *London Clubland: A Cultural History of Gender and Class in Late Victorian Britain*. New York: Palgrave Macmillan, 2011.

Miller, Bonnie. *From Liberation to Conquest: The Visual and Popular Cultures of the Spanish-American War of 1898*. Amherst: University of Massachusetts Press, 2011.

Miller, Laura J. "The Best-Seller List as Marketing Tool and Historical Fiction." *Book History III* (2000): 286–304.

Mitchell, John G. "A Man Called Bird." *Audubon Magazine 89* (March 1987): 81–104.

Mitchell, Lee Clark. *Westerns: Making the Man in Fiction and Film*. Chicago: University of Chicago Press, 1996.

———. "'When you call me that …': Tall Talk and Male Hegemony in *The Virginian*." *PMLA 102* (January 1987): 66–77.

Mitchell, S. Weir. *Characteristics*. 1891. New York: The Century Co., 1905.

———. *Constance Trescot*. 1905. New York: The Century Co., 1910.

———. *Doctor and Patient*. 1887. 3rd ed. Philadelphia: J. B. Lippincott, 1898.

———. *Dr. North and his Friends*. 1900. New York: Century, 1905.

———. *Fat and Blood: and How to Make Them*. 2nd ed. 1878. Introduction by Michael S. Kimmell. Walnut Creek, CA: AltaMira Press/Rowman and Littlefield, 2004.

———. *Fat and Blood: An Essay on the Treatment of Certain Forms of Neurasthenia and Hysteria*. 1877. 8th ed. Ed. with additions by John K. Mitchell. Philadelphia: J. B. Lippincott, 1902.

———. *The Guillotine Club and Other Stories*. New York: The Century Co., 1910.

———. *Hugh Wynne: Free Quaker, Sometime Brevet Lieutenant-Colonel on the Staff of His Excellency General Washington*. 1896. New York: The Century Co., 1898.

———. *In War Time*. 1884. New York: The Century Co., 1905.

———. *Lectures on Diseases of the Nervous System, Especially in Women*. London: J. & A. Churchill, 1881.

———. *Wear and Tear, Or Hints for the Overworked*. Philadelphia: J. B. Lippincott, 1871.

———. *Wear and Tear, Or Hints for the Overworked*. 5th ed. 1887. Introduction by Michael S. Kimmell. Walnut Creek, CA: AltaMira Press/Rowman and Littlefield, 2004.

Mojica, Monique. "Of Borders, Identity and Cultural Icons: A Rant." *CTR 125* (2006): 35–40.

Moon, Krystyn R. *Yellowface: Creating the Chinese in American Popular Music and Performance, 1850s-1920s*. New Brunswick, NJ: Rutgers University Press, 2005.

Morgan, Charles. *The House of Macmillan (1843–1943)*. London: Macmillan, 1944.

Morison, Elting E., ed. *The Letters of Theodore Roosevelt: The Years of Preparation 1868–1900*. 2 Vols. Cambridge, MA: Harvard University Press, 1951.

Morris, Edmund. *The Rise of Theodore Roosevelt*. New York: Ballantine Books, 1980.

Morrison, Toni. *Paradise*. New York: Alfred A. Knopf, 1997.

———. *Playing in the Dark: Whiteness and the Literary Imagination*. New York: Vintage Books-Random House, 1993.

Mott, Frank Luther. *Golden Multitudes: The Story of Best Sellers in the United States*. New York: R. R. Bowker, 1947.

"Mrs. Mary Newell, Leader of Indians." [obituary] *New York Times*, October 29, 1938: 19.

Murdoch, David Hamilton. *The American West: The Invention of a Myth*. Reno: University of Nevada Press, 2001.

Nemerov, Alexander. "Doing the 'Old America': The Image of the American West, 1880–1920." Truettner, *The West as America*, 285–343.

———. *Frederic Remington and Turn-of-the-Century America*. New Haven, CT: Yale University Press, 1995.

New Zealand *Freelance*, September 19, 1905.

New Zealand *Observer*, August 5, 1905: 17.

Ngai, Mae M. *Impossible Subjects: Illegal Aliens and the Making of Modern America*. Princeton, NJ: Princeton University Press, 2004.

Nicholas, Liza J. *Becoming Western: Stories of Culture and Identity in the Cowboy State*. Lincoln: University of Nebraska Press, 2006.

Nye, Eric W., and Sheri I. Hoem, eds. "Big Game on the Editor's Desk: Roosevelt and Bierstadt's Tale of the Hunt." *New England Quarterly 60:3* (September 1987), 454–65.

O'Connor, Harvey. *The Astors*. New York: Alfred A. Knopf, 1941.

Ohmann, Richard. *Selling Culture: Magazines, Markets, and Class at the Turn of the Century*. London: Verso, 1996.

Olson, Lee. *Marmalade and Whiskey: British Remittance Men in the West*. Golden, CO: Fulcrum Publishing, 1993.

O'Neal, Bill. *The Johnson County War*. Austin, TX: Eakin Press, 2004.

Osborn, Henry Fairfield. "Preservation of the Wild Animals of North America." Grinnell, *American*, 349–73.

"Outing in New Hands." *New York Times*, February 15, 1900.

Owens, Louis. "White for a Hundred Years." Graulich and Tatum, *Reading* The Virginian, 72–88.

Packard, Chris. *Queer Cowboys and Other Erotic Male Friendships in Nineteenth-Century American Literature*. New York: Palgrave Macmillan, 2005.

Palmer, R. Barton. "An Untypical Typicality: Screening Owen Wister's *The Virginian*." *Nineteenth-Century American Fiction on Screen*. Ed. R. Barton Palmer. Cambridge: Cambridge University Press, 2007. 219–45.

Parker, John W. "James Ephraim McGirt: Poet of 'Hope Deferred.'" *The North Carolina Historical Review 31.3* (July 1954): 321–35.

Patterson, Donald I., ed. *Letters from Old Friends and Members of the Wyoming Stockgrowers Association: Reminiscences of Pioneer Wyoming Cattle Barons in their Original Words*. Cheyenne, WY: Medicine Wheel Books, 2004.

Payne, Darwin. *Owen Wister: Chronicler of the West, Gentleman of the East*. Dallas, TX: Southern Methodist University Press, 1985.

Payne, James Robert. "Afro-American Literature of the Spanish-American War." *MELUS 10.3* (1983): 19–32.

Penrose, Charles B. *The Rustler Business*. Douglas, WY: Douglas Budget, [1959].

Pfeifer, Michael J. *Rough Justice: Lynching and American Society, 1874–1947*. Urbana: University of Illinois Press, 2004.

Philips, James. "The Little-Known Negro Rough Riders." *The Negro History Bulletin 27.3* (1963): 59.

Pickett, W. D. "Nights with the Grizzlies." Roosevelt and Grinnell, *American*, 212–39.

Pokagon, Simon (Potawatomi). *O-gî-mäw-kwe Mit-i-gwä-kî, Queen of the Woods*. Hartford, MI: C. H. Engle, 1899.

———. *The Red Man's Greeting*. Hartford, MI: C. H. Engle, 1893.

"Politics Disturbs Indian Fete Here." *New York Times*, September 29, 1928.

Porter, Kenneth W. "Negro Labor in the Western Cattle Industry, 1866–1900." 1969. *Peoples of Color in the American West*. Ed. Sucheng Chan et al. Lexington, MA: D. C. Heath, 1994. 158–67.

Posey, Alexander. *The Fus Fixico Letters*. Ed. Daniel F. Littlefield, Jr., and Carol A. Petty Hunter. Foreword by A. LaVonne Brown Ruoff. Lincoln: University of Nebraska Press, 1993.

"Professional Women to Hold Exposition." *New York Times*, May 3, 1926: 28.

Pullen, Frank. "'A Perfect Hailstorm of Bullets': A Black Sergeant Remembers the Battle of San Juan Hill in 1899." *History Matters: The U.S. Survey Course on the Web*. http://historymatters. gmu.edu. Accessed January 21, 2007.

Punke, Michael. *Last Stand: George Bird Grinnell, the Battle to Save the Buffalo, and the Birth of the New West*. New York: HarperCollins/Smithsonian, 2007.

Putnam, George Haven. "An Analysis of a Scheme for International Copyright, Suggested by Mr. R. Pearsall-Smith." 1887. *The Question of Copyright*. Comp. George Haven Putnam. New York: G. P. Putnam's Sons, 1891.

———. "Roosevelt, Historian and Statesman." *The Winning of the West II*. By Theodore Roosevelt. *The Works of Theodore Roosevelt: National Edition*. Vol. IX. New York: Charles Scribner's Sons, 1926. ix–xix.

Radway, Janice A. *A Feeling for Books: The Book-of-the-Month Club, Literary Taste, and Middle-Class Desire*. Chapel Hill: University of North Carolina Press, 1997.

Rattenbury, Richard C. *Hunting the American West: The Pursuit of Big Game for Life, Profit, and Sport, 1800–1900*. Missoula, MT: The Boone and Crockett Club, 2008.

Ravage, John W. *Black Pioneers: Images of the Black Experience on the North American Frontier*. Salt Lake City: University of Utah Press, 1997.

Razack, Sherene. "Race, Space, and Prostitution: The Making of the Bourgeois Subject." *Canadian Journal of Women and the Law 10.2* (1998): 338–76.

Razack, Sherene, ed. *Race, Space, and the Law: Unmapping a White Settler Society*. Toronto: Between the Lines, 2002.

"Real and Make-Believe Indians Join in Park Ceremony in Honor of Red Veterans." *New York Times*, May 10, 1925: 1.

Red Fox St. James. "What Would You Do?" *Indian Tepee 9.1* (1927): 2.

Reid, Margaret. *Cultural Secrets as Narrative Form: Storytelling in Nineteenth-Century America.* Columbus: Ohio State University Press, 2004.

Reid, Captain Mayne. *The Scalp-Hunters; Or, Romantic Adventures in Northern Mexico.* London: The Standard Library Company, 1851.

Reiger, John F. *American Sportsmen and the Origins of Conservation.* 3rd ed. Corvallis: Oregon State University Press, 2001.

Reiger, John F., ed. *The Passing of the Great West: Selected Papers of George Bird Grinnell.* New York: Winchester Press, 1972.

Remington, Frederic. "A Scout with the Buffalo-Soldiers." *The Century: A Popular Quarterly* 37 (April 1889): 899–912.

———. *The Collected Writings of Frederic Remington.* Ed. Peggy and Harold Samuels. Garden City, NY: Doubleday, 1979.

———. "Colonel Roosevelt's Pride." *Harper's Weekly,* August 27, 1898: 848.

———. "A Gallop through the Midway." *Harper's Weekly,* October 7, 1893: 996.

———. *John Ermine of the Yellowstone.* 1902. Introduction by Gary Scharnhorst. Lincoln: University of Nebraska Press, 2008.

———. "Natchez's Pass." *Harper's Monthly Magazine* 102 (February 1901): 437–43.

———. "Policing the Yellowstone." *Harper's Weekly,* January 12, 1895: 35–38.

———. *Sundown Leflare.* New York: Harper & Brothers, 1899.

———. *The Way of an Indian.* London: Gay & Bird, 1906.

———. "With the Fifth Corps." *Harper's New Monthly Magazine* 97 (November 1898): 962–75.

"Remington's Novel." *New York Times,* December 13, 1902.

Repplier, Agnes. *Agnes Irwin: A Biography.* Garden City, NY: Doubleday, 1934.

Richardson, Heather Cox. *West from Appomattox: The Reconstruction of America after the Civil War.* New Haven, CT: Yale University Press, 2007.

Rinehart, Mary Roberts. *Lost Ecstasy.* New York: George H. Doran, 1927.

Robbins, William G. *Colony and Empire: The Capitalist Transformation of the American West.* Lawrence: University Press of Kansas, 1994.

Robinson, Corinne Roosevelt. *My Brother Theodore Roosevelt.* New York: Charles Scribner's Sons, 1921.

Robinson, Forrest G. *Having It Both Ways: Self-Subversion in Western Popular Classics.* Albuquerque: University of New Mexico Press, 1993.

———. "The Virginian and Molly in Paradise: How Sweet Is It?" *Western American Literature 31.1* (May 1986): 27–38.

Rogers, Archibald. "Big Game in the Rockies." Roosevelt and Grinnell, *American,* 90–128.

Rogin, Michael Paul. *Blackface, White Noise: Jewish Immigrants in the Hollywood Melting Pot.* Berkeley: University of California Press, 1996.

Roosevelt, Elliott. "A Hunting Trip in India." Roosevelt and Grinnell, *Hunting,* 107–22.

Roosevelt, Theodore. "A Colorado Bear Hunt." *Scribner's Magazine* 38 (October 1905): 387–408.

———. "A Wolf Hunt in Oklahoma." *Scribner's Magazine* 38 (November 1905): 513–32.

———. "The Boone and Crockett Club." *Harper's Weekly,* March 18, 1893: 267.

———. "The Cavalry at Santiago." *Scribner's Magazine* 25 (April 1899): 420–40.

———. "Coursing the Prongbuck." Roosevelt and Grinnell, *American,* 129–39.

———. "Hunting in Cattle Country." Roosevelt and Grinnell, *Hunting,* 278–317.

———. *Hunting Trips of a Ranchman: Sketches of Sport on the Northern Cattle Plains.* 1885. New York: G. P. Putnam's Sons, 1886.

———. *Ranch Life and the Hunting Trail.* New York: The Century Co., 1888.

———. "Remarks on Balloting and Copyright." *North American Review 146.375* (February 1888): 221.

———. *The Rough Riders.* 1899. New York: Charles Scribner's Sons, 1920.

———. "What 'Americanism' Means." *The Forum* 17 (March–August 1894): 196–206.

———. "Wilderness Reserves." Grinnell, *American,* 23–51.

———. *The Winning of the West.* 4 vols. New York: G. P. Putnam's Sons, 1889–1896.

Roosevelt, Theodore, and George Bird Grinnell, eds. *American Big-Game Hunting: The Book of the Boone and Crockett Club.* New York: Forest and Stream Publishing Co., 1893.

————. *Hunting in Many Lands: The Book of the Boone and Crockett Club*. New York: Forest and Stream Publishing Co., 1895.

Rose Bibliography (Project). *Analytical Guide and Indexes to* The Colored Magazine, 1900–1909. Westport, CT: Greenwood Publishing, 1974.

Ryan, Mary P. "Gender and Public Access: Women's Politics in Nineteenth-Century America." *Feminism, The Public and The Private: Oxford Readings in Feminism*. Ed. Joan Landes. NY: Oxford University Press, 1998.195–222.

Sabo, Lewis. "When Wagon Trails Were Dim." *The Pacific Northwesterner* [newsletter] 28.2 (Spring 1984): 23–31.

"Sales of Books During The Month." *Bookman 2.1* (August 1895): 72.

Sampson, Alden. "A Bear-Hunt in the Sierras." Roosevelt and Grinnell, *Hunting*, 187–219.

Samuels, Peggy, and Harold Samuels. *Frederic Remington: A Biography*. Garden City, NY: Doubleday & Co., 1982.

————. *Teddy Roosevelt at San Juan: The Making of a President*. College Station: Texas A&M University Press, 1997.

Samuels, Peggy, and Harold Samuels, eds. *The Collected Writings of Frederic Remington*. Garden City, NY: Doubleday, 1979.

Sandoz, Mari. *Cheyenne Autumn*. 1953. Introduction by Alan Boye. Lincoln: University of Nebraska Press, 2005.

Savage, W. Sherman. *Blacks in the West*. Westport, CT: Greenwood Press, 1976.

Saxton, Alexander. *The Rise and Fall of the White Republic: Class Politics and Mass Culture in Nineteenth-Century America*. 1990. Foreword by David Roediger. New York: Verso, 2003.

Schaefer, Jack. *Shane: The Critical Edition*. Ed. James C. Work. Lincoln: University of Nebraska Press, 1984.

Scharnhorst, Gary. "Introduction." Remington, *John*, v–xvi.

Schimmel, Julie. "Inventing 'the Indian.'" Truettner, *The West as America*, 149–89.

Schofield, Brian. *Selling Your Father's Bones: The Epic Fate of the American West*. London: Harper Press, 2008.

Schubert, Frank N. "Buffalo Soldiers at San Juan Hill." *Army.Mil: The Official Homepage of the United States Army*. www.army.mil/cmh-pg/documents/spanam/bssjh/shbrt-bssjh.htm. Accessed January 21, 2007.

————. "The Suggs Affray: The Black Cavalry in the Johnson County War." *The Western Historical Quarterly 4.1* (January 1973): 57–68.

Schultz, James Willard. *Blackfeet Tales of Glacier National Park*. 1916. Introduction by Darrell Robes Kipp. Helena, MT: Riverbend Publishing, 2002.

————. *My Life as an Indian: The Story of a Red Woman and a White Man in the Lodges of the Blackfeet*. 1907. New York: Skyhorse Publishing, 2010.

————. *Signposts of Adventure: Glacier National Park as the Indians Know It*. Boston: Houghton Mifflin, 1926.

Schurman, Lydia Cushman. "The Effect of Nineteenth-Century 'Libraries' on the American Book Trade." *Scorned Literature: Essays on the History and Criticism of Popular Mass-Produced Fiction in America*. Ed. Lydia Cushman Schurman and Deidre Johnson. Westport, CT: Greenwood Press, 2002. 97–121.

————. "Nineteenth-Century Reprint Libraries: When a Book Was Not a Book." Bold, *US*, 81–96.

Scott, Edward Van Zile. *The Unwept: Black American Soldiers and the Spanish-American War*. Montgomery, AL: The Black Belt Press, 1996.

Seelye, John. *War Games: Richard Harding Davis and the New Imperialism*. Amherst: University of Massachusetts Press, 2003.

Shapiro, Michael Edward. "Remington The Sculptor." *Frederic Remington: The Masterworks*. Michael Edward Shapiro and Peter H. Hassrick. New York: Harry N. Abrams in association with The Saint Louis Art Museum, 1988. 170–233.

Sheldon, Charles. *The Wilderness of the North Pacific Coast Islands*. New York: Charles Scribner's Sons, 1912.

Silber, Nina. *The Romance of Reunion: Northerners and the South, 1865–1900*. Chapel Hill: University of North Carolina Press, 1993.

Simon, Rita. *Public Opinion and the Immigrant: Print Media Coverage, 1880–1980.* Lexington, MA: Lexington Books/D. C. Heath, 1985.

Simpson, Mark. "Immaculate Trophies." *Essays on Canadian Writing 68* (1999): 77–106.

———. "Powers of Liveness: Reading Hornaday's *Camp-Fires.*" *The Culture of Hunting in Canada.* Ed. Jean L. Manore and Dale G. Miner. Vancouver: University of British Columbia Press, 2006. 56–85.

Slotkin, Richard. *The Fatal Environment: The Myth of the Frontier in the Age of Industrialization, 1800–1890.* New York: Atheneum, 1985.

———. *Gunfighter Nation: The Myth of the Frontier in Twentieth-Century America.* New York: Atheneum, 1992.

———. *Regeneration through Violence: The Mythology of the American Frontier, 1600–1860.* Middletown, CT: Wesleyan University Press, 1973.

———. "The 'Wild West.'" *Buffalo Bill and the Wild West.* Brooklyn: The Brooklyn Museum, 1981. 27–44.

Smalley, Andrea L. "'Our Lady Sportsmen': Gender, Class, and Conservation in Sport Hunting Magazines, 1873–1920." *Journal of the Gilded Age and Progressive Era 4.4* (October 2005): 355–80.

Smith, Andrew Brodie. *Shooting Cowboys and Indians: Western Films, American Culture, and the Birth of Hollywood.* Boulder: University Press of Colorado, 2003.

Smith, Helena Huntington. *The War on Powder River.* New York: McGraw-Hill, 1966.

Smith, Henry Nash. *Virgin Land: The American West as Symbol and Myth.* Cambridge, MA: Harvard University Press, 1950.

Smith, Sherry L. *Reimagining Indians: Native Americans through Anglo Eyes, 1880–1940.* New York: Oxford University Press, 2000.

Smith, Wm. Lord. "An African Shooting Trip." Grinnell and Roosevelt, *Trail and Camp-Fire,* 78–123.

Solomon, Barbara. *Ancestors and Immigrants: A Changing New England Tradition.* Cambridge: Harvard University Press, 1956.

"Some Vaudeville Headliners." *New York Times,* May 4, 1902.

Spence, Mark David. *Dispossessing the Wilderness: Indian Removal and the Making of the National Parks.* New York: Oxford University Press, 1999.

Spiro, Jonathan Peter. *Defending the Master Race: Conservation, Eugenics, and the Legacy of Madison Grant.* Hanover, NH: University Press of New England/Burlington: University of Vermont Press, 2009.

Splete, Allen P., and Marilyn D. Splete. *Frederic Remington: Selected Letters.* New York: Abbeville Press, 1988.

Spring, Agnes Wright. *The Cheyenne Club: Mecca of the Aristocrats of the Old-Time Cattle Range.* Kansas City: Don Ornduff, 1961.

Stange, Mary Zeiss. *Woman the Hunter.* Boston: Beacon Press, 1997.

Stern, Madeleine B. *Imprints on History: Book Publishers and American Frontiers.* Bloomington: Indiana University Press, 1956.

Steward, T. G. *The Colored Regulars in The United States Army.* 1904. New York: Arno Press and The New York Times, 1969.

Stickney, Mary E. *Brown of Lost River: A Story of the West.* New York, D. Appleton, 1900.

Stiles, T. J. *The First Tycoon: The Epic Life of Cornelius Vanderbilt.* New York: Alfred A. Knopf, 2009.

Stimson, Henry L. "The Ascent of Chief Mountain." Roosevelt and Grinnell, *Hunting,* 221–37.

Stokes, Frances K. W. *My Father Owen Wister—and—Ten Letters Written by Owen Wister to his Mother during his First Trip to Wyoming in 1885.* Laramie, WY: n.pub., 1952.

Stoler, Ann Laura. *Haunted by Empire: Geographies of Intimacy in North American History.* Durham, NC: Duke University Press, 2006.

Streeby, Shelley. *American Sensations: Class, Empire, and the Production of Popular Culture.* Berkeley: University of California Press, 2002.

Strouse, Jean. *Morgan: American Financier.* London: The Haverill Press, 1999.

"The Sunday Concerts." *New York Times,* March 30, 1902.

"Sunday Concerts." *New York Times,* October 23, 1904.

Szasz, Ferenc Morton. *Scots in the North American West, 1790–1917.* Norman: University of Oklahoma Press, 2000.

Tatum, Stephen. *In the Remington Moment.* Lincoln: University of Nebraska Press, 2010.

Taylor, Antony. *Lords of Misrule: Hostility to Aristocracy in Late Nineteenth- and Early Twentieth-Century Britain.* Basingstoke: Palgrave Macmillan, 2004.

Taylor, Ned [St. George Rathborne]. *Ted Strong's Rough Riders; Or, The Boys Of Black Mountain.* The Young Rough Riders Weekly *1.* New York: Street & Smith, 1904.

Taylor, Ned [William Wallace Cook]. *King of the Wild West's Haunt; or, Stella's Escape from Sacrifice.* Rough Rider Weekly *102.* New York: Street & Smith, 1906.

———. *The Young Rough Riders in the Rockies; or, A Fight in Midair.* Young Rough Riders Weekly *38.* New York: Street & Smith, 1905.

Taylor, Quintard. *In Search of the Racial Frontier: African Americans in the American West, 1528–1990.* New York: W. W. Norton, 1998.

Tebbel, John. *A History of Book Publishing in the United States. Volume II. The Expansion of an Industry 1865–1919.* New York: R. R. Bowker, 1975.

"Theodore Roosevelt." Grinnell, *American,* 13–22.

Thomas, Evan. *The War Lovers: Roosevelt, Lodge, Hearst, and the Rush to Empire, 1898.* New York: Little, Brown and Co., 2010.

Thomas, Lately. *A Pride of Lions: The Astor Orphans, The Chanler Chronicle.* New York: William Morrow and Company, 1971.

Thompson, Lewis S. "Cherry." Grinnell and Roosevelt, *Trail and Camp-Fire,* 51–77.

Thweatt, Hiram H. *What the Newspapers Say of the Negro Soldier in the Spanish-American War.* Thomasville, GA: n.pub., n.d.

Toll, Jean Barth, and Mildred S. Gillam, eds. *Invisible Philadelphia: Community through Voluntary Organizations.* Philadelphia: Atwater Kent Museum, 1995.

Tolnay, Stewart E., and E. M. Beck. *A Festival of Violence: An Analysis of Southern Lynchings, 1882–1930.* Urbana: University of Illinois Press, 1995.

Tompkins, Jane. *West of Everything: The Inner Life of Westerns.* New York: Oxford University Press, 1992.

Tonkovich, Nicole. "Guardian Angels and Missing Mothers: Race and Domesticity in *Winona* and *Deadwood Dick on Deck.*" *Western American Literature* 32.3 (November 1997): 241–64.

Townsend, Kim. *Manhood at Harvard: William James and Others.* Cambridge, MA: Harvard University Press, 1996.

Trachtenberg, Alan. *The Incorporation of America: Culture and Society in the Gilded Age.* New York: Hill and Wang, 1982.

———. *Shades of Hiawatha: Staging Indians, Making Americans 1880–1930.* New York: Hill and Wang, 2004.

Trefethen, James B. *An American Crusade for Wildlife.* New York: Winchester Press and The Boone and Crockett Club, 1975.

———. *Crusade for Wildlife: Highlights in Conservation Progress. A Boone and Crockett Club Book.* Harrisburg, PA: The Stackpole Co., and New York: Boone and Crockett Club, 1961.

Truettner, William H., ed. *The West as America: Reinterpreting Images of the Frontier, 1820–1920.* Washington, DC: Smithsonian Institution Press, 1991.

Turnbull, Margaret. *The Close-Up.* New York: Harper & Brothers, 1918.

Turner, Frederick Jackson. "The Significance of the Frontier in American History." *Annual Report of the American Historical Association for the Year 1893.* Washington, DC: GPO, 1894.

Tuttle, Jennifer S. "Indigenous Whiteness and Wister's Invisible Indians." Graulich and Tatum, *Reading* The Virginian, 89–112.

———. "Rewriting the West Cure: Charlotte Perkins Gilman, Owen Wister, and the Sexual Politics of Neurasthenia." *The Mixed Legacy of Charlotte Perkins Gilman.* Ed. Catherine J. Golden and Joanna Schneider Zangrando. Newark: University of Delaware Press, 2000. 103–21.

Van Nuys, Frank. *Americanizing the West: Race, Immigrants, and Citizenship, 1890–1930.* Lawrence: University Press of Kansas, 2002.

Vivian, Thomas. *The Fall of Santiago.* New York: R. F. Fenno, 1898.

Vorpahl, Ben Merchant. *Frederic Remington and the West: With the Eye of the Mind.* Austin: University of Texas Press, 1978.

———. "Henry James and Owen Wister." *The Pennsylvania Magazine of History and Biography* 95.3 (July 1971): 291–338.

Vorpahl, Ben Merchant, ed. *My Dear Wister: The Frederic Remington-Owen Wister Letters.* Palo Alto, CA: American West Publishing, 1972.

Wadsworth, Sarah. *In the Company of Books: Literature and Its "Classes" in Nineteenth-Century America.* Amherst: University of Massachusetts Press, 2006.

Waldrep, Christopher. *The Many Faces of Judge Lynch: Extralegal Violence and Punishment in America.* New York: Palgrave Macmillan, 2002.

Walker, Cheryl. *Indian Nation: Native American Literature and Nineteenth Century Nationalisms.* Durham, NC: Duke University Press, 1997.

Walker, Francis A. "Immigration and Degradation." *The Forum* 11 (August 1891): 634–44.

Ward III, George Baxter. "Bloodbrothers in the Wilderness: The Sport Hunter and the Buckskin Hunter in the Preservation of the American Wilderness Experience." PhD Dissertation, University of Texas, Austin, 1980.

Warner, Jr., Sam Bass. *The Private City: Philadelphia in Three Periods of Its Growth.* Philadelphia: University of Pennsylvania Press, 1968.

Warren, Louis. *Buffalo Bill's America: William Cody and the Wild West Show.* New York: Alfred A. Knopf, 2005.

———. *The Hunter's Game: Poachers and Conservationists in Twentieth-Century America.* New Haven, CT: Yale University Press, 1997.

———. Review of *Hunting and the American Imagination*, by Daniel Justin Herman. *The Journal of American History* 89. 2 (2002): 621–22.

Warshow, Robert. "The Gentleman with a Gun." *Encounter* 2.3 (March 1954): 18–25.

Washington, Booker T., N. B. Wood, and Fannie Barrier Williams. *A New Negro for a New Century.* 1900. New York: Arno Press and The New York Times, 1969.

Watts, Sarah. *Rough Rider in the White House: Theodore Roosevelt and the Politics of Desire.* Chicago: University of Chicago Press, 2003.

Weiner, Mark S. *Americans without Law: The Racial Boundaries of Citizenship.* New York: New York University Press, 2006.

Westermeier, Clifford P. *Who Rush to Glory: The Cowboy Volunteers of 1898.* Caldwell, ID: The Caxton Printers, 1958.

White, Corporal Charles Fred. *Plea of the Negro Soldier and a Hundred Other Poems.* Easthampton, MA: Press of Enterprise Printing Company, 1908.

White, G. Edward. *The Eastern Establishment and the Western Experience: The West of Frederic Remington, Theodore Roosevelt, and Owen Wister.* 1968. Austin: The University of Texas Press, 1989.

White, Richard. "Frederick Jackson Turner and Buffalo Bill." *The Frontier in American Culture.* Ed. James R. Grossman. Berkeley: University of California Press, 1994. 7–65.

Whitney, Caspar. "The Santiago Campaign." *Harper's New Monthly Magazine* 97 (October 1898): 795*–818*.

———. *A Sporting Pilgrimage: Riding to Hounds, Golf, Rowing, Football, Club and University Athletics.* New York: Harper & Brothers, 1894.

Whitney, Casper [sic] W. "The Cougar." Roosevelt and Grinnell, *Hunting* 238–54.

Whitney, Caspar, George Bird Grinnell, and Owen Wister. *Musk-Ox, Bison, Sheep and Goat.* New York: The Macmillan Company, 1904.

Whittaker, Frederick. "Dime Novels: A Defence by a Writer of Them." *New-York Daily Tribune,* March 16, 1884: 8.

———. *Parson Jim, King of the Cowboys; or, The Gentle Shepherd's Big "Clean Out."* Beadle's Dime Library 215. New York: Beadle & Adams, 1882.

Will, Barbara. "The Nervous Origins of the American Western." *American Literature* 70.2 (June 1998): 293–316.

Williams, Raymond. *Resources of Hope: Culture, Democracy, Socialism.* Ed. Robin Gable. London: Verso, 1989.

Williams, Roger D. "Old Times in the Black Hills." Roosevelt and Grinnell, *American*, 73–89.

———. "Wolf-Coursing." Roosevelt and Grinnell, *Hunting*, 318–57.

Wilson, Christopher P. *The Labor of Words: Literary Professionalism in the Progressive Era.* Athens: The University of Georgia Press, 1985.

Wise, Jennings C. *The Red Man in the New World Drama: A Politico-Legal Study with a Pageantry of American Indian History*. Ed., rev., and introduction by Vine Deloria, Jr. New York: The Macmillan Company, 1971.

Wister, Fanny Kemble, ed. *That I May Tell You: Journals and Letters of the Owen Wister Family*. Wayne, PA: Haverford House, 1979.

———. *Owen Wister Out West: His Journals and Letters*. Chicago: University of Chicago Press, 1958.

Wister, Owen. "Educating the Polo Pony." *Outing 36.3* (June 1900): 296–99.

———. "Em'ly." *Harper's New Monthly Magazine 87* (November 1893): 941–48.

———. "The Evolution of the Cow-Puncher." *Harper's New Monthly Magazine 91* (September 1895): 602–17.

———. "Extra Dry." O. Wister, *Members*, 207–28.

———. "Hank's Woman." *Harper's Weekly*, August 27, 1892: 821–23.

———. "Hank's Woman." O. Wister, *Jimmyjohn*, 251–88.

———. "How Lin McLean Went East." *Harper's New Monthly Magazine 86* (December 1892): 135–47.

———. *The Jimmyjohn Boss and Other Stories*. New York: Harper & Brothers, 1900.

———. *Lady Baltimore*. New York: Macmillan, 1906.

———. *Lin McLean*. New York: Harper & Brothers, 1897.

———. *Members of the Family*. New York: Macmillan, 1911.

———. "The Mountain Sheep: His Ways." Whitney, Grinnell, and Wister, *Musk-Ox*, 167–226.

———. "Owen Wister Graphically Views Life of Dr. S. W. Mitchell." *The Philadelphia Press*, April 5, 1914.

———. *Philosophy 4: A Story of Harvard University*. 1903. New York: Macmillan, 1911.

———. "A Pilgrim on the Gila." O. Wister, *Red*, 211–80.

———. "Preface." *The Virginian*. Rev. ed. *The Writings of Owen Wister*. Vol. 4. New York: Macmillan, 1928. vii–xv.

———. *Red Men and White*. New York: Harper & Brothers, 1895.

———. *Romney and Other New Works about Philadelphia*. Ed. James A. Butler. University Park: Pennsylvania State University Press, 2001.

———. *Roosevelt: The Story of a Friendship 1880–1919*. New York: Macmillan, 1930.

———. "Spit-Cat Creek." O. Wister, *Members*, 67–88.

———. "The Story of Chalkeye: A Wind River Romance." *American West 21* (January-February 1984): 37–52.

———. *The Virginian: A Horseman of the Plains*. 1902. New York: Macmillan, 1904.

———. *When West Was West*. New York: Macmillan, 1928.

———. "Where It Was." O. Wister, *Members*, 229–75.

———. "The White Goat and His Country." Roosevelt and Grinnell, *American*, 26–60.

———. "The Wilderness Hunter." *Outing 39.3* (December 1901), 251–55.

———. "The Winning of the Biscuit Shooter." *Harper's New Monthly Magazine 88* (December 1893): 52–57.

Wister, Owen, and Kirke La Shelle. *The Virginian: A Play in Four Acts*. Introduction and Notes by N. Orwin Rush. Tallahassee, FL: n.pub., 1958.

Wister, Sarah Butler. "The Early Years of a Child of Promise." F. K. Wister, *That*, 69–126.

Wister, Sarah Butler, and Agnes Irwin, eds. *Worthy Women of Our First Century*. Philadelphia: J. B. Lippincott, 1877.

Wister, Sarah Butler, Agnes Irwin, and Benoni Lockwood. *Brisée*. Philadelphia: J. B. Lippincott, 1862.

Womack, Craig S. *Red on Red: Native American Literary Separatism*. Minneapolis: University of Minnesota Press, 1999.

Woods, Lawrence M. *British Gentlemen in the Wild West: The Era of the Intensely English Cowboy*. New York: Free Press, 1989.

Worden, Daniel. *Masculine Style: The American West and Literary Modernism*. New York: Palgrave Macmillan, 2011.

Wylder, Delbert E. *Emerson Hough*. Southwest Writers Series 19. Austin, TX: Steck-Vaughan, 1969.

———. *Emerson Hough.* Twayne's United States Authors Series 397. Boston: Twayne, 1981.

Yates, Norris W. *Gender and Genre: An Introduction to Women Writers of Formula Westerns, 1900–1950.* Albuquerque: University of New Mexico Press, 1995.

"The Yellowstone National Park Protection Act." Roosevelt and Grinnell, *Hunting,* 403–23.

Young, James Rankin. *Reminiscences and Thrilling Stories of the War by Returned Heroes.* Grand Rapids, MI: P. D. Farrell Co., 1898.

Zimmermann, Warren. *First Great Triumph: How Five Americans Made Their Country A World Power.* New York: Farrar, Straus and Giroux, 2002.

Zitkala-Ša. *American Indian Stories.* 1921. Introduction by Susan Rose Dominguez. Lincoln: University of Nebraska Press, 2003.

———. *Dreams and Thunder: Stories, Poems, and The Sun Dance Opera.* Ed. P. Jane Hafen. Lincoln: University of Nebraska Press, 2001.

———. "The Soft-Hearted Sioux." *Harper's Monthly Magazine 102* (March 1901): 505–08.

Films

Blazing Saddles. Dir. Mel Brooks. Warner Brothers, 1974.

Cheyenne Autumn. Dir. John Ford. Warner Brothers, 1964.

Daniel Boone, Trailblazer. Dir. Albert C. Gannaway and Ismael Rodriguez. Republic Pictures, 1956.

A Fistful of Dollars (Por un puñado de dólares). Dir. Sergio Leone. United Artists, 1967 (Unidis 1964).

Heaven's Gate. Dir. Michael Cimino. United Artists, 1980.

High Noon. Dir. Fred Zinnemann. United Artists, 1952.

Hondo. Dir. John Farrow. Warner Brothers, 1953.

My Darling Clementine. Dir. John Ford. Twentieth Century Fox, 1946.

Once Upon A Time in the West (C'era una volta il West). Dir. Sergio Leone. Paramount Pictures, 1969. (Euro International Film, 1968).

One-Eyed Jacks. Dir. Marlon Brando. Paramount Pictures, 1961.

The Ox-Bow Incident. Dir. William A. Wellman. Twentieth Century Fox, 1943.

Posse. Dir. Mario Van Peebles. Gramercy Pictures, 1993.

The Searchers. Dir. John Ford. Warner Brothers, 1956.

Sergeant Rutledge. Dir. John Ford. Warner Brothers, 1960.

Shane. Dir. George Stevens. Paramount Pictures, 1953.

The Squaw Man. Dir. Cecil B. DeMille. Jesse L. Lasky Feature Play Co., 1914.

Stagecoach. Dir. John Ford. United Artists, 1939.

The Virginian. Dir. Cecil B. DeMille. Jesse L. Lasky Feature Play Company, 1914.

The Virginian. Dir. Tom Forman. Al Lichtman/Preferred Pictures, 1923.

The Virginian. Dir. Victor Fleming. Paramount Pictures, 1929.

The Virginian. Dir. Stuart Gilmore. Paramount Pictures, 1946.

The Virginian. NBC, September 19, 1962–September 9, 1970.

The Virginian. Dir. Bill Pullman. Turner Network Television, 2000.

Wild Wild West. Dir. Barry Sonnenfeld. Warner Brothers, 1999.

INDEX

Page numbers in *italics* refer to illustrations.

Brooks, Mel 236
Browder, Laura 215
Brown, Arthur Erwin 40
Brown, Bill 91
Brown, Corporal 147
Brown of Lost River (Stickney) 220
Brownsville Raid 163, 167
Buck Taylor (Ingraham) 91, 92
Buckley, Gail 158
Buffalo Bill *see* Cody, Bill
Buffalo Bill and the Indians (Altman) 235
Buffalo Bill's Wild West 18, 36, 91, 128, 146,
    163–64, 211, 216, 219, 253n9, 255n50,
    255n52, 259n18
Buffalo Bulletin (Wyoming) 8
"The Buffalo Horse" (Remington) 185
Buffalo Soldiers *see* African American soldiers
Butler, James A. 117, 247n22
Butler, Private 147, 155–56

Cabot family 100
Cadwalader, John 62
Cadwalader family 58, 62
Callahan, S. Alice 218–19, 228
Camp-Fires in the Canadian Rockies (Hornaday)
    187
Campeau, Frank 12, 180
Cannadine, David 69
Carby, Hazel V. 225
Carey, Joseph M. 13
Carlisle Indian School 209, 211, 219
Carnegie, Andrew 62, 73, 184
Carpenter, Cari 214
Carter, Thomas H. 196, 197, 204, 257n58
Cashin, Herschel V. 157, 158
"A Cavalrymen's Breakfast" (Remington) 152
Cawelti, John xx, 97, 260n2
censorship 8, 94, 184
Century Magazine 89, 182
    The Century Co. 223
Champ, Abraham 13
Champion, Nate 1, 6–8, 12, 76
Chaney, Lon 237
Chanler, Margaret Terry "Daisy" 18, 29, 30, 31,
    98–99, 101, 104, 105, 117, 127, 128, 129
Chanler, William 51–52, 131
Chanler, Winthrop xvii, *xviii*, 3, 18, 29–31, 33,
    39, 54, 58, 74, 75, 172, 174, 241
    and African Americans 131
    familial rhetoric 104
    hunting tales 30, 43, 102, 104
    marriage 30, 98–99, 101, 104
    and Native women 102
    and Remington 36
    Spanish-American War 146
    and Wister 18, 64–65, 75, 98
Channing, William Ellery 122

Characteristics (Mitchell) 62
"The Charge" (Remington) 152
"Charge of the Rough Riders" (Remington)
    154–55, *155*
"Charge of the 24th and 25th Colored Infantry"
    156
Charles Scribner's Sons *see* Scribner's
Charleston 64, 89, 90, 107, 108, 114–15, 123,
    131, 166, 252n60
cheap libraries 82, 83–84, 85–86, 89
Chesnutt, Charles 139
Cheyenne Autumn (Ford) 233, 239–40
Cheyenne Autumn (Sandoz) 213, 233
Cheyenne Club 4, 6, 8, 11, 12, 68–73, *69*, 74, 75,
    78, 79, 82, 83, 91, *134*, 175, 198, 206,
    256n15
    violence 76–77
Cheyenne Daily Leader 5
The Cheyenne Indians (Grinnell) 25, 212
Cheyenne Nation 25, 192, 202, 209, 211, 212,
    213, 233, 239
Cheyenne Sun 5, 94, 249n86
Chicago Herald 8
Chicago Tribune 153
Chief Mountain 189, 194, 196, 215
Child, Lydia Maria 181
children's books 86, 132, 149–52, 197–205; *see
    also* young readers
Chinese Exclusion Act 169, 186, 255n1
Chinquilla, Princess 207, 208, *208*, 209–15, 240,
    259n5, 259n11, 259n18
Cimino, Michael 8, 174
citizenship 19, 48, 53, 161, 169–70, 172, 175,
    177, 188, 205, 214, 215
Civic Club 109, 111–13, 114, 116, 117, 122, 123,
    126, 129, 252n58
    Bulletin 116–17, 125–27, 210, 259n6
Clark, Horace B. 22
Clark, J.J. 253n6, 253n10
Clark, Walter Van Tilburg 239
Clarke, Lieutenant 152
class
    division 57, 68, 70, 74, 92–93, 94, 95, 105,
        117, 153, 162, 174, 176, 177, 191,
        223–24
    high-class vaudeville 210
    middle class 33, 102, 176, 188
        magazines 145, 219
    nouveau riche 15, 58, 64
    upper class 11, 22, 26, 42, 57, 73, 109, 139, 192
        beleaguered 2, 8, 40, 53, 58, 102, 181, 196, 210
        enclaves 32, 44, 97, 122, 124, 130
        and marketplace 56, 60, 66, 67, 75
        and publishers 80–82, 83, 86
        and West 56, 60, 65–66, 68, 133, 166, 172,
            190
    working class 40, 176

Pawnee Hero Stories and Folk Tales (Grinnell) 36
Payne, Darwin 105, 107, 245n24
Payne, James Robert 151
Penn, Arthur 235
Penrose, Boies 59, 77
Penrose, Charles B. 8, 59, 77–78, 79
Penrose, Dick 78
Perkins, Maxwell 187
Petter, Mrs 213
Petter, Rodolphe 212, 213
Philadelphia 1, 8, 15, 56, 83, 108, 109, 112,
    113, 114, 123, 125, 129, 131, 135, 160;
    see also Civic Club, Philadelphia Club,
    Rittenhouse Club
  aristocracy 27, 28, 40, 44, 56, 57–58, 65, 67,
    77, 99, 105, 107, 111
  Board of Education 117
  Evening Home for Boys 121
  fictionalized 62–63, 65, 90, 108, 238
  politics 131, 252n58, 259n6
Philadelphia Club 2, 3, 8, 55–56, 57, 58, 59, 65,
    67, 86, 95, 108, 113, 135, 179
Philadelphia Ledger 228
Philips, James 144
Philosophy 4 (Wister) 178
Pickett, W. D. 42
Piegan 194, 195, 201–3, 221, 257n55; see also
    Blackfeet, Pikuni
Pikuni 193, 194, 222
"Pilgrim on the Gila" (Wister) 134
Plains Indians Wars 171
"playing Indian" (Deloria) 45, 188–89, 191, 202,
    215
Plessy, Homer 137
Plunkett, Horace 69, 71
Pokagon, Simon 216–18, 231, 260n42
popular print culture 1, 90, 91, 142, 205, 207,
    209, 213, 218, 223, 230–1, 232; see also
    dime novels, mass culture, publishing
popularization of the West xvii, xix, 3, 15, 17, 23,
    34, 46, 56, 92, 133, 207, 208, 209, 219, 231
populism 91
Porcellian Club 2, 4, 8, 28, 30, 31, 32, 36, 66, 68,
    245n28
Posey, Alexander Lawrence 227–30, 231,
    260n37, 260n42; see also Fus Fixico
    letters
Posse (Van Peebles) 164–65, 239
Potawatomi Tribe 217
power relations 73–74, 75, 130, 222, 223
preservation see conservation
press propaganda 6–7
prints 156–57, 161
"The Problem" (Gilmore) 158
Publishers' Weekly 87
publishing xix, 2, 12, 38, 56, 80–90, 94, 103,
    121, 207

alternative 132, 158, 159, 160, 161, 208, 218,
    223, 224–25, 227
  battles 81, 83–87, 93, 94, 95, 173
  cheap 37, 80, 82, 86, 89, 90, 92, 93, 94, 149, 155
  mass xvii, 80, 81, 83
  "quality" 3, 37, 46, 56, 80, 81, 82, 83, 85, 87,
    89, 90, 92, 149, 155, 176, 183, 219, 222,
    223, 230
Puck 149, 150, 174, 175
Pulman, Bill 235
Punke, Michael 16, 40, 48, 67, 101
Putnam, George Haven 80, 84; see also G. P.
    Putnam's Sons

racism 2, 11, 13, 32, 40
  against African American soldiers 143–44,
    162, 163, 255n49
  against African Americans 155, 186, 227
  in dime novels 92, 150–52
  and films 211, 235–37, 239
  frontier club 40–41
  in Grant 32, 182, 186, 187
  Immigration Restriction League 176–77
  against Indigenous peoples 52, 97, 131, 143,
    165, 211, 219
  and lynching 10, 165
  Remington 152
  in Wister 9, 12, 135, 166, 180
  and WSGA 13
Radcliffe College 100, 109, 129
The Rainbow Trail (Grey) 48
Ranch Life and the Hunting Trail (Roosevelt)
    36, 90
ranching xvii, xix, 4–5, 9, 11, 20–21, 56, 66,
    68–69, 75, 76, 80–81, 128, 132, 135,
    148, 204, 218
Rankin, U.S. Marshal 77
Ransom, Fletcher C. 156
Ravage, John 132, 253n4, 255n40
Ray, Nick 1, 6, 8, 11, 12, 76
Razack, Sherene 130
Red Bird see Zitkala-Ša
Red Fox Saint James 214
The Red Man's Greeting (Pokagon) 217
Red Men and White (Wister) 36, 135, 190
Red Wing, Lillian 211, 234
Reid, Margaret 243n1
Reid, Mayne 24, 25, 93
Reiger, John F. 16, 23, 42, 101
Remington, Eva Caten 102, 128
Remington, Frederic xvii, xviii, 3–4, 36, 54, 102,
    155, 172, 177, 243n4, 245n47, 245n50,
    255n43
  and African Americans 132, 137, 152–53, 154,
    167, 255n41
  anti-immigrant 177
  art-works 152, 153, 154, 177, 185